Applying Anthropology in the Global Village

Applying Anthropology in the Global Village

Editors

Christina Wasson
Mary Odell Butler
Jacqueline Copeland-Carson

Walnut Creek, California

LEFT COAST PRESS, INC.
1630 North Main Street, #400
Walnut Creek, CA 94596
http://www.LCoastPress.com

ISBN 978-1-61132-085-5 hardcover
ISBN 978-1-61132-086-2 paperback

Library of Congress Cataloging-in-Publication Data:

Applying anthropology in the global village / Christina Wasson, Mary Odell Butler, and Jacqueline Copeland-Carson, editors.
    p. cm.
  Includes bibliographical references and index.
  ISBN 978-1-61132-085-5 (hardcover : alk. paper) —
  ISBN 978-1-61132-086-2 (pbk. : alk. paper)
1. Applied anthropology. 2. Villages. 3. Community life. 4. Community development. 5. Culture and globalization. I. Wasson, Christina. II. Butler, Mary Odell. III. Copeland-Carson, Jacqueline.
  GN397.5.A674 2011
  306—dc23
          2011029638

Printed in the United States of America

∞™ The paper used in this publication meets the minimum requirements of American National Standard for Information Sciences—Permanence of Paper for Printed Library Materials, ANSI/NISO Z39.48—1992.

Cover design by Piper Wallis.
Cover photograph: Street scene from Jaipur, India, January 2011. Photograph by Patricia Cukor-Avila.

Contents

Introduction

Global-Local Connections: The View from Applied Anthropology

Jacqueline Copeland-Carson, Mary Odell Butler, and Christina Wasson

> In the globalized world that is ours, maybe we are moving towards a global village, but that global village brings in a lot of different people, a lot of different ideas, lots of different backgrounds, lots of different aspirations.
>
> Lakhdar Brahimi, Former Special Ambassador to the United Nations (quoted in Keisler 2005)

Throughout the world, the "village" has been both a place and an imagined community of harmony and cooperation (Anderson 1983). Today, the trope of the village has been extended to the "global village," a metaphor for the complex interconnections of the contemporary world. Thinkers from Marshall McLuhan to Bill Gates have imagined and located the global village in new social relations created by international commerce, travel, communications, and the World Wide Web (McLuhan 1962, 1964; Gates n.d.). But the twenty-first century's expanding global relationships are a double-edged sword. The very processes and technologies that bring us into ever-closer connection also create new opportunities for cooperation and conflict. As a social reality, the global village brings with it accelerated and escalating worldwide war, environmental degradation, pandemics, and more. As an imagined community, however, the global village inspires humanity's desire for a future of shared peace and prosperity, unleashing powerful global and local movements for human rights and social justice, such as the recent democratic uprisings in Tunisia, Egypt, and Libya.

Anthropology was born of villages—both large and small—whose early theoretical conceptualizations are now largely recognized as fictions of our field's colonial past, figments of a popular imagination of a mythic simpler time. *Applying Anthropology in the Global Village* highlights the contributions of today's applied anthropologists who are working at the cusp of new social relations and localities emerging in today's global economy. Our work has shown us that current theoretical formulations of place and identity do not fully capture the complexities of this era. At the same time, an alternative paradigm that fully expresses the nuances, tensions, creativity, new possibilities, social relations, conflicts, and challenges of the times is difficult to define. The "global village" as we construe it here is not a social theory or even a future that we necessarily espouse. Instead, it is a placeholder social construct with widespread cultural resonance that we use to orient this book's core question: how do we understand, represent, explain, and influence the complex social relations that are emerging in our increasingly global world? Instead of imposing a definitive answer from established social or cultural theory, we recognize that associations of people, places, and identities—such as those inherent in various notions of the global village—cannot simply be taken as givens, but must be part of the research context to be studied (Gupta and Ferguson 1997). This book presents grounded ethnographic case examples from applied projects that might suggest new paradigms to inform theory across the multiple disciplines and fields in which we work.

Anthropology's development has been driven in large part by the effort to create paradigms that explain the astounding complexity of human experience. As the world has become increasingly interconnected, anthropologists are challenged to explain a contemporary social reality that seems qualitatively different from previous historical eras. Overnight international travel, instantaneous finance, and new information and communication technologies make our lives at once global and local. This book explores the global locality, the complex mosaic in which people live their lives in the first part of the twenty-first century. Now more than at any time in history, people are embedded in a multilayered community combining the global and the local, the innovative and the traditional, and the visible and invisible sociopolitical currents that run through their communities. These new environments are dynamic, ever-emerging, and rapidly shifting over time and space. Today, every human being on the planet negotiates these global localities. This context poses new challenges for all who seek to understand humans and their capacity to adapt to change. We consider how anthropologists apply their discipline to help resolve human problems in these new kinds of communities that emerge as people become intensely linked by global forces.

Anthropology provides a useful lens for understanding the complex changes of our increasingly global world. This field has contributed multiple theories to help explain the rapid-fire changes of a new social reality (see Appadurai 1996; Hannerz 1992; Marcus 1998; Ong and Collier 2004). But this book is not another anthropological treatise on the abstracted concept of globalization. Our purpose in this volume is not to propose new theories of globalization, although there are novel theoretical perspectives in some of the chapters.

Rather, we seek to illustrate the new connections and tensions that cut across various local contexts—villages, corporations, public agencies, and others—in an increasingly interconnected world, based on case studies from practicing and applied anthropologists. As applied anthropologists, we seek to develop new understandings of cultural systems at the nexus of the global and the local. Our work is unavoidably translocal. At the same time, our projects are not geared merely to passive descriptions of cultural systems as they change. Our work is often used actively to change, resist, and transform global-local interactions.

As applied anthropologists, we help solve some of society's most pressing challenges. The human experience of globalization has turned much of the received wisdom of earlier generations of anthropologists on its head. A lot of what we thought we knew three decades ago no longer pertains as the world becomes more interconnected. Anthropologists have been at the center of these events because they are increasingly called on by policy makers, planners, businesses, agencies, and many others to understand how globalization affects peoples' lives.

The authors in this volume are all anthropologists. Although much of our work focuses on applying anthropology to practical problems, we are also scholars who build theory to explain the effects of global change on people. Anthropological practice requires a synthetic approach that explores how different levels of sociopolitical organization interact in dynamic ways. To understand community life that is shaped by processes of globalization, we have developed new ways of thinking about community that incorporate issues of transnational power and hegemony (Edelman and Haugerud 2005). In this volume, we hope to highlight the multiple ways that contemporary anthropologists combine theory and practice to understand the global locality.

Each chapter is a critical self-study of an applied anthropologist's effort to understand and shape the impact of translocal dynamics from various vantage points. Passmore and others examine how global ideologies such as neoliberalism influence public programs and ways that project leaders attempt to redirect them. The chapters by Butler, Iris, and Copeland-Carson examine how global migration can influence issues as diverse as public health, community development, and senior services in cities and agencies. Dewey's chapter examines the local-global connections in the international sex trade, particularly how policy makers and advocates attempt to influence its impact on eastern European women. Clarke shows how modern transportation networks connect localities to the global economy, bringing both positive and negative impacts for women and low-income people, and the multiple ways that anthropologists address these issues. Fiske, focusing on her climate change advocacy, shows how the intersection and collision of local and global forces can influence project outcomes. Squires and Wasson demonstrate the ways that applied anthropology of information and communication technology (ICT) projects can highlight the unique ways that consumers localize global communications technologies. Using the translocal context of university-based public health training programs, Pinsker shows how program design and practices reflect the tensions and connections of local and global dynamics. Finally, Schensul and Butler's conclusion considers the potential implications of these case studies for an applied translocal anthropology.

Anthropology in Practice

The practice of anthropology provides an important perspective and information to help the field and society more broadly understand and address the challenges of global complexity. Anthropology is useful for understanding and managing the accelerated structural changes caused by globalization because we view people as situated in complex, changing social systems, and have for much of our history.

The first several generations of anthropologists were absorbed with understanding the "glue" that held people together in communities and in systems that reached across time and space. This is still a central focus of the discipline. However, the effort to fit people into a sociocultural context has become more challenging in recent years because of the almost continual augmentation of connectivity across the planet. Today, the relevant "community" may be a neighborhood, a city, a nation, a pastoral nomadic tribe, a kinship group, or a diaspora. Normally it is several of these at the same time. Community may extend across many localities and members may even speak different languages on a daily basis. People living in a locality move in a wide array of differing realms that overlap in multiple ways, are often dependent on one another, and are not cognitively recognized as distinct by those who live in these realms.

There has been much controversy in the past century about how community can be usefully defined in the face of sociocultural change coming from many directions, even prior to the current age of globalization (Delanty 2003; Hyland and Brimhall 2005). Although it has not been considered valid to close one's community to outside influences, even heuristically, for at least a half-century, it is part of anthropology that we view people's life in situ. This means that practitioners have a special requirement to clarify the linkages among multiple layers of human activity. Our work is commissioned by people and organizations that plan to use our findings in some way. If we fail to adequately map the overlaps and fissures in the experiences of people's lives, those who support and fund our work may misdirect their own efforts to address issues arising from global forces. We do not have the luxury to pretend that global dynamics do not affect the local projects with which we work.

Our efforts to establish and understand community require us to tease out the relevant connections from the complex layers in which people live. Although we use theory to orient our understanding of project contexts, our careers depend on unpacking these frameworks—concepts such as "community," "development," and "globalization"—to accurately identify, explain, and even influence the worldviews and actions of people for our clients or employers.

We try very hard to obtain and communicate the perspectives of the populations with which we work, speaking their language as much as possible in an effort to translate the viewpoints of these groups to program sponsors, policy makers, and government institutions. We also translate the perspectives of clients to the communities with which we work. This can and often does lead to a culture-broker role in which the anthropologist bridges organizational languages and cultures. The role of culture broker can be difficult, and should be entered into with awareness and humility. The anthropologist practitioner is not necessarily a native of either community. Careful investigation and cross-checking of both information and opinion are essential to avoid miscommunication that would make things worse rather than better.

Reflections on Globalization Theory

Although we do not envision this as a book on globalization, it is an important dimension of many of the chapters in this volume. "Globalization" is a broad rubric that encompasses a wide range of phenomena associated with the growing connectivity of communities and humans around the world. Because of the vast literature on globalization, we would like to clarify our use of the term in this volume.

The globalization framework as we consider it here builds on prior scholarship in the anthropology of globalization (see Appadurai 1996; Edelman and Haugerud 2005; Hannerz 1996; Inda and Rosaldo 2002; Lewellen 2002; Trouillot 2003), including the following concepts:

- Globalization involves complex and disjunctive flows of capital, people, commodities, images, and ideologies. Although it is important to examine the economic dimensions of globalization, other aspects must be investigated as well (Appadurai 1996; Inda and Rosaldo 2002). For example, anthropologists have extensively criticized neoliberalism and the logic of the marketplace as an appropriate framework for social interventions (Passmore, this volume; Edelman and Haugerud 2005).

- Globalization is always accompanied by local adaptation. In other words, while processes of globalization may promote the spread of Western goods and practices, these goods and practices are adapted by local peoples to fit into their own cultural systems of meaning. Phenomena ranging from hip-hop music to McDonald's have taken on surprisingly different meanings around the world (Condry 2006; Watson 1997).
- Globalization is increasingly multicentric (see Hannerz 1992). Today it is not only the United States and European countries that direct the flow of global capital and cultural forces. The current recession and a growing body of literature highlight the growing global impact of nonwestern countries, particularly Brazil, Russia, India, and China (Fishman 2006; Pelle 2007). This era of multicapitalism complicates conventional notions of globalization, requiring more attention to South-South interactions as well as the ascendance of Asian global powers. Practicing anthropologists create important windows into which we can see how these emerging powers influence globalization.
- The traditional anthropological notion that cultures have clear geographical boundaries has been replaced by an awareness that this is no longer true, if indeed it ever was. One effect of globalization is the deterritorialization of cultures due to migration flows and the worldwide spread of media, information, and images (Butler, this volume; Appadurai 1996; Gupta and Ferguson 1997; Kearney 1995).

While drawing on these scholarly insights from the anthropology of globalization, our experience as practitioners attunes us to the creative ways that people "on-the-ground" are attempting to reshape, resist, and even transform global dynamics and structures. This effort to integrate theory and practice allows us to contribute to the topic of globalization in several different ways.

- We emphasize the human face of globalization through our lived experience working with local groups that have been profoundly affected by the forces of globalization.
- We show how existing theories can be tested by application in the field. Some ideas may sound reasonable, but may not map very well onto observed situations on the ground.
- The process of engaging in practical actions has led us to new ideas and new theory development. For instance, one area in which we contribute is the effort to theorize how positive social change happens, and how we as practitioners can effectively contribute to such processes. Although there are growing literatures on aspects of this issue, such as social movement theory and complexity theory, it is still a fascinating but emerging area (Edelman 2001; Geyer 2003; Guidry and Kennedy 2000; Kiel and Elliott 1996; Mosko and Damon 2005; Nash 2005; Smith and Chatfield 1997).

Applied anthropologists today work in a variety of contexts trying to address social problems and new opportunities created by the global economy. For instance, the expansion of wealth in countries such as China, India, and Brazil has created a new demand for consumer electronics as well as a heightened need to address the potential negative environmental impact of increased consumption. At the same time, there is a growing disparity between haves and have-nots in many parts of the world. The economic crisis that developed in 2008–2009 spread from one national economy to another with a rapidity that had never been seen before because of the unprecedented number of international linkages among financial institutions. Aided by easy credit and liberalizing economies, in just a decade globalizing forces created a worldwide economic boom that bubbled and then burst (Tett 2009).

As the Great Recession unfolded, globalization moved from being the market's new invisible hand to a visceral experience in many people's daily lives (Rampbell 2009). The shell-shocked, formerly middle-class family now living in a Sacramento tent city, the new Madoff poor, the foreclosed Nevada homeowner, the 60-somethings who now need to indefinitely defer retirement, and the legions of suddenly unemployed in cities and towns throughout the world have taken an unpleasant crash course in the human costs of globalization. Similarly, we see the rise of global pandemics and accelerating climate change around the globe. Applied anthropologists' work on projects in many areas such as environmental protection, public health, community development, social service, and consumer electronic design offer new opportunities to better understand the localization of these global dynamics and resolve the new challenges that can emerge as a result.

One of this volume's strengths comes from its synthesis of anthropological thinking about social change with the concrete experience of anthropologist practitioners working in the global arena. Our jobs expose us to the new cultures and culture changes that are developing as communities seek to sustain their existence in the face of globalizing processes. Applied anthropologists compile empirical data on the ramifications of global forces through social systems. We facilitate change, act as advocates, and as culture brokers. At the same time, our work is also constrained by forces that relate to contemporary social change, such as neoliberal government policies and multinational corporate interests, and our reflections on these constraints provide further insights.

Anthropologists in Practice

Anthropologists address the impact that global connectedness has on people's lives. This book focuses on the experiences of practicing anthropologists who have used anthropology to address, clarify, or resolve cultural questions. The work of such anthropologists is normally commissioned and funded by an agency or organization with a need to understand some phenomenon with which they themselves are working. Practice is not defined by a work environment. Practitioners of anthropology may be located in corporations, nonprofit organizations, government agencies, universities, or as independent consultants.

Many of us who consider ourselves practitioners combine institutional settings and roles into jobs with multiple complementary components, as we are called upon to diagnose problems, identify theoretical approaches to them, develop research designs, implement research, and synthesize and report results. Moreover, our work tends to change many times during our careers, as we move up organizational hierarchies or as we experiment with different challenges (Clarke, this volume; Wasson 2006b). In the practice of our discipline, we can draw upon the richness of anthropology and combine it with the insights of other scientists in novel, interdisciplinary ways.

Regardless of where we work today, at some point in our career, all of us have worked as practitioners and draw on those experiences for this volume. The training and experience that practicing anthropologists have accumulated in working across many kinds of change allow them to address complex social problems and facilitate the efforts of organizations and communities seeking to address the challenges of globalization in arenas such as public health, the environment, design, organizational culture and change, aging, human rights, human services, international development, food security, community development, and the military. Depending on their roles, practitioners may intervene at widely different points in change processes, from grassroots activism to the development of federal policies.

We have both formal and informal influence as practitioners. Usually a product of our research is a written report intended to address client needs. We may also publish in the peer-reviewed literature, although academic publication can be constrained by the confidentiality agreements of our clients and funders. Despite these constraints, practitioners have a long track record of academic contributions to anthropology and other fields (see Copeland-Carson 2005; Ervin 2004; Farmer 1999; Hyland and Brimhall 2005; Schensul and LeCompte 1999; Singer and Baer 1995; Van Willigen 1980; Wasson 2006b; Wulff and Fiske 1987). It is our hope that this volume will build on and extend that body of work.

Scholar-Practitioners

This volume presents a model for the application of anthropological theory in practice, and the use of practitioner experience to enlarge anthropological perspectives on contemporary human issues. All anthropologists are to some degree both scholars and practitioners. A distinction between those who are scholars and those who practice does not reflect the ways in which anthropologists work in the twenty-first century. Defining our work as either scholarship or practice undermines our own capacity—indeed that of all anthropologists—to understand and address the social conditions we encounter.

In this volume, we explore the potential of anthropology as an agent of social change while demonstrating its limits and complexity, and suggest some ways in which anthropology can further strengthen its public role and impact. The concept of the scholar-practitioner emphasizes the integral nature of both components to the anthropological endeavor. The idea of the scholar-practitioner has been implicit in anthropological practice since the era of the public intellectuals of previous generations, such as Margaret Mead, who sought to apply anthropological insights to the problems of modern society (Eddy and Partridge 1978; Patton 2005). In the last decade, the integration of theory and practice has become an explicit focus of attention in anthropology (Baba 2000, 2009; Copeland-Carson 2005; Wasson 2006b).

We integrate scholarly and practical approaches by examining how theory influences action and how practice contributes to theory. By intertwining practice and scholarship, we are able to offer a perspective that goes beyond solutions to specific social problems to contribute to a broader theoretical understanding of how global processes operate across time, space, and culture (Butler 2005). In addition, as we reflect on our own research processes, we hope that our work will add to the theory of practice—a "set of ideas that explains the role of practice inside and outside the discipline" (Baba 2000:21)—and reinforces the training of future practitioners.

Common strands that link us to each other and to communities are explored throughout the volume. None of our chapters presents simple stories of how we interact with the world to understand, facilitate, or ameliorate change. We seek instead to show the complexities and challenges that we encounter as we try to bridge multiple points of view in the context of global change. The chapters represent our accounts of events and their meanings, recognizing that other participants in projects may see things differently. We view this volume as an effort to move forward the ongoing dialogue within anthropology and with our partners in other disciplines to strengthen anthropology's positive impact on our globalizing world.

Audiences for This Volume

We have tried to write the book in a way that is accessible to a broad range of readers. However, there are two primary audiences for this book, each with multiple constituencies.

One audience for this book is anthropologists who want a perspective on the practice of anthropology in the global context. This group of people includes academic anthropologists, students, scholar-practitioners, and practitioners.

Most especially, we hope to reach students and beginning anthropologists whose careers will take form in this new, more complex environment.

Many anthropologists have written about transnational dynamics, usually from the perspective of globalization. The more widely known publications have come from academic anthropologists who often developed good theoretical frameworks, but did not link them to practical applications (Appadurai 1996; Edelman and Haugerud 2005; Lewellen 2002). Prior publications on globalization by practicing anthropologists are scattered across many sources, and have not previously been pulled together into a coherent book-length exploration. We hope to provide one such resource to our colleagues in anthropology.

Another audience is those who are not anthropologists but who work—or might seek to work—with anthropologists. This group includes colleagues on interdisciplinary teams, employers, clients, or other stakeholders in the projects on which anthropology practitioners work. In this category, we may also include members of general public who have an interest in what practicing anthropologists do, and what they can contribute to understanding the effect of global change on people's lives around the world.

Structure of Chapters

In the chapters that follow, anthropological contributions to the challenges of the complex global environment are explored in depth, from a first-person perspective. The authors examine a topic that they engage with in their own work; the chapter topics were selected to highlight the breadth and variety of areas in which anthropologist practitioners are making a difference.

To help readers navigate the book, all of the authors have followed the same four-part structure in the design of their chapters:

- Introduction. In this section, authors summarize the global issues in their field.
- An Anthropological Perspective on Their Field. In this section, authors provide an overview of how an applied anthropology perspective on their field can deepen our understanding of globalization's dynamics and impacts.
- Case Examples. In this section, authors present ethnographic stories and examples from their research that illuminate the kinds of work being done by anthropology practitioners in this field.
- Conclusions. Here, authors identify key lessons learned and recommendations that deepen our understanding of global issues.

We invite you to follow your interests in choosing the order in which you read the chapters. They do not need to be read in a particular sequence; each one can stand on its own.

Acknowledgments

The editors would like to express their deep appreciation to the chapter authors for participating in a community that was a model of collaborative intellectual engagement and warm collegial support. This is the second shared project for most participants, the first having been an edited volume on the lives of women anthropology practitioners (Wasson 2006a). The community thus existed continuously from 2004 until the publication of this book in 2011. Its extended lifespan allowed for many fascinating conversations over the years via e-mail, teleconferences, and at conferences. The relationships that formed will undoubtedly continue to grow in the future.

Second, the editors and authors would all like to express their gratitude to the School for Advanced Research (SAR), and particularly Nancy Owen Lewis, for hosting a short seminar for the book project in May 2008. The opportunity to spend several days together at SAR in focused review and discussion was invaluable in allowing us to formulate the themes and goals of the book, and in providing momentum for the project.

We also would like to thank Robert Packwood for conducting an extensive literature review for us on the anthropology of globalization. Robert completed his master's degree in the Department of Anthropology, University of North Texas, and worked for Christina Wasson as research assistant while he was there. His review of the literature was thoughtful, detailed, and rapidly executed; it was a pleasure to work with him.

This book is dedicated to the countless residents, colleagues, and other partners from many disciplines, communities, and backgrounds with whom we have worked. We hope that this book not only chronicles the daunting social challenges facing the world but also bears witness to their tireless and inspiring efforts to make a difference.

References

Anderson, Benedict
    1983 Imagined Communities. New York: Verso Books.
Appadurai, Arjun
    1996 Modernity at Large: Cultural Dimensions of Globalization. Minneapolis: University of Minnesota Press.
Baba, Marietta L.
    2000 Theories of Practice in Anthropology: A Critical Appraisal. NAPA Bulletin 18:17–44.
    2009 Disciplinary-professional Relations in an Era of Anthropological Engagement. *Human Organization* 68(4):380–91.
Butler, Mary
    2005 Translating Evaluation Anthropology. *In* Creating Evaluation Anthropology: Introducing an Emerging Subfield. NAPA Bulletin 24:17–30.

Condry, Ian
2006 Hip-hop Japan: Rap and the Paths of Cultural Globalization. Durham: Duke University Press.

Copeland-Carson, Jacqueline
2005 "Theory-building" Evaluation Anthropology: Bridging the Scholarship-versus-Practice Divide. NAPA Bulletin 24:7–16.

Delanty, Gerard
2003 Conceptions of Europe: A Review of Recent Trends. *European Journal of Social Theory* 6(4):471–88.

Eddy, Elizabeth M., and William L. Partridge
1978 The Development of Applied Anthropology in America. *In* Applied Anthropology in America, Elizabeth M. Eddy and William L. Partridge, eds. Pp. 3–45. New York: Columbia University Press.

Edelman, Marc
2001 Social Movements: Changing Paradigms and Forms of Politics. *Annual Review of Anthropology* 30:285–317.

Edelman, Marc, and Angelique Haugerud
2005 The Anthropology of Development and Globalization: From Classical Political Economy to Contemporary Neoliberalism. Malden, MA: Blackwell.

Ervin, Alexander M.
2004 Applied Anthropology: Tools and Perspectives for Contemporary Practice. Boston: Allyn & Bacon.

Farmer, Paul
1999 Infections and Inequalities: The Modern Plagues. Berkeley: University of California Press.

Fishman, Ted C.
2006 China, Inc. How the Rise of the Next Superpower Challenges America and the World. New York: MacMillian.

Gates, Bill
n.d. BrainyQuote.com. Available at: http://www.brainyquote.com/quotes/quotes/b/billgates384628.html. Accessed June 26, 2011.

Geyer, Robert
2003 Beyond the Third Way: The Science of Complexity and the Politics of Choice. *British Journal of Politics and International Relations* 5(2):237–57.

Guidry, John A., and Michael D. Kennedy
2000 Globalizations and Social Movements: Culture, Power, and the Transnational Public Sphere. Ann Arbor: University of Michigan Press.

Gupta, Akhil, and James Ferguson
1997 Culture, Power, Place: Explorations in Critical Anthropology. Durham, N.C.: Duke University Press.

Hannerz, Ulf
1992 Cultural Complexity: Studies in the Social Organization of Meaning. New York: Columbia University Press.

Hannerz, Ulf
1996 Transnational Connections: Culture, People, Places. London and New York: Routledge.
Hyland, Stanley E., and Robert E. Brimhall
2005 Evaluation Anthropology in Community Development/Community Building. *In* Creating Evaluation Anthropology: Introducing an Emerging Subfield. NAPA Bulletin 24:125–37.
Inda, Jonathan Xavier, and Renato Rosaldo
2002 The Anthropology of Globalization: A Reader. Malden, MA: Blackwell.
Kearney, M.
1995 The Local and the Global: The Anthropology of Globalization and Transnationalism. *Annual Review of Anthropology* 24:547–65.
Keisler, Harry
2005 A Conversation with Lakhdar Brahimi, United Nations Special Envoy. University of California. Berkeley, CA: Regents of the University of California, April 3, 2005. Available at: http://globetrotter.berkeley.edu/people5/Brahimi/brahimi-con6.html.
Kiel, L. Douglas, and Euel W. Elliott
1996 Chaos Theory in the Social Sciences: Foundations and Applications. Ann Arbor: University of Michigan Press.
Lewellen, Ted C.
2002 The Anthropology of Globalization: Cultural Anthropology Enters the 21st Century. Westport, CT: Bergin & Garvey.
Marcus, George E.
1998 Ethnography Through Thick and Thin. Princeton: Princeton University Press.
McLuhan, H. Marshall
1962 The Gutenberg Galaxy: The Making of Typographic Man. Toronto: University of Toronto Press.
1964 Understanding Media: The Extensions of Man. New York: McGraw Hill.
Mosko, Mark S., and Frederick H. Damon
2005 On the Order of Chaos: Social Anthropology and the Science of Chaos. New York: Berghahn.
Nash, June C.
2005 Social Movements: An Anthropological Reader. Malden, MA: Blackwell.
Ong, Aihwa, and Stephen J. Collier (eds.)
2004 Global Assemblages: Technology, Politics, and Ethics as Anthropological Problems. Malden, MA: Blackwell.
Patton, Michael Q.
2005 The View from Evaluation. NAPA Bulletin 24:31–40.
Pelle, Stefano
2007 Understanding Emerging Markets: BRIC by Brick. New York/New Delhi: Sage Publications.

Rampbell, Catherine
2009 "Great Recession": A Brief Etymology. *The New York Times*, March 11, 2009. Available at: http://economix.blogs.nytimes.com/2009/03/11/great-recession-a-brief-etymology/. Accessed June 26, 2011.

Schensul, Jean J., and Margaret D. LeCompte
1999 Ethnographer's Toolkit: 7 Volume Boxed Set. Walnut Creek, Calif.: AltaMira Press.

Singer, Merrill, and Hans Baer
1995 Critical Medical Anthropology. Amityville, N.Y.: Baywood Publishing Co.

Smith, Jackie, and Charles Chatfield
1997 Transnational Social Movements and Global Politics: Solidarity Beyond the State. Syracuse: Syracuse University Press.

Tett, Gillian
2009 Fool's Gold. New York: Free Press.

Trouillot, Michael-Rolph
2003 Global Transformations: Anthropology and the Modern World. New York: Palgrave Macmillan.

Van Willigen, John
1980 Anthropology in Use: A Bibliographic Chronology of the Development of Applied Anthropology. Pleasantville: Redgrave Publishing.

Wasson, Christina (ed.)
2006a Making History at the Frontier: Women Creating Careers as Practicing Anthropologists. NAPA Bulletin 26.
2006b Making History at the Frontier. *In* Making History at the Frontier: Women Creating Careers as Practicing Anthropologists, Christina Wasson, ed. NAPA Bulletin 26:1–19.

Watson, James L.
1997 Golden Arches East: McDonald's in East Asia. Stanford, CA: Stanford University Press.

Wulff, Robert M., and Shirley J. Fiske
1987 Anthropological Praxis: Translating Knowledge into Action. Boulder: Westview Press.

1

Global Localities and the Management of Infectious Disease

Mary Odell Butler

Introduction

The more I have worked with the issue of global influences in the context of public health—or in any other context for that matter—the less certain I have become about what it means to talk about culture in a global sense. Much of what I know has been brought into question by all this change. Yet, anthropology has met this challenge with innovative concepts and approaches to traditional notions of culture, aided in no small part by applied anthropologists who work with this change every day, on the ground.

In the twenty-first century, we are all challenged to examine our understandings of how people organize themselves and how they act under these changing conditions. A vast literature on globalization describes the many aspects of global change, including in markets and capital, increases in migration and return migration, the detachment of work from locality, global tourism, daily communication among people over the Internet and social media (see Appadurai 1996; Edelman and Haugerud 2005; Hannerz 1996; Inda and Rosaldo 2002; Lewellen 2002; Trouillot 1995). In this chapter, I focus explicitly on the increase in connectivity of communities across the globe as it affects the transmission and control of infectious diseases.

As it turns out, the spread of disease is one example of a much broader phenomenon. As I write this, the nations of the Mediterranean and the Middle East are witnessing uprisings by citizens against governments they perceive as oppressive. The rapid spread of the idea that people can be successful in resisting authoritarian control is a new kind of contagion,

21

one that is spread by the flow of information over the Internet and social media. The world is now linked densely by streams of "capital, people, commodities, images, and ideologies," which results in borders becoming "increasingly porous, allowing more and more peoples and cultures to be cast into intense and immediate contact with each other" (Inda and Rosaldo 2002:2). The proliferation of linkages among communities facilitates the flow of ideas, commodities, and information as well. As the connectedness of the world increases, people are increasingly living in complex, multilayered communities with individuals who are themselves embedded in multiple contexts that overlap and interlock in many ways.

The visions of the world from the perspectives of anthropologists and public health professionals are distinct from one another but, as we will see, they are also complementary. Seen through the anthropological lens, people live embedded in culture, a shared understanding they acquire as part of their experience living and interacting with other humans in families, kin groups, communities, and nations. Culture is not a static entity, but a complex matrix made up of multiple exposures of people to other people directly or indirectly through education, literature, and media. The culture that shapes human life is not necessarily explicit and articulated. It is the task of the anthropologist to untangle and explain culture in such a way that those who live it will recognize the anthropologist's description as correct. Anthropologists do this by asking people to tell us how they perceive the world and then assembling the perspectives of many into a description. The unit of anthropological analysis is the community, usually but not always defined geographically.

This perspective differs from that of public health in significant ways. Public health is grounded in the idea that it is the job of government to protect the public health—the health of communities. This requires monitoring, service delivery, and the development of policies for disease prevention or control for people living in some kind of government jurisdiction. Public health is usually described by measuring something, be it disease incidence and prevalence, risk factor distribution, or behavior change. The usual unit of public health intervention is the individual living in a designated territory. People will accept public health interventions if they understand the rationale behind them. There is a vast literature on health behavior designed to predict how individuals will act in response to such interventions (see Bandura 1986, 2004; Green and Kreuter 1991; Guo et al. 2011; Prochaska and DiClemente 1983).

There is also common ground on which we can communicate and build. Both fields are concerned with the responses of communities of people to challenges, in this case from health, disease, environmental degradation, and exposures to dangerous substances. We both tend to think in terms of geographic jurisdictions as the unit of study or action, a concept that is under increasing pressure from the shifting nature of community due to global flows of people and diseases. We share an understanding of the role of policy and political power in determining what happens to people "on the ground." And we both take an ethical stance that recognizes the respect due to the people with whom we work, the critical nature of informed consent in interventions, and the commitment to do no harm.

The case of collaboration between public health and anthropology in addressing global health issues illustrates the essential nature of inter-disciplinary approaches to global problems. The academic disciplines in which we are educated do not change rapidly in response to changes in the larger world, yet the issues that we address in our professional lives will mutate many times in our careers. Professional education continues far beyond the university, especially for anthropological practitioners, and much of what we learn, we learn from colleagues and clients in other fields. To maintain our edge in responding to emerging problems, we must cultivate flexibility and an open mind to what we can learn from others. Work across disciplinary boundaries in response to complex problems of social change is synergistic. Entirely new approaches can result from such collaboration.

To illustrate the way practicing anthropologists develop these new approaches in response to change, I will talk about tuberculosis (TB). TB is a companion of migration. Thus it is the global health problem par excellence, one that requires a global solution. TB is one of those diseases all too often attributed to the cultural practices of sufferers that result in unhygienic living conditions, failure to take advantage of preventive health services, and refusal to seek and maintain timely treatment. The basic causes of TB do in fact lie in the conditions of poverty and inequality (Farmer 1999). However, the first key anthropological insight into TB is that it is not culture that is to blame; it is poverty. Few middle-class Americans will ever know someone who is infected with TB, at least until measures to control the disease among the poor and the displaced fail. The disease is painfully familiar to the poor of all countries who are at continuing high risk because of crowded housing, poor nutrition, lack of resources to detect and treat the disease, or absence of the political will to intervene.

How then do we understand where TB happens, to whom it happens, and how to intervene? I will consider public health measures to control tuberculosis in terms of global localities. Global localities are home to communities that embed people simultaneously in many contexts—local, regional, national, and international. They are far less dependent on geographic space than are the communities that anthropologists have traditionally studied. Global localities are not geographically continuous, but consist of people linked into communities across the earth by kinship, shared cultural experience, communication, migration, and travel. The lived experience of community is different at different times as people's relationships to geography, culture, employment, and worldwide interconnection via the Internet and social media evolve. Linkages to the outside and to each other may be different for the young and the old in the same households, and yet the global locality is experienced by people as community, the cultural world in which they function.

In the sections that follow, I describe the global movements of infectious diseases and the public health models that have evolved to contain them based on my own observations of public health policy and practice over 20 years as an anthropologist working on the evaluation of public health programs. I call on a growing body of fairly contentious literature on what public health should look like as contact among people and their microorganisms intensifies, and draw from anthropological thinking about globalization to explore its implications for public health approaches to infectious disease. I look at the application and applicability of the public health model as it has been refined over the last century in one situation, the control of tuberculosis in the U.S.-Mexico border.[1] Finally, I discuss the role of anthropology and anthropological practitioners in addressing problems of public health in the global locality.

Public Health in a Global Context

Many of the afflictions of the twenty-first century are diseases for which proven medical interventions are available to ameliorate or eliminate adverse consequences of disease even for those living with poverty, malnutrition, poor housing, and neglect. What is missing are the political will, the health infrastructure, and the health policies needed to make remedies available to those who need them. As a result, the world's poor, wherever they live, are dying of diseases that are almost unknown to most people in wealthier countries.

The movement of people and their diseases across localities and boundaries is a significant characteristic of the new global environment. Business, travel, tourism, urbanization, and international migration have not only moved us from one place to another but have facilitated the movement of infectious diseases in ways unprecedented in more sedentary times (Gushulak and McPherson 2007). Diseases that have spread with people into new places include HIV/AIDS, cholera, dengue fever, malaria, and tuberculosis (Morse 1995; Wilson 1995, 2010). The consequences of migration for infectious diseases are especially grave because migratory populations are often the poor, the sick, and the powerless displaced by economic conditions, national disasters, or wars (Carballo and Nerukar 2001; Farmer 1996, 1999; Ioannidi-Kapolou 2010). Modernization itself leads to changes in production and to ecological degradation that bring people into close contact both with microbes and each other. No one is safe. Today, infectious disease is concentrated in the poor and the disenfranchised population. Microbes are not constrained by boundaries and economic differences, however. Globalization has facilitated the spread of infectious diseases in ways that have yet to make their full consequences felt among the advantaged populations who usually make policy decisions that affect the health and welfare of the poor.

The global spread of infectious diseases is nothing new. Diseases have always accompanied people as they have moved across territory with trade, armies, and resettlement of human populations. Syphilis emerged in Europe in 1495, three years after Columbus first landed in the Americas and during a time of intensification of long-distance warfare in Europe and the Middle East. Opinion is still divided over whether syphilis was a new disease that emerged from previous illnesses caused by a closely related organism, whether it came from the Far East along trade routes, or whether it was "Montezuma's Revenge" brought to Europe from the Americas (Quetel 1990:34–37). Regardless of its origin, it had catastrophic effects on the population of Europe. Similar stories can be told about many other diseases. Each time the world has experienced a dramatic increase in connectivity, infectious diseases have entered history as an unintended companion of new opportunities (Apostolopoulos and Sonmez 2010; Porter 1999; Zinsser 1934).

The present movement of infectious disease is different from those of the past in its scale and the speed with which epidemic disease moves across space. Unprecedented numbers of people routinely travel across international boundaries with the speed made possible by modern travel. The spread of the H1N1 virus is a case in point. Influenza ("flu") is a respiratory disease of greater or lesser severity spread by an unstable, rapidly mutating set of viral strains with a marked ability to move from animal populations to humans. The flu with which we are most familiar is a seasonal variety concentrated during the winter months. However, flu is very unpredictable, so public health authorities maintain a high level of vigilance for new flu strains or strains newly appearing in human populations.

The current "novel" H1N1 virus was first detected in Mexico in mid-April 2009. By the beginning of May, the disease had been reported in 21 countries (in addition to Mexico and the United States) with a total of 1,882 probable or confirmed cases (Morbidity and Mortality Weekly Report [MMWR] 2009). By June 11, when the World Health Organization (WHO) declared that a global pandemic of H1N1 was in place, the disease had been reported in 74 countries with almost 29,000 laboratory-confirmed cases (WHO 2009). For the period August 30,

2009, to January 9, 2010, the Centers for Disease Control (CDC) reported more than 61,000 cases in the U.S. and its territories with 1,779 confirmed fatalities (MMWR 2010).

The spread of H1N1 outside of Mexico has a clear link to international travel. In May 2009, of 178 cases worldwide for which a travel history was available, 84 percent reported recent travel to Mexico (MMWR 2009). Nor is H1N1 the only recent worldwide epidemic of a serious respiratory disease. The 2003 epidemic of Severe Acute Respiratory Syndrome (SARS) in 2002–2003 is another example. SARS is a serious respiratory disease of unknown etiology that apparently originated in Guandong Province, China, and moved with travelers to 11 countries in little more than a month after it was first reported by the Chinese Ministry of Health (MMWR 2003a, 2003c).

Like H1N1 and SARS, TB is a serious respiratory disease that moves with human populations. It is highly infectious, with an airborne route of transmission that disproportionately affects those of low socioeconomic status, crowded living conditions, and poor nutrition. It occurs at a very high rate in immigrant populations. In 2007, 58 percent of TB cases in the United States in persons of known origin were in foreign-born persons. In addition, 77 percent of Latinos and 96 percent of Asians with newly diagnosed cases of TB were foreign born (MMWR 2008). In one study in New Jersey, it was found that the incidence of TB in the foreign population increased from 20 percent in 1986 to 37 percent in 1995 (Liu et al. 1998).

Although the disease has been present for longer than anyone knows, it declined steadily in Europe and the United States over most of the twentieth century. Beginning in 1985, the decline first leveled off and then began to reverse itself in spite of the availability of effective treatments for most cases of TB. The resurgence of TB is attributed to a lack of funding and commitment on the part of public health agencies to control of the disease (Institute of Medicine [IOM] 2000).

The Public Health System

To understand the factors that govern the management of tuberculosis, we need to look briefly at how public health is organized. Public health as classically construed builds on a basic model for how the health of the community should be protected by preventing, detecting, and controlling diseases and conditions leading to ill health. Public health is a governmental function, although public health agencies may work in collaboration with private organizations. Public health agencies normally have responsibility for preventing and controlling health problems for a population living in a defined territory. In the United States, the protection of public health is a function largely reserved to the states with policy advice and technical assistance coming from the federal level, policy making and the maintenance of vigilance over population health at the state level, and the delivery of public health services at the local level (Buttery 1992). Management of infectious disease within countries is the responsibility of national agencies, most commonly ministries of health, that are responsible for providing both preventative and treatment services to their populations. In poor and middle-income nations, public health policy and practice are also affected by many layers of policy and technical assistance from the WHO, other United Nations (UN) agencies, and nongovernmental organizations (NGOs) (Last 1992:1130).

In 1988, the IOM defined public health as consisting of three essential functions: assessment, assurance, and public policy (IOM 1988:42–47). Assessment includes the monitoring of the health of populations and the initiation of interventions at the community level, for example to investigate and control outbreaks of serious infectious diseases.

The assurance function ensures that appropriate health services are available to the population to manage common health problems. In the United States, assurance is reserved to the private sector largely through private and limited public (Medicare/Medicaid) health insurance, sometimes reinforced by services from public health clinics and federally funded community health centers. An alternative model is found in Britain, Canada, and the Scandinavian countries where assurance of health services is the responsibility of the public sector, although often a private health care system parallels the public service (Porter 1999).

The policy function is focused on assessing the fit between available infrastructure and the needs of communities and populations. It is centered in government but is now widely shared with private entities, especially those with an interest in the provision of health care. A second IOM report, *Future of Public's Health in the 21ˢᵗ Century,* argues for an intersectoral approach to public health planning that brings private and public partners together to achieve improvements in the public health (IOM 2003:2–3). This reflects a general movement toward privatization of public functions in the United States over the past two decades (see Passmore in this volume).

For any health system, these three elements—assessment, assurance, and policy development—must be part of the public health enterprise. If they are not, the system fails in one or more ways: to detect disease, control outbreaks, ameliorate the illness of those already ill to minimize further disease, and/or ensure the well-being of both individuals and communities. For example, most of us are well aware that the U.S. system has failings on the assurance front for the poor and vulnerable, a problem that is reflected in an uncertain and unstable health policy

(IOM 2001:225–29). This problem is vastly increased if we take the observation to the global level. Viewed as a global system, the availability of health services for the poor and even for the middle class is seriously deficient in many countries.

The distribution and uses of power is central to anthropological thinking about how humans respond to inequities in the distribution of benefits and risks. Public health is a political system; like all political systems, it has discontinuities that are not part of the organizational chart but still affect the effectiveness with which public health systems operate. Unofficial communication channels are as important in public health as they are in any other human organization. Public health epidemiologists live in a community in which there is a network of acquaintance that accommodates much of the daily activity of public health. In the United States, many public health epidemiologists went through a small group of training programs such as the CDC Epidemic Intelligence Service (EIS) program (Thacker 2006). The "old school tie" of the EIS is sometimes a much faster means of communication of disease outbreaks than the more official surveillance channels, as the State Epidemiologist responsible for disease control in one state telephones his colleague in a second state to verify the presence of cases that might signal an outbreak (Butler 1990, 1991).

Integrating public health on a global scale is essential to protect the highly mobile populations of the twenty-first century from infectious diseases once thought to be under control as well as new diseases coming from changes in the relationships of humans to nature and to each other. International cooperation in the control of emerging infectious diseases across national boundaries goes back at least to the middle of the nineteenth century (Bashford 2006; Fidler 2001). However, this kind of cooperation has been negotiated disease by disease and is not robust to changes in political and economic conditions. For instance, infectious diseases may reemerge because of unilateral relaxation of a health policy. Until recently, dengue, a mosquito-borne illness that causes a hemorrhagic fever, was uncommon in the Americas because in the 1950s and 1960s the Pan-American Health Organization (PAHO) maintained environmental measures to control *Aedes aegypti,* the vector of yellow fever as well as of dengue. The United States discontinued its participation in the Aedes eradication program in 1970, and support for the program gradually eroded in other countries. By 1995, dengue hemorrhagic fever had become endemic in much of the Americas (Briseño-Garcia et al. 1996; Farley 2004:297; Gubler and Clark 1995; Morse 1995).

A global health paradigm will require international acceptance of common systems of surveillance, nomenclature, laboratory practice, and regularization of modes of concerted action in the case of transnational diseases. At times, it may necessitate the acceptance across borders of disease control measures that conflict with liberalization of trade as, for example, is the case with tobacco control and international tobacco marketing (Porter 1999:299). These kinds of action require some sacrifice of national sovereignty in the interest of global disease prevention and control. Some commentators on the evolution of global health systems argue for a shift from an international health paradigm to a global health system in which the needs of the population of the globe are given priority over those of any participating nation (Brown et al. 2006; Yach and Bettcher 1998a, 1998b). Most countries are very hesitant to relinquish any of their sovereignty over public health within their borders.

There is no international legal basis for establishing binding requirements for infectious disease response across national boundaries and for ensuring compliance. The WHO is the UN agency officially responsible for global health acting in concert with an array of NGOs, private foundations, aid programs, and other international agencies. Current practice in controlling international threats from infectious diseases calls for cooperation with UN International Health Regulations administered by WHO. WHO cannot legally or politically call for increases in public health infrastructure in member nations, and there is no mechanism for enforcement of international regulations. One author calls it a fundamental paradox in international law that globalization frustrates international efforts to control infectious disease by eroding the sovereignty of national public health systems that must develop the component health policies and programs for any international response (Fidler 1996).

The capacity of nations to implement programs to address their own health needs has been diminished by a shift of funding and technical assistance away from public agencies toward an "unruly mélange" of public-private partnerships (Buse and Walt 1997). An increased emphasis on market forces and privatization of multiple functions in the 1980s and 1990s led international health funders to channel funds to NGOs and private voluntary organizations (PVOs). These organizations provide health benefits to participating countries and are often significant parts of the public health system in poor countries. Ministries of Health in poor countries are unlikely to decline such offers of help. Nor is it inherently wrong to support programs in poor countries with private funds. However, the privatization of public health functions can compromise the capacity of health programs in middle-income and poor nations to manage health within their borders, to reinforce their own health infrastructure, and to collaborate effectively to mitigate global health threats.

Public-private partnerships in global health follow a trend in the public sector to use this kind of arrangement to achieve important health goals as WHO's influence has declined because of budget constraints and political rivalries in the UN system (Brown et al. 2006). However, under this scenario, national Ministries of Health have less influence on holistic public health agendas and implementation of their own national priorities. If funding is available to address malaria, malaria will be addressed regardless of national needs. Private funding raises the possibility that funding of international health programs may be biased toward the interest of donor countries and partners as it diminishes the capacity of recipient countries to identify and address their own health priorities (Buse and Walt 1997; Walt and Buse 2001).

Over the past decade, there has been devolution of health to the local level both in the United States and elsewhere at the very time when international cooperation has become critical to ensuring health on a global basis. The rationale for this comes from the neoliberal assumption that localities should be able to set their own priorities based on local needs. All too often this means that health must compete for funding with roads, schools, and other desperate needs in poor communities. Managing health at the local level is not feasible because critical infectious diseases are not local (Butler 1996).

An Anthropological Perspective on Public Health

There are two levels at which the problem of public health in the global locality can be addressed by anthropology. First, we will explore the role of anthropological theory in understanding specific problems that human communities face with respect to global health. Second, we will look at the role of anthropological practice in brokering interdisciplinary study of global health as a human problem. Conceptually, we must build new frameworks for looking at global issues. What is to be the unit of analysis in which an ethnographic inquiry can be structured in researching global health problems? Are local programs reflective of "errors in implementation" of an international or national plan? Or is local experience the focus of inquiry that informs the design and management of the public health programs?

Anthropologists and epidemiologists tend to think in terms of the spatial placement of things—the nation, the community, or some other locality. Our instincts may lead us to be satisfied with and to agree on explanations that fail to encompass the entire scope of global issues. I have never done an evaluation of a public health program in which the public health staff involved was not concerned with the geographic representativeness of findings. The public health model views disease control as jurisdictional—based on a specific population dwelling in an identified and contiguous geographic space within which an intervention can be managed. Anthropology can help to expand the field in which public health problems are understood by using ethnographic approaches to move thinking about public health problems from a focus on "health risk behavior" at the local level to a focus on the cultural embeddedness of all human experience at multiple levels of organization.

Anthropologists are taught to understand the embeddedness of local happenings in state and national political and economic systems. We are permitted to bracket "our people" for purposes of description, but any explanation of what we see requires us to link our observation to conditions impinging from the outside. This perspective on the embeddedness of human life in larger systems is especially critical in the consideration of public health because discontinuities in policies and commitments between the national and the local level can have dire consequences for the poor at the bottom of the hierarchy. Anthropologists have frequently pointed out situations in which national policy was far removed from the needs of who are vulnerable to the worst ravages of infectious disease (see Briggs and Mantini-Briggs 2003; Farmer 1999). The assumption that goodwill and dedication on the part of local staff will lead to a positive outcome in terms of peoples' lives is wishful thinking at best in the absence of good national policy and the staff and funding needed to implement it.

New models are needed for accommodating local conditions within programs for managing the spread of infectious disease on a transnational and translocal basis. National public health programs are built with an assumption that a technically sound public health action should work anywhere, and yet it is difficult for those who are not members of local communities to accurately identify those most in need and to provide services in a way that they can be accepted and used (Briggs and Mantini-Briggs 2003; Manderson and Whiteford 2000). It requires a perspective on public health problems, communities, interventions, and responses to them that is systemic, capable of accommodating diversity, and responsive to local and individual needs while providing technically sound public health interventions. Health professionals have a firm control of the technical aspects of public health, but may fail to fully engage the sociocultural complexity of health problems on the ground. The delivery of interventions in variable and complex contexts is an area where anthropologists can help if they can devise ways to communicate and cooperate with public health professionals on the one hand and the populations receiving interventions on the other.

Anthropologists can build an ethnographic understanding of community life in the globalizing world that may not be accessible from the outside and may be quite different from that of policy makers. For example, government agencies tend to perceive geographic boundary zones as a territory with a line through it. However, the people who live there perceive it as a single community (Donnan and Wilson 1999). The presence of a national border is part of their environment, one that they cross and cross again for activities of daily life. It does not look the same in the border region as it does from the national capitals. U.S. immigration policy emphasizing the control of traffic across the U.S.-Mexico border stands in stark contrast to the observable flow of people across the border for school, work, shopping, and other activities of daily life. From the local perspective, the border area is a single place—a home—where local, regional, and national realities are mapped on a single ground and derived from both history and contemporary conditions. The experience of hegemony and power as perceived by people who respond to interventions are critical to interpreting what happens on the ground.

The "global locality" as it is observed may seem incomprehensible, an unpredictable and irrational set of events. This is a problem in what Jean and John Comaroff call "Ethnography on an Awkward Scale," with pressures from history and from all levels of government manifested in the cultural behavior of local life (Comaroff and Comaroff 2003). The task of unraveling all this complexity requires teasing out causality from the national and local systems in which people function and within historical frameworks that are unspoken but still mold the present (Trouillot 1995). All public health programs are subject to these forces that are behind the scenes from a strictly local perspective. It is no longer permissible, even heuristically, to close off the outside for the purpose of examining localities.

New approaches to multisite ethnography promise to enhance our ability to model general processes in localities by embedding several communities in a single research inquiry. While acknowledging macro-level systems, this emergent form of ethnography traces cultural constructions across time and space rather than confining the inquiry to a single site embedded in a world system (Marcus 1995). By considering cultural meanings and objects (such as diseases) as the subject of study rather than localities, the ethnographer becomes open both to variations in the manifestation of the thing observed and to the connections that are built across sites by shared understandings and challenges. Thus, we can build ethnographies of migrants that are grounded in multiple sites defined by connections established by the presence and movement of people (Rouse 1991). This is a far cry from the traditional ethnographic focus on relatively static communities embedded in larger constructs such as nation-states, capitalism, developing economies, and many others. This new conceptualization of the ethnographic endeavor provides a flexible means to understand the subjective experience of migrants in a global environment where the conditions of life change rapidly across time and space.

The global environment requires new ways of understanding communication across the boundaries that humans create to set themselves apart from one another. Problems of communication and miscommunication are especially clear around international borders, but we can also define and address borders that are not geographic, but rather are ethnic, translocal, and transnational. Moreover, boundaries may shift and disappear with new means of communication. As Arjun Appadurai points out, a migrant worker in the United States can maintain his or her membership in his home community through Internet participation in community activities (Appadurai 1996:2ff). Similarly, discontinuities do not necessarily exist across communities that incorporate an international boundary.

Especially interesting in the context of global health planning is the application of complex adaptive system (CAS) models to study the emergence of global solutions to social, ecological, and economic problems arising from local interactions (Lansing 2003). CAS models arose in physics and mathematics and have been used to model physical and biological systems. In anthropology, they have been applied to simulate the formation of settlements among the thirteenth-century Anazazi (Dean et al. 2000) and to understand the management of very large irrigation systems by Balinese farmers (Lansing et al. 1998).

CAS models posit that one of several possible semistable states emerge from chaotic processes in component interconnected localities. The number of possible stable states (called attractors) that develop depends on the density of interconnections among the component elements (localities) in the system. CASs are dynamic, and perturbations in localities can move the system from one attractor to another. The dependence of the global system on the panoply of local events and the capacity of CASs to model the effects of local change on larger systems can help us visualize the dynamics of multiple local events on global processes.

Anthropology can also provide methodological advantages to the study of global changes in public health by using tools of ethnography to understand how people define membership and non-membership in groups. One element of our stock in trade as anthropologists is identifying and making intelligible the multiple understandings of events that participants in public health events bring to the table. The etic/emic distinction is one way to do this that many of us have used at one time or another. Emic is the view from the perspective of the "native"; etic, the view of the outsider (Harris 1968; Pike 1954).

The definition of insiders and outsiders is, of course, relative to the perspective of the investigator. In the case of public health, the "native" is a member of a group of people in need of some kind of service or product. The "outsider" is all too often the person who is trying to provide the service (the program). Sometimes program recipients or even local health providers do not consider outside health personnel to be members of their "tribe," an attitude that can drastically hinder the implementation of public health interventions. Anthropological research teaches us how to transcend these kinds of barriers by brokering collaboration between building rapport with those who run the programs and those who are expected to use them. Anthropologists are trained to enter communities as outsiders and negotiate access to the insider perspective. The combination of a systems perspective and the way that we do ethnography prepare us to describe the social-political organization of public health whether it is manifest or not.

Anthropology can take a lead in forging interdisciplinary approaches to generate rich understandings of complex public health problems. To do this, we must change some of our own ways of doing our work. The model of the single anthropologist studying a single community is passing into history. Among practitioners in particular, modes of partnership are developing in which the anthropologist actively supports the emergence of community-based approaches that empower indigenous communities to manage their own development (Hill and Baba 2006; Uquillas and Larreamendy 2006). A number of projects in which local communities have worked with teams of anthropologists and other professionals to develop local responses to global health problems are presented in Whiteford and Manderson (2000).

Case Example: Tuberculosis Control at the U.S.-Mexico Border

I will illustrate the complexity of locality in addressing global health issues by examining an evaluation that I and several colleagues undertook in partnership with the CDC to assess a binational program to improve the control of TB in the U.S.-Mexico border region.[2] The U.S.-Mexico Binational TB Referral and Case Management Project (Pilot Project) was a well-designed and intensely collaborative binational effort to ensure the completion of therapy for patients with TB who travel across the border between the United States and Mexico by providing referral and case management for active cases of TB on both sides of the border.

The evaluation that I will describe was funded by the CDC under a contract with the Battelle Centers for Public Health Research and Evaluation to provide evaluation technical assistance to this project. The project that was evaluated was also funded by the CDC with some financial support from the U.S. Agency for International Development (USAID) and large in-kind contributions from many partners on both sides of the border.

The Context of the Pilot Project

The border is a special case of the global locality in which local solutions to health problems must be embedded in national systems of two nations with sovereignty over their own health systems. There are two important contextual issues that affected this program: the specific health threat from TB and the exacerbation of this threat in a population that migrates between two national health systems.[3]

TB is a serious infectious disease that is concentrated in populations that live in crowded housing conditions with inadequate health care. The awful toll of TB on the poor has been dramatically documented by medical anthropologists who have worked in poor communities (Farmer 1999). Untreated TB normally kills patients within five years, the majority within 18 months. If appropriately treated, it can almost always be cured, even if the individual is coinfected with HIV.

The treatment regime for TB is complicated, usually requiring a combination of drugs taken over a period of 6 to 12 months. Treatment can be uncomfortable, with a variety of side effects, and people start feeling better early in the course of treatment, making premature termination of TB therapy is a serious problem. If TB is not eliminated by completion of the treatment regime, the microorganism sequesters in the body to reemerge when treatment is discontinued. Even worse, partially treated TB selects for a variety of drug-resistant forms, including multiply drug-resistant TB, for which there is little or no available treatment (MMWR 2003b).

Effective public health action against tuberculosis is costly and difficult to maintain among the poor, who may have little control of their daily lives. TB control requires conscientious case management, reliable referral, and good data systems to monitor patients, ensure delivery of treatment, and detect loss of cases to follow-up. A major component of TB therapy is monitoring treatment and maintaining compliance with treatment, often by direct observation on the part of health care workers of the patient ingesting the drug (directly observed therapy, or DOT). Patient education is another important TB control measure. Patients must understand the urgency of compliance with treatment and completion of treatment for him- or herself, but also for their family and the community.

Maintaining compliance with treatment is hindered by the very conditions in which TB is most easily transmitted, especially residential instability due to frequent movement of people in search of work or other opportunities. Because TB moves with people, the U.S.-Mexico border is an important locus of TB transmission for both countries. It is estimated that about one million people cross the U.S.-Mexico border daily between California, Arizona, New Mexico, and Texas on the U.S. side and Baja California, Sonora, Chihuahua, Coahuila, Nuevo Leon, and Tamaulipas on the Mexican side. This area is characterized by a high incidence of TB, higher than the average for either country. Based on 1997 data, the case rate per 100,000 population can be calculated as 9.0 for the four U.S. border states (compared with 7.4 for the United States) and 34.7 per 100,000 for the Mexican border states (compared with 24.8 for all of Mexico).[4] MMWR data published in 1998 showed that 18 percent of Mexican border cases are resistant to isoniazid, and another 6 percent are multidrug resistant (MMWR 1998).

There are two kinds of population movements at the U.S.-Mexico border. One is the movement of a large stable resident population over the border on a fairly regular basis for school, work, services, and shopping, staying for a few hours to a few days. A second kind of migration occurs among individuals bound for the United States who come from all over Latin America and even from the rest of the world. They move to the border cities where they spend several months waiting for an opportunity to cross into the United States, legally or otherwise. Once they arrive on the U.S. side, they leave the border region as quickly as possible to join families in Houston, Chicago, and other U.S. cities, or to enter rural migratory labor flows. While in the border region, they live in very crowded housing with poor nutrition and few health services, an optimal situation for the transmission of TB from the sick to the well. The short-term migration serves to maintain a reservoir of untreated TB on the border while the long-term migration moves TB from the reservoir of cases at the border to the interior of both countries.

Description of the Pilot Project

The Pilot Project was implemented in March 2003 as a demonstration project in two sets of "sister cities": San Diego-Tijuana and El Paso–Ciudad Juarez. There was great interest along the border in the project and by the time Battelle joined the team in 2004, operations had expanded to several other locations. The project was built around the basic elements of TB control: tracking and monitoring of infected persons to initiate and ensure completion of treatment; identification of domestic and other close contacts of infected persons; and screening and treatment of these potentially infected persons (MMWR 2003b).

The Pilot Project included a tracking and surveillance system based on the principles of good public health and the requirements of TB case management in a population with the specific characteristics of the border populations (i.e., linguistic and cultural diversity and mobility within a multinational jurisdiction). The Pilot Project offered to providers on both sides of the border a referral protocol for managing patients with TB receiving treatment in health facilities in the border area that planned to move to communities across the border for more than one month.

Providers were to notify the system when a patient was referred, and patients were provided with a Binational Health Card summarizing important facts about their case and its treatment as well as referral contact numbers. The patients were given referral information and asked to present the TB card when they reported to the clinic at their destination. The provider at the receiving clinic could then call the toll-free number on the card to obtain medical information needed to resume and hopefully complete the patient's treatment. Providers also agreed to update the patient record in the database when a referral was completed and the patient was under care of a new provider.

Referrals were supported by two electronic databases, one in each country. Data from the databases in the United States and Mexico were submitted to the CDC on a quarterly basis and structured to provide case-level information on a set of indicators chosen to support tracking of TB cases and maintenance of their treatment. This information was shared with partners collaborating on the project for use in TB control efforts.

The Pilot Project intelligently built on existing infrastructure in the border region to produce a strong partnership that surpassed previous collaborations. Many of the local organizations that participated in the project had been established at the border for a long time (Hopewell 1998). They already had in place many of the networks, programs, and data infrastructure needed to accomplish the goals of the program. Ten Against TB was one of the early cooperative efforts involving 10 border states in the United States and Mexico in TB control efforts. The Binational/ Migrant Tuberculosis Tracking and Referral Project (TBNet), a project of the Migrant Clinicians Network based in Austin, Texas, conducts a system quite similar to the Pilot Project that focuses on migrants but is also available to border area residents. Cure TB ran the Binational Tuberculosis Referral Program, operated by the San Diego Health Department, and managed referrals across the California border. The Cure TB database, maintained by project staff in San Diego, served as the clearinghouse for Pilot Project data. A third such project is Project Juntos, which provided such services in the Ciudad Juarez–El Paso–Las Cruces area. The successes of the Pilot Project in mounting a response to binational TB cases was in no small part due to the skilled, experienced staff in these local programs.

Evaluation of the Pilot Project

I was involved in the evaluation of the Pilot Project as the project director supported by an evaluation team that had two other anthropologists as well as a statistician and computer specialists. Our team was brought into the project at the end of its first year of implementation under a contract to provide program evaluation support to the CDC. Our charge on this project was to help the partners determine if the Pilot Project was effective in maintaining better tracking and case management of TB, identify factors that contributed to its success or failure, and determine whether the evidence supported an extension of the Pilot Project to other parts of the border.

The evaluation of the project was participatory. The questions to be asked and the protocol to be used were developed by an Evaluation Working Group (EWG) comprising a subset of collaborating partners in the project from both countries. This ensured participation by front-line health workers in the design of the inquiry, the implementation of the evaluation, and hopefully the utilization of its results. The evaluation team developed a logic model mapping how the project was expected to achieve its objectives and specified the evaluation questions to be addressed. Battelle then worked with the CDC to design the evaluation and to complete data collection and analysis.[5]

Outcome of the Pilot Project Evaluation

Operationally, the Pilot Project went well in spite of a number of start-up difficulties and a few problems that were never resolved, and perhaps cannot be resolved. Whereas coordination central to the project required a single locus of data management, there were two participating organizations with long histories of tracking TB cases and managing the data. This led to some early discussion over which of a series of existing databases would form the backbone of the case management data to be collected. After some discussion, the collaborative workgroup crafted a resolution that defined a separate data management role for each of these two entities.

The process within health departments worked well, and most of the partners were pleased with it. Health personnel and public health staff who participated in the program felt that the project was a model for effective and productive collaboration of a large number of organizations across the U.S.-Mexico border, extending even to the federal level in both countries. Stakeholders in the project told us that it demonstrated what could be accomplished with good binational collaboration. This is in no small part due to the unceasing effort on the part of CDC and the National Tuberculosis Program (NTP) in Mexico to promote ongoing meetings and discussions of the Pilot Project, both the successes and the struggles, broadly among a large number of organizations. The commitment of the partners to this project extended to their active participation in the evaluation.

There can be no doubt that the Pilot Project strengthened the collaboration of health personnel across the border, not only locally but also along the length of the border. In spite of some initial disagreements about who would do what, there was a division of labor in which people from multiple border communities exchanged information on a regular basis and collaborated in getting the job done. Although there were existing partnerships across the border prior to the Pilot Project, they tended to be local, bringing together single sets of "sister cities" located immediately across the border from each other and geographically comprising a single community, such as San Diego-Tijuana, El Paso–Ciudad Juarez, and Brownsville-Matamoros. By the time the project ended, there was a single forum for communication of TB control activities along the length of the border. Moreover, the capacity to track patients at least in principle extended far into the United States, if not into Mexico. This brokering of new collaborations was a major contribution of the Pilot Project to the improvement of health planning in the border region.

The patients in the focus groups appreciated the binational TB card because it allowed them obtain and continue treatment when moving between health care clinics on both sides of the border. There was anecdotal evidence that possession of a binational card improved TB treatment even in cities that were not part of the Pilot Project. However, interviews with providers suggested that patients sometimes misunderstood the role of the card and felt that it would either facilitate their movement across the border or that it would be used to identify them as sick and bar them from crossing. As expected, patients lost to follow-up were extremely difficult to contact. We reached only four of 20 candidates identified by clinic personnel as individuals who had entered the program, received a card, and failed to appear in the destination clinics for follow-up.[6] Of the four patients reached, two reported that they had finished their TB treatment at sites that did not participate in the Binational Pilot Project.

In spite of its organizational successes, the Pilot Project had a modest impact on the management of TB in terms of ability to track and manage cases. Few of the patients who received cards on one side of the border appeared as referrals at the other side. In the 12 months of the Pilot Project, the number of patients who received a card and actually moved was estimated by comparison of the Pilot Project database with U.S. tuberculosis surveillance data maintained by the U.S. Public Health Service and the Mexican NTP. Of 488 patients receiving cards in the United States, 130 appeared in the databases across the border, whereas only 17 of the 793 patients receiving a card in Mexico appeared in U.S. surveillance data.[7] Of patients appearing in the database, 40 U.S. patients completed treatment in Mexico, whereas six Mexican patients completed treatment in the United States.[8]

It is entirely possible that the partners in Mexico needed more time than was available during the Pilot Project to adapt its existing reporting system to the binational project. Case reporting and data management are much more centralized in Mexico than in the United States, requiring some time for data to move through channels. Before any case originating in Mexico could be incorporated in the Pilot Project database, it needed to be transmitted in hard copy from the clinic first to the state, then to the region of several states, and finally to the NTP, where it was incorporated into the NTP data reports. Only then could it travel back down the system to be submitted by the clinic to the Cure TB database. Also, there is a lack of computers at the local health centers in Mexico so that much of the case data from Mexico were managed in hard copy. This reinforces the idea that standardization of infrastructure and data systems to be consistent with intensive public health tracking is necessary as part of any effort to facilitate infectious disease surveillance across international borders.

Policy makers in both countries were interested in extending the Pilot Project beyond the border area, and argued that the Pilot Project would be much more effective if it incorporated interior communities in both countries to capture patients with TB migrating from longer distances. They also indicated that a referral system was already in place for patients in the border region before the Binational Card program was established, and they saw little need for the program for patients who remained in the border community.

The cost of any potential replication of the Pilot Project was a concern for many stakeholders, including burden on staff, direct costs of the program, and indirect costs of identifying and treating patients with TB. The cost of the Pilot Project did not accurately reflect the cost of a full implementation of this kind of system. For example, the labor burden imposed on public health staff was acceptable in the Pilot Project, but would need to be addressed in a more systematic way for it to be replicated and sustained. Policy makers in both the United States and Mexico said that there was unlikely to be additional money for this project given other priorities in their public health systems. In both countries, but especially in the United States, with its private means of delivering health services, there was uncertainty about the economic viability of finding and identifying new patients with TB without adequate funding to expand treatment services for those patients identified.

The Role of Anthropology in the Pilot Project Evaluation

The incorporation of an anthropological perspective with its focus on the human experience of TB as mediated by culture and community permitted us to identify and describe fracture lines in the Pilot Project that were not visible from a strictly public health model for TB control. As public health, the benefits of tuberculosis control across the border were so great that providers and policy makers from both sides embraced the Pilot Project with great enthusiasm. Yet, the program failed to successfully track patients outside of the border itself.

There were a number of reasons for this, some cultural and some structural. In spite of excellent collaboration in the border region, there is a level of suspicion about the hegemony of the United States in many areas of border life. This impedes full cooperation to some degree in almost any program. In the case of the Pilot Project, partners on both sides of the border were so hesitant to offend each other that hard questions could not be addressed. The decrease in U.S. funding and the slow movement of data through the Mexican health system and any discussion of undocumented migrants were important issues that could not be tackled because of perceived political sensitivity. For collaboration to be truly effective, open communication among partners must be brokered in some way that is culturally appropriate to both sides. Anthropologists are specialists at building this kind of communication.

The Pilot Project did not distinguish between the two kinds of migrating populations even though they presented very different public health problems. This distinction was not made because there was no distinction of migrant types in the public health regulations of either country. This was reasonable from a strictly public health perspective. However, a complete understanding of the spread of tuberculosis requires an understanding of this difference. Movement of population across the border and movement between the border and areas in the interior of the country have different policy implications. Within-border migration is mostly local among people living sedentary lives in a border community that straddles the frontier. Local migrants are easier to track for ongoing TB treatment than those who come from deep in the interior of either country, spend a brief time in the border region, and then move on to join relatives in the interior of the destination country. The latter group experiences TB in a geographically discontinuous community in which tracking based on a geographically defined public health infrastructure is much more difficult. There is undoubtedly overlap in these populations as people from the border communities travel to interior cities and as migrants from the interior build lives in the border region. However, most people belong to one population or the other. The Pilot Project could have channeled limited resources more precisely to the population that posed the greatest risk of significant TB transmission in both countries had it been able to target activities toward the highest-risk group.

Management of TB in the border region has consequences that reach far beyond the geographic border itself. Fewer people would be lost to follow-up if health officials could act on an understanding of how social organization in both communities of origin and communities of destination embed the movement of people—and their illnesses—from place to place. People who migrate from deep in Mexico to deep into the United States are not by and large the border populations who have a lifelong familiarity with U.S. institutions. They are people who were raised in Mexico with a Mexican understanding of the world, and they need to learn to live in the United States. This includes learning how to access health care in a very different health system.

The expectation that migrants would access treatment at their destination was probably asking too much of people who may not have a command of the English language and who have little understanding of how health care works in the United States. Differences in how services are accessed in the United States and Mexico were poorly understood by some patients. Many immigrants find the health system in the United States hard to navigate. For the Pilot Project to have achieved its goals, it needed to complete the process of bridging localities from the beginning of the migration to the completion of treatment at the other end. Outreach to patients at their destination would have done this, and in fact such outreach is common to domestic TB programs in both the United States and Mexico. This connection was not made by the Pilot Project, probably because of the cost and logistical difficulty of setting up such a structure in cities distant from the border.

Cultural and personal factors that determine health-seeking behavior are also important here. Why did so few people appear in the surveillance system at the destination of migration? Our data suggest that there was some anxiety about the linkage of the TB card to immigration status. There was no connection, of course, but some patients were nervous about carrying a piece of paper across the border, either because they might be held up trying to enter the United States or because they were afraid that they would not be admitted to the country if they had TB.

Managing TB across many localities was challenging. The treatment and control of infectious diseases occurs at the local level because this is where people get sick and are treated. However, the management of health issues that arise in faraway places requires a conceptualization of health care services that incorporates a broader definition of health into its planning. Health planning must transcend the traditional public health paradigm that focuses on health threats originating in the local environment to anticipate and accommodate a broader field of disease origin. This is politically difficult—as health care for the poor always is—but there is a cultural lag as well in moving beyond what has always been to anticipate new disease threats. If you do not anticipate, you are always in emergency response mode.

Conclusions: The Practice of Anthropology in Global Public Health

This study teaches us that anthropologists can help conceptualize health as a matter of community rather than one of individuals afflicted with disease. The public health model tends to consider health problems in terms of individual risk behaviors with interventions geared to facilitating the compliance of individuals with health regimes. This study illustrates the inadequacy of trying to keep individuals within the purview of the health system until TB treatment is completed. When individuals move rapidly and over great distances, the system itself must be modified to improve the access of individuals to continuing services. The ability of the Pilot Project to reduce the number of individuals who are lost to treatment because of migration was limited because the locality in which this might have been accomplished stretched far beyond the border region. An understanding of how communities function to incorporate individuals into a social framework independent of geography is needed to reconceptualize disease control in the global locality.

Methodologically, the most important thing about the project was its participatory nature. Every step in the evaluation—design, implementation, and analysis—was produced by the Pilot Project's Evaluation Working Group. Although the EWG recognized the importance of our evaluation expertise, all draft designs were reviewed, discussed, and accepted by the EWG. This kind of collaboration with participants in research, the vetting of knowledge with the subject, is inherent to the ethnographic approach, even as practiced by the "lone wolf" anthropologist. For those of us who do anthropology for use by stakeholders, it is a very good way to ensure that the questions asked are properly focused, not subject to misinterpretation, and likely to produce valid data for people to use in improving their action toward some purpose. In this project, the participatory approach was used partially because of the political sensitivity of a program implemented in an international locality. In part, it was used because of funding limitations. However, it was so productive in this case that it should always be at least considered in projects requiring collaboration among groups of people.

The anthropological approach to community illustrates inherent limitations of the traditional public health model based on governmental sovereignty over territory. This leaves global health up to voluntary cooperation, which may or may not be strong enough to achieve policy objectives. Collaboration between "sister cities" on both sides of the border was excellent and went back for many years. People managing health in the border region knew each other personally and had worked together on many programs in the past. Moreover, interviews with public health professionals in both countries revealed that they understood the patterns of migration across the border and into the interior of each country. They recognized patterns in which migration streams connected communities in Mexico and in the United States, but lacked the authority or the funding to apply what they knew to the management of TB across the border. Lacking national authority and significant funding, they could not act on their knowledge of migration patterns to institute tracking of patients with TB into the interior of either country.

Perhaps more than anything else, anthropological practice at the border provides us with an opportunity to examine the way in which global localities are to be understood. My work as an evaluator supporting federal agencies in assessing their own work meant that I was always looking at local programs on the ground as exemplars of federal ideas of what kinds of programs would work to improve health and human services at the local level. Yet from the anthropological perspective, local programs were always shaped by local needs, whatever the federal concept of an intervention might be. At the same time, the alternatives available to localities were critically shaped by national and international health systems. Ways of modeling localities within larger dynamic systems, now emerging as anthropological tools, will shape future work to understand local responses to global systems.

The perspective that I as an anthropologist brought to the understanding of community was also helpful in this project. Community is conceptualized in many different ways by social scientists: as a geographic locality, a subpopulation within a larger settlement or organization, a group of people with a shared culture with or without a geographic basis. We see that community is all of those things under some conditions. The definition of community as people live it can only be constructed from the vision of those who live in it. This understanding is often not articulated by members. They know who is in the community and who is not, but developing knowledge of boundaries requires careful ethnographic work grounded in experience with diverse communities.

Although we have learned to conceptualize the community in terms that extend beyond locality, this perspective is still not intuitive to many anthropologists. I was trained to study "peasant" communities, which were acknowledged to exist in a larger context and to be influenced by the political economy of nation-states. These contextual factors, however, were treated either as noise to be considered and factored out, or as stimuli to local change. The concept of the global locality is a recent phenomenon in anthropology as well as in many other social sciences.

Anthropologists must sometimes unlearn what they know if they are to be sensitive to the effects of their intuitive understanding of community in global contexts such as the border. As anthropologists, we tended to think of the border as a locality with a culture typical of this geographic context. This is true in one sense, but border communities cannot be understood apart from their embeddedness in two countries. Individuals with TB move from households in the border region to households in Chicago and Houston and Los Angeles. TB control on the border is critically affected by health policies and their implementation in both countries.

To understand the factors underlying local perceptions and anxieties around infectious diseases, one must consider context in developing multinational health programs. Context is part and parcel of the health situation, one that will not sort itself out easily. Differences in the organization of public health in the United States and Mexico are exacerbated by a history of perceived power differentials between the U.S. authorities and those in Mexico, a legacy of the history of the border (Heyman 1994). To accommodate political considerations in the evaluation of the Pilot Project, we needed to ensure that all of those who used the system on both sides of the border had input into the evaluation design and an opportunity to talk about it as it proceeded. It was important to be able to read the subtle cues of noncommunication and miscommunication that are a danger in any exchange between Anglos and Latinos in the border region.

The political paralysis that can arise in considering binational programs in the border region results in a limited ability to solve problems because it is not acceptable even to admit that they are there. There was tremendous good will on both sides and at all levels in the Pilot Project, yet concerted action was hampered because no one could talk about the fact that U.S. hegemony over the project and the slow movement of Mexican data across the frontier meant that timeliness of response was not possible.

The Pilot Project was lost to other priorities in both Mexico and the United States. This demonstrates a big problem in global health (i.e., that translocal and transnational problems may be eclipsed by more politically urgent priorities within each country). In spite of the importance of the border from a public health standpoint, its problems may have a low priority for attention and resources in both national capitals. The U.S.-Mexico border is among the wealthiest parts of Mexico and the poorest parts of the United States, yet it was difficult to establish a priority for addressing needs of the border population in either country. Policy makers in Washington, Atlanta, and Mexico City were less interested in the border as reflected in staff, funds, and programming. In the United States, the project was defunded to support other CDC priorities. In Mexico, the national staff devoted to the program was genuinely interested in its success. However, once again, funding limited what they could do. In both countries, health officials were very interested in the implications of the program for managing TB in internal areas of the country. In the United States, the program was rapidly expanded to Chicago and Tennessee. The stakeholders in Mexico broadly agreed that they would be most interested in replicating the program in internal regions of the country where most cases originate.

One must plan realistically around both the public and private health organizations in participating countries for a multinational health program to succeed. The capacity of middle-income and poor countries to participate in global public health collaborations depends critically on development and maintenance of strong public health infrastructures at the national level in all countries that bring health problems to the global health discussion. National public health systems must have the organization, qualified staff, and funding to deliver on commitments that they make to global disease control. This will require a global commitment to public health in the interest not only of nation-states but also of the health and safety of the world as a whole.

Technical assistance alone will not be enough. For global health to be protected, all countries must be able to provide for the surveillance, health service, and policy needs of their own population. The CDC has recognized this in several global health programs designed to build the capacity of partner nations to reinforce their own public health infrastructure. Ministries of Health participating in one of these programs—the Field Epidemiology Training Program—identified the training of local public health staff in the administrative infrastructure of managing and delivering services as a top priority. More traditional measures for directly combating infectious diseases with the cooperation of public and private international health agencies have taken a backseat to the reinforcement of local infrastructure (Butler 1998). However, unilateral programs of this kind can be problematic if those who implement them are not willing to let the direction and management of in-country programs rest with participating nations.

From a policy perspective, global public health must be *public* health, based on health and disease of a population over which a nation has sovereignty rather than on the disease priorities of private donors. There must be a public infrastructure. Private organizations depend on funding of sponsors, may not be sustained, and may have commercial or political interests that are not congruent with the health priorities of countries benefiting from their largesse. Although public health responses address specific diseases, public health itself cannot be disease-specific. Diseases change, migrate, increase, and decrease in epidemiologic importance.

The public health *system* must maintain vigilance and response for a population, not a disease. Finally, public health must manage the health of communities, not individuals, although health services may be delivered to individuals as part of a community response.

All of these factors map onto the observation of local programs. For example, inaccessibility of health care at the local level may result from inadequate funding, poor management, the history of minority clients with local providers, or other empirically determined factors. All of this collapses into a single context in which people make health decisions. My clients have understood that they need to take a multilayered local perspective, which may extend over more than one community. They have sought an anthropologist to help refine their approach to doing this. The approach itself, however, is not new to them.

Anthropologists traditionally envisioned themselves as lone investigators working to contribute to the understanding of the human condition by their special expertise in the understanding of "their people." This model dominated anthropology departments even when I was a student 25 years ago. To some extent it still does, although it has been the subject of some critique (Fox 1991). Practitioners of anthropology have been forced to move away from this perspective by the needs of our clients. We are asked to focus on a specific problem rather than upon disciplinary perspectives with the goal of creating something that supports an action to be undertaken by our clients. To do this well, we mobilize teams to address complex problems in interdisciplinary ways that transcend individual disciplinary expertise. We must work with economists, statisticians, and epidemiologists while staying in touch with the fact that our understanding does not make us economists, statisticians, or epidemiologists. This professional interdependency is very helpful to addressing many issues of globalization, including global public health.

If we want to help, we must respect the understanding of professionals in other disciplines. Epidemiologists are masterful at investigating the circumstances directly affecting diseases and they are aware of local events that impinge on disease transmission. They may underestimate the significance of contextual forces that, although not obviously linked to a disease, affect people's ideas and behaviors in ways that affect disease transmission. Anthropologists understand that a disease cannot be abstracted from people in designing interventions, that one size will not fit all because the context varies. The disease is not embedded in a context; the context is part of the disease (Schoepf 2001). However, the systems perspective is not unique to anthropologists any more than are culture, sensitivity, ethnography, or the study of sociocultural processes. Public health people also think in terms of systems, as do many other disciplines. Anthropologists are trained to view as a central issue some of the things that public health people regard as context, thus strengthening joint projects. Often, I have been brought onto an interdisciplinary team to help discern and articulate the dynamic interactions of health systems and multiple levels of context in understanding why people respond to public health programs in the ways that they do.[9] In these situations, I have learned from others as I hope they have learned from me.

When I began this project, I thought that I understood public health as a cultural system with an ideology that guided the efforts of public health practitioners worldwide, an organization of agencies and individuals empowered to implement the policies thereby developed, and a technology for delivering public health that at least in principle could ameliorate the suffering of the world, subject of course to political and economic barriers. This turned out to be too simple a view in the global context. I now recognize that the political and economic conditions in which public health is practiced are not simply barriers to be overcome but are integral to the operation of public health systems at both the global and the local levels, part of the system itself. Public health lies embedded in both a global public health system and local politics that have a very immediate impact on the ability to identify, access, and use even those health services that are available to them. It all looks different depending on who you are and how much power you have to define priorities and ask for what you need.

I must admit that I remain uncertain about how to apply the culture concept that I learned in graduate school to the situation in the border region. As an anthropologist, I buy into Geertz's assertion that you cannot have humans without culture (Geertz 1973). But the way I learned to understand culture as a bounded thing that can be described in some finite way does not work as well in practice as it did in my dissertation fieldwork. In the multicultural, multilocal, contingent, and fluid society of the border, where do we find the limits of culture, and what are we left with when we do? It may be a culture concept that is too broad to illuminate or too narrow to account for what we see in the global locality. It is our shared challenge to pioneer theories and methods that can be applied in the global context without turning away from what is valuable in the anthropological and the public health traditions. Moreover, I believe that the practice of anthropology in the global system will be one of the ways we get there. Anthropologists no longer have the option of studying tribes, villages, and urban neighborhoods as if they could be conceptually isolated. No longer can we pursue our discipline as though it were the only one with which we need to be concerned. Our ways of understanding the world are emerging from the world that is coming to be. But then, maybe it has never been any other way.

Notes

1. The work that I describe was not undertaken for the purpose of this chapter and hence the data collection did not probe these questions with informants as deeply as I would have had the project been directed to the issues I address here. Most of what I observed in this case emerged in interviews with policy makers in the border region and illustrated things that others have observed in similar situations. However, the suggestions in the chapter would be well served by empirical testing directed specifically to these questions.

2. The research described in this chapter was conducted by the Battelle Centers for Public Health Research and Evaluation under Contract Number 200-2001-00121, Task Order 8. The project was based on a participatory partnership with the CDC and the Mexican NTP. Mary Odell Butler was the Battelle Project Leader. Other Battelle staff members involved in the project were Rodolfo Matos, MA, and Kendra Versendaal, MPH. Maureen Wilce was the CDC Technical Monitor for this project (see Butler et al. 2006).

3. There is much common ground between the U.S. and Mexican health systems. Like the United States, Mexico has a national public health structure (the Secretario de Salud) and state health departments. Moreover, many Mexican public health officials have studied for some period of time at the CDC or in U.S. schools of public health. However, there are also important differences. In the United States, the prevention and control of infectious diseases, including reporting, is a state responsibility, with the CDC (the federal agency) providing support, training, and technical assistance. In Mexico, in spite of a decentralization of public health functions in the past decade, most decisions about public health are still made at the federal level. Mexico has an additional layer of public health organization, the regional health departments, in addition to the federal, state, and local levels. Each of these levels has its own rights and responsibilities, which cannot be directly inferred from the organization of public health in the United States. These differences demand great political sensitivity to different ways of doing things and the bracketing of frustrations that come up in the search for common ground.

4. Computed from data presented at the November 1997 Meeting of Ten Against TB, an international partnership of border states that has worked together since 1995 to improve TB prevention and control in the border area.

5. This evaluation used a mixed-method approach common in anthropological practice and emphasized the need for anthropologists to work effectively with specialists across many disciplines. In addition to three anthropologists, the project team included epidemiologists, physicians, nurses, an economist, a statistician, and data management specialists. Data collection strategies integrated aggregation of data from the national tuberculosis databases maintained in both countries as well as two local

databases compiled for the project. Interviews with key stakeholders at the local, state, and federal levels in both the United States and Mexico were conducted during site visits to the border as well as to Washington, Mexico City, and Atlanta. We also visited U.S. Immigration Control and Enforcement (ICE) detention facilities in El Paso and San Diego to discuss the experience of staff with the Pilot Project, their perspective on how well it operated and barriers that they encountered, and issues surrounding the transmission and use of clinical information. Interviews were conducted in Spanish or English, depending on the participant's preference. All focus groups were conducted in Spanish. A wide range of skills and experience were needed to cover all of this activity. No individual would have had the knowledge needed to mount this evaluation without the support of others.

6. The sample used here was not random. The clinics had very little data available to them for patient follow-up. The 20 patients in this group were those for whom clinics thought they had good contact information. In fact, most of these individuals could not be reached after multiple attempts.

7. This is probably an underestimate, since Mexican patients would need to seek treatment in the United States to appear in U.S. surveillance data. Nonetheless, the number is very small.

8. These data come from a joint presentation by the NTP of Mexico, the CDC, and Battelle at the annual World TB Day meeting held in El Paso, Texas, on April 4, 2005.

9. To give one U.S. example, usage of publicly funded breast and cervical cancer screening programs by individual women depends on the funding of the program from the federal level, implementation by health agencies in states, and the availability and reputation of services at the local level (Abed et al. 2000).

References

Abed, Joanne, Barbara Reilly, Mary O. Butler, et al.
    2000 Comprehensive Cancer Control Initiative of the Centers for Disease Control and Prevention: An Example of Participatory Innovation Diffusion. *Journal of Public Health Management and Practice* 6(2):79–92.
Apostolopoulos, Yurghos, and Sevil Sonmez
    2010 Demographic and Epidemiological Perspectives on Human Movement. *In* Population, Mobility and Infectious Disease, Yorghos Apostolopoulos and Sevil Sonmez, eds. Pp. 3–17. New York: Springer.
Appadurai, Arjun
    1996 Modernity at Large: Cultural Dimensions of Globalization. Minneapolis: University of Minnesota.
Bandura, Albert
    1986 Social Foundations of Thought and Action: A Social Cognitive Theory. Englewood Cliffs, NJ: Prentice-Hall.

Bandura, Albert
2004 Health Promotion by Social Cognitive Means. *Health Education and Behavior* 31(2):143–64.

Bashford, Alison
2006 Global Biopolitics and the History of World Health. *History of the Human Sciences* 19(1):67–88.

Briggs, Charles L., and Clara Mantini-Briggs
2003 Stories in the Time of Cholera: Racial Profiling during a Medical Nightmare. Berkeley, CA: University of California Press.

Briseño-Garcia, Baltasar, Hector Goméz-Dantés, Enid Argott-Ramírez, et al.
1996 Potential Risk for Dengue Hemorrhagic Fever: The Isolation of Serotype Dengue-3 in Mexico. *Emerging Infectious Diseases* 2(2):133–35.

Brown, Theodore M., Marcus Cueto, and Elizabeth Fee
2006 The World Health Organization and the Transition from International to Global Public Health. *American Journal of Public Health* 96(1):62–72.

Buse, Kent, and Gill Walt
1997 An Unruly Mélange? Coordinating External Resources to the Health Sector: A Review. *Social Science and Medicine* 45(3):449–63.

Butler, Mary O.
1990 Results of the NNDSS Surveillance Evaluation. Presented at the Annual Meeting of the Council of State and Territorial Epidemiologists. Bolton's Landing, NY, April 11, 1990.
1991 An Evaluation of the National Electronic Telecommunications System for Surveillance (NETSS). Final report to the Centers for Disease Control and Prevention, Office of Program Planning and Evaluation and Epidemiology Program Office (Contract No. 200-88-0642, Task 8). Arlington, VA: Battelle, June 1991.
1996 Building Public Health Infrastructure in Bolivia: Cultural Assumptions and Program Impact. Presented at the Annual Meeting of the Society for Applied Anthropology, March 30, 1996.
1998 Evaluation of the Field Epidemiology Training Program (FETP)— Final Report. Report to the Centers for Disease Control and Prevention, Epidemiology Program Office and Office of Program Planning and Evaluation (Contract No. 200-96-0599, Task No. 3). Arlington, VA: Battelle, April 1998.

Butler, Mary O., with Rodolfo Matos and Kendra Versendaal
2006 Evaluation of the US-Mexico Binational TB Referral and Case Management Project. Report to the Centers for Disease Control and Prevention, Division of Tuberculosis Elimination and Office of Strategic (Contract No. 200-2001-00121, Task No. 8). Arlington, VA: Battelle, July 20, 2006.

Buttery, C. M. G.
1992 The Provision of Public Health Services. *In* Maxcy-Rosenau-Last Public Health and Preventive Medicine, J. M. Last and R. B. Wallace, eds. Pp. 1113–28. Norwalk, CT: Appleton and Lange.

Carballo, Manuel, and Aditi Nerukar
2001 Migration, Refugees and Health Risks. *Emerging Infectious Diseases* 7(3)Supplement:556–60.

Comaroff, Jean, and John Comaroff
2003 Ethnography on an Awkward Scale: Postcolonial Anthropology and the Violence of Abstraction. *Ethnography* 4(2):147–79.

Dean, Jeffrey S., George J. Gumerman, Joshua M. Epstein, et al.
2000 Understanding Anazazi Culture through Agent-based Modeling. *In* Dynamics in Human and Primate Populations, T. Kohler and G. Gumerman, eds. Pp. 179–205. New York: Oxford University Press.

Donnan, Hastings, and Thomas M. Wilson
1999 Borders: Frontiers of Identity, Nation and State. Oxford: Berg.

Edelman, Marc, and Angelique Haugerud
2005 The Anthropology of Development and Globalization: From Classical Political Economy to Contemporary Neoliberalism. Malden: Blackwell.

Farley, John
2004 To Cast Out Disease: A History of the International Health Division of the Rockefeller Foundation. New York: Oxford University Press.

Farmer, Paul
1996 Social Inequalities and Emerging Infectious Diseases. *Emerging Infectious Diseases* 2(4):259–69.
1999 Infection and Inequalities: The Modern Plagues. Berkeley, CA: University of California Press.

Fidler, David P.
1996 Globalization, International Law and Emerging Infectious Diseases. *Emerging Infectious Diseases* 2(2):77–84.
2001 The Globalization of Public Health: The First 100 Years of International Health Diplomacy. *Bulletin of the World Health Organization* 79(9):842–49.

Fox, Richard G.
1991 Introduction: Working in the Present. *In* Recapturing Anthropology: Working in the Present, Richard G. Fox, ed. Pp. 1–16. Santa Fe: School of American Research Press.

Geertz, Clifford
1973 The Impact of the Concept of Culture on the Concept of Man. *In* The Interpretation of Cultures, C. Geertz, ed. Pp. 33–54. New York: Basic Books.

Green, Lawrence W., and Marshall W. Kreuter
1991 Health Promotion Planning: An Educational and Environmental Approach, 2nd Edition. Mountain View, CA: Mayfield.

Gubler, Duane J., and Gary G. Clark
1995 Dengue/Dengue Hemorrhagic Fever: Emergence of a Global Health Problem. *Emerging Infectious Diseases* 1(2):55–57.

Guo, Boliang, Anthony Fielding, Stephen Sutton, and Paul Aveyard
　2011 Psychometric Properties of the Processes of Change Scale for Smoking Cessation in UK Adolescents. *International Journal of Behavioral Medicine* 18(1):71–78.
Gushulak, Brian D., and Douglas W. McPherson
　2007 Migration in a Mobile World: Health Population Mobility and Emerging Disease. *In* Population, Mobility and Infectious Disease, Yorghos Apostolopoulos and Sevil Sonmez, eds. Pp. 283–300. New York: Springer.
Hannerz, Ulf
　1996 Transnational Connections: Culture, People, Places. London and New York: Routledge.
Harris, Marvin
　1968 The Rise of Anthropological Theory. New York: Crowell.
Heyman, Josiah McC
　1994 The Mexico-United States Border in Anthropology: A Critique and Reformulation. *Journal of Political Ecology* 1:43–66.
Hill, Carol, and Marietta L. Baba
　2006 Global Connections and Practicing Anthropology in the 21st Century. NAPA Bulletin 25, C. E. Hill and M. L. Baba, eds. Pp. 1–13.
Hopewell, Jillian
　1998 Cross-Border Cooperation: A Case Study of Binational Tuberculosis Control. *In* U.S.-Mexico Border Health: Issues for Regional and Migrant Populations, J. Gerard Power and Theresa Byrd, eds. Pp. 89–102. Thousand Oaks, CA: Sage Publications.
Inda, Jonathan Xavier, and Renato Rosaldo
　2002 The Anthropology of Globalization: A Reader. Malden: Blackwell.
Institute of Medicine (IOM)
　1988 The Future of Public Health. Washington, D.C.: The National Academy Press.
　2000 Ending Neglect: The Elimination of Tuberculosis in the United States. Washington, D.C.: The National Academy Press.
　2001 Crossing the Quality Chasm. Washington, D.C.: The National Academy Press.
　2003 The Future of the Public's Health in the 21st Century. Washington, D.C.: The National Academy Press.
Ioannidi-Kapolou, Elizabeth
　2010 Health Barriers and Inequities for Migrants. *In* Population, Mobility and Infectious Disease, Yorghos Apostolopoulos and Sevil Sonmez, eds. Pp. 41–54. New York: Springer.
Lansing, J. Stephen
　2003 Complex Adaptive Systems. *Annual Review of Anthropology* 32:183–204.
Lansing, J. Stephen, James Kremer, and Barbara B. Smuts
　1998 System-Dependent Selection, Ecological Feedback and the Emergence of Functional Structure in Ecosystems. *Journal of Theoretical Biology* 192:377–91.

Last, John M.
1992 International Health. *In* Maxcy-Rosenau-Last Public Health and Preventive Medicine, John M. Last and Robert B. Wallace, eds. Pp. 1129–39. Norwalk, CT: Appleton and Lange.

Lewellen, Ted C.
2002 The Anthropology of Globalization: Cultural Anthropology Enters the 21st Century. Westport, CT: Bergin & Garvey.

Liu, Zhiyuan, Kenneth L. Shilkret, John Tranotti, et al.
1998 Distinct Trends in Tuberculosis Morbidity among Foreign-Born and US-Born Persons in New Jersey, 1986 through 1995. *American Journal of Public Health* 88:1064–67.

Manderson, Lenore, and Linda M. Whiteford
2000 Introduction: Health, Globalization and the Fallacy of the Level Playing Field. *In* Global Health Policy, Local Realities: The Fallacy of the Level Playing Field, L. M. Whiteford and L. Manderson, eds. Pp. 1–19. Boulder, CO: Lynne Reinner Publishers.

Marcus, George E.
1995 Ethnography in/of the World System: The Emergence of Multi-Sited Ethnography. *Annual Review of Anthropology* 24:95–117.

Morbidity and Mortality Weekly Report (MMWR)
1998 Population-based Survey for Drug-Resistance of Tuberculosis—Mexico 1997. *Morbidity and Mortality Weekly Report* 47(18):372–75.
2003a Outbreak of Severe Acute Respiratory Syndrome—Worldwide, 2003. *Morbidity and Mortality Weekly Report* 52(11):226–28.
2003b Treatment of Tuberculosis, American Thoracic Society, CDC and Infectious Disease Society of America. *Morbidity and Mortality Weekly Report* 52(RR-11): 1–77.
2003c Revised U.S. Surveillance Case Definition for Severe Acute Respiratory Syndrome (SARS) and Update on SARS Cases—United States and Worldwide. *Morbidity and Mortality Weekly Report* 52(49):1202–06.
2008 Trends in Tuberculosis—2007. *Morbidity and Mortality Weekly Report* 57(11):281–85.
2009 Update: Novel Influenza A (H1N1) Virus Infections—Worldwide, May 6, 2008. *Morbidity and Mortality Weekly Report* 58(17):453–58.
2010 Update: Influenza Activity—United States, August 30, 2009–January 9, 2010. *Morbidity and Mortality Weekly Report* 59(50):1651–55.

Morse, Stephen S.
1995 Factors in the Emergence of Infectious Diseases. *Emerging Infectious Diseases* 1(1):7–15.

Pike, Kenneth
1954 Language in Relation to a Unified Theory of the Structure of Human Behavior, Vol I. Glendale: Summer Institute of Linguistics.

Porter, Dorothy
1999 Health, Civilization and the State. London: Routledge.

Prochaska, James O., and Carlo DiClemente
    1983 Stages and Processes of Self-Change in Smoking: Toward an Integrative Model of Change. *Journal of Consulting and Clinical Psychology* 5:390–95.
Quetel, Claude
    1990 History of Syphilis. Baltimore, MD: Johns Hopkins Press.
Rouse, Roger
    1991 Mexican Migration and the Social Space of Post-Modernity. *Diaspora* 1:8–23.
Schoepf, Brooke G.
    2001 International AIDS Research in Anthropology: Taking a Critical Perspective on Crisis. *Annual Reviews of Anthropology* 30:335–61.
Thacker, Steven B.
    2006 Epidemiology at CDC. *Morbidity and Mortality Weekly Report* 55(supplement):3–6.
Trouillot, Michel
    1995 Silencing the Past: Power and the Production of History. Boston: Beacon Press.
Uquillas, Jorge E., and Pilar Larreamendy
    2006 Applied Anthropology in Ecuador: Development, Practice, and Discourse. NAPA Bulletin 25, Carol E. Hill and Marietta L. Baba, eds. Pp. 14–34.
Walt, Gill, and Kent Buse
    2001 Editorial: Partnership and Fragmentation in International Health: Threat or Opportunity? *Tropical Medicine and International Health* 5(7):467–71.
Whiteford, Linda M., and Lenore Manderson (eds.)
    2000 Global Health Policy, Local Realities: The Fallacy of the Level Playing Field. Boulder, CO: Lynne Rienner Publishers.
Wilson, Mary
    1995 Travel and the Emergence of Infectious Diseases. *Emerging Infectious Diseases* 1(2):39–45.
    2010 Population Mobility and the Geography of Microbial Threats. *In* Population, Mobility and Infectious Disease, Y. Apostolopoulos and S. Sonmez, eds. Pp. 21–39. New York: Springer.
World Health Organization (WHO)
    2009 New Influenza A (H1N1) Virus: Global Epidemiologic Situation. *Weekly Epidemiological Record* 84:249–57.
Yach, Derek, and Douglas Bettcher
    1998a The Globalization of Public Health I: Threats and Opportunities. *American Journal of Public Health* 88(5):735–38.
    1998b Globalization of Public Health II: The Convergence of Self-Interest and Altruism. *American Journal of Public Health* 88(5):738–41.
Zinsser, Hans
    1934 Rats, Lice and History: A Chronicle of Pestilence and Plagues. New York: Little, Brown.

2

Engendering Transport: Mapping Women and Men on the Move

Mari H. Clarke

Introduction: Transport, Gender, and Global-Local Connections

Highways, bridges, waterways, railways, airports. Bicycles, footpaths, donkeys, rickshaws. Modes of transport do not ordinarily evoke images of anthropological field research sites: they are merely viewed as means for anthropologists to travel there. Similarly, engineers designing transport infrastructure do not usually think of anthropologists as valuable colleagues with knowledge and skills that can help increase the sustainability of their project outcomes. These preconceptions lead to missed opportunities because transport, with its huge financial investments and tremendous potential for both positive and negative impacts on people, is a very strategic area for anthropological practice. Moreover, there is compelling evidence that anthropologists can make a difference there.

The scholarship and practice of transport anthropologists appear in the margins of literature in anthropology and other disciplines, yet the dramatic social and economic changes created by roads and other modes of transport linking local landscapes with urban centers, other countries, and continents as well as the spatial dimensions of transport, provide rich material for reshaping our anthropological understanding of cultural change, global-local linkages, and core sociocultural identities such as gender. Transport is not simply a mode of connection between places, but is itself a gendered space where important sociocultural processes are at work, one that further pushes the boundaries of how anthropologists understand concepts of culture, community, and gender and the global and local processes transforming them.

In this chapter, I examine anthropological contributions to our understanding of gender and related sociocultural issues in transport and make the case for why and how gender and transport is a promising area for anthropological practice and scholarship. I explore the ways in which the expansion of transport networks was a catalyst of and also accelerated by globalization, resulting in positive and negative impacts on poor women and men in low-income and transition countries. I also briefly describe challenges faced by development agencies engaged in gender and transport initiatives and highlight key applications of anthropological concepts and methods in this context. I then narrate stories of five anthropologists applying anthropology innovatively in gender and transport in various countries and international development organizations. I conclude with insights about future prospects for transport anthropology in mapping spatial dimensions of gender and transport and making a difference for women and men in an increasingly globally connected world.

Global Expansion of Transportation: The Good, the Bad, and the Ugly

Advances in transportation, energy, and telecommunications technology have facilitated rapid global integration of economic processes and information exchange as well as movement of women and men to burgeoning urban centers and across borders. At the same time, advances in technology and communications have extended motorized means of transport beyond the elite to the wider public by dramatically reducing the cost and increasing speed, efficiency, and customer volume. The dramatic decline of transport and communications costs over time facilitated global economic integration (Leautier and Lerner 2003).

The expansion of transport networks has had many positive impacts on the lives of women and men in low-income countries: increasing access to markets for labor and goods, reducing the cost of taking goods to market, creating access to health and other services, expanding educational opportunities, and facilitating civic participation. Clean, safe, and affordable transport provides an important means to help developing countries achieve the United Nations Millennium Development Goals for reducing global poverty, particularly those focused on to education, health, women's empowerment, and environmental sustainability (German Technological Corporation [GTZ] 2005; United Nations Economic and Social Council [UN/ECOSOC] 2004; World Bank 2007a, 2008).

There is also a darker side to the expansion of transport networks. Inequitable distribution of benefits from these networks has exacerbated existing gender and income disparities. The global flow of people, information, and capital has contributed to major global crises in finance, food, energy, and health such as the spread of HIV/AIDS (Lema et al. 2003).

Transport can also increase environmental pollution and deforestation, and can escalate injuries and deaths from traffic accidents (World Health Organization [WHO] 2004). Greenhouse gases, emitted by most motorized transport, contribute significantly to global climate change, which affects the lowest-income countries the most, even though they contribute the least emissions (GTZ 2010). Expanding transport networks can also expedite the trafficking of women, children, drugs, and weapons (Asian Development Bank [ADB] n.d.).

The construction and repair of roads and other modes of transport displaces people residing or working in the pathway. By the year 2000, more than 200 million people had been displaced by development projects (Cernea 2000; de Wet 2005). In Mumbai, India, 60,000 people were moved from the edges of the railway to reduce accidents and allow faster train speeds (Dickson n.d.). The Jamuna Bridge Project in Bangladesh required relocation of an estimated 65,000 people, and the Jingjiu Railway Project in the People's Republic of China involved displacement of about 210,000 people (ADB 1995).

In response to current financial and food crises, the scale of global investment in transport infrastructure has increased. The World Bank Infrastructure Recovery and Assets Platform invested \$45 billion in infrastructure between 2009 and 2012. World Bank President Robert B. Zoellick explained that "investments in infrastructure can provide the platform for job creation, sustainable economic growth and overcoming poverty, and help jump start a recovery from the crisis" (World Bank 2009a). This major increase in large infrastructure investment pushes social risk management to the forefront given the sheer volume of social impact assessments required to ensure that the projects are implemented in a socially sustainable manner.

Despite substantial transport investments by the World Bank, other donors, national governments, and the private sector, many poor people worldwide, particularly women, walk on paths and tracks, along the edges of roads with no pedestrian walkways, and over narrow footbridges or through streams. Some use bicycles and motorbikes or ride donkeys (Barwell and Dawson 1993; Porter 2002). Frequently, rural and urban transport planning decisions focus on increasing the miles and numbers of roads, rail track, or runways to speed up the flow of goods and people to grow economies, overlooking the needs and priorities of the poor, minorities, the elderly, and women. Many planners assume that transport projects benefit everyone and thus are "gender neutral." However, transport thus designed is neither "gender neutral" nor equitable in its impact (Fernando and Porter 2002; Graeco 2002; International Forum for Rural Transport and Development [IFRTD] 2004, 2010; Peters 2002; van Riet 2008). Fortunately, these perspectives are changing (Fernando 2010).

The Gender Divide in Transport Benefits and Risks

In international development organizations, "gender" is often used as a synonym for "women" because the term is confusing to many. It is important to clarify that gender is about *both* women and men, their socially defined roles and responsibilities, and the power and other relations between them.[1] Like race, ethnicity, and class, being male or female shapes individuals' opportunities to participate in the economy and society (Organisation for Economic Co-operation and Development, Development Assistance Committee [OECD/DAC] 2004; World Bank 2002a). Looking at gender in transport means assessing the different needs of males and females for and uses of transportation as well as barriers to their access, mobility, and economic opportunities to guide selection, design, and implementation of transport policies and projects.

The interface between gender and transport in a globally interconnected economy is a complex one characterized by unequal distribution of risks and benefits based not only on gender but also age, ethnicity, location (rural/urban), wealth, and other characteristics (Graeco 2002; Peters 2002). Gender and transport issues are grounded in broader gender inequalities[2] in access to land, labor, financial, and product markets, the gendered division of labor, and associated time poverty (Clarke 2008a; Graeco 2002; van Riet 2008).

Time is an economic good and a key dimension of development as well as a constraint on economic participation, particularly for women. Men and women play multiple roles (productive, reproductive, and community management), but men generally focus on a single productive role and play other roles sequentially. Most women need to juggle all their roles at the same time and balance competing claims on limited time. As a result, their labor time is much more constrained and inelastic than men's. Thus, women face tradeoffs in time allocation between different productive activities, between market and household tasks, and between meeting short-term economic and household needs and long-term investment in capacity and human capital. Women's time and income poverty often reinforce each other, with negative impacts for women, their families, and communities (Blackden 2003; Blackden and Wodon 2006; Quisumbing 2003).

Gender inequality exists at different levels: household, community, regional, national, and transnational (Bennett 2003; World Bank 2006, 2007c). At each level, social norms, cultural values, and formal and informal laws and policies constrain women's access to infrastructure services, markets, and civic participation as well as their ownership of land, businesses, and other property. At each level, reducing gender inequalities contributes to poverty reduction, economic growth, and empowerment of poor women and men (Bennett 2003), but strategic, practical approaches are required to do so (Grown 2006; Mehra and Gupta 2006). At all levels it is important to ensure that women, minority, and indigenous groups gain a voice in decision making about transport programs affecting them (Graeco 2002; Porter 2002; van Riet 2008).

Limited access to transport usually takes a heavier toll on women and girls than on males. Females are responsible for nearly all the "invisible" domestic tasks such as processing food, providing firewood and water, and caring for the elderly and sick. Rural women and girls in many countries walk several hours daily, collecting wood and water, carrying it on their heads or backs. In Africa, roughly 70 percent of all household and market goods are head-loaded, predominantly by women. In some areas, travel by foot can consume up to eight hours a day (Blackden and Wodon 2006; Malmberg-Calvo 1994a; Peters 2002; Porter 2002). Time spent on this travel limits females' education and economic opportunities, restricting them to activities compatible with domestic tasks (Blackden and Wodon 2006; Quisumbing 2003). Rural transport and gender professionals are asking why we have not provided alternatives to this extremely inefficient use of human energy and potential (IFRTD 2010).

Limited road access has human costs as well. There is a clear link between road access and distance to schools and girls' enrollment levels (Peters 2002). Around the world, every minute, a woman dies in childbirth, when many of these deaths could be prevented by access to emergency medical care, which requires passable roads and affordable transport services (Babinard and Roberts 2006; White Ribbon Alliance for Safe Motherhood [WRA] 2002).

Most urban transport schedules are based on peak-hour travel to work in the city center, yet many women travel during off-peak hours, making several stops during each journey to take children to school, visit relatives, and engage in community activities on their way to work, which is termed "trip chaining." Transport pricing often makes trip chaining more expensive than traveling directly to work. Fares are frequently unaffordable for poor women. The safety of pedestrians and nonmotorized vehicles (e.g., bicycles or rickshaws) seldom receives attention. Personal security is often overlooked, leaving women and girls vulnerable to gender-based violence and crime in dimly lit streets and access points for public transport (Kudat 1998; Kunieda and Gautier 2007; Montgomery and Roberts 2008).

When households and businesses are displaced by transport projects, the heaviest impacts are often shouldered by women, who struggle to provide safe water, feed their children, care for the sick and elderly, and provide shelter in an unfamiliar environment, often without the help of social support networks disrupted by resettlement. Too often, compensation for displacement and resettlement is allocated to male heads of households, who do not necessarily share it with other household members. Women and others with use rights but no titles to land are seldom compensated (ADB 2003; Mehta 2002).

Global financial and food crises have increased the gender-based poverty gap, particularly in countries lacking fiscal resources to cushion the impacts of these crises, high infant and child mortality, and low rates of female schooling. Other than Afghanistan, all of the countries at highest risk for these negative impacts are in Africa (Sabarwal et al. 2009). Africa has the world's lowest levels of rural road access[3] as well at 0 to 32 percent of the population. Without road access, infrastructure for water and electricity cannot be developed and access to markets, agricultural inputs, schools, and health care is extremely limited (Roberts et al. 2006). Given the low population density in most of Africa compared with low-income Asian countries, roads cost roughly twice as much. This translates into much higher transport costs for rural African households (Torero and Chowdhury 2005).

Addressing Gender and Transport Issues: Opportunities and Challenges

Micheael Cernea was an early advocate for analysis of the social dimensions of international development, including transport. In his book *Putting People First,* he argued that "people are—and should be the starting point, the center and the end of each development effort" (Cernea 1985; Cook 1991). By the late 1990s, transport had entered the gender mainstreaming[4] agendas of major development agencies. The Swedish International Development Agency commissioned a gender analysis of infrastructure and poverty (Masika and Baden 1997); the Canadian International Development Agency (CIDA) conducted a review of infrastructure projects that integrated gender (CIDA 1998); the Asian Development Bank initiated a series of practical guides on good practices (Pulley et al. 2003); the World Bank launched a Gender and Transport Thematic Group (1998); and the Organization for Economic Cooperation and Development issued the report "Why Gender Matters in Infrastructure" (OECD/DAC 2004) along with tip sheets for mainstreaming gender in specific sectors. The World Bank Group Gender Action Plan (2007–2010), "Gender Equality as Smart Economics," placed a strong emphasis on infrastructure as a base on which the other economic sectors build and through which women's access to labor, land, financial, and product markets and empowerment can increase (World Bank and International Finance Corporation [IFC] 2006). International nongovernmental organizations (NGOs) and web-based networks such as the Gender and Transport Network and the IFRTD have also championed gender and transport issues. The private sector role is growing as corporate social responsibility is increasingly an investor priority.

Recent donor agency self-evaluations of gender mainstreaming efforts[5] revealed that strong policies for gender equality had not translated into significant results in transport and other infrastructure projects. Regional development banks, country donors, and United Nations agencies made greater progress on gender equality in social sectors, such as health and education, than in economic sectors such as infrastructure and private sector development (ADB 2006; Fernando 2010; Lateef 2007; Norwegian Agency for Development Cooperation [NORAD] 2006; OECD/ DAC 2007; Swedish International Development Cooperation Agency [SIDA] 2004; UN/ECOSOC 2004; United Kingdom Department for International Development [DFID] 2005; World Bank and IFC 2010).

A retrospective on gender and transport by the IFRTD acknowledged both progress and challenges (IFRTD 2010). Good practice examples have encouraged greater social inclusion[6] and participation of women in planning, implementation, and monitoring of transport projects as well as labor-based road construction and improved transport services. However, much remains to be done to empower women there (Fernando 2010). Nite Tanzarn asked: "Why are we still raising the issues put forward by others decades ago? Is it lack of commitment, understanding, capacity, or methodological tools?" (Tanzarn 2010:4). She noted that gender specialists and transport experts still have different ways of thinking and doing and barely understand each other's sector, resulting in a "cosmetic" treatment of gender in transport. This inadequate cross-sector communication may partly explain why transport projects have improved women's visibility but rarely increase women's bargaining power and empowerment in the sector[7] (Tanzarn 2010).

Development agencies and ministries of transport face numerous challenges to integrating gender in transport projects. One is time: transport project managers face a tension between tight project timeframes and the more extensive time required for consultations and social and gender assessments. Mandatory analyses such as those for procurement, financial management, and safeguards[8] take precedence over social and gender analysis. Although evidence indicates that participatory, inclusive approaches are more sustainable, they are also more management and resource intensive. Many transport staff feel that addressing gender and other social issues increases the complexity of projects that are already challenging.

Financial resources for social and gender assessments of transport projects are also limited. Task teams are frequently asked to address multiple, competing themes (e.g., gender, HIV/AIDS, climate change, governance) with no extra funding. Client countries are usually reluctant to invest borrowed resources in social and gender analysis and pilot activities. Thus, task teams regularly need to request trust funds for this work.

A third challenge is the limited availability of country-level expertise in gender and other social dimensions of transport. Few transport agencies have gender or social development specialists. World Bank social development specialists are often deployed to address narrowly defined displacement and resettlement safeguards for the rapidly growing transport portfolio rather than broader gender and other social issues. Client country reluctance presents a fourth challenge: gender and transport issues are often a "hard sell" to ministers of transport in client countries who want visible, infrastructural outcomes from borrowed money. Many decision makers lack awareness of the gender and other social dimensions of transport. Finally, there are few direct incentives: reward structures for advancing within organizations focus largely on the economic bottom line of transport rather social inclusion and gender equality (Clarke 2007; DFID 2005; SIDA 2004; Tornqvist and Lam 2005; World Bank 2010d).

An Anthropological Perspective on Engendering Transport Spaces

Some of the anthropological concepts and methods that guide transport anthropologists working in international development organizations include learning the "language" and "culture" of other professions, giving voice to local communities, applying a holistic approach to frame analysis in a broader context and look at cross-sectoral linkages, triangulating qualitative and quantitative research methodologies.

Learning the "Language" and "Culture" of Other Disciplines

Learning the language and cultural meanings of others is central to anthropological research. This is also essential for practitioners, whether or not they conduct research in a formal sense, to avoid the communication barriers described in the previous section. Transport anthropologists need to learn the "language" and professional "culture" of transport engineers and economists. This is essential to translate the gender dimensions of transport risks and benefits into terms that make sense and respond to the practical, "on-the-ground" realities of transport construction, maintenance, and services as well as development economics.

Reidar Kvam has described a communication gap between the "linear" approach of engineers who want "nuts and bolts" solutions to concrete problems and the "messy" approach of social scientists who explore the complexities of social and gender dimensions residing at the margins of roads (Kvam 2010). Road engineers tend to see a solution to lack of access to markets in terms of building a road from one point to another, or strive to reduce HIV/AIDS infection rates among transport workers through contract requirements for HIV/AIDS prevention training for construction workers. In contrast, social scientists examine a complex array of social, political, and cultural factors affecting choice of routes and uses and impacts of roads for different social groups as well as the gendered nature of HIV/AIDS transmission.

Gloria Davis has characterized anthropologists' equally daunting challenge of understanding and communicating with economists. Whereas anthropologists and other social scientists focus on people as members of groups, economists usually focus on individuals. Whereas anthropologists examine different groups' responses to a wide range of social factors such as norms and values, economists focus on individual responses to economic interests such as information and incentives. Economists emphasize inputs or outputs, whereas anthropologists highlight process. Economists assume an expert or advisory stance, whereas anthropologists generally adopt a listening and learning stance, trying to understand the meanings and values of other groups. Whereas an economic approach is technically rigorous and quantitative, an anthropological approach is holistic, contextual, qualitative, and participatory, though it may include quantitative elements. Where the economic approach is too simple and reductionistic to adapt to diverse contexts, the anthropological approach is often too complex and particularistic to be policy relevant (Davis 2004).

Transport anthropologists need to serve as translators of different professional languages and cultures to facilitate development of a common vision for addressing transport and gender issues in terms understandable to all parties, and foster cross-fertilization of conceptual frameworks and methods among disciplines.

Giving a Voice to Local Communities

Anthropologists value and seek to understand nuances of traditional knowledge to interpret its meanings. Transport anthropologists craft ethnographic methodologies to capture the voices of local women and men often excluded from decision making about transport that affects their lives and create channels for those voices to reach transport decision makers. They also delve into the interstices between the social, political, and economic structures that shape gendered and other spaces to understand and change the ways they limit mobility and access to transport and an array of opportunities. For example, Maria Gutierrez used participatory planning to understand gender relations and overcome gender stereotypes in highland Peru, which empowered women to play leadership roles in road maintenance microenterprises and local governance.

Framing Gender in Its Broader Sociocultural Context

Gender is an abstract concept that often poorly resonates with transport specialists, who may equate gender with women's rights issues rather than men's and women's different roles and responsibilities. Too often, analyses of gender and transport focus only on women's transport burdens and lack of mobility, access, and voice, ignoring men's constraints and potential to champion women's empowerment. A holistic anthropological perspective can frame gender and transport in a broader sociocultural context in concrete terms that make sense to non-anthropologists. However, it is very important to avoid the complex and often ambiguous anthropological jargon and "thick description," which prompts transport experts to throw up their hands and say that they cannot take on larger social issues. They want to see the implications of male and female differences in needs, risks, and benefits in operational terms; that is, translated into project management approaches such as definition of objectives, outcome indicators, activities, and budgets at actual points in the transport project cycle. Although this may appear to be a dilemma for anthropologists operating in the intersection of theory and practice, it need not be if they approach other disciplines as "cultures" with "languages" that they need to learn and use to translate anthropological theory into practice in those domains. This translation also fosters cross-fertilization of concepts and methods that benefits anthropology and other disciplines.

Looking at the Big Picture

A holistic perspective enables anthropologists to look beyond sector-specific "silos" to the bigger cross-sectoral picture to identify nontransport solutions to transport problems, foster multisectoral project approaches, and facilitate synergies among projects in different sectors. For example, bringing piped water to a village reduces the time women travel to collect water. Building more local markets reduces the distance women and men travel to sell their produce or goods (Carr and Hartl 2010; Starkey 2001). Digital phones can enable grassroots health workers to access expert advice without transporting patients to distant health facilities (Babinard and Roberts 2006).

A holistic perspective also helps anthropologists look at global-local linkages. They analyze factors affecting the spread of HIV and other infectious diseases along cross-border transport corridors (Kudat 2000; Lema et al. 2003; World Bank 2009b), examine the human impacts of greenhouse gases and explore the options for green transport (Fiske, this volume; GTZ 2010), or expand the understanding of factors driving human trafficking across borders and through ports to other continents (ADB n.d.; Dewey, this volume).

Triangulating Research and Evaluation

Anthropologists have enriched gender and transport research and evaluation of project outcomes by combining various quantitative and qualitative methods to balance the strengths and weaknesses of both types of data through "triangulation," a mixed-method approach designed to reduce bias and provide a more in-depth picture of the topic of study (Bamberger 2000; Bamberger et al. 2006). Thus, they enrich the findings with a better understanding of the "how" and "why" as well as the "what" of development outcomes. For example, Ayse Kudat rigorously applied multiple methods in her assessment of an urban transport design in Turkmenistan to provide convincing evidence why institutional reforms were also needed to reduce poverty (Kudat 1996).

Case Examples: Anthropologists in Action Addressing Gender and Transportation

During my work on gender and transport at the World Bank, I discovered the innovative approaches of other anthropologists on a range of gender and transport issues. Thus, before sharing my own experience, I present the stories[9] of those who broke anthropological ground before me on gender and transport over the past 30 years. Collectively, we have worked for a wide range of international development agencies, country donors, international NGOs, interdisciplinary networks, academic institutions, and private sector corporations. Our roles have included scholars, consultants, and development agency and NGO employees. Although these narratives by no means encompass all of the anthropologists working on gender and transport, they give a sense of the range and scale of contributions that transport anthropologists can make in international development endeavors around the world.

Building the Social Assessment Practice: Ayse Kudat

Ayse Kudat's interest in transport came from early research guided by diffusion theory; she concluded that human evolution was also transport evolution, because humans moved to new places to survive and succeed. After managing extensive monitoring and impact studies in the early 1980s for the Kenya Rural Road Access Program (Kudat 1989; Kudat and Woods 1981) and coordinating the second and third World Conferences on Women, Kudat joined the World Bank in 1988 as a transport anthropologist. At the center of her work at the World Bank was social assessment: the systematic investigation of social processes and factors that affect development impacts and results. Social assessment combines social analysis and participatory processes to identify affected people and involve them in determining project-related social issues and identifying the means to address them (Davis 2004).

Kudat led an initiative that clarified the purpose of social assessment, formalized key elements, and made social assessment more systematic and rigorous. Formally linking the objectives of social assessment to poverty reduction and other positive social outcomes (such as enhancing the social inclusion of women, minorities, and other often excluded groups;

strengthening social cohesion; increasing social capital; and reducing adverse social impacts), she positioned it in the development mainstream. Kudat and her colleagues conducted and published social assessments that served as models (e.g., Cernea and Kudat 1997; Kudat 1996). Through this and later work, the idea of social assessment was widely disseminated inside and outside the World Bank and increasingly mainstreamed in World Bank country programs and national policies in various countries (Davis 2004).

Social assessments provide an important entry point for addressing gender and other social issues in transport (Kudat 1998; World Bank 2006). Social assessments conducted by Kudat in Central Asia provided a platform for poor urban women and men to voice their views about changes needed in the transport system. Her 1995 assessment of the potential impact of a transport project design for Ashgabat Turkmenistan revealed that privatization of transport, as a part of the emergence of a market economy, had resulted in increased fares and reduced access to transport services for the poor, particularly women, who responded by shifting to employment within walking distance of their homes (Kudat 1998). These findings influenced the project designers to incorporate institutional reforms to serve the needs of low-income groups. These reforms significantly improved poor women's access to transport services and eliminated revenue leakage. Kudat addressed similar problems and impacts elsewhere in Central Asia. Kudat currently consults for British Petroleum, assessing the social impact of oil pipelines and associated construction, including access roads and developing resettlement action plans.

In Kudat's view, anthropologists' most important contributions in transport are raising awareness about positive and negative impacts of transport on people and identifying what can be done to make transport more beneficial to different groups of people. Social assessments and impact assessments play a very important role in achieving this. Anthropologists' hands-on multidisciplinary experience across sectors and continents is also valuable.

Navigating the Winds of Change in Bangladesh Inland Waterways and Beyond: Reidar Kvam

Reidar Kvam first ventured into transport anthropology as an advisor to Bangladesh's Inland Water Transport Authority. He headed a team assessing the country boat sector, the second largest source of livelihoods after agriculture, to help increase the competitiveness of country boatmen who were losing business to truck transporters. He traveled as a participant observer with boatmen, helped them move boats stuck on sandbars, learned community aspects of this informal sector, and helped boatmen organize to protect themselves from police harassment. He also conducted community outreach to encourage boatmen to adopt new approaches (Kvam et al. 1991;

Palmer et al. 2002). Kvam worked in several positions as the sole social scientist in development programs at the United Nations Food and Agriculture Organization, United Nations Economic and Social Commission for Asia, and the Norwegian Agency for Development Cooperation. In 1996, he joined a community of social scientists at the World Bank hired to address social impacts of resettlement for large infrastructure construction. This growing social scientist community collaborated to develop common approaches to resettlement and other social development issues, building on the pioneering work of Cernea and Kudat. The establishment of the Social Development Group in 1997 helped mainstream these approaches into projects and analytical work (World Bank 2005a).

Kvam's first World Bank assignment was in Andhra Pradesh, India, "fixing" the problem of government resistance to compensation for squatters whose livelihoods were displaced by a major state highway project. This is a common problem facing the World Bank and other development agencies. He met with men and women in affected communities as well as government officials and transport engineers. He learned that the government viewed growing crops or operating shops in the right of way for the road as illegal, and hence ineligible for compensation.

Kvam also discovered a semantic dimension of the problem. Indian law used the term "compensation" for payment to legal owners of land taken by the state under eminent domain, transferring title from private owners to the state. Officials refused to compensate squatters because they felt it would legitimize unlawful land occupancy. When asked if they would be willing to provide assistance to men and women displaced by the road, the government agreed. This, along with good collaboration within the World Bank team, enabled significant reduction of negative impacts on local populations through local consultations and better designs. This approach became a model for similar projects throughout India.

Kvam worked with Kudat, Cernea, and others in the World Bank social development community, gradually establishing approaches and methodologies that strengthened integration of social dimensions in the World Bank's work, including general terms of reference that positioned social scientist inputs at the beginning of the transport project design process rather than after design completion. The group established criteria for participatory approaches, social assessment, integration of gender, and other social concerns, as well as transport and other sector-specific guidelines for social analysis. Social impact and participation indicators have been incorporated into standardized project documents (World Bank 2005a, 2005b, 2006). Social issues, including gender, gradually became key aspects of the internal audit process.[10] Kvam currently leads the Policy and Quality Assurance Unit at the IFC.

In Kvam's view, anthropologists working inside development organizations can influence decision makers to address gender and social dimensions of transport and become decision makers themselves. They need to lead analytical work on social and gender analysis of unequal risks and benefits in project impacts, facilitate participatory approaches giving voice to excluded groups in affected communities, and translate findings into operational terms that transport engineers understand. One of the key lessons from mainstreaming social assessment in World Bank procedures was that consistency in messages and approaches among social scientists has a greater impact than an array of diverse approaches and studies in a large development organization.

Anthropologists working on the outside of development organizations can influence the transport agenda through applied research, advocacy, and public education. However, the credibility and acceptance of their advice depends on their understanding of technical transport realities and offering constructive and solutions-oriented recommendations.

"I Did Not Know I Had Rights"—Women and Rural Road Work in Peru: Maria Teresa Gutierrez

After graduate work exposed her to theories of gender exclusion and the links between social relations and power, Maria Gutierrez consulted for the Peru Rural Roads Project, financed by the World Bank and InterAmerican Development Bank. The project aimed to reduce rural isolation and poverty in poor highland areas, populated largely by indigenous people, by expanding the transport network through rehabilitation and maintenance of rural roads, developing community-based rural road maintenance microenterprises, improving local road planning and management, and strengthening local capacity to engage in economic activities (World Bank 2007c).

Gutierrez served as regional coordinator for the "Local Development Window," which stimulated entrepreneurial activities to take advantage of improved road conditions. For example, the Sauce Lake community commercial fishing initiative, driven largely by women, provided income to 61 families. Increased access to fish income improved child nutrition, increasing alertness and performance in school (World Bank 2007c).

This work increased Gutierrez's understanding of accessibility and mobility constraints faced by women trying to reach services and markets. Participatory rural planning with all-women and all-men groups enabled her to identify opportunities to address both women's and men's needs. One of the most significant outcomes of the consultations with women was the addition of footpaths to the rehabilitation agenda of the project. Passable footpaths enabled previously isolated women and men to access markets with greater impact on poverty reduction than road repair (Clarke 2008b; World Bank 2007c).

Gutierrez assumed the role of gender specialist for the Peru Rural Roads Project and responded to a request from *Provias Rurale,* the implementing agency, for gender training for technical specialists to enable them to train local people working in road maintenance microenterprises. She convinced *Provias Rurale* that she needed to work directly with local women and men to understand the perceptions, power relations, and gender stereotypes constraining women's participation in roadwork.

Her development of gender-informed training programs combined focus group discussions, participatory workshops, and interviews to better understand local perceptions, relationships, and levels of difficulty as well as gender stereotypes associated with road maintenance work. Interviews with spouses of microenterprise members examined gender relations, agricultural activities, and the impact of the microenterprise income on the family economy and life expectations (Gutierrez 2006).

The year-long training for road maintenance workers looked at gender relations in households, agricultural activities, road maintenance organizations, community, and local government by role playing common everyday situations. These role-plays raised awareness of the gendered division of labor, women's heavy workload, sex discrimination, and domestic violence. To counter views that roadwork was a man's job because it requires great strength, she developed a matrix of 20 activities differentiated by gender, level of difficulty, ability, and expertise. Participants realized that force alone was not enough to produce quality roadwork; resource management, quality control, and negotiation and reconciliation skills were also important (Gutierrez 2006).

In the months after the training, women's roles in decision-making positions within the maintenance microenterprises began to increase. Women on road teams improved the quality and efficiency of the work, in part by ensuring that male workers stayed on the job instead of getting drunk. Given their positive effect on productivity and quality of roadwork, road maintenance monitors recommended placing women on all teams. As community perceptions concerning female leadership changed, women became more actively involved in community organizations and activities, and their contributions were recognized. This was not an easy process. Rural women had to conquer personal barriers such as fear and shame of working on the road as well as *machismo* and other cultural barriers (Gutierrez 2009).

By the end of the project in 2007, 24 percent of the microenterprise members were women, more than doubling the 10 percent project target. In rural road committees, women comprised 21 percent of the members, 46 percent of the treasurers, 18.7 percent of the secretaries, and 4.6 percent of the presidents. Male and female members of road microenterprises became civic leaders, participated more in local elections as voters and candidates, and facilitated collaboration between communities (Caballero and Alcahuasi 2007; Clarke 2008b; World Bank 2007c).

Since 2008, Gutierrez has worked for the Internal Labor Organization as a technical specialist and gender focal point for the Employment and Intensive Investment Program in the Employment Policy Department.

In Gutierrez's view, anthropologists can contribute to increasing awareness that routine activities and patterns of mobility differ for women and men and affect their needs and priorities. For women in particular, management of time and social relations are important means of social support and mobilization. Anthropologists can identify gendered spaces and distances to inform the development of appropriate transport and foot trails. They can enhance the understanding of cultural practices that can affect project outcomes both positively and negatively and demonstrate the value of local resources and knowledge.

Ground Truthing—Mapping Mobility and Access in Lesotho: Wendy Walker

Wendy Walker worked as a World Bank consultant in the Africa Region Social Development Unit, reviewing the Africa Transport portfolio to identify how to more effectively address the social dimensions of the projects. She worked closely with the Africa Transport unit and made several trips to "ground truth" specific project findings (Walker and Sagna 2002).

One of the ground-truthing sites was Lesotho, where she met Ministry of Public Works staff and heard their concerns about how to prioritize transport investments, consult with communities, conduct social assessments, and use monitoring and impact evaluation. She also discovered a geographic information systems (GIS) database for the road network under construction in two different divisions of the Ministry. Drawing on her previous experience using GIS in research in Madagascar, she introduced the idea of using GIS as a consultation and decision support tool. Impressed by her approach, the task team leader for the Lesotho transport project obtained funds for Walker and others to assess the GIS database. As a result of the study, Ministry transport leaders became aware of the potential benefits of including gender and transport data in a multisectoral data-sharing network protocol to improve analysis and decision making. They also clarified their vision for the uses of the GIS database.

With the Ministry on board, Walker obtained another grant to pilot a methodology on social assessment and participatory mapping to identify social, transportation, and physical constraints to mobility and access as a basis for a consultation process for prioritizing roadworks using the GIS database. Previous social assessments for transport projects had focused only on costs of transport and access to specific destinations, with little attention to residents' mobility and access patterns within areas larger than specific communities. This broader view was particularly important for understanding the gender dimensions of transport. Women's travel by foot was invisible—uncounted in transport assessments focused only on the cost of motorized travel from one point to another.

Spatial analysis of mobility and access and the georeferenced collection of data are growing in the transport sector. Participatory mapping is widely used to complement GIS data on specific features such as roads, health services, markets, and water sources, with information on livelihoods and contexts in which people live. Walker and her team added women's and men's mobility and service access to the map by using a global positioning system (GPS) to plot participatory access and mobility maps onto the GIS database (Vajjhala and Walker 2009).

Using this methodology, the team found significant differences between women's and men's mobility and additional constraints for the elderly. Men had the greatest range of mobility and traveled primarily along the road, whereas the women's range was narrower and focused on footpaths perpendicular to the road. Women's travel times were much longer than those of men, especially when traveling with children. The elderly had great difficulty collecting their pensions. Social structure and the gendered dimensions of livelihoods played an important role in determining women's and men's access and mobility. Lack of cash and social constraints often prevented women from using public transport or even intermediate means of transport (IMTs) such as donkeys. Addressing these gender and age differences will have enormous positive impacts through greater attention to rehabilitation of footpaths and their connections to existing roads, improving transport service regularity and affordability, facilitating access to and ownership of IMTs, and making mobile health and pension services available (Walker et al. 2005).

Following the pilot, Walker guided the Ministry of Transport team in designing an extensive social assessment and monitoring methodology for the Lesotho Integrated Transport Project, which is still being used today with the interactive database for the national road network. In addition to its use for data storage and analysis, this GIS database also serves as a communication tool, facilitating participation of stakeholders at the local level in prioritizing roadworks. Thus, the GIS database provides a means to integrate local and community perspectives into national plans to better address local needs.

Walker followed up with another small grant to pilot a methodology for analysis of transport and health issues in Demographic and Health Surveys (DHSs). She collaborated with DHS teams in Lesotho, Ethiopia, and Ghana. Transport-related data routinely collected in DHSs includes ownership of transport (motorized and nonmotorized) by household, barriers to health care access for women, HIV/AIDS knowledge and experience of both women and men, and time required to access water. The DHS team in Lesotho agreed to add additional household-level questions on the time to access health clinics, mode of access to clinics, main health centers accessed, and IMT and vehicle ownership. She incorporated DHS data into the GIS database for the national road network to provide a picture of macro-level inputs and outcomes.

Walker's work integrated the social and spatial analysis of transport into the GIS database at three levels: first, as an analytical and decision support tool for the Ministry, integrating multisectoral data (location of schools, clinics, roads, populations, etc.); second, as an analytical and monitoring tool for social assessment and impact evaluation; and third, as a means to integrate nationwide data sources for analysis of macro-level and social impacts of transport investments.

In Walker's view, a major contribution of anthropologists in gender and transport is raising transport decision makers' awareness of the multiple transport stakeholders and transport users, particularly those who are invisible in standard transport surveys such as women, children, non-motorized transport users, and pedestrians. Transport planners tend to think that if they build a road, the services and customers will come to use the road. They overlook the gender-based control of money within the household, social restrictions to mobility, multiple transport needs, and other issues affecting access and mobility differently for women and men. Transport anthropologists need to understand appropriate entry points for gender and other social issues in the transport project cycle.

Making Transport Work for Women and Men: Mari Clarke

In my study of the changing household economy in rural Greece, I documented the importance of road and sea transport in linking the peninsula of Methana to the larger Greek economy (Clarke 1988). I was interested in the role of transport in part because I was already involved in international development work and aware of its importance for access to health care, education, and economic opportunities. I was also influenced by the regional analysis approach of anthropologist Carol Smith (Smith 1976), which was built on Wallerstein's notions of the world system and core-periphery relationships (Wallerstein 1974). She led me to look at links, such as roads, between local communities and the state. Another factor was my work on multidisciplinary archaeology teams in Greece focused on interpreting material culture and tracing early trade routes (Clark-Forbes 1976). Most important, my attention to transport reflected the perspectives of men and women in Methana, who routinely used the opening of the road as a historical reference point for describing events. The road brought them electricity, running water, a bus service, and access to cook stoves and gas cylinders to fuel them. Seeking these benefits of the road, local people labored to help complete it.

More than a decade later, after working on gender issues in various sectors with the U.S. Agency for International Development (USAID), the Asian

Development Bank, the Millennium Challenge Corporation, and several NGOs (Clarke 2006), I was invited to tackle gender and transport at the World Bank. My task was refining and repackaging reports from the Gender and Rural Transport Initiative, which supported pilot projects, gender studies, country workshops, capacity building, advisory services, and information dissemination on gender and transport (Banjo 2003; Sub-Saharan Africa Transport Policy Program [SSATP] 2007). It was part of an effort launched by the Gender and Development Group in the late 1990s to demonstrate that gender issues applied in the "hard" sectors such as transport as well as the "soft" sectors, such as education, health, and population, on which most World Bank gender work had focused (Bamberger and Lebo 1999; Rankin 1999). This task evolved into a much larger, global CD-ROM and web-based *Gender and Transport Resource Guide*—a virtual library of case studies, training manuals, issues papers, research and conferences reports, web sites, and other resources. I had learned from past experience in development agencies that it is essential to learn and correctly use the "language" of professionals with different disciplinary backgrounds. This assignment gave me a valuable introduction to transport language and operational realities.

I later served as senior gender specialist for "Capacity Building for Mainstreaming in Gender in Transport Projects," aiming to create a cadre of transport and gender "champions" among World Bank transport staff and their country counterparts. I guided gender reviews of transport projects in Africa, Europe and Central Asia, Latin America and the Caribbean, and South Asia as well as gender analysis of specific transport projects and issues, such as urban transport and post-conflict environments. In addition, I designed and delivered training workshops and materials and updated the *Gender and Transport Resource Guide* with new documents and emerging issues such as climate change.

I also provided technical support for several transport projects. My support to projects in Vietnam was especially extensive and culminated in the design and delivery of a gender and transport workshop for the Ministry of Transport staff. I assisted the Mekong Delta Transport Infrastructure Development Project, which aims to improve access to markets for businesses, farmers, and the poor by reducing physical and institutional bottlenecks in the main transport corridors of the Mekong Delta region. The project includes national road corridors, national inland waterway corridors, and smaller feeder roads and waterways connecting the poor to supply corridors. Gender issues were addressed only in the resettlement action plan, not in the project design components (World Bank 2007c).

I reviewed various drafts of the project implementation plan with a focus on gender issues. To translate my comments into operational terms, I prepared a matrix showing project objectives and indicators aligned with specific potential gender issues that could affect outcomes related to increased market access for poor women and men. The approved project implementation plan specified sex-disaggregated beneficiary data collection and analysis of gender differences in access, mobility, and use of transportation. I also reviewed and revised the terms of reference for the consulting group conducting the baseline survey and final evaluation to clarify the gender requirements of the task so that they would not "disappear" when the baseline study commenced.

The scope of the monitoring and evaluation task expanded to include the Northern Delta Transport Project. Aiming to strengthen local monitoring and evaluation capacity and reduce reliance on foreign experts, a contract was awarded to a Vietnamese firm. Their first-draft baseline survey instrument inadequately addressed gender differences in transport access and use. We asked them to sex-disaggregate data on transport ownership, use, and travel time and add questions on multitask travel ("trip chaining") and male and female roles in transport projects. We also stressed the importance of clear definition of units of analysis such as "household membership" as a part of instructions for data collectors to ensure that the data would be comparable. This process was important, not only to assess gender differences in transport access and use, but also to ensure validity and reliability of the survey data and support local capacity building. An added challenge for me was the limitation of my assistance to emails and videoconferences (Clarke 2010b).

By the time that we conducted the gender and transport workshops with the Ministry of Transport in October 2010, the baseline survey had been completed for the Mekong Delta Transport Infrastructure Development Project and preliminary data were available. We invited the lead researcher to give a presentation. His initial response was a series of number tables summarizing responses to every question in the survey. I looked at the data and offered suggestions for analyzing trends and making comparisons between males and females; I also urged him to replace number tables with bar and pie charts to communicate trends more clearly to workshop participants.

His charts showed that, despite strong national commitment to women's economic empowerment in all sectors, women walk and use nonmotorized transport (bicycles) significantly more than men and spend more time traveling. Women travel more to get fuel for the household and to work on the family farms, and spend less on their travel. In contrast, men travel more to the post office and the public telephone, and spend more money on more motorized travel. Women combine several tasks in one trip much more than men. Men have more information about transport projects than women and are more involved in project decision making and supervision. Women's project participation is largely limited to project implementation (Hai 2010). When the small group discussions among Ministry of Transport staff included potential approaches for addressing these trends, I realized that we had come a long way since the start of my technical support.

The Ministry of Transport supported the idea of gender and transport workshops because the proposed content was grounded in the operational realities of transport, rather than general discussions of gender mainstreaming. In preparation for the workshop, I learned that the Third Rural Transport Project had received a grant to conduct a pilot project that trained 1,533 minority women to maintain 51 kilometers of road in remote, mountainous areas where contracting firms were reluctant to take equipment. Their efforts provided accessibility to previously isolated communities and increased community awareness of the importance of road maintenance. Income earned by women road workers contributed to family livelihoods, enabled more investment in their children's education, and increased their voice in community and household decision making (Tran 2010; Tran et al. 2010; World Bank 2010c).

The manager of the Third Rural Transport Project agreed to give a presentation on the pilot project. In addition, she arranged for participation of Ministry of Transport and Women's Union speakers and facilitated the workshops. Her transport team played a leading role in carrying out a daunting logistics plan. This included translation of all workshop materials into Vietnamese, printing, simultaneous translation during both workshops, and projection of all PowerPoint presentations in English and Vietnamese in Hanoi and Ho Chi Minh City, as well as arranging transport and lodging for Ministry of Transport participants from the provinces.

Working with the Vietnamese World Bank transport staff in the country office was a wonderful process of teamwork. This enabled us to deliver a high-quality, well-received workshop that raised awareness of gender issues among Ministry of Transport decision makers and project implementation staff as well as World Bank staff. Workshop participants generated a number of recommendations to mainstream gender in their work (Clarke 2010b). One specific outcome of the workshop was the extension of the pilot women's road maintenance project. Another was my support in the integration of gender and transport in the transport training institute curriculum. Without the country office staff's insights and active engagement, we would not have been able to achieve these outcomes.

Conclusions: Whither Transport Anthropology?

The five transport anthropology narratives clearly demonstrate their contributions to development practice, putting women and men first. Less apparent are their innovative contributions to anthropological theory and methods by mapping the spatial dimensions of gender and transport. Both are important for the future of transport anthropology.

Putting Women and Men First in Transport Development

The narratives illustrate how transport anthropologists make a difference translating anthropological concepts and methods into operational terms at key entry points in the development process, including analytical work, technical support, training, advocacy, and social safeguards to maximize the positive impacts of development on different groups of people. Anthropologists have thus transformed development processes, agendas, and organizational culture.

Analytical Work

Analytical work, such as that of Kudat, Gutierrez, and Walker, applying social and gender analysis sheds light on gender differences in transport access, use, risks, and benefits. This can give voice to those seldom heard; recognize "invisible" stakeholders such as pedestrians, users of nonmotorized transport, women, children, the elderly, and the handicapped; identify gendered spaces; and raise awareness of the importance of local knowledge. Analytical work can take many forms such as poverty and social impact assessments, policy analyses, case studies of specific transport projects, participatory mapping of mobility, and access to transport, transport portfolio reviews, baseline surveys, and impact evaluations.

Technical Support

Technical support to transport teams, such as Kvam's in India and mine in Vietnam, focuses on entry points for addressing gender over the project cycle. In each phase, standard project documents provide opportunities to incorporate gender and other social issues into the blueprints and due diligence for projects. Examples include: project concept notes; project appraisal documents, including summaries of social and environmental assessments and resettlement action plan; implementation plans and operational handbooks; and the results framework and baseline survey that provide the basis for monitoring and impact evaluation. Terms of reference for analytical work conducted in preparation, during, and after the completion of a project are important entry points needed to ensure that gender issues are examined.

Training and Capacity Building

Anthropologists, such as Gutierrez, have applied their participant observation, cross-cultural communication, and analysis skills along with participatory approaches in various types of training and capacity building for local communities, roadworkers, transport implementers, and transport decision makers in the public and private sectors, raising awareness of the diverse, human face of transportation, its differential impacts on social groups, and methods for listening to local women and men to learn about their needs, constraints, perceptions, and priorities.

Influencing Decision Making

Both Kudat and Kvam became decision makers in their own right as they moved into management positions in the World Bank and the IFC. Anthropologists also influence transport decision makers by presenting research findings in compelling ways that speak to the needs and interests of the sector and the country. They can, as Walker did, develop planning tools for decision makers that provide a voice for the people affected by transport projects. They can also develop "scripts" for transport staff to make the case to decision makers in Ministries of Transport, as I did in my work in Vietnam. Anthropologists working outside of development agencies can play important roles in advocacy for gender and transport issues and conduct research grounding practical recommendations in sound evidence.

Social Safeguards

Anthropologists have a long history documenting development impacts on communities. When the World Bank began hiring social scientists to address the impacts of large infrastructure investments, Michael Cernea led the way in developing an involuntary displacement and resettlement policy informed by anthropological research, including Thayer Scudder's and Elizabeth Colson's study of the forced resettlement of the Gwembe Tonga in Zambia (Cernea 1985; Scudder 1993). This was followed by a policy protecting the rights and resources of indigenous peoples. Similar social safeguard policies are now widely used internationally by most major financial institutions lending to the public and private sectors (World Bank 2010b). The World Bank, the IFC, and other donors continue to refine social safeguard policies and procedures, guided by anthropologists such as Reidar Kvam. Other anthropologists continue research to improve the impacts of resettlement programs (Cernea 2010; Koenig 2005).

Anthropologists' analytical work, technical support, training, advocacy, and social safeguards have influenced development decision-making processes and reshaped the development agenda in the World Bank where social development, social assessment, and social safeguards have moved into the mainstream of an international development bank driven by business and economic principles.

Pushing Boundaries of Understanding Spatially

The spatial aspect of transport planning lends itself to mapping gendered and other social spaces as well as meanings that women and men assign to changing elements of their landscapes. Gender analysis of everyday use of pathways across landscapes and how places and spaces are used, valued and struggled over expands understanding of local and larger social and power relations shaping their use, value, and meaning (Rocheleau et al. 1995).

Long before sociocultural anthropologists studied transport, archaeologists explored its spatial dimensions, tracing land and sea routes across different times and cultures. They deployed interdisciplinary teams using aerial and satellite photography, surface survey, historic records, and archaeological excavation to interpret social, political, and economic organization, gender differences, and cultural expressions of patterned movement reflected in material culture (Arnold and Wicker 2001; Snead et al. 2009).

Few sociocultural anthropologists outside of development organizations have conducted and published research focused on transport. For example, Emilio Moran examined the positive and negative socioeconomic and environmental impacts of settlements along the Transamazon Highway (Moran 1981), and Gina Porter examined rural mobility and social inequality in Africa (Porter 2002). A number of anthropologists, guided by postmodernist theory, are examining multiple ways in which road spaces simultaneously connect and disconnect people, places, and things. They analyze road narratives as a means through which people make sense of the colonial or socialist past as well as present changes and asymmetries associated with the global economy (Dalakoglou 2010; Harvey 2005; Klaeger 2009; Masquelier 2002; Roseman 1996; Thomas 2002; Trankell 1993).

For example, Adeline Masquelier links a paved road and the deadly spirits surrounding it to Niger's history of forced labor and bloodshed on roads constructed to serve foreign interests, emergent capitalism, foreign assistance, and a high traffic accident rate in a Sahelian context where travel has long been a necessity for survival. She characterizes the road as "a hybrid space that condenses past histories at the same time that it concretizes perils and possibilities of modern life" (Masquelier 2002:829). Penny Harvey and Hannah Knox conducted ethnographic research on roads in Andean and Amazonian Peru, looking at how technologies and knowledge which they require and produce both materialize and operationalize the state and the economy and how "roads as territorial connectors rely on standardisations of space into socially and administratively defined domains, which in turn enable mobilities that come to constitute the very fabric of a cohesive and integrated nation" (Harvey and Knox 2006:6).

Dimitiri Dalakoglou discusses how the physical and social construction, uses, and perceptions of a cross-border highway between Greece and Albania encapsulate the transition to a market economy, new nationalisms, massive emigration to Greece, and the asymmetric globalization of sovereignty in a postsocialist country on the European economic periphery. He suggests that anthropological research is focusing more on roads because transport networks and flows of vehicles, people, and things on them are increasingly extensive and complex with enormous social as well as material impacts on culture (Dalakoglou 2010).

The transport anthropology narratives presented earlier also point to the significance of the spatial dimension for pushing the boundaries of anthropological understanding of culture, community, gender, and global-local connections and, as scholar practitioners, using that understanding to facilitate change. Maria Gutierrez nuanced the understanding of community and culture in highland Peru by examining gendered spaces in highland Peru, which facilitated change in gender stereotypes empowering women. Wendy Walker's use of participatory mapping with GIS in Lesotho added women's and men's access and mobility spaces to the understanding of gender and translated this into development planning. Reidar Kvam focused on spaces at the margins of roads in India inhabited by squatters and hawkers, viewed as illegal by transport officials. Kudat demonstrated how privatization diminished economic spaces occupied by poor women in urban Turkmenistan and the need to facilitate expansion of those spaces.

Looking to the future, spatial analysis of gendered dimensions of global-local transport linkages, cross-fertilized with concepts from other disciplines, adds another dimension to the anthropological understanding of culture, community, gender, and global-local linkages. Future transport anthropology needs to engage and foster dialogue between anthropologists approaching transport as an object for narrative analysis and critique and those learning the transport "language" as a means to transform development agendas. Electronic footprints of both streams of work such as the "Anthropology of Highways and Byways" blog and the GATNET (Gender and Transport Network) listserv provide channels for such communication and reflect the global-local nature and future of anthropological scholarship and practice in transport anthropology.

Acknowledgments

My sincere appreciation for the time and experiences shared by Ayse Kudat, Reidar Kvam, Maria Gutierrez, and Wendy Walker. Many thanks for the insightful comments on drafts of this chapter provided by Phuong Thi Minh Tran, Thuy Bich Nguyen, Dung Anh Hoang, Paul Vallely, Daniel Mont, Baher El Hifnawy, Nina Batt, George Banjo, Michael Bamberger Jennifer Collier, and Christina Wasson.

Notes

1. This is adapted from the definition widely used by gender specialists: "Gender refers to the socially constructed roles and socially learned behaviors and expectations associated with males and females" (World Bank 2002).

2. "Gender equality" refers to equality under the law, equality of opportunity (rewards for work, equality of access to human capital, and other productive resources), and equality of voice (ability to influence and contribute to the development process) (World Bank 2002).
3. The rural road access measures the percentage of the population that lives within 2 kilometers of an all season road. A low rural access index correlates with low economic growth (Roberts et al. 2006).
4. "Gender mainstreaming is a strategy for making women's as well as men's concerns and experiences an integral dimension of the design, implementation, monitoring, and evaluation of policies and programs in all political, economic and societal spheres so that women and men benefit equally" (UN/ECOSOC 1997).
5. There have been extensive debates about the gender mainstreaming approach that have not directly addressed gender and transport issues and thus are not discussed here. For example, see Mehra and Gupta (2006) and Walby (2005).
6. Social inclusion refers to change in institutions such as the development policies, social norms, and behaviors that provide an opportunity for marginalized groups to increase their voice and access to assets (Alsop et al. 2006; Kabeer 2001; World Bank 2005a).
7. Empowerment is a process of enhancing individual or group capacity to make strategic choices and transform those choices into actions and outcomes as agents of positive social change (Alsop et al. 2006; Kabeer 2001; World Bank 2005a).
8. The objective of the World Bank and other international development bank safeguards policies is to prevent and mitigate undue harm to people and their environment in the development process. For more details see http://go.worldbank.org/WTA1ODE7T0.
9. These narratives are based on conversations and e-mail communications with the featured individuals as well as a review of their writings and others writing about them.
10. For more information, see http://web.worldbank.org/WBSITE/ EXTERNAL/PROJECTS/QAG/0,,contentMDK:20067126~menuP K:114865~pagePK:109617~piPK:109636~theSitePK:109609,00.html.

References

Alsop, Ruth, Mette F. Bertelsen, and Jeremy Holland
    2006 Empowerment in Practice: From Analysis to Implementation. Washington, D.C.: World Bank.
Arnold, Bettina, and Nancy Wicker
    2001 Gender and the Archaeology of Death. Lanham, MD: AltaMira Press.
Asian Development Bank (ADB)
    1995 Social Safeguards Policy.

Asian Development Bank (ADB)
2003 Gender Checklist: Resettlement.
2006 Implementation Review of the Policy on Gender and Development.
n.d. Lao People's Democratic Republic East-West Corridor Project—Reconsidering Highway Traffic: Women, Children and HIV/AIDS.

Babinard, Julie, and Peter Roberts
2006 Maternal and Child Mortality Development Goals: What Can the Transport Sector Do? Washington, D.C.: World Bank Transport Sector Board Transport Paper TP-12.

Bamberger, Michael
2000 Integrating Quantitative and Qualitative Research in Development Projects: Directions in Development. Washington, D.C.: World Bank.

Bamberger, Michael, and Gerry Lebo
1999 Gender and Transport: A Rationale for Action. Washington, D.C.: World Bank.

Bamberger, Michael, Jim Rugh, and Linda Mabry
2006 Real World Evaluation: Working Under Budget Time, Data and Political Constraints. Thousand Oaks, CA: Sage Publications.

Banjo, George
2003 Gender and Rural Transport Initiative: Presentation on Process and Initial Lessons for Gender and Transport Thematic Group. Washington, D.C.: World Bank.

Barwell, Ian, and Jonathon Dawson
1993 Roads are Not Enough: New Perspectives on Rural Transport Planning in Developing Countries. Sterling, VA: Stylus Publishing.

Bennett, Lynn
2003 Empowerment and Social Inclusion: A Social Development Perspective on the Cultural and Institutional Foundations of Poverty Reduction. Washington, D.C.: World Bank, Social Development.

Blackden, Mark
2003 Too Much Work and Too Little Time, Gender Dimensions of Transport, Water and Energy. Paper presented at a World Bank—sponsored training event in Arusha, Tanzania, February 3–7.

Blackden, Mark, and Quentin Wodon (eds.)
2006 Gender, Time Use, and Poverty in Sub-Saharan Africa. Washington, D.C.: World Bank.

Caballero, Lutz, and Nerida Alcahuasi
2007 Gender in Peru: Can Women be Integrated into Transport Projects? En Breve. Analytical Note Series No. 112. Washington, D.C.: World Bank Latin America and Caribbean Region.

Canadian International Development Agency (CIDA)
1998 Building Bridges, a Review of Infrastructure Service Projects Addressing Gender Integration. Ottawa: CIDA.

Carr, Marilyn, and Maria Hartl
2010 Lightening the Load: Labor Saving Technologies and Practices for Rural Women. Bourton-on-Dunsmore, U.K.: International Fund for Agricultural Development and Practical Action Publishing.

Cernea, Michael (ed.)
1985 Putting People First: Sociological Variables in Rural Development. Second expanded edition 1991. World Bank. New York: Oxford University Press.
2000 Impoverishment Risks and Reconstruction: A Model for Population Displacement and Resettlement. *In* Risks and Reconstruction: Experiences of Resettlers and Refugees, Michael Cernea and Chris McDowell, eds. Pp. 11–55. Washington, D.C.: World Bank.
2010 Broadening the Definition of "Population Displacement": Geography and Economics in Conservation Policy. *In* Resettling Displaced People: Policy and Practice in India, Hari Mohan, ed. Pp. 85–119. London: Routledge.

Cernea, Michael, and Ayse Kudat
1997 Social Assessments for Better Development Case Studies in Russia and Central Asia. Washington, D.C.: World Bank.

Clark-Forbes, Mari
1976 Farming and Foraging in Prehistoric Greece. *Annals of the New York Academy of Sciences* 268:127–42.

Clarke, Mari
1988 The Transformation of Households on Methana, Greece, 1931–1987. Ph.D. dissertation, Department of Anthropology, University of North Carolina at Chapel Hill.
2006 Pursuing International Development Through a Gender Lens: Reflections on a Nonlinear Career Path in Applied Anthropology. *In* Making History at the Frontier: Women Creating Careers as Practicing Anthropologists. National Association for the Practice of Anthropology Bulletin 26:32–54.
2007 Progress Report on Dissemination of Gender and Transport Good Practice. Unpublished report prepared for the World Bank Transport Department, Washington, D.C.
2008a Thematic Note on Rural Roads. *In* Gender and Agriculture Sourcebook. Pp. 372–82. Washington, D.C.: World Bank, Food and Agriculture Organization (FAO), International Fund for Agricultural Development (IFAD).
2008b Rural Roads and Innovation Activity Profile: Peru Rural Roads. *In* Gender and Agriculture Sourcebook. Pp. 407–10. Washington, D.C.: World Bank, FAO, IFAD.
2010a Technical Support for the Mekong Delta Transport Infrastructure Project. Prepared for the Capacity Building for Mainstreaming Gender in Transport Initiative. Washington, D.C.: World Bank.
2010b Making Transport Work for Women and Men in Vietnam: Workshop Report. Washington, D.C.: World Bank.

Clarke, Mari
   2010c Making Transport Work for Women and Men: Tools for Task Teams. World Bank Social Development, http://web.worldbank.org/WBSITE/EXTERNAL/TOPICS/EXTSOCIALDEVELOPMENT/0,contentMD K:22511004~pagePK:148956~piPK:216618~theSitePK:244363,00.html.
Cook, Cynthia
   1991 Social Analysis in Rural Road Projects. In Putting People First, Michael Cernea, ed. Pp. 395–427. New York: Oxford University Press.
Dalakoglou, Dimitris
   2010 The Road: An Ethnography of the Albanian-Greek Cross-border Motorway. American Ethnologist 37(1):132–49.
Davis, Gloria
   2004 A History of the Social Development Network in the World Bank, 1973–2002. World Bank Social Development Paper 56.
de Wet, Chris, ed.
   2005 Development Induced Displacement: Problems, Policies and People. London: Berghahn Press.
Dickson, Eric
   n.d. Community Participation in Resettlement: An Alternative to Evictions. London: London School of Economics.
Fernando, Prianthi
   2010 Recognizing the Care Economy. IFRTD Forum News 15(3):4.
Fernando, Prianthi, and G. Porter (eds.)
   2002 Balancing the Load: Women, Gender and Transport. London: Zed Books.
German Technological Corporation (GTZ)
   2005 Transport Matters: Contributions of the Transport Sector Towards Achieving the Millennium Development Goals. Eschborn, Germany: GTZ.
   2010 Reducing Emissions Through Sustainable Transport. Prepared by Anne Binsted, Holger Dalkman, Daniel Bogarat, and Ko Sakamoto. Eschborn, Germany: GTZ.
Graeco, Margaret
   2002 Gender, Social Inclusion and Rural Infrastructure Services. Washington, D.C.: World Bank.
Grown, Karen
   2006 Quick Impact Initiatives for Gender Equality: A Menu of Options. Levy Economics Institute, Bard College Working Paper Number 462.
Gutierrez, Maria
   2006 I Did Not Know I Had Rights: The Process of Training Workers in Peruvian Rural Roads Infrastructure Project. Paper Presented at the First International Conference on Gender and Transportation, Port Elizabeth, South Africa, August 27–30.
   2009 Gender Participation in Infrastructure Investment Programs and Rural Transport. Paper presented at FAO, IFAD, International Labor Office (ILO) Workshop on Gaps, Trends and Current Research on the

Gender Dimensions of Agricultural and Rural Employment: Differentiated Pathways out of Poverty, Rome, Italy, March 31–April 2.

Hai, Do Phu
2010 Addressing Gender Issues in the Mekong Delta and Northern Delta Transport Monitoring and Evaluation. Presentation at the "Making Transport Work for Women and Men" Workshop, Hanoi, Vietnam, October 26.

Harvey, Penny
2005 The Materiality of State Effect: An Ethnography of a Road in the Peruvian Andes. *In* State Formation: Anthropological Perspectives, Christian Krohn-Hansen and Knut G. Nustad, eds. Pp. 216–47. Cambridge: Pluto Press.

Harvey, Penney, and Hannah Knox
2006 Research Report on Roads to Development: Uneven Development and the Politics of Knowledge. Manchester, U.K.: Economic and Social Research Centre for Research on Socio-Cultural Change.
2010 Delivering Social Change: An Anthropological Approach to the Ethnography of Place. *In* Understanding Social Research: Thinking Creatively about Method, A. Dale and J. Mason, eds. London: Sage Publications.

International Forum for Rural Transport and Development (IFRTD)
2004 From Rhetoric to Practice: Mainstreaming Gender in Transport. *IFRTD Forum News* 11(1):1–63.
2010 Gender and Transportation: Why Are We Still Talking about Head Loading? *IFRTD Forum News* 15(3).

Kabeer, Naila
2001 Resource, Agency Achievements: Reflections on the Measurement of Women's Empowerment. *In* Discussing Women's Empowerment: Theory and Practice, B. Sevefjord et al., eds. Pp. 18–57. Stockholm: SIDA Studies No. 3.

Klaeger, Gabriel
2009 Religion on the Road: The Spiritual Experience of Road Travel in Ghana. *In* The Speed of Change: Motor Vehicles and People in Africa 1890–2000, J. B. Gewald, S. Luning, and K. Van Walraved, eds. Pp. 169–94. Leiden: Brill.

Koenig, Dolores
2005 Enhancing Local Development in Development-induced Displacement and Resettlement Projects. *In* Development Induced Displacement: Problems, Policies and People, Chris de Wet, ed. Pp. 105–48. London: Berghahn Press.

Kudat, Ayse
1981 Participation of Women in Rural Access Program in the Kenya. Nairobi: United Nations Settlement Program UN HABITAT.
1989 Participation of Women in Rural Road Maintenance in SubSaharan Africa. Washington, D.C.: World Bank.

Kudat, Ayse
    1991 A Discussion Note on Women and Transport in Africa. Africa
    Infrastructure Symposium. Washington, D.C.: World Bank.
    1996 A Case Study for Social Support of Transport in Ashgabat.
    Washington, D.C.: World Bank.
    1998 A Working Paper on Social Assessment for an Urban Transport
    Project. Washington, D.C.: World Bank.
    2000 Integrating HIV/AIDS in Transport Planning. World Bank,
    Subshaharan Africa Transport Unit.
    2001 Working Paper on a Model for Social Impact Monitoring for Rural
    Transportation. Washington, D.C.: World Bank.
Kudat, Ayse, and Dennis Woods
    1981 A Baseline Study of Rural Access Roads in Kenya. Nairobi: Ministry
    of Transport and Communications.
Kudat, Ayse, Stan Peabody, Ovezdurdy Muhammetberdiev, and Klaus Moeltner
    1997 Strengthening Ashgabat's Urban Transport Sector. *In* Social
    Assessments for Better Development Case Studies in Russia and Central
    Asia, Michael Cernea and Ayse Kudat, eds. Pp. 165–86. Washington,
    D.C.: World Bank.
Kunieda, Mika, and Aimee Gautier
    2007 Gender and Urban Transport: Smart and Affordable. Module
    7a. Sustainable Transport Sourcebook for Policy Makers in Developing
    Countries. Eschborn: GTZ.
Kvam, Reidar
    2010 Gender-Responsive Social Analysis in Transport Projects. Paper pre-
    sented at the Workshop on Designing Inclusive Transport Operations,
    January 28. Washington, D.C.: World Bank.
Kvam, Reidar, Colin Palmer, and Nazibar Rahman
    1991 Navigating the Winds of Change: Mechanization of Country Boats
    in Bangladesh. Oslo: Norwegian Agency for Development Cooperation
    (NORAD).
Lateef, Shireen
    2007 Gender Mainstreaming at ADB. Paper presented at UN
    Expert Group Meeting on Financing Gender Equality and Women's
    Empowerment, Oslo, Norway, September 4–7.
Leautier, Frannie, and Andrew Lerner
    2003 Perspectives on Globalization in Infrastructure. Washington, D.C.:
    World Bank Institute Working Paper.
Lema, Antoine, Stephen Brushett, Negede Lewi, et al.
    2003 Taming HIV/AIDS on Africa's Roads. SSATP Technical Note 35.
Malmberg-Calvo, Christina
    1994a Case Study on the Role of Women in Rural Transport: Access of
    Women to Domestic Facilities. SSATP Working Paper 11.
    1994b Case Study on Intermediate Means of Transport Bicycles and
    Rural Women in Uganda. SSATP Working Paper 12.

Masika, Rachel, and Sally Baden
   1997 Infrastructure and Poverty: A Gender Analysis. Report prepared for the Gender and Equality unit, SIDA by BRIDGE. International Development Studies, Sussex University, United Kingdom.
Masquelier, Adeline
   2002 Road Mythologies: Space, Mobility, and the Historical Imagination in Post-colonial Niger. *American Ethnologist* 29(4):829–56.
Mehra, Rekha, and Geeta Rao Gupta
   2006 Gender Mainstreaming: Making It Happen. Washington, D.C.: International Center for Research on Women.
Mehta, Lyla
   2002 The Double Bind: A Gender Analysis of Forced Displacement and Resettlement. Paper presented at Workshop on Engendering Resettlement Polices and Programs in India, New Delhi, India, September 12.
Montgomery, B., and Peter Roberts
   2008 Walk Urban, Demand, Constraints, and Measurement of the Urban Pedestrian Environment. Washington, D.C.: World Bank.
Moran, Emilio
   1981 Developing the Amazon: The Social and Ecological Impact of Settlement Along the Transamazon Highway. Bloomington: Indiana University Press.
Norwegian Agency for Development Cooperation (NORAD)
   2006 Lessons from Evaluation of Women and Gender Equality in Development Cooperation. Synthesis Report 2006/1, Oslo: Norway.
Organisation for Economic Co-operation and Development, Development Assistance Committee (OECD/DAC)
   2004 Why Gender Matters in Infrastructure. Working Group on Gender and Equality. Paris: OECD/DAC.
   2007 Gender Equality and Aid Delivery: What Has Changed in Development Cooperation Agencies since 1999? Paris: OECD/DAC.
Palmer, Colin, Farhad Ahmad, Ana Bravo, and Priyanthi Fernando
   2002 Rural Water Transport Literature Review. London: IFRTD.
Peters, Deike
   2002 Gender and Transport in Less Developed Countries. Paper commissioned by United Nations Environment and Development (UNED) Forum for Expert Workshop on Gender Perspectives for the Earth Summit 2002, Berlin, Germany, January 10–12.
Porter, Gina
   2002 Living in a Walking World: Rural Mobility and Social Equity Issues in SubSaharan Africa. *World Development* 30(2):285–300.
Pulley, Tulin Akin, Shireen Latif, and Ferdousi Sutana Begum
   2003 Making Infrastructure Work for Women in Bangladesh. Manila: ADB.
Quisumbing, Agnes
   2003 What Have We Learned from Research on Household Allocation. *In* Household Decisions, Gender, and Development: A Synthesis of

Recent Research, Agnes Quisumbing, ed. Pp. 1–16. Washington, D.C.: IFPRI.

Rankin, Elizabeth
1999 Gender and Transport: A Strategy for Africa. Washington, D.C.: World Bank.

Roberts, Peter, K. C. Kyam, and Radula Rastogi
2006 Rural Access Index: A Key Development Indicator. World Bank Transport Sector Board Transport Paper TP 10.

Rocheleau, Diane, Barbara Thomas Slayter, David Edmunds
1995 Gender Resource Mapping: Focusing on Women's Spaces in the Landscape. *Cultural Survival Quarterly* 18(4):62–68.

Roseman, Sharon
1996 How We Build the Road: The Politics of Memory in Galicia. *American Ethnologist* 23(4):836–60.

Ruiz Abril, Maria Elena
2005 Making Rural Roads Work for Both Women and Men: The Example of Peru's Rural Road Program. Promising Approaches in Gender and Development. World Bank Gender and Development, electronic document, http://siteresources.worldbank.org/INTGENDER/Resources/PeruRRPFINAL.pdf.

Sabarwal, Shwetlena, Nistha Sinha, and Mayra Buvinic
2009 The Global Financial Crisis: Assessing Vulnerability for Women and Children: Policy Brief. Washington, D.C.: World Bank.

Scudder, Thayer
1993 Development-induced Relocation and Refugee Studies: 37 Years of Change and Continuity among Zambia's Gwembe Tonga. *Journal of Refugee Studies* 6(2): 123–52.

Smith, Carol (ed.)
1976 Regional Analysis Volume I: Economic Systems. New York: Academic Press.

Snead, James, Clark Erickson, and Andres Darling (eds.)
2009 Landscapes of Movement: Trails, Paths, and Roads in Anthropological Perspective. Philadelphia: University of Pennsylvania Press.

Starkey, Paul
2001 Local Transport Solutions: People, Paradoxes and Progress: Lessons Arising from the Spread of Intermediate Means of Transport. SSATP Working Paper 56.

Sub-Saharan Africa Transport Policy Program (SSATP)
2007 Gender and Transport Resource Guide. Electronic document, http://www4.worldbank.org/afr/ssatp/Open.aspx?id = 693.

Swedish International Development Cooperation Agency (SIDA)
2004 Integrating Gender Equality into Development Cooperation—Lessons Drawn from the Recent Evaluations by SIDA and the European Commission. Joint Seminar, Brussels, November 27–28.

Tanzarn, Nite
2010 Challenges of Addressing Gender in the Transport Sector. *IFRTD Forum News* 15(3):4.

Thomas, Philip
  2002 The River, the Road and the Rural-Urban Divide: A Post-colonial Moral Geography from Southern Madagascar. *American Ethnologist* 29(2):366–91.
Torero, Maximo, and Shyamal Chowdhury
  2005 Increasing Access to Infrastructure for Africa's Poor. 2020 Africa Conference Brief 16. Washington, D.C.: International Food and Policy Research Institute.
Tornqvist, Annika, and Ky Tu Lam
  2005 Assessment of the Trust Fund for Gender in the World Bank (GENFUND). Washington, D.C.: World Bank.
Tran, Phuong Thi Minh
  2010 Paths to Development: Ethnic Minority Women Rehabilitate Bac Ha Roads. Paper presented at the Making Transport Work for Women and Men Workshop, Hanoi, Vietnam, October 26.
Tran, Phuong Thi Minh, Nguen Thi Hien, and Le Ngoc Hung
  2010 Report on the Assessment of the Social Impact and Cost Effectiveness of Rural Road Maintenance with Local Women's Participation. Washington, D.C.: World Bank.
Trankell, Ing-Britt
  1993 On the Road in Laos: An Anthropological Study of Road Construction and Rural Communities. Uppsala, Sweden: Uppsala Research Reports in Cultural Anthropology.
United Kingdom Department for International Development (DFID)
  2005 Evaluation of DFID Development Assistance: Gender Equality and Women's Empowerment. London: DFID.
UN Economic and Social Council (UN/ECOSOC)
  1997 Mainstreaming the Gender Perspective into All Policies and Programs in the United Nations System. Report of the Secretary General E/1997/100. Geneva: UN/ECOSOC.
  2004 Issues Paper Prepared for Discussion on Mainstreaming Gender in UN Operations. Geneva: UN/ECOSOC.
UN Millennium Project
  2005 Taking Action: Achieving Gender Equality and Empowering Women. Task Force on Education and Gender Equality. New York: UN Millennium Project.
Vajjhala, Shalini, and Wendy Walker
  2009 Roads to Participatory Planning: Integrating Cognitive Mapping and GIS for Transport Prioritization in Rural Lesotho. Washington, D.C.: Resources for the Future Discussion Paper 09-26.
van Riet, Marinke
  2008 The Unbalanced Load: Mainstreaming Gender in the New World Bank Transport Business Strategy. Response for IFRTD, May 22. London: IFRTD.

Walby, Sylvia
    2005 Gender Mainstreaming: Productive Tensions in Theory and Practice. *Social Politics: International Studies in Gender State and Society* 12(3):321–43.
Walker, Wendy, and Cheikh Sagna
    2002 Social and Poverty Issues/Impacts in the Africa Transport Sector. Washington, D.C.: World Bank Africa Regional Transport Unit. December.
Walker, Wendy, Shalini Vajjhala, Thasi Phomane, et al.
    2005. Ground Truthing: Mobility Mapping and Access in Rural Lesotho. Washington, D.C.: World Bank and Lesotho Ministry of Public Works.
Wallerstein, Emmanuel
    1974 Capitalist Agriculture and the Origins of the European World Economy in the Sixteenth Century. New York: Academic Press.
White Ribbon Alliance for Safe Motherhood (WRA)
    2002 Saving Mothers Lives: What Works. Washington, D.C.: WRA.
World Bank
    2002 Engendering Development through Gender Equality in Rights, Resources, and Voice. New York: Oxford University Press.
    2005a Empowering People by Transforming Institutions: Social Development in Bank Operations. Washington, D.C.: World Bank.
    2005b Gender Responsive Social Analysis: A Guidance Note. Washington, D.C.: World Bank.
    2006 Social Analysis in Transport Projects: Guidelines for Incorporating Social Dimensions into Bank-supported Projects. Washington, D.C.: World Bank.
    2007a Global Monitoring Report: Confronting the Challenges of Gender Equality and Fragile States. Washington, D.C.: World Bank.
    2007b Implementation Completion and Results Report for the Second Peru Rural Roads Project. Washington, D.C.: World Bank.
    2007c Mekong Delta Transport Infrastructure Development Project, Project Appraisal Document. Washington, D.C.: World Bank.
    2008 Safe, Clean and Affordable Transport for Development: The World Bank Group's Transport Business Strategy 2008–2012. Washington, D.C.: World Bank.
    2009a World Bank to Invest $45 Billion in Infrastructure to Help Create Jobs and Speed Crisis Recovery [Press Release]. Washington, D.C.: World Bank.
    2009b Transport Against HIV/AIDS: Synthesis of Experience and Best Practice Guidelines. Transport Sector Board Paper 25.
    2010a Mainstreaming Gender in Road Transport: Operational Guidance for World Bank Staff. Transport Sector Board Paper 25.
    2010b Safeguards and Sustainability Policies in a Changing World: An Independent Evaluation of World Bank Group Experience. Washington, D.C.: World Bank.

World Bank
2010c Pathways to Development: Empowering Local Women to Build a More Equitable Future in Vietnam. Vietnam Country Office, World Bank.
2010d Making Infrastructure Work for Women and Men: A Review of World Bank Infrastructure Projects 1995–2009. Social Development Department, World Bank.

World Bank and IFC
2006 Gender Equality as Smart Economics: A World Bank Group Gender Action Plan. Washington, D.C.: World Bank.
2010 Gender and Development: A Review of World Bank Support 2002–2008. Washington, D.C.: Independent Evaluation Group, World Bank.

World Health Organization (WHO)
2004 World Report on Safety and Injury Prevention. Geneva: World Health Organization.

3

Housing Interests: Developing Community in a Globalizing City

Jacqueline Copeland-Carson

Introduction: Global Migration and U.S. Community Development

It's a truism and almost an understatement to say that the global economy has linked communities in unprecedented ways. Global flows of people, technology, ideas, and capital have fundamentally changed local communities, and the U.S. is no exception. Immigrants and refugees, especially from countries in Africa, Asia, and Latin America, are reshaping the face of U.S. communities. Newcomers, like generations of U.S. immigrants before them, bring new energy and resources to communities, revitalizing declining urban neighborhoods and increasing tax revenues. At the same time, their language and cultural diversity can present new challenges for public and private institutions attempting to provide basic housing and other services. Migration has long been a key force in globalization. However, reactions to the increasing immigration of racial and religious minorities such as Muslims in the late twentieth century have created especially visceral tensions. Today U.S. community development anthropologists work to help cities adapt to this new diversity, including expanding housing and economic opportunity to immigrants.

This chapter examines how I worked with community, corporate, foundation, and other leaders to understand and meet the housing needs of Somali immigrants and other religious minorities, who migrated to Minneapolis-St. Paul (the Twin Cities), Minnesota, during the 1990s and early 2000s. Somalis, most of whom were Muslim, had cultural prohibitions against paying or receiving interest that were a barrier to both home and business ownership in the United States, which are of course two keys to economic mobility in the United States. Whereas interest-free finance products are common now in the United States, 10 years ago there were limited options for Minnesotan and other Muslims as well as religious minorities in other parts of the country. Here, I describe how I used anthropological concepts and methods such as culture and ethnography as well as my training as an urban planner and Africa area specialist to help leaders develop a non–interest-based mortgage tool for the Twin Cities' growing Somali immigrant community as well as others facing similar challenges. My goal in this project was to promote system change that would open up new economic opportunity for all Minnesotans, including low-income religious minorities.

This chapter has three primary goals. First, it shows how the anthropological lens can provide windows into how often-overlooked, "hidden in plain view" global dynamics influence local institutions and communities. Second, it examines how anthropologists can practically apply the discipline's theories and methods to understand and promote accessible services and social change. Third, it concludes by arguing that U.S. community development practitioners of all disciplinary backgrounds become more adept at culturally appropriate practice, recognizing that refugees and other poor people have social innovations that could expand economic opportunity for all. Fourth, it recommends that anthropologists adopt a "praxis" lens that consciously integrates theory and practical experience to better help communities promote social justice. A praxis perspective can open up new windows into globalization's challenges as well as possible innovations to resolve them. Finally, it suggests that community development anthropologists and other specialists in the field cultivate more of a "translocal" perspective to better understand how the active mixing of local and global development practices and experiences influence the regions in which they work and study.

An Anthropological Perspective on U.S. Community Development

Community development is a multifaceted field with varied definitions. Essentially, it is the planned, systematic effort to improve a place or people's quality of life, power, or economic opportunity. Although in the U.S. the field has roots in the early twentieth-century settlement house movement, community development became a movement in the post–Civil Rights era as the country attempted to address Jim Crow's legacies of concentrated ghettos and rural poverty.

Today, like its international development counterpart, it has become a full-fledged industry with many disciplines and subfields. Some community development anthropologists focus on housing, economics, environment, social services, or some combination of issues. Cutting across these subfields is the array of public and private institutions that implement such activities, including multilateral bodies, government agencies, for-profit or nonprofit corporations, grassroots voluntary organizations, religious groups, and others. Practitioners can work at multiple systems levels. Some focus on macro policy issues and related institutions. Others focus on more local level development in regions, cities, or neighborhoods. Yet others, like me, focus on connecting macro policies and systems to local level needs and assets.

Community development specialists can also specialize in any number of functional areas, including finance, needs assessment, program design/development, evaluation, or management. Also, of course, depending upon the functional area, there are different subissues, such as indigenous, public or philanthropic community development finance, program evaluation, and so on. For example, although I have occasionally worked with government funders as in the case highlighted here, I have worked mostly with foundations and other philanthropies to fund local-level community development. Much of my scholarship, speaking, and activism as of late has documented and promoted indigenous philanthropy for social change and development. Currently, my professional focus is funding, evaluating, strengthening, and promoting community-based organizations and programs. Throughout my career, I have worked across the continuum of roles that constitute community development, including grantmaking, fundraising, and managing programs. I also took on executive and consulting roles where I designed and managed policies, programs, and strategies; managed staff; and collaborated with boards to promote a broader social change mission.

Community development anthropologists can have multiple area and topical specialties. We also often take on advocacy roles in our personal lives. Table 3.1 summarizes my own focus areas, which center on philanthropy and evaluation. It illustrates one particular example of the ways in which theory, practice, and advocacy can combine in a community development anthropologist's career. For other examples of community development anthropologists' integration of theory, practice, and advocacy, see Copeland-Carson (2004), Hyland (2005), Schensul (2005), and Odendahl (1990).

Regardless of the particular type of community development that anthropologists engage with, there are common ties that bind us. Community development anthropologists specialize in the social and cultural dynamics of housing and economic development and change—what is often called "the human factor." As is the case with applied anthropologists working in many fields, we recognize that cultural values, power, and social structures all influence community prospects. Thus, instead of just developing urban policy, buildings, or finance, we consider how different

Table 3.1. Theory, Practice, and Advocacy in a Community Development Career

	Theoretical Focus *Basic and secondary research areas as well as related university teaching*	Practice Focus *Where I work and/or apply my research?*	Geographic/Culture Area Focus *Regions, social groups, and institutions from anthropological training as well as current practice and ongoing study*	Advocacy Focus *How I promote my social mission?*
Anthropological training, research, and teaching that are the basis of my scholarship and practice	Identity formation, organization of cultural diversity, social theory, culture theory, evolutionary theory, social network theory, ethnohistory, African and South Asian studies			
Philanthropy	• Migration • Cultural diversity • Social change	• Philanthropic grantmaking and management • Community development • Microfinance and international remittances • African diaspora philanthropy • Social media • Strategic planning, forecasting, and future studies • Advisory services to donors, "alternative philanthropy" • Social entrepreneurs and innovators • Immersive philanthropy, volunteerism, and socially responsible travel services	• Africa (West Africa as well as Kenya and South Africa), South Asia, Diasporas, and U.S. cities • Philanthropic foundations • Cross-sector funding collaborative	• Building the women's philanthropy movement • Promoting grassroots philanthropy for social change among diverse African-descent communities • Promoting social justice and equity • Creation of personal donor-advised funds and other mechanisms to support such activities (e.g., donation of book proceeds or speaking honoraria)
Evaluation	• Indigenous knowledge systems	• Cross-cultural evaluation • Program evaluation and logic modeling • Social change evaluation and impact assessment	• Foundations, nonprofits, international NGOs	• Pro bono evaluation and coaching services to nonprofit organizations serving low-income communities

institutions and social groups have diverse agendas, needs, or interests that need to be considered. Community development anthropologists also consider how various trends in the field can become ideologies that subtly influence project priorities and outcomes. For example, the growing use of market-based approaches such as social entrepreneurship, as well as efforts to profit from poverty, euphemistically referred to as "the bottom of the pyramid," can devolve into exploitative development practices (Prahalad 2005; Rivlin 2010). At the same time, such approaches can provide alternative sources of capital for personal self-improvement and even foundation grants to organizations that advocate for social justice. By making the inherent cultural values driving projects clear, community development anthropologists can help reshape goals and outcomes.

In addition to bringing a critical eye to ideology, like other applied anthropologists, we often start our work by deconstructing the very concepts of community and development as understood by different stakeholders. Sometimes our community development ethnographies are to uncover and explain diverse perspectives; other times, our role is to align or use them to improve project or community outcomes. Much of the research and learning we do is participatory, using ethnographic research methods, but it is also ethnographic in that we use anthropological and other theories to interpret what we learn and communicate findings in ways that multiple stakeholders can understand within their community or organizational cultures.

Furthermore, we often take on a "systems view" that considers how the parts of a community—various constituencies, institutions, and histories—interact, conflict, and change over time. This inherently inter-disciplinary perspective is very useful in typical project contexts where constituents and policy makers have differing backgrounds and training.

We can take on a variety of roles as bridges among powerful institutions, community-based groups, and activists, including advocate, activist, technician, manager, planner, and many others (Copeland-Carson 2005b). And our cross-cultural training and theory are critical to our capacity to take on these different roles. For example, my background as an Africanist anthropologist has proven indispensable; it not only taught me about African communities, their migration, and diaspora dynamics, but also sensitized me to the cross-cultural issues in community development that have proven ubiquitous in U.S. community development work, especially with increased migration from Africa, Asia, and Latin America.

The impact of sociocultural issues is becoming more recognized in U.S. community development as globalization and migration intensify. Immigrants and refugees not only bring new languages, foods, and ethnicities. They also bring new community development practices. For example, although this is obvious to the handful of scholars who study these issues and residents who practice them, immigrants, refugees, and people of color give money and time—called "philanthropy" and "volunteerism"—for collective goals and projects just as the majority community does. Often these are ancient practices adapted to contemporary needs. For example, rotating savings clubs are a major immigrant and refugee resource for community development off the radar screen of many professionals in the field. Immigrants and refugees send remittances not only to assist extended family members, but also to build schools and clinics and provide other services in the world's poorest regions. As U.S. communities have become more diverse with worldwide migration, studying these indigenous finance practices as well as promoting more grassroots influence on neighborhood development policy has become a key component of my research and practice (see Copeland-Carson 2005a, 2005b, 2007). Globalizing cultural influences do not stop at community development finance. For example, foundations and other public funders are very interested in knowing whether the nonprofit agencies they fund are representative of their communities. Their leaders, however, are not necessarily knowledgeable about clan or ethnic dynamics that might influence nonprofit governance and representation, and foundations are not typically diverse enough to have experts from these communities on their staffs or boards, which deprives them of an important source of cultural knowledge and competence.

Community development anthropologists can help cities resolve globalization's challenges in many ways, including identifying new needs; uncovering social innovations from many cultures to address them; creating policies, programs, and procedures for the times; and designing, managing, or evaluating such programs. The case presented here examines how I convened Muslim and Christian religious leaders, activists, nongovernmental organizations (NGOs), foundations, bankers, the Minneapolis Federal Reserve, and the U.S. Department of Housing and Urban Development (HUD) to understand and accept non–interest-based finance, a longstanding, ancient practice in Islamic countries, to promote homeownership and business opportunities for its growing Somali immigrant community as well as others who had cultural prohibitions against paying or receiving interest.

In the following section, I recount the experience, emphasizing lessons learned from what I call "anthropological praxis," the blending of scholarship from basic academic research with the knowledge of anthropologists applying these theories and methods to resolve public problems. I argue that anthropologist practitioners working at the intersection of the field's theoretical and applied knowledge may be particularly attuned to the ways that new social phenomena such as globalization affect local communities and institutions.

Case Example: Profile of a Globalizing City (ca. 2000)

In the 1990s, the Twin Cities of Minnesota, the largely liberal land of Vice President Hubert Humphrey and Governor Jesse Ventura as well as Senators Paul Wellstone and Al Franken, lovingly gibed in the stories of Garrison Keillor, underwent a dramatic demographic shift that is still reshaping its civic discourse and culture.

During the 1990s, Minnesota's unemployment rate was about 2 percent—the lowest in the country. There was a labor shortage even for the most entry-level positions, with companies providing signing bonuses to attract bank tellers and meat packers. These booming economic conditions, including one of the highest concentrations of Fortune 500 companies (Target, Land O' Lakes, General Mills, and Medtronic are all headquartered there), relatively low crime levels, strong public infrastructure, an active religious community, and a longstanding Scandinavian-based ethic of "Minnesota Nice" emphasizing civic engagement, social responsibility, philanthropy, and mutual support, attracted millions of people from throughout the U.S. and the world. Notwithstanding the fact that in July 2011, Minnesota had to shut down many basic government services due to budget shortfalls, from the 1970s through 1990s it had a well-deserved national reputation as what a 1973 cover story from *Time* magazine titled "Minnesota: A State that Works" (American Scene 1973).

Starting in the 1990s, the region experienced a dramatic growth in its African refugee and immigrant population, including mostly Somalis but also significant numbers of Ethiopians, Sudanese, Nigerians, Kenyans, Sierra Leoneans, Ghanaians, and others. By the 2000 U.S. Census, the Twin Cities had the nation's most diverse black population based on ethnicity and country of origin, including one of the highest concentrations of college-educated blacks as well as the country's largest Somali, Hmong, Tibetan refugee, and urban Native American communities. Not all newcomers were immigrants or refugees from other countries. Overall, during a two-decade period, Minnesota had one of the country's highest levels of in-migration. Included were professionals from all over the country, as well as low-income people from declining industrial areas in midwestern cities such as Gary, Indiana, and Chicago, diversifying the region politically, culturally, and ethnically and drawing it more tightly to the global economy.

Although the newcomers were seeking the good life in Minnesota, long-time Minnesotans were not always so sure how much they wanted to share it. It is easier to be liberal and accepting in a community where, as a *Wall Street Journal* reporter writing about the state's unprecedented demographic changes in a 1999 article noted, "a mixed marriage once meant the marriage of a Norwegian and a Swede" (Johnson 1997). This globalizing urban area began experiencing new pressures that were even more challenging, given its different racial makeup, than the Great Migration of mostly Europeans to the area in the early twentieth century.

Employers had to determine how to allow Muslim employees to pray during the work day, as required by Islam, while respecting the rights of non-Muslim workers too; YMCAs had to decide whether to let Muslim girls swim in their scarves and full body coverings, as required by Islam's modesty principles; high schools had to resolve sometimes violent tensions between African-American and African immigrant students, while school districts had to educate students representing almost 80 different languages. Lawyers had to determine how to advocate for Hmong women escaping arranged or polygamous marriages. Bankers had to figure out if and how to open checking accounts for undocumented Latino business owners. City health officials had to determine whether African hair-braiding shops should be subject to cosmetology laws that did not take such practices into account. And social service officials had to respond to a growing and alarming Native American teen suicide rate as young people felt caught between the worlds of the hardcore inner city and the reservation.

This period of accelerated social change was fraught with challenges but also new possibilities. The fabric of Minnesota's good life was seriously tested as its communities responded to the new diversity as the 1990s and 2000s unfolded. A racially charged mayoral race unseated the two-term African-American female mayor of Minneapolis. So-called "white flight" from urban public schools grew as neighborhoods and student bodies became more diverse and, coincidentally, public education funding declined, eroding the state's once touted educational system. There were growing and alarming disparities between minority and white Minnesotans along almost every social indicator.

Social Innovation in the Twin Cities

Despite these pressures, Minnesota's social compacts die hard; enterprising newcomers, along with their more established Twin Cities partners, created new ways to build communities. During this period, a number of high-profile initiatives emerged as leaders attempted to shape these new public issues. These efforts attempted to build bridges between newcomer and established communities, incorporate immigrants and refugees, and address the growing concentrations of poverty, especially in communities of color.[1]

Immigrants and refugees opened small businesses along declining inner city commercial corridors, slowly reviving them and their surrounding neighborhoods. Service providers, with the help of public and private funders, convened to address unmet immigrant/refugee service needs. Corporate leaders recognized that newcomer communities were also new markets that they could tap. The state has among the country's highest levels of giving and volunteerism, and its companies have set national standards for social responsibility and corporate giving. Philanthropy and civic involvement were seen as enlightened self-interest, as healthy, educated communities made better customers and employees.

Supported by a booming economy and expanded philanthropic funding, Hmong, African, and Latino newcomers also created nonprofits to address their community needs and tap the new markets they brought for social innovation donations. In the case of the diverse African immigrant nationalities and religions, several created nonprofits with novel "Pan-African" governance and programs to accommodate the diversity of their communities and respond to the fact that government and foundation funders were less likely to support clan-, village- or tribally defined organizations.[2] The combined entrepreneurial and social sector activity in this then-thriving economy, along with gains in education, eventually catapulted many new immigrants/refugees into the middle class at the same time the concentration of poverty in the region's U.S.- and foreign-born communities of color continued. This remarkable change and innovation continues, even though it had been stressed by the early century's economic volatility.

Unlearning Mortgage "Sins"

Since my anthropology and urban planning graduate school days in the early 1980s, I had studied and practiced community development with a focus on housing, first in Nigeria, West Africa, and later throughout the U.S. I was particularly interested in culturally appropriate housing development as well as diversity, community formation, and social networks in cities throughout the world. Other experiences prepared me to help address the cross-cultural and social challenges facing the Twin Cities in this period. I had worked for many years as a foundation executive who designed, managed, and funded initiatives to address social issues, such as reducing poverty and promoting homeownership, jobs, and other wealth-building strategies. But despite all my exposure to cross-cultural community development issues, I was not quite prepared for what I encountered when I started working with HUD's Twin Cities office.

In the late 1990s, the Clinton/Gore administration, recognizing that the new pressures of globalization and demographic and other socioeconomic change in U.S. cities might have outpaced federal agencies' capacity to keep pace, created the Community Builders Fellowship Program.

This was part of the administration's effort to reform and improve federal services. HUD's primary departments—Community Development, Fair Housing, Federal Home Administration (FHA), and Multi-Family Housing—had a notorious reputation for working in silos, even though each typically funded the very same neighborhoods through HUD's various regional offices.[3] Fellows were selected from a national applicant pool of interdisciplinary development professionals to be full-time two-year internal consultants who would create new initiatives that integrated and updated HUD's programs.

I was selected to be one of these Community Builders Fellows. Given my interest and experience in housing development, I decided to support FHA's Faith-based Homeownership Initiative, created by the administration to do outreach about FHA mortgages and other tools to expand homeownership in low-income communities.

Thinking like a typical anthropologist, I interpreted "faith" in broad terms to mean the various religious traditions represented in a community. I developed a list of diverse religious leaders, including Christian ministers, Muslim imams, rabbis, and others, to whom I should speak to let them know how FHA-backed mortgages could help low-income congregants become successful homeowners. I also wanted to learn more about their communities' housing issues and get advice on how FHA could better publicize and explain its programs.

I was initially shocked and confused when a prominent Somali imam whom I interviewed early on told me "Well, it's great that the government has all these ways to help struggling people buy homes. But in my community, all these mortgages and interest will just send people to hell. Getting a mortgage is a sin" (Somali Imam explaining the community's reluctance to take on mortgages, personal communication, 1999).

Others explained that there was great ethical conflict and debate among Minnesota Muslims about how to resolve the conundrum of a growing need and market demand for homeownership and the lack of culturally appropriate mortgage products. Some segments of the community took a "when in Rome do as the Romans do" approach, sometimes receiving special dispensation from their imams to take on the *sin* of a mortgage because no other finance options were available in the U.S. Others would pool resources with extended family members and attempt to pay cash for a home. I even met a devout Muslim and successful architect, earning well into six figures, who was still a renter because he had been saving money for almost 15 years so he could pay cash to buy a house in Minnesota's thriving and increasingly expensive market.

As I continued my conversations with many imams and activists in the state's diverse Muslim community, I discovered that for many the Koran prohibited both the payment and receipt of interest. In fact, a rabbi also told me of a small Orthodox Jewish community in a Minneapolis suburb with a similar interpretation of the Talmud. He explained that "strictly speaking, Judaism renders all interest as inherently usurious because it... just involves a privileged class taking advantage of a poor class. It creates permanent debtors and creditors and is not good for society" (Twin Cities rabbi explaining Judaism's perspective on usury, personal communication, October 1, 1999).

Through outreach to ministers active in the housing justice movement, I also learned that this same strict interpretation of the Bible was a driving force in the original formation of Habitat for Humanity, the Christian-based housing NGO made famous by Jimmy Carter that uses sweat equity, donations, and grants to build houses for low-income families throughout the world and provides interest-free mortgages. So a social equity philosophy, rooted in faith, was the basis of many Minnesota Muslims', Orthodox Jews', and some Christian groups' aversion to either paying or receiving interest.

Now this was difficult for someone who had spent her career managing nonprofit endowments and promoting homeownership to understand. As I continued my exploration, I decided to talk with an African-American imam who also happened to be the director of a nonprofit housing development agency, thinking that with our similar backgrounds and career missions, he could help me understand. He explained, "You see, for many Muslims the Koran teaches that this time value of money thing is just a way that rich people made up to rip off poor people. Money is just a piece of paper. It has no tangible value on its own, unlike this chair or this table that has a real value" (African-American Imam and director of a nonprofit housing development agency, personal communication, 1998).

The look of consternation on my face must have been clear, because he went on to give me an example that helped me to finally grasp the issue.

> Maybe this will help you understand. You are a *homeowner*, right? But think about it, do you really *own* that house? Every month you pay the bank more than the house is worth for the right to live there. And you'll probably end up paying for the next 30 years. So, you don't really own anything right now. The bank really owns your house. This is the fundamental problem many Muslims have with paying interest period—for a house, a car, a business. They know they don't necessarily own anything; they just own debt (African-American Imam and director of a nonprofit housing development agency, personal communication, 1999).

Although certainly an overstatement for educational effect, with hindsight, the irony and wisdom of this imam's core cautions about the potential dangers of interest-bearing mortgages seemed prophetic of the

2007–2010 U.S. foreclosure and predatory lending crises. This moment of epiphany helped me to understand how something as seemingly fundamental as paying interest—an article of faith for most Americans and certainly anyone in the community development field—was a real religious and cultural taboo for many Minnesota Muslims and others. The Minnesota housing industry, and indeed, most of the country, was proceeding as if interest-based mortgages were the universal means of purchasing a home, although clearly they were not.

From Epiphany to Systems Change

However, making the case to HUD officials—let alone banking and philanthropic leaders—would require more than my sharing the stories of Minnesota religious minorities who felt the system did not provide the tools necessary for them to become homeowners. When I described what I learned to one of my FHA colleagues, s/he exclaimed, "so what, now will I have to speak Somali to do my job? A mortgage is a mortgage whether they call it interest or something else"—a clear signal that taking on this project would not be the easiest way to fulfill my fellowship obligations. Despite some staff members' initial reservations, fortunately, the HUD office's senior leadership was committed to ensuring that it was serving the entire public, as were other public officials who eventually became partners.

Essentially, I mixed anthropological methods such as ethnographic interviewing, participant observation, and cross-cultural comparisons with the compilation of demographic and market data to prove my case and build alliances. The first step was to further my knowledge of cross-cultural finance, particularly in Muslim countries and communities throughout the world, as interest-free loans were not yet a common option in the United States. The core research question was, "Given that all countries are part of a global capitalist system that runs on credit, interest payments, equity investments, and dividends, how could any Muslim country or person be 'interest free?' Was this just a semantic issue or a real cultural barrier for Minnesota Somalis and other religious minorities, a public obligation for the government and a possible market opportunity for businesses?"

Without getting deeply into all the technical details of interest-free or, in Arabic, *riba*-free financing, there is an ancient tradition of equity-based financing in all the world's major religions. Essentially, riba-free principles prohibit not only the payment of interest but all potentially exploitative financial practices, such as derivatives and predatory lending. A financier would buy a house, business, or other capital asset at what might be best understood as a wholesale price, adding a markup that would include fees for concrete administrative services and a profit.

The financier would sell the house to a buyer, who is considered a co-investor; the buyer then pays back the loan and fees in agreed-upon installments. Because these various fees are for real assets—that is, not for what would be considered an artificial commodity like interest, the time value of money—they are considered an equity investment, which is allowed in Islam, producing an ethical and legitimate profit. It is broadly similar to a lease-purchase agreement in U.S. terms. In instances where a national government receives international loans through a multilateral body such as the International Monetary Fund (IMF) or the World Bank and includes the required "interest" in its loan payments, this is considered the "sin" that unavoidably accompanies life in the modern world that is appropriately absorbed by a secular, political administration. However, there is an active debate in some Muslim countries about whether it is ethical for national and other government bodies to accept interest-bearing money under any circumstances. Islamic housing agencies and banks in such countries repackage international financing into riba-free loans along conventional Islamic underwriting, amortization, and repayment terms.

Riba-free Islamic finance has been growing worldwide, fueled both by the growth of Islam as well as concerns about escalating national and personal debt, as Western-based finance systems penetrate the world's markets. Other alternative finance mechanisms, such as micro- and cooperative finance as well as bartering, actually created millennia ago by indigenous societies throughout the world, also continue to grow. The institutionalization, regulation, and taxation of such practices is also expanding as more people in Western countries, including the United States, explore them as survival tools, especially as credit access declined in the early twenty-first century's economic downturns.

After providing myself a basic education in riba-free financing, the second step was to assemble the demographic data to describe the United States' and Minnesota's potential riba-free mortgage market. I convened an advisory body of Muslim clerics, activists, nonprofit leaders, and realtors as well as non-Muslim foundation officials, bankers, and federal agency representatives, most notably the Minneapolis Federal Reserve Bank and Fannie Mae, establishing a "Cross-Cultural Mortgage Finance Working Group."

Although recruiting Muslim clerics and activists was not difficult, as they were delighted that someone was taking up their cause, attracting bankers was another matter altogether. Let's just say that even the term "non–interest-based mortgage" was an oxymoron to many in the initiative's formative stages. Eventually, however, I was able to sustain the working group, which met for a year under HUD auspices to learn about the cultural barriers to homeownership for religious minorities and the various types of alternative finance strategies. This involved my acting as a sort of research center, compiling and translating cross-cultural finance information and data about Minnesota's growing Muslim market.

I did not, of course, use the terms "anthropological" or "ethnographic" in any of this work. Instead, various euphemisms such as "culturally appropriate financing," "cultural markets," or "cultural communities" were sufficient to convince public officials and bankers that the need for riba-free mortgages was real for this "market" even though this was only a semantic issue for non-Muslims. Basically, I facilitated what anthropologists would call an "emic" perspective on mortgage finance.

Part of our strategy was to build a public profile for our work to legitimize religious minorities' homeownership needs as a tool of inclusion and not special interests. The initiative was designed to organize a series of high-profile public meetings about the community's homeownership needs, put in terms of both new market opportunities as well as the need to expand economic opportunity for low-income minorities. Meeting agendas typically involved participants sharing stories of "culture clashes," as devout Muslims of various backgrounds attempted to finance their mortgages in a system that did not provide a sufficient array of options. One participant, a Muslim Nigerian realtor, shared the stories of clients who were perpetual renters because of these barriers. Another, a Somali single mother with a household that included six children and two elders, and whose husband had died in her home country's long civil war, told of the inherent challenges of finding suitable rentals that would accept large families. Men were the primary public spokespersons for the Somali community at this time. I made a deliberate effort to recruit and encourage women's participation. Several noted that they were often not sought out for such roles, as male leadership was more prominent and accessible to mainstream institutions, and women's public leadership was not encouraged in many of their communities in Somalia. My prior ethnographic research with a Pan-African women's group introduced me to a diverse network of Somali and other African Muslim women that I tapped for inclusion in the working group. Today, Minnesota's Somali women are now taking on more prominent public leadership roles as they are throughout Africa and the Somali diaspora.

Over time, these stories—auto-ethnographic vignettes, really—combined with my research briefs documenting similar issues in other cities to create a kind of culturally immersive experience for public officials and funders. It had the practical effect, as well, of extending and diversifying all participants' social networks, providing more direct access to the community's leadership for the grassroots participants, and more connections to a new constituency's leadership for the public officials. Interestingly, several of the participants have, over the years, extended their civic participation, including gaining seats on public agency boards and even running for public office.

All working group participants were interested in meeting the needs of residents with religious beliefs that made homeownership less feasible. However, there were more institutionally specific interests as well. Banking officials were interested in allying themselves early with the Muslim and African immigrant market, becoming the bank of choice. Research among immigrants demonstrated strong brand loyalty. For example, Minnesota Latinos had strong brand loyalty to specific banks that were willing to provide services to undocumented workers early in the community's settlement, when it was not common in the industry. HUD and the Federal Reserve were concerned about a growing number of class action suits filed by American Muslim organizations claiming that interest-based financing was inherently discriminatory. In addition, foundations, community activists, and nonprofits were motivated by the goal of increasing access to homeownership.

During the course of our year-long cross-sector education and industry awareness process, the Hennepin County Government, also a working group member, created a non–interest-based financing tool for its tax-for-feited sale program (homes essentially repossessed by the government for long-term failure to pay property taxes). This was probably the first such program by a branch of Minnesota government and by a member of our working group. Our collaborative study and outreach led to our holding a technical conference cohosted by the Federal Reserve in 2000. Much of my conference design work involved selecting presenters who could credibly present a range of new non–interest-based mortgage models that were emerging in various parts of the United States. Several of the expert presenters were U.S.-born Muslim converts, including African Americans and white Americans who were experts in culturally appropriate financing vehicles. Other conference design challenges were providing for Muslim prayer and dietary restrictions while being sensitive to the needs of non-Muslim participants, all in a conference and catering center located at the Minneapolis Federal Reserve building. In addition, advised by the Muslim participants, I was careful not to choose a date that conflicted with religious observances, especially Ramadan, a period requiring fasting during the day for Muslims. Prayer needs were accommodated using a technique I had witnessed in religiously diverse regions of Nigeria. I set aside gender-specific contemplation rooms that anyone could use for activities that required some level of privacy, including nursing, meditation, or prayer. Thus, even the meeting design required cultural sensitivity, listening to both the needs and ideas of diverse working group participants.

The working group meetings and the conference attracted press attention (see Gendler 2000). I received a couple of complaints and even one death threat by phone at the HUD office. For example, one day, after a series of press reports about housing issues in the Somali immigrant/ refugee community, a member of the public angrily called to ask me, "I was wondering how I could convert to 'Somali Islam' to get one of those free houses." After I explained that I was not qualified to counsel him on spiritual matters and offered to refer him to an imam for guidance, he yelled, "That's what's wrong with this damned community. The government and foundations keep bringing those people to the U.S. where they don't belong." This was a couple of years before 9/11, and I imagine that subsequently the public response would have been even more severe, and engaging such a diverse range of institutions in the initiative would have been less feasible.

Soon after the conference, my HUD fellowship expired. However, an expanded working group continued to meet, sponsored by the Federal Reserve's community relations department, ultimately culminating in a non–interest-based mortgage pilot developed by the Fannie Mae Foundation, a key working group partner. And, as noted by Wafiq Fannoun, one of our working group members and a Muslim community development specialist interviewed for this case study, "Today there are many riba-free tools for Muslims. But that wasn't true in these early days. The HUD working group brought the issue to the attention of the broader community, making it possible to do something about it" (Mutombu 2005). Later in the 2000s, an enterprising Somali banker, Hussein Samatar, who had been an officer with a major bank in the region, created the African Development Corporation (www.adc.org), a nonprofit development corporation specializing in these riba-free financing instruments. This organization has become a major force in promoting homeownership and small business development in the region's African immigrant community. Also, a long-time community development advocate, Mike Temali, director of the Neighborhood Development Center (www.ndc.org), created one of the country's first domestic riba-free business finance loan programs, although Saudi-backed banks in the United Kingdom had been providing such loans in the U.S. since the 1990s. A booming economy no doubt made it easier for both nonprofit and corporate financiers to create such products. Despite 9/11, growing prejudice against even law-abiding Muslims, and the economic decline, interest-free finance programs became an established alternative to conventional financing by the end of the first decade of the new millennium, albeit still used by a minority of Minnesotans and other Americans. Islamic finance, because it did not charge interest, escaped some of the pitfalls of the conventional, interest-based finance systems that almost brought down the world's economy. By 2010, there were $500 billion in riba-free loan assets in the United States, and the market was booming.

However, it is not without controversy. There are those who argue that the fees and markups charged by these loans are merely interest in other cultural clothing. Furthermore, some claim that fees charged to U.S.-based riba-free purchasers is either just as expensive or, in some cases, more expensive than their conventional finance counterparts. Thus, Islamic or other alternative finance may, in some cases, be as exploitative as the supposedly usurious loans they are supposed to counterbalance. Moreover, it is not clear if such riba-free financed loans in the United States have lower foreclosure rates than interest-based ones. Nonetheless, at least in Minnesota, religious minorities and others with interest-free requirements have an expanded set of choices, all monitored by federal agencies and fair-lending activists, to finance businesses and homes.

Lessons Learned for Applied Global Anthropology and Beyond

Searching for Inclusion

Even though anthropology does not always practice it well, the field is strongly shaped by a social justice philosophy. Anthropology students are taught that diversity is a cultural resource. Sometimes in a particular power system or historical moment, cultural difference can become a barrier to social justice or even basic survival. Our basic orientation as anthropologists, however, is to promote inclusion, pushing the public—as presented through policies, institutions, and officials—to encompass all social groups. One never knows when what was once seen as a "fringe" or marginal cultural practice, such as the growing worldwide use of interest-free loans or microfinance during credit-restricted times, might help a broader constituency. Just as biologists promote biodiversity as a natural resource, anthropologists promote diverse cultural practices as a way to help people survive and adapt to changing times. We not only celebrate and promote cultural variation, but we also, as the cliché goes, promote "unity in diversity"—the notion that people from different backgrounds can define common goals and interests. Working together, they can learn from each other, breaking down barriers of race, class, religion, and ethnicity to build mutual networks of support and community. Certainly, these basic anthropological principles of diversity and inclusion drove my initial interest in ensuring that the needs of religious minorities were included in homeownership financing policies and products. In the community development and philanthropy field, this cross-cultural bridge-building is often called either "community convening" or "cross-sector convening." Using the terms familiar to the nonprofit, philanthropic, and corporate stakeholders involved in the project was critical to its success, even though the anthropological side of my brain certainly conceptualized it as a means to increase cross-cultural understanding while expanding economic opportunity.

The Power of a Cross-Cultural Lens
Globalization's impact can manifest itself in unexpected ways. Even the most seasoned practicing anthropologists can miss its nuances if they don't engage in careful use of their field's tools. The basic culture concept in anthropology—that social groups have differing worldviews that are true for them even if they contradict the researcher's own experience—is fundamental to understanding and addressing the cultural barriers that can arise as cities become more diverse and global. This principle enabled me to eventually understand that riba-free mortgages were a legitimate need in the Somali market. The approach also helped me to present interest-based mortgages not only as an economic tool, but as a "culturally specific way of financing the purchase of capital assets," as I often explained it to bankers. Furthermore, it enabled me to translate these needs into the cultures and languages of the government, foundations, and banking to craft a legitimate social justice and business argument for interest-free housing. A cross-cultural lens also allowed me to patiently listen to the perspective of some development industry peers that it was a temporary community need that would pass with assimilation. Applying the culture concept as a framework to understand and build common ground across these conflicting interests and perceptions was essential to the initiative's success.

Native Anthropology
Anthropology in globalizing cities can involve practicing in one's own community, which presents special opportunities and challenges. As a long-time community development specialist, I was also practicing a form of native anthropology in this initiative. Applying reflexive ethnographic research techniques that consider and make apparent one's own hidden cultural biases became critical in helping me recognize and credibly teach in culturally compelling terms that the need for an interest-free mortgage option was real in a globalizing city with a growing Muslim community.

Mixing Scholarship and Practical Ethnography in Real Power Systems
A number of skills were critical to establish trust with local groups and move forward effectively with this project. They included creating community rapport, tapping established social networks and crafting new ones, active listening, demonstrating authentic empathy, meeting people in their neighborhoods and institutions, and participatory planning that gave leaders a sense of ownership in the reform strategies.

I avoided surveys, as they are often off-putting to disadvantaged people, and instead engaged in in-depth, open-ended interviews. Although these interviews were important, they were not sufficient to prove the case to various public and private sector agencies. I also had to draw on and translate scholarship from multiple disciplines, including cross-cultural, international, and Islamic finance. In addition, I had to pull together primary data, as only limited research had been conducted previously, to profile Minnesota's growing Muslim market. Anthropologists working in global contexts must mix research methods to document and communicate information in compelling ways that move diverse institutions and audiences. To fully effect social change in our increasingly digital world, this means more than translating flyers and reports into multiple languages. It may also require using new social media, such as virtual communities and videos, in instances where our clients or constituents participate in such communities.

Any collaborative work of this nature involves navigating the agendas and territorial issues of diverse institutions and cultures. Remaining humble, admitting what one does not know, acknowledging and highlighting community expertise, and understanding local political dynamics are all critical skills. One must position oneself as a neutral convener devoted to expanding opportunity, inclusive of everyone, when working on culturally specific projects designed to remove barriers for a particular ethnicity or religious group.

On the Limits of Praxis

For anthropologists working to address social problems, it is critical to remember that whether we like it or not, we are unavoidably also a part of the system we are trying to change. This role requires a particularly sensitive reflective anthropology—a kind of sensor for the insidious ways that good intentions can inadvertently aggravate injustice. This perspective will help avoid, although it cannot completely prevent, the "antipolitics" that can often ultimately undermine social change efforts. For example, it was important to not just create alternative programs. It was also critical to give voice to the need for both regulation and community-based advocacy to avoid exploitative overpricing of these new products. But even with these measures, over time it is difficult to prevent the system's tendency toward exploitation as evidenced by the predatory and unethical practices that helped to cause the world's worst recession. It may sometimes require stepping outside of the neutral convener role to take sides as an advocate for the less powerful. Applied anthropology, even when inclusive, cross-culturally sensitive, and praxis-oriented, is no more of a panacea to social inequity than any other field. Recognizing its limits can embolden interdisciplinary, interethnic, cross-sector collaboration, and advocacy necessary to maximize the chances for sustainable change.

Conclusions: Toward a Translocal Community Development Praxis

In the past 30 years, U.S. community development has become an industry with a wide range of conventional wisdom and core practices that are often taken for granted. But cultural change has accelerated for everyone in the globalizing city. Just as anthropologists can no longer take for granted that the majority represents a community's needs and norms, community development specialists cannot presume that their conventional tools will work in diverse cultural populations. Moreover, the culturally diverse techniques represented in such communities may not be "backwards cultural barriers." In fact, they may be just the cultural resource that can resolve the broader community's challenges, as suggested by Muhamad Yunus's Nobel Prize–winning application of ancient microfinance practices in the developing world and now in the United States. Community development practitioners, whatever their training and background, need to become more cross-culturally competent to be effective in globalizing contexts, even in such seemingly "culture-proof" arenas as housing finance and economic development.

Globalization's varied influences on U.S. cities are pervasive. They affect people's everyday lives at both the macro level of economies as well as the micro level of community services. The Twin Cities' interest-free housing case shows that to understand and promote social change, anthropologist practitioners must work all levels of a social system. This approach not only strengthens our work as practitioners, but also can contribute to social and cultural theory in anthropology and other fields. As Levitt (1997) suggests, the nongovernmental sector is taking on an increasingly important role in managing the global flow of people, ideas, and capital. Ethnography in the applied contexts of this Twin Cities housing project demonstrates how social and political dynamics are being shaped by globalization. The complex dynamics of diversity and cross-sector collaboration in the Twin Cities case presented here demonstrate how globalization is blurring the lines of the government and public sector (Fisher 1997). Community development anthropologists take on important roles in creating cross-sector alliances that balance these relationships. At the same time, just as Ferguson (1994) shows in Lesotho, a kind of "anti-politics" can creep into community development projects where initial goals become co-opted in the inherently inequitable power system that limits the poor's access to basic rights and services like housing.

The Twin Cities have become what anthropologist Arjun Appadurai describes as "translocalities," world cities at the nexus of global flows of people, ideas, and resources (Appadurai 1996; Copeland-Carson 2004). Today, more than ever before, social life in U.S. neighborhoods is at once local and global. Basic community development notions, such as "community" as geographically defined, or interest-based finance, are not givens. People are remixing their concepts of identity, community, and development itself as the global and local meet in America's cities.

For example, activists are resisting the overuse of neoliberal approaches to community development that equate access to housing or capital as magical cures for poverty. As the current foreclosure debacle shows, many affordable mortgage finance schemes may have, in fact, ultimately increased poverty instead of reducing it. A current countervailing trend is to promote grassroots community engagement, advocacy, and diversity as well as the public accountability and social equity, aided by government regulation, as fundamental components of a community development project. Of course, effectively preventing market abuses in a period of declining public resources is exceedingly challenging as governments across the country cut agency budgets. The increasingly important role of the "third sector" in filling the public watchdog function of government is not surprising, especially in our present politically deadlocked climate. However, progressive ideologies are no more immune than their neoliberal counterparts to the potential inequities inherent in any market over time.

A "translocal" perspective, sensitive to cultural and other innovations emerging in globalized cities and how they can be used as tools of resistance and social transformation, can expand opportunities, not only for immigrants but for all residents. To work effectively in globalizing contexts, we must practice a kind of translocal anthropology: sensitive to the intersections, intercultural collisions, and new energy created when the local and global meet, and less reverent of increasingly irrelevant divisions between theory and practice. With such a lens, we can help policy makers and even grassroots leaders see and resolve emerging community challenges that may be hidden in plain view. Such challenges may be removed from constituents' direct experience. Furthermore, policy makers may rely on an ideology, bureaucracy, or mission that cannot nimbly or quickly adjust to changing needs or opportunities. We can get behind the scenes of the "party line" to uncover the taken-for-granted assumptions, rules, and power dynamics that govern institutions and their community relations.

Anthropology can, does, and must have an obligation to resolve the complex challenges and opportunities that globalization presents. We should bear witness to and document the good, the bad, and the ugly of globalization through praxis, linking basic with applied research. Theory and practice in the real world are the basis of a contemporary field that remains relevant today and in the future.

Notes

1. Among these initiatives were the Itasca Group, a coalition of business leaders convened to encourage companies to address racial dispari- ties and poverty; the Institute on Race and Poverty at the University of Minnesota, which, under the leadership of first John Powell and then Myron Orfield, did groundbreaking public policy research doc- umenting disparities in housing and economic opportunity; Nexus Community Partners (formerly known as Payne Lake Community Partners), a coalition of innovation foundations and nonprofits, includ- ing McKnight, Knight, McNeely, and other national and local foun- dations, the Cities of Minneapolis and St. Paul Twin Cities LISC, and the Neighborhood Development Center (see www.nexuscp.org); Twin Cities RISE!, a coalition of corporations to provide employment opportunity for the lowest-income men of color; The Minneapolis Foundation's "Minnesota Nice or Not" public information campaign, and many other initiatives, too numerous to mention, that were cre- ated during this period to help the region constructively address the new public challenges that emerged as the Twin Cities became a more diverse, globalizing metropolitan city.

2. Among this new crop of culturally-based nonprofits were the Hmong American Partnership, Asian Community Development Corporation, the African Development Center, the Latino Economic Development Center, Stairstep Initiative, the Somali Confederation, People of African Communities Everywhere, the Phillips Powderhorn Cultural Wellness Center, Casa de Esperanza, Comunidades Latinas Unidas en Servicio, American Indian Community Development Corporation, Harvest Preparatory School, an Afrocentric charter school serving elementary and middle school students, and Ain Dah Yung (an American Indian social services agency).

3. Community Development primarily administers a block grant program that supports the urban and economic development plan of metropolitan areas; Fair Housing enforces antihousing discrimination laws; the Federal Home Administration (FHA) manages the federal government's insur- ance program that backs private mortgages for lower income buyers; and Multi-Family Housing develops and administers public housing programs. For more on HUD, go to www.hud.gov.

References

American Scene
  1973 Minnesota: A State that Works. *Time* Magazine, August 13. Available at: http://www.time.com/time/magazine/article/0,9171,907665,00.html. Accessed July 7, 2011.

Appadurai, Arjun
1996 Modernity at Large: Cultural Dimensions of Globalization. Minneapolis: University of Minnesota Press.
Copeland-Carson, Jacqueline
2004 Creating Africa in America: Translocal Identity in an Emerging World City. Philadelphia: University of Pennsylvania Press.
2005a Embracing Diversity in Contemporary Black Philanthropy: Toward a New Conceptual Model. *In* Black Philanthropy: New Directions for Philanthropic Fundraising, Patrick Rooney, ed. 48:77–87.
2005b Applying Theory and Method in Evaluation Anthropology: The Example of the South Bronx's Comprehensive Community Revitalization Project. *In* Creating Evaluation Anthropology: Introducing an Emerging Sub-field, Mary Odell Butler and Jackie Copeland-Carson, eds. NAPA Bulletin 25:89–106. Berkeley: University of California Press.
2007 Kenyan Diaspora Philanthropy: Key Practices, Trends and Issues. *In* The Global Equity Initiative of Harvard University and the Philanthropic Initiative, March 2007. Available at: http://www.tpi.org/downloads/pdfs/Kenya_Diaspora_Philanthropy_Final.pdf. Accessed July 7, 2011.
Ferguson, James
1994 The Anti-Politics Machine: "Development," Depoliticization, and Bureaucratic Power in Lesotho. Minneapolis: University of Minnesota Press.
Fisher, William F.
1997 Doing Good? The Politics and Antipolitics of NGO Practices. *Annual Review of Anthropology* 26:439–64.
Gendler, Neal
2000 Lenders Look for a Way Around Islamic Barrier to Homeownership. *Minneapolis-St. Paul Star Tribune*, February 29, P. 01B.
Hyland, Stanley (ed.)
2005 Community Building in the Twenty-first Century. Santa Fe: School of American Research Press.
Johnson, Dirk
1997 Ethnic Change Tests Mettle of Minneapolis Liberalism. *Wall Street Journal*, October 18, pp. A1, A8.
Levitt, Peggy
1997 Transnationalizing Community Development: The Case of Migration between Boston and the Dominican Republic. *Nonprofit and Voluntary Sector Quarterly* 26(4):509–26.
Mutombu, Chingwell
2005 Notes from Case Study Interview with Wafiq Fannoun, Former Cross-Cultural Mortgage Finance Working Group Member, U.S. Department of Housing and Urban Development, 2000.
Odendahl, Teresa
1990 Charity Begins at Home: Generosity and Self-Interest among the Philanthropic Elite. New York: Basic Books.

Prahalad, Coimbatore K.
   2005 The Fortune at the Bottom of the Pyramid: Eradicating Poverty through Profits. Philadelphia: The Wharton School Press.
Rivlin, Gary
   2010 Broke, U.S.A.: From Pawnshops to Poverty, Inc.—How the Working Poor Became Big Business. New York: Harpers Collins.
Schensul, Jean J.
   2005 Strengthening Communities through Research Partnerships for Social Change: Perspectives from the Institute for Community Research. *In* Community Building in the Twenty-First Century, Stanley Hyland, ed. Pp. 191–218. Santa Fe: School of American Research Press.

4

Policy, Applied Feminist Anthropological Practice, and the Traffic in Women[1]

Susan Dewey

"Who is accusing us? Where are they?" These questions, shouted by a furious Uzbek man on trial for sex trafficking, echoed throughout the nearly empty Armenian courtroom. He was the chief defendant in the first court case[2] to employ Armenian antitrafficking legislation, and stood accused together with his mother and sister of coercing eight women from the Central Asian republic of Uzbekistan into prostitution in Armenia. The women had returned to Uzbekistan with funds and assistance provided by various organizations, and thus the defendants argued for the dismissal of their case because it was effectively without victims. Taking events related to this trial as its case study, this chapter will address a central question: what can the perspective of a practicing feminist anthropologist reveal about the complex convergence of local and global forces that created this predicament?

Introduction: Sex Trafficking as a Global Phenomenon

A number of global issues complicate the answer to the Uzbek defendant's questions, including the historically unprecedented rise in the numbers of women who choose international migration and sex work from a limited number of survival strategies available to them (Gamburd 2000; Hondagneu-Sotelo 2001; Keough 2006; Parreñas 2001). The phrase "the traffic in women" generally, but by no means always, refers a situation of real or invented indebtedness that serves as a justification for a woman turning over a significant portion of her sex work–related earnings to a third party who facilitated her travel across an international border.

Threats of violence against the woman or her family may be used as a means of control by the person who is profiting from her work. The sense of insecurity and fear that this creates is compounded by the often-illegal nature of the activities involved, such as the use of false or altered documents to cross borders, the bribery of border guards and police, and the stigma associated with prostitution even in countries where there are no laws against it. Even when a woman is entitled to be in a country because she holds a tourist or student visa, her marginal status as an illegal worker and a prostitute discourages her from approaching the police or organizations that could assist her.

Most international policy and national legislation bear resemblance to the United Nations Protocol to Prevent, Suppress and Punish Trafficking in Persons, Especially Women and Children, Supplementing the United Nations Convention against Transnational Organized Crime. Often referred to in abbreviated form as "the Palermo Protocol," it defines sex trafficking as activity that involves the "threat or use of force or other forms of coercion, of abduction, of fraud, of deception, of the abuse of power or of a position of vulnerability...[to engage in] the exploitation of the prostitution of others or other forms of sexual exploitation" (United Nations [UN] 2000).

The Palermo Protocol carefully distinguishes sex trafficking from sex work, a now-popular term encompassing prostitution as well as other forms of transactional sexual behavior that was originally coined in response to a late-1970s political environment that labeled all forms of sex work antifeminist (Leigh 1997:225). Debates regarding the differences between sex trafficking and sex work have taken on a particularly contentious tone in recent decades, as have the burgeoning number of institutions, groups, and individuals involved in antitrafficking activities, all with their own wildly variant motivations for engaging with the issue, ranging from humanitarian idealism to xenophobia.

Indeed, many critics have argued that such concerns about the subject expressed by governments, international organizations, and activist groups began to take place just as economic crises, many of which were prompted by the collapse of the Soviet Union and the implementation of structural adjustment programs throughout Asia and Africa, created the conditions of economic constraint and hardship that encourage voluntary labor migration (Agustín 2007; Chew 2005; Sharma 2005). It is thus unsurprising that the most significant debate on the relationship between globalization and sex trafficking centers on the issue of the set of circumstances a woman must undergo to be considered a "victim of trafficking" entitled to service provision and legal assistance measures, as opposed to sex workers ineligible for such benefits.

This question is particularly contentious because those with the power to define the behaviors and experiences that constitute "trafficking" are polarized into two camps, one holding that prostitution is a form of violence against women, and the other arguing that it should be recognized as a form of work. As we shall see in this chapter's case study, the lack of clarity regarding this issue and appropriate responses to it has enormous implications for public policy and its implementation. Members of the first camp, which includes the U.S. government and some feminist activists (Barry 1996 [1986]; Farley 2004; Jeffreys 2008), believe that the criminalization of prostitution is a necessary step toward ending the traffic in women. The U.S. government maintains what it terms a "zero tolerance policy" toward prostitution so extreme that it refuses to fund any international initiatives that provide services to sex workers.[3] This policy is quite paradoxical given that many women who become victims of trafficking according to most definitions of the term have previously sold sex as a survival strategy and thus could potentially be targeted by the numerous U.S.-funded antitrafficking projects through existing local agencies and nongovernmental organizations (NGOs) that have experience assisting sex workers. As such, these initiatives deliberately separate sex workers from victims of trafficking in ways that neither reflect reality nor address the needs of the population they purport to serve.

Partially in response to this paradoxical exclusion, the second camp argues that prostitution should be recognized as a legal form of work or, at the very least, as an enduring reality that warrants a more pragmatic approach. They argue that criminalization renders sex workers invisible to those in positions of privilege, thus placing them at greater risk of violence and abuse by both clients and the police. As such, it has been argued that the contemporary North American and Western European response to trafficking "supports the neoliberal economic interests of corporations, multilateral aid agencies, policy experts and national governments" (Kempadoo 2005:36) rather than sex workers. Critics of these laws and policies (Doezema 2010; Sharma 2003) believe that bifurcating sex workers into the deceptively neat categories of either "prostitute" or "victim of trafficking" effectively ignores the realities of women's lives and their efforts to support themselves and their families.

Yet, scholars and activists on both sides of this debate generally do agree that a woman's likelihood of engaging in sex work, whatever the degree of coercion involved in doing so, dramatically increases in situations of poverty and limited life choices, such as the ones discussed in this case study. This chapter is set in Armenia, a small nation nestled in the Caucasus Mountains and surrounded by Iran, Georgia, Azerbaijan, and Turkey, the latter two of which it has a bitter history of conflict.[4] After

Armenia received independence from the Soviet Union in 1991, massive emigration ensued in response to the country's numerous sociopolitical and economic crises. This atmosphere of pervasive emigration and, for those who remain in Armenia, difficulties in finding work, has resulted in a situation in which trafficking has become an issue of concern.

A Feminist Anthropological Perspective on Sex Trafficking

I arrived in Armenia in late summer 2004, curious to learn how this global problem manifested itself in a local context. My central goal as a researcher was to ascertain the impact of then-nascent antitrafficking laws upon female migrants who had sold sex outside their home country. To carry out this research, I knew that I had to embed myself in the everyday workplace environment of an organization specifically tasked with carrying out antitrafficking work, particularly one that provided direct assistance to women who self-identified as victims of trafficking. I chose the International Organization for Migration (IOM) because it is the sole international organization solely dedicated to the needs of migrants and displaced persons throughout the world.

IOM was a particularly nuanced and dynamic field site because of the numerous and sometimes insurmountable hurdles its staff members face, including low overall resources, frustration with limited impact, problems in interacting with socially stigmatized groups, and the burden of determining individuals' eligibility for assistance programs. This is further complicated by the gravity of the life-changing (and, indeed, potentially life-destroying) decisions staff members must make as part of the sometimes conflicting set of obligations they face while simultaneously attempting to assist clients, cooperate with governments and law enforcement officers, and work within legal and financial restrictions. One Armenian IOM staff member characterized the difficulties inherent in the job as "you have to think like a cop and act like a humanitarian, all in your second language," a statement which exposes just one of the numerous points of tension regarding the dominance of international organizations by Western European and North American interests, languages, and high-ranking staff members.

During the course of my research I functioned as a full-time unpaid member of the IOM office staff, assisting in whatever capacity other staff deemed necessary on a daily basis. I attended meetings both inside and outside the office, I helped write and edit reports, and, most important, I was able to witness the complex set of everyday struggles that frame individual and organizational efforts to put antitrafficking legislation and policy into practice in situations that are, at best, incredibly complex.

IOM was thus both my field site and my point of entry into interviews and meetings with highly placed officials who otherwise would not have provided me with the same levels of candor had I been a complete outsider to their world.

Throughout my research I used a feminist anthropological perspective, a form of inquiry and analysis which had its nascence during the North American women's movement of the 1960s and 1970s, and has grown exponentially since that time due to the incorporation of gender and women's studies programs and departments on many college campuses.[5] Feminist anthropological research, broadly defined, analyzes aspects of culture from women's perspectives while simultaneously acknowledging that scientific objectivity is at best an illusion. Feminist anthropologists recognize that their work is explicitly political and that it, like other forms of scholarly analysis, represents a particular perspective rather than an objective account of reality. In this vein, feminist philosopher Donna Haraway notes that "the codes of the world are not still, waiting only to be read," (1988:593) and argues that all accounts of marginalized populations risk replicating "the god trick" of positivist science, which she believes to assume the possibility of rational, invisible, and omniscient authorial voice free of bias.

Most feminist anthropologists believe that gender is a set of culturally constructed behavioral norms that vary considerably from place to place. One of the most important implications of this belief is that once we acknowledge that gender norms have a very limited (if any) biological basis, it becomes clear that there is nothing "natural" about the attributes ascribed to particular genders. Nonetheless, as recent anthropological work has shown, the fact that gender is culturally constructed does not preclude it from carrying enormous weight. This is particularly evident in recent ethnographic studies of sexuality (Blackwood 2005; Boellstorff 2005; Manalansan 2003), all of which emphasize the enormous power that cultural notions of normativity wield in individual lives.

Feminist anthropologists frequently note the ways in which these cultural constructions of gender have very real manifestations that can be quite detrimental. One example is the enduring existence of feminized labor, work performed primarily by women and characterized by low pay, temporality, and limited amounts of respect accorded to it. Yet despite the cross-cultural frequency with which women are accorded lower status than their male peers, feminist anthropologists pay careful attention to the ways that women exert their will even in systems or situations that limit their ability to do so. This human ability to act, known as agency, provides much analytical fodder but is definitely not confined to the rarefied sphere of intellectual debate. Indeed, the continued existence of high rates of maternal mortality for women living in poverty, female infanticide, and deaths caused by intimate partner violence are all sobering reminders that sexism continues to exert deadly force upon women's lives.

Recent anthropological literature on agency has stressed how individuals' human ability to act is shaped by both immediate social realities and the intersections of global media, religious doctrines, and human rights discourses. This scholarship (Bierlich 2007; Clarke 2004; Smilde 2007; Vilaça 2010) emphasizes how agency has been reconfigured due to the increased interconnectedness often referred to as globalization.[6] Feminist anthropologists whose research focuses upon sex work have made considerable contributions to scholarly understandings of agency by underscoring the complex strategies women engage in as part of their individual strategies for social mobility (Brennan 2004; Kelly 2008; Wardlow 2006; Zheng 2009).

Like their counterparts in other applied subfields of anthropology, applied feminist anthropologists distinguish themselves through their commitment to research that promotes political and social change. Yet feminist anthropologists face some unique challenges in carrying out their work due to the high value that anthropologists of all persuasions place upon cultural relativism, the principle that ethnographic researchers should not engage in moral judgment. This presents applied feminist anthropologists with a dilemma when they find themselves faced with cultural practices that seem clearly to disadvantage women.

Feminist debates over cultural relativism and human rights are ongoing in anthropology and in the interdisciplinary feminist academic literature. Female genital cutting (also known as female circumcision) and the various forms of garments worn by some religious Muslim women (often described as "veiling") constitute two salient examples of particularly heated debates regarding cultural practices that may or may not be construed as oppressive to women. Feminist anthropological scholarship on female genital cutting, for instance, notes that these predominantly sub-Saharan African cultural practices constitute a rite of passage for young girls into womanhood rather than a violation of their human rights akin to mutilation (Boyle 2005; Gruenbaum 2000). Similarly, Muslim women's decision to wear head-coverings and other religious garments has become a particularly contentious debate regarding their ability to freely choose such a form of expression. Feminist literature on the subject notes the frequency with which such debates are implicated in broader polemics regarding migration and translocal culture and citizenship (Shirazi 2003; Tarlo 2010; Winter 2009).

In the case of sex trafficking and, indeed, sex work, such debates about the ability of women to make choices freely are perhaps even more constrained. This is only further complicated by the emergence of human rights instruments, including the Palermo Protocol, that emphasize the desired universality of, for instance, women's rights to equal participation in society and freedom from violence. These human rights discourses are presumed universally relevant, yet are almost exclusively originated and disseminated by Western European and North American organizations. Notably, such discourses are increasingly used by populations outside these geographical regions in ways that illuminate gendered points of tension in local communities (Helms 2003; Puri 2008).

The most recent feminist scholarship on the gendered nature of the global political economy speaks to the complex cultural flows that aid in the social construction of gender. This work sharply contrasts with earlier anthropological research, which tended to focus almost exclusively on the locally bounded nature of gender and its associated cultural forms. In focusing upon the intersections between neoliberal[7] economic reforms, feminized migration, and labor practices, as well as the meanings ascribed to citizenship and its accompanying rights and privileges, this burgeoning new literature presents a complex portrait of factors that inform women's lives (Caldwell 2006; Ong 2006; Parreñas 2008; Salzinger 2003).

Feminist anthropology is uniquely able to use both theory and method in understanding sex trafficking because of its long history of examining the nuances of privilege while developing methodological tools that encourage researchers to elicit multiple perspectives (Hawkesworth 2006; Hill Collins 2008). With its nascence in the women's movement, feminist anthropology is both an activist discipline that encourages social transformation upon more equitable grounds and a scholarly field with a rich ethnographic tradition. This integrative approach is particularly effective in analyses of how individuals inhabit perspectives in particular cultural systems, including bureaucratic organizations (Carr 2009, 2010).

The central tenets of applied feminist anthropology thus provide an excellent lens through which to understand why the eight women returned to Uzbekistan without testifying in court, and thereby arrive at nuanced answers to the questions posed by the Uzbek man on trial. The practice of applied feminist methods in the field, particularly the ability to recognize agency within constraint, can also help concerned parties (henceforth known as "stakeholders") understand how the lines between prostitution and sex trafficking are never as clear in women's lives as they might seem in policy documents and legislation. As this chapter's case study will make eminently clear, applied feminist anthropology's chief contribution to understandings of sex trafficking is an insistence that effective assistance measures must account for the complex realities of everyday life.

Case Examples: "The Uzbek Returns"

We now return to the questions shouted by the Uzbek man in the courtroom on charges of sex trafficking. None of the eight women he and his family were accused of coercing into prostitution was willing to testify, and the defendants unsurprisingly used this as evidence that the case was unfounded. The literal invisibility of the victims was compounded by the lack of precedent in prosecuting a trafficking case and an almost tangible sense of apathy that filled the nearly empty courtroom and the global antitrafficking system in which it was embedded.

This court case, which took place in 2004, was pursued under the Armenian Criminal Code's Section 132, which was added in 2003 to recognize trafficking as a criminal offense defined as the use of force, fraud, or coercion to profit from the sexual exploitation of others. Trafficking in Armenia is punishable by a fine ranging from $6,900 to $11,500 (300 to 500 times the monthly minimum wage), up to one year of correctional labor, or one to four years in prison. The maximum sentence is eight years in prison, which may be imposed if an organized group commits the crime, if the perpetrator makes use of life-threatening violence or the threat thereof, or if the crime involves a minor or results in the death of the victim.

As illustrated in Figure 4.1, the case began when eight Uzbek women filed a complaint with the Armenian police that alleged they had been held against their will in an Uzbek-managed Armenian illegal brothel for more than one month. The police arrested the illegal brothel's managers, an Uzbek family of three, and then contacted the activist director of a shelter for women deemed victims of trafficking, who agreed to house the Uzbek women. The shelter's activist director, funded by a multilateral aid package from IOM and the U.S. Agency for International Development (USAID) through antitrafficking funding supplied by North American policy makers, was bound by the rules mandated by the latter. As the stakeholder responsible for gathering information and making assessments of the eight women's eligibility for assistance in returning to their home country, the IOM became intimately involved in their case.

An enormous controversy immediately arose between USAID and IOM regarding the pregnancy of one of the Uzbek women, who had conceived during a paid sexual encounter with a client. Two key pieces of legislation passed by North American policy makers prohibit the use of U.S. donor funds to pay for abortions: the 1973 Helms Amendment to the Foreign Assistance Act of 1961, which states that "no foreign assistance may be used to pay for the performance of abortion as a method of family planning," and the 2001 Mexico City Policy, which requires international NGOs to certify that "they will not perform or actively promote abortion as a method of family planning as a condition of receiving… assistance" (USAID 2007). U.S. law forbids the use of its donor funds to finance abortion in other countries due to the influence of religious conservatives on the formation of international policy.

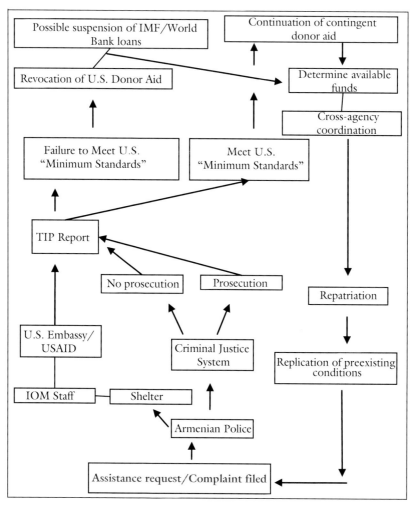

Figure 4.1. Visualizing the Case Study

The IOM eventually acted in conjunction with the shelter's activist director to assist the woman in obtaining an abortion in the interests of her rights and emotional stability, but the question of the controversial termination of her pregnancy remains extremely relevant in this case. The activist-director and IOM were bound by the laws made in North America, which in turn were passed in response to broader antiabortion campaigns led by religious right-wing voters, none of whom will likely ever encounter the Uzbek woman whose body became the ultimate object of their political views. Yet because the question of the abortion might be viewed as a human rights issue by visiting representatives of international and development organizations based in Europe and North America, both the activist-director and IOM needed to be extremely careful to handle the case with the knowledge that their actions would later be under scrutiny by such representatives, who might resent the interference of right-wing U.S. politics in the operations of a multilaterally funded international organization.

Local government bureaucrats also held a powerful stake in the case due to Armenia's heavy dependency upon U.S. foreign aid to Armenia (Ishkanian 2003, 2008). The case had the potential to result in the suspension of all U.S. donor aid to Armenia due to provisions in The Victims of Trafficking and Violence Prevention Act of 2000 (TVPA), which established an Office to Monitor and Combat Trafficking in Persons that compiles an annual Trafficking in Persons Report (TIP Report). This report describes trafficking and efforts to combat it in almost every country and is compiled in conjunction with U.S. embassies throughout the world. TIP Reports divide countries into four tiers (including one known as the "watch list"), based upon assessments of the efficacy of individual governments' antitrafficking activities. These standards are composed of a checklist of nine criteria that assess government involvement in trafficking, punishment of traffickers, assistance to victims, cooperation with extradition and international investigations, recognition of victim rights, and prevention of double victimization by the legal system (U.S. Congress 2000).

Placement in the lowest category of Tier Three indicates that a country has failed to take "significant actions to bring itself into compliance with the minimum standards for the elimination of trafficking in persons" (U.S. Department of State 2004). Due to this possibility for aid suspension, government bureaucrats were eager to present a positive assessment of their involvement in the case to visiting representatives of international and development organizations based in Western Europe and North America, who might also prove vital sources of aid. As such, the judiciary in the case was under strong local government pressure to ensure a conviction, as was the local government itself by the Western European and North America–based funding organizations and governments.

The next major hurdle in handling "The Uzbek Returns" began when logistical questions of support arose between the IOM offices in Armenia and Kazakhstan, as no equivalent office existed in Uzbekistan. A flurry of emails between the Chief of Mission in Armenia and the Counter-Trafficking Program Coordinator in Kazakhstan documents the intricacies of organizing the return of eight women and underscores how difficult it is to facilitate the safe reintegration of victims of trafficking into their home environment. In some ways, it also revealed the vast networks of customs officials, border guards, and immigration authorities that traffickers have to bypass or co-opt into their world to sustain their operations. The return of the Uzbek women was paid for by a multilateral aid–funded project titled "Combating Trafficking in Central Asia," which covered Kazakhstan, Tajikistan, and Uzbekistan and had a set amount of funds reserved for the voluntary return of victims of trafficking. The total cost for all eight of the women to be returned to their homes in Namangan was approximately U.S. $7,000 including airfare, temporary housing in Tashkent, and spending money. IOM officials in Kazakhstan recommended that the U.S. $150 that the women would be provided with to facilitate their safe journey home be given to them by an escort only after their arrival in Tashkent to ensure that law enforcement authorities would not steal it at the airport.

A smaller point of contention then arose regarding which language the women should use to complete a series of questionnaires about their experiences as victims of trafficking. The IOM mission in Armenia felt that what they called the "international language" of English should be used, but IOM authorities in Kazakhstan argued that Uzbek or Russian, a second language common to all, should be substituted to ensure clarity. IOM Armenia eventually compromised by using forms in English translated from conversations conducted in Russian with the Uzbek women by IOM staff members in Armenia, as the forms had already been printed in English and many staff members felt that they should not be wasted due to budgetary constraints. This underscores the complexities of the situation as well as the disturbing propensity of international organizations to focus an enormous amount of energy on matters of little importance relative to the gravity of the problems facing the Uzbek women. Discussions about the women's reintegration into Uzbek life centered on the assumption that they would immediately be identifiable to airport authorities and those in their home region as victims of trafficking and, by default, be stigmatized as prostitutes. This was a matter of major concern to both Armenian and Kazakh IOM staff members, who wanted to maximize the women's chances of completing a safe transition into their former lives. The unspoken theory on both sides of the return coordination effort was that the women's provocative clothing, status as travelers in a small, all-female group between two post-Soviet countries, and behavioral cues would allow strangers to identify them as easy to exploit. In other words, the relatively privileged staff assisting the women assumed that they were somehow "marked" as sex workers.

The idea of the Uzbek women as "marked" reveals a set of assumptions the relatively privileged staff members at international and NGOs sometimes share about sex workers as somehow culturally distinct from other women. The word "prostitute" is often seen as an identity and permanent professional category rather than a noun describing a woman who has engaged in the exchange of sex for something of value perhaps as part of a temporary role she has taken on as a survival strategy. This conflation of sex work with a static condition of immorality and marginalization highlights the gendered reality that while the Uzbek (and other) women may try to negotiate the knowledge that their actions mark them in a negative way by wearing less provocative clothing, a number of factors also work against their efforts. Corrupt border guards and other law enforcement officials may assume that women with little education, professional experience, and no place of employment have no reason to be traveling internationally, and so discrimination against such women becomes not so much a matter of "what she was wearing" as "what she was doing."

Knowledge of assumptions about their behavior and moral characters by outsiders definitely informed the behavior and choice of language that the eight women used with IOM staff members so that it became almost impossible to determine the real degree of knowledge the women had about the type of work they would do in Armenia prior to their arrival. Victims of trafficking are well aware of the stigma that marks them as sex workers and may be ashamed of the choices they have been forced to make because of their unstable economic circumstances and social marginalization. Only one of the Uzbek women was adamant that she knew she was coming to Armenia to perform sex work, while the other seven insisted they had been promised jobs as waitresses in a café. It seems highly unlikely that eight women traveling together outside of the country for the first time would not have some sort of discussion en route to their destination about the type of work they were going to do once they arrived. While this is by no means an argument which implies that all victims of trafficking know the conditions they will be working in once they reach their country of destination, the discontinuity in opinion among the Uzbek women does suggest that there are profound gaps in education and authority between workers at international and nongovernmental organizations and trafficked women, which can serve to silence victimized women in a very real way.

The result of such gaps is that in some (but by no means all) cases, job titles such as "waitress," "dancer," or "entertainer" may serve as code words that mask the reality: women know they will have to sell sex upon their arrival in a new country. Such code functions to preserve cultural notions of morality in the presence of outsiders, especially the relatively privileged individuals who make up the staff of most organizations designed to assist victims of trafficking. By tailoring the reality of their situation to fit the neatly circumscribed typologies most international and nongovernmental organizations have for victims of trafficking, women are able to not only preserve some degree of dignity in what has the potential to be an extremely humiliating situation, but also to exercise agency in a space where very little room exists to do so otherwise. Yet the agency exhibited by the Uzbek women closely resembles Scott's (1985) "weapons of the weak" in their decision not to testify in the court case or their use of linguistic code to preserve cultural notions of female propriety.

Advance knowledge of the circumstances women find themselves in once they arrive in the country they have been trafficked to is of course tempered by the reality that desperate and impoverished people who are offered what they perceive as their only chance to earn money for themselves and their families are not likely to ask many questions about the conditions under which they will have to work. The discourses of naiveté and trickery presented in many analyses of sex trafficking thus may not be entirely representative of the way in which women's anxieties about their futures and very real lack of choices temper their ability to inquire about what circumstances await them in a new country or even to effectively seek help from organizations designed to assist them.

After the return of the eight women to Uzbekistan, the IOM had maintained regular contact with the Uzbek trafficking victims via email and had learned that the Uzbek family was allegedly threatening the safety of their accusers, making this a case in which the victims were supposedly not even safe in their own homes. Such reports definitely informed the sense of urgency to pursue a conviction among almost all concerned in the global antitrafficking system in Armenia. The brother and sister entered a guilty plea while their mother, who had previously been charged with trafficking in Uzbekistan, professed her innocence. All three had refused the services of a lawyer by claiming they had no real hope for a fair trial and insisted that although they did bring the eight Uzbek women to Armenia to engage in sex work, they should not be charged with trafficking because the women had gone willingly with full knowledge that they would work as prostitutes upon their arrival. The defendants, who did not speak Armenian, presented their closing statement in mutually intelligible Russian to the judge and insisted that they should be sent back to Uzbekistan because they had already been in prison for nine months. The judges sentenced the brother, mother, and sister to four, four and a half, and two years in prison, respectively.

The tone of the posttrial staff meeting was one of resignation rather than happiness at the conviction, with the IOM Chief of Mission pausing briefly after lighting a cigarette to announce, "Yes, they'll bribe someone and be back in Uzbekistan by the end of the year." The overall sentiment was that no real victory had been won, and the consensus held that only a tiny fraction of a broader trafficking network between Tbilisi (Georgia), Baku (Azerbaijan), and Dubai had actually been exposed in the courtroom. His acknowledgment, along with staff awareness that repatriating women did little more than replicate the very circumstances that they had initially sought to escape, doubtless contributed to this sense of defeat despite the judge's sentence.

Conclusions: Lessons Learned

This case study raised a number of vexing complexities inherent in putting antitrafficking law and policy into practice, the most sobering of which is the reality that those who formulate and enact policies with enduring impacts on women's bodies and lives may not always understand crucial factors at work in many sex workers' lives. This cognitive gap compounds sex workers' social invisibility by rendering many antitrafficking initiatives ineffective from their very inception, resulting in women's double victimization by both institutionalized corruption endemic in many post-Soviet states and the very organizations that seek to assist them.

Using an applied feminist anthropological perspective reveals that female migrants like the Uzbek women are deeply disadvantaged by definitions and characterizations of sex trafficking that are far too simplistic to take the complex realities of their lives into account. The deeply embedded nature of gender discrimination and violence against women in all societies throughout the world presents particularly difficult challenges to those tasked with designing public policy and legislation designed to prevent and respond to sex trafficking. Accordingly, this chapter will conclude with several suggestions for changes to the contemporary global antitrafficking system. Although I had neither the seniority nor the power to implement these changes during my fieldwork, I would argue that the case study and other arguments presented in this chapter illuminate the broad range of roles played by applied anthropologists.

One of the biggest lessons I learned in the course of my research was that while I have absolute freedom as an academic to write about less-than-successful cases such as the one described here, I would not necessarily be able to do so as an employee of an international organization or NGO. As such, my role as an applied feminist anthropologist will continue to lie primarily in research and publishing findings that offer recommendation for policy change.

The Power of Language and Definitions

This chapter's case study underscores how bureaucracy evinces a kind of invisible agency in which a culture with its own rules and codes of behavior emerges in tandem with the needs and responsibilities of the organization itself, and how this culture informs the decisions made by those tasked with carrying out its daily operations. This invisible agency explains why so many individuals I met in the course of my research simultaneously lamented the inefficacy of efforts to assist women deemed "victims of trafficking" and yet continued to pursue strategies that were clearly ineffective. Part of the reason why such assistance measures often had unintended negative consequences is that such women constitute a population invisible to most policy makers, who thus fail to see the agency they demonstrated as part of broader strategies to improve their lives.

The way that a particular organization defines prostitution and sex trafficking directly affects the social services provided to women who sell sex in any capacity. Monica O'Connor and Grainne Healy, as part of their antiviolence work, have noted that the view of prostitution as a form of violence against women leads to service provision outcomes that label clients as abusers, thus obscuring the complex ways of thinking about gender and power that inform their decisions. Conversely, the authors argue that viewing prostitution as a form of work can result in a lack of social incentives for governments and organizations to assist sex workers because of its depiction as a career choice, thus protecting the health and anonymity of male clients by screening prostitutes for sexually transmitted diseases (O'Connor and Healy 2006).

Female sexuality is a subject of tension and a matter of enormous concern in every culture, so it is unsurprising that ideas about agency, consent, and choice are so hotly debated with respect to sex work. Both ways of defining expose the gendered power inequalities that influence the ways sex workers are treated, and yet the sobering consequence of the global antitrafficking system's reach is that its subjects are, at best, blurry, ill-defined, and often objectified through the assumptions relatively privileged policy makers hold about sex workers. This is particularly true in reference to prevailing definitional standards of sex trafficking. Even though the global antitrafficking system ostensibly exists to assist women who are labeled "victims of trafficking," such women's voices often remain submerged in antitrafficking discourse unless they fit neatly into narratives of victimization.

Feminist anthropological studies of sex workers' lives have clearly demonstrated that all forms of sex work involve some degree of coercive force, ranging from economic need to gender inequality broadly defined (Brennan 2004; Day 2007; Hoigaard and Finstad 1992). Paradoxically, sex workers are often defined by those who are the most removed from their everyday existence; as a result, their self-identities and what they are required to have suffered to qualify as "trafficked" depends upon who is doing the defining rather than what they have actually experienced.

The "trafficked woman" and her "trafficker" are thus constructed as hollow bodies, empty figures to be filled up with the assumptions of the relatively privileged staff members at most international organizations, governments, and NGOs. This way of operating differentially positions migrant sex workers as either unwanted migrants in need of rescue or help- less, enslaved victims. From the point of view of the migrant sex worker, who is ostensibly the center of need from which the global antitrafficking system emanates, the situation is much more complex. Trafficking cases often feature the complex circumstances resulting from undocumented migration, in which prostitution or survival sex might be but one of the many difficult aspects of daily survival. It is particularly difficult to identify the lines between consent and coercion in such circumstances. Although sex workers are in the best position to offer information about the dynam- ics of their everyday lives, a number of sociopolitical forces constrain their ability to be heard by those in positions of authority over them, includ- ing the stigma that surrounds sex work even for those who claim to be staunch advocates of human rights.

Such stigma results in a resounding, albeit unspoken, "We can't hear you" from policy makers to sex workers, whereas sex workers' internaliza- tion of this results in an acknowledgment akin to "You can't (and won't) hear me." Even when sex workers are consulted for advice, this reality constrains the terms upon which others hear them, so that although their stories might be listened to and even featured in reports, books, and argu- ments for more donor funding and antitrafficking policies and legisla- tion, sex workers are unlikely to be *heard* as a source of real potential change. In a bitter case of irony, the real authorities on the issue are cast as the only actors who are not "experts," a title assigned in this system through formal education and affiliation with a particular organization and its philosophy.[8]

Similar difficulties regarding definition and understanding surround an equally obscure figure: the individual who facilitates migration for the woman who is or will become a sex worker. This facilitator, variously known as "trafficker," agent, or smuggler, assists with migration for those who do not have access to legally issued travel documents. The facilita- tor may view their actions as a simple service provision (albeit often for an exorbitant fee) that allows migrants the possibility of improving their lives on their own terms. As one specialist at IOM Sarajevo noted, "Some people don't even realize they are traffickers, because they've been help- ing people cross the border their entire lives. It is a business to them, but now that we have this new term ["trafficking"], it changes everything."

Anthropologists of all persuasions assert that language organizes the way that individuals experience and view the world. Applying a femi- nist anthropological approach to the question of definitions necessar- ily involves interrogating the premises underlying the terms involved. Linguist Deborah Cameron notes that feminist analysis of language use "attempts to understand the role of language in the conflicts and power struggles that shape relations between men and women" (2006:1). Yet, this power struggle also extends to institutions and public policy formation in ways that directly affect women's lives (e.g., Marcus 1992). Clearly, policy makers and NGO workers need to move toward definitions of trafficking that more accurately reflect women's lived experiences.

The Need to Listen to Evidence-based Research and Life Experiences

Many feminist fieldworkers (Brennan 2004; Katsulis 2010; Kelly 2008; Zheng 2009) have documented connections between women's increased economic reliance on sex work and the rise of neoliberal labor practices, in which those in positions of power and privilege have increasingly less direct contact with or responsibility for those who work at the lowest levels of the same industry (Ehrenreich and Hochschild 2004; Newman 2008). Yet, paradoxically, these established and research-based notions in feminist anthropology have yet to enter into policy discourse, a problem that sociologist Ronald Weitzer (2005) has noted in other areas of sex work research and policy formation.

There are very real legislative and policy implications for societies that fail to incorporate the lived experiences of women who self-identify as "victims of trafficking" or the research of scholars and activists that focus upon this issue. In the Armenian context, the fact that trafficking is criminalized is relatively meaningless if elements of the crime are not defined clearly enough to facilitate effective prosecution. Maximum sentences for those convicted of trafficking are often extremely low and do not recognize the offense as a serious crime; in Armenia, the maximum punishment for trafficking resulting in the death of a victim is eight years of imprisonment. Most worrying is the fact that, as illustrated in this chapter's case study, no workable mechanisms are in place for the protection of individuals who choose to testify against those accused of trafficking, which leaves them vulnerable to violence, intimidation, threats, and even murder. This situation is further complicated by the reality that many individual activists and organizations working on trafficking-related issues in Armenia face a situation in which, as a condition of receiving donor funds, they must consistently follow rules defined in a country far from their own.

Donor Dependency and the Perils of the "Top-Down" Approach

USAID has been the single largest donor to Armenia since its independence in 1991 through its grants to Armenian NGOs and other organizations based in the country (Ishkanian 2008:133). Understandably, all actors involved in the court case described in this chapter's case study had a vested interest in a conviction to retain these funds. At the time of my research, Armenia was located on the Tier Two watch list of the tier system mandated by the Victims of Trafficking and Violence Prevention Act, a status that indicates that although a country has taken some steps to combat an especially significant trafficking problem, it is still far from taking "reasonable steps" (U.S. Department of State 2004) to resolve it.

At the time of the trial described in this chapter's case study, Armenian NGOs and government offices needed to demonstrate to U.S. representatives who compile the TIP Report that it was making "significant efforts" (U.S. Department of State 2004) to bring itself into compliance with U.S. minimum standards. Prosecution was an essential element of this demonstration, as assignment to Tier Three could prompt the suspension of U.S. assistance and jeopardize aid and loans from the International Monetary Fund and the World Bank (U.S. Department of State 2004:28).

The reductive set of extremely clear-cut criteria that make up the tier system is ineffective due to the reality that just because a country meets the terms defined by the United States does not mean that trafficking is being effectively dealt with by a given government. Premises underlying the minimum standards for prevention rely upon the assumption that the checks and balances of U.S.-style democracy exist everywhere, that justice systems function with impartiality, that citizens feel free to express their concerns about institutional corruption without fear of repercussions or loss of position, and that prosecution is the answer to ending trafficking; in essence, that all countries operate exactly like an idealized version of the United States. Despite its reductive nature, however, the tier system depicts trafficking as an abstract problem by lumping countries with extremely different socioeconomic and cultural systems together without consideration of the ways in which individual justice systems and gender norms function in particular countries.

Final Thoughts

In my case, using an applied feminist anthropological perspective revealed that the global antitrafficking system is sufficiently flawed and involuted to recommend its complete reconfiguration. An equitable response to this global issue will not simply replicate the current state of unfairly distributed privilege, but should instead focus on how current migration policies are akin to feudal privilege (Ong Hing 2006). The current global antitrafficking system fails to recognize the manifold ways in which individuals negotiate their lack of privilege in ways that often circumvent the law precisely because they see no other options readily available to them. Hence, this chapter's case study resulted in little more than the removal of the problem from sight by relocating it back to its point of origin. By illuminating the broader structural inequalities that make this seem a desirable solution to all parties except those the system intended to help, applied feminist anthropology clearly exposes the untenability of current antitrafficking policies to offer alternatives that could result in real change.

Notes

1. This chapter draws partially upon research findings presented in my book *Hollow Bodies: Institutional Responses to Sex Trafficking in Armenia, Bosnia and India* (Dewey 2008).
2. The trial took place in October 2004.
3. The legal impetus for this policy stems from the United States Leadership Against HIV/AIDS, Tuberculosis and Malaria Act of 2003, which refuses any form of U.S. aid to "any group or organization that does not have a policy explicitly opposing prostitution and sex trafficking" (U.S. Congress 2005:5).
4. An estimated 1.5 million Armenians were murdered during the dissolution of the Ottoman Empire, of which Armenia had been a part since the early 1500s (Balakian 2004; Miller and Miller 1999). From September 1989 until 1994, Azerbaijan and Turkey imposed a blockade of Armenian fuel and supply lines in a dispute over Azerbaijan's claim to the Armenian territory of Nagorno-Karabakh, a decision that was particularly devastating in the wake of the 1988 Spitak earthquake, which took 25,000 lives and devastated almost half of the country (Frelick 1994).
5. Like all academic scholarship, feminist anthropology is a product of the historical circumstances in which it was performed. For examples of what could be considered feminist anthropology written prior to the advent of the North American women's movements of the 1960s and 1970s, see Lurie 1999 [1966]. For excellent examples of feminist anthropology written during the height of the women's movement, see Boserup (1970), Murphy and Murphy (1974), Reiter (1975), Stack (1974), and Weiner (1974). Work published since that time is generally more concerned with how gender shapes the human experience in various cultures, and can be found in Abu-Lughod (2000), Behar (1993), Blackwood (2000), Freeman (2000), Martin (1989), and Tsing (1993).
6. This chapter follows Held et al.'s definition of globalization "as a process (or set of processes) which embodies a transformation in the spatial organization of social relations and transactions—assessed in terms of their extensity, intensity, velocity and impact—generating transcontinental or interregional flows and networks of activity, interaction, and the exercise of power" (1999:16).
7. Geographer David Harvey defines neoliberalism as "a theory of political economic practices that proposes that human well-being can best be advanced by liberating individual entrepreneurial freedoms and skills within an institutional framework characterized by strong private property rights, free markets, and free trade. The role of the state is to create and

preserve an institutional framework appropriate to such practices.... State interventions in markets (once created) must be kept to a bare minimum because, according to the theory, the state cannot possibly possess enough information to second-guess market signals (prices) and because powerful interest groups will inevitably distort and bias state interventions (particularly in democracies) for their own benefit" (Harvey 2005:2).

8. In her ethnography of drug addiction treatment programs in the United States, anthropologist Summerson Carr notes that "realizing oneself as an expert commonly entails figuring others as less aware, knowing, or knowledgeable, and therefore establishing differential relationships between people, words, and valued objects, such as inner states" (2010:225).

References

Abu-Lughod, Lila
2000 Veiled Sentiments: Honor and Poetry in a Bedouin Society. Berkeley, CA: University of California Press.

Agustín, Laura
2007 Sex at the Margins: Migration, Labour Markets and the Rescue Industry. London: Zed Books.

Balakian, Peter
2004 The Burning Tigris: The Armenian Genocide and America's Response. New York: HarperCollins.

Barry, Kathleen
1996 [1986] The Prostitution of Sexuality: The Global Exploitation of Women. New York: New York University Press.

Behar, Ruth
1993 Translated Woman: Crossing the Border with Esperanza's Story. Boston: Beacon Press.

Bierlich, Bernhard
2007 The Problem of Money: African Agency and Western Medicine in Northern Ghana. Oxford: Berghahn Books.

Blackwood, Evelyn
2000 Webs of Power: Women, Kin, and Community in a Sumatran Village. New York: Rowman & Littlefield Publishers, Inc.
2005 Gender Transgression in Colonial and Postcolonial Indonesia. *Journal of Asian Studies* 64(4):849–79.

Boellstorff, Thomas 2005
The Gay Archipelago: Sexuality and Nation in Indonesia. Princeton, N.J.: Princeton University Press.

Boserup, Ester
1970 Women's Role in Economic Development. London: George Allen and Unwin.

Boyle, Elizabeth Heger
2005 Female Genital Cutting: Cultural Conflict in the Global Community. Baltimore: Johns Hopkins University Press.

Brennan, Denise
2004 What's Love Got to Do With It? Transnational Desires and Sex Tourism in the Dominican Republic. Durham, N.C.: Duke University Press.

Caldwell, Kia Lilly
2006 Negras in Brazil: Re-envisioning Black Women, Citizenship, and the Politics of Identity. Piscataway, N.J.: Rutgers University Press.

Cameron, Deborah
2006 On Language and Sexual Politics. London and New York: Oxford University Press.

Carr, Summerson
2009 Anticipating and Inhabiting Institutional Identities. *American Ethnologist* 36(2):317–36.
2010 Scripting Addiction: The Politics of Therapeutic Talk and American Sobriety. New Brunswick, N.J.: Princeton University Press.

Chew, Lin Lap
2005 Reflections by an Anti-Trafficking Activist. *In* Trafficking and Prostitution Reconsidered: New Perspectives on Migration, Sex Work and Human Rights, Kamala Kempadoo, Jyoti Sanghera, and Bandana Pattanaik, eds. Pp. 65–80. London: Paradigm Publishers.

Clarke, Kamari Maxine
2004 Mapping Yoruba Networks: Power and Agency in the Making of Transnational Communities. Durham: Duke University Press.

Day, Sophie
2007 On the Game: Women and Sex Work. London: Pluto Press.

Dewey, Susan
2008 Hollow Bodies: Institutional Responses to Sex Trafficking in Armenia, Bosnia and India. Sterling, VA: Kumarian Press.

Doezema, Jo
2010 Sex Slaves and Discourse Masters: The Construction of Trafficking. London: Zed Books.

Ehrenreich, Barbara, and Arlie Russell Hochschild
2004 Global Woman: Nannies, Maids and Sex Workers in the New Economy. London: Owl Books.

Farley, Melissa
2004 Bad for the Body, Bad for the Heart: Prostitution Harms Women Even if Legalized or Decriminalized. *Violence against Women* 10(10):32–40.

Freeman, Carla
2000 High Tech and High Heels in the Global Economy: Women, Work, and Pink Collar Identities in the Caribbean. Durham, N.C.: Duke University Press.

Frelick, Bill
1994 Faultlines of Nationality Conflict: Refugees and Displaced Persons from Armenia and Azerbaijan. *International Journal of Refugee Law* 6(4):581–619.

Gamburd, Michelle Ruth
2000 The Kitchen Spoon's Handle: Transnationalism and Sri Lanka's Migrant Households. Ithaca, NY: Cornell University Press.

Gruenbaum, Ellen
2000 The Female Circumcision Controversy: An Anthropological Perspective. Philadelphia: University of Pennsylvania Press.

Haraway, Donna
1988 Situated Knowledges: The Science Question in Feminism and the Privilege of Partial Perspective. *Feminist Studies* 14(3):575–99.

Harvey, David
2005 A Brief History of Neoliberalism. Oxford: Oxford University Press.
2007 A Brief History of Neoliberalism. Oxford: Oxford University Press.

Hawkesworth, Mary
2006 Feminist Inquiry: From Political Conviction to Methodological Innovation. New Brunswick, NJ: Rutgers University Press.

Held, David, Anthony McGrew, David Goldblatt, and Jonathan Perraton
1999 Global Transformations: Politics, Economics, and Culture. Stanford: Stanford University Press.

Helms, Elissa
2003 Women as Agents of Ethnic Reconciliation? Women's NGOs and International Intervention in Postwar Bosnia-Herzegovina. *Women's Studies International Forum* 26(1):15–33.

Hill Collins, Patricia
2008 Black Feminist Thought: Knowledge, Consciousness, and the Politics of Empowerment. New York: Routledge.

Hoigaard, Cecilie, and Liv Finstad
1992 Backstreets: Prostitution, Money and Love. University Park, PA: Penn State University Press.

Hondagneu-Sotelo, Pierrette
2001 Doméstica: Immigrant Workers, Cleaning and Cooking in the Shadows of Affluence. Berkeley, CA: University of California Press.

Ishkanian, Armine
2003 Importing Civil Society? The Emergence of Armenia's NGO Sector and the Impact of Western Aid on Its Development. *Armenian Forum: A Journal of Contemporary Affairs* 3(1):7–36.
2008 Democracy Building and Civil Society in Post-Soviet Armenia. Abingdon, UK: Routledge.

Jeffreys, Sheila
2008 The Industrial Vagina: The Political Economy of the Global Sex Trade. London: Spinifex Press.

Katsulis, Yasmina
2010 Sex Work and the City: The Social Geography of Health and Safety in Tijuana, Mexico. Austin: University of Texas Press.

Kelly, Patty
    2008 Lydia's Open Door: Inside Mexico's Most Modern Brothel. Berkeley: University of California Press.
Kempadoo, Kamala
    2005 Victims and Agents: The New Crusade Against Trafficking. *In* Global Lockdown: Race, Gender and the Prison Industrial Complex, Julia Sudbury, ed. Pp. 35–56. New York: Routledge.
Keough, Leyla
    2006 Globalizing "Postsocialism": Mobile Mothers and Neoliberalism on the Margins of Europe. *Anthropological Quarterly* 79(3):431–61.
Leigh, Carol
    1997 Inventing Sex Work. *In* Whores and Other Feminists, Jill Nagle, ed. Pp. 225–31. New York: Routledge.
Lurie, Nancy Oestreich
    1999 [1966] Women and the Invention of American Anthropology. Prospect Heights, IL: Waveland Press.
Manalansan, Martin
    2003 Global Divas: Filipino Gay Men in the Diaspora. Durham: Duke University Press.
Marcus, Sharon
    1992 Fighting Bodies, Fighting Words: A Theory and Politics of Rape Prevention. *In* Feminists Theorize the Political, Judith Butler and Joan Scott, eds. Pp. 385–403. New York: Routledge.
Martin, Emily
    1989 The Woman in the Body: A Cultural Analysis of Reproduction. Boston: Beacon Press.
Miller, Donald E., and Lorna Touryan Miller
    1999 Survivors: An Oral History of the Armenian Genocide. Berkeley: University of California Press.
Murphy, Yolanda, and Robert F. Murphy
    1974 Women of the Forest. New York: Columbia University Press.
Newman, Katherine
    2008 Chutes and Ladders: Navigating the Low-Wage Labor Market. Cambridge: Harvard University Press.
O'Connor, Monica, and Grainne Healy
    2006 The Links between Prostitution and Sex Trafficking: A Briefing Handbook. Technical Report. Coalition against Trafficking in Women and the European Women's Lobby on Promoting Preventative Measures to Combat Trafficking in Human Beings for Sexual Exploitation.
Ong, Aihwa
    2006 Neoliberalism as Exception: Mutations in Citizenship and Sovereignty. Durham: Duke University Press.
Ong Hing, Bill
    2006 Deporting Our Souls: Values, Morality and Immigration Policy. Cambridge: Cambridge University Press.

Parreñas, Rhacel Salazar
    2001 Servants of Globalization: Women, Migration and Domestic Work. Stanford: Stanford University Press.
    2008 The Force of Domesticity: Filipina Migrants and Globalization. New York: New York University Press.
Puri, Jyoti
    2008 Gay Sexualities and Complicities: Rethinking the Global Gay. *In* Gender and Globalization in Asia and the Pacific: Method, Practice, Theory, Kathy E. Ferguson and Monique Mironesco, eds. Pp. 59–79. Honolulu: University of Hawai'i Press.
Reiter, Rayna
    1975 Toward an Anthropology of Women. New York: Monthly Review Press.
Salzinger, Leslie
    2003 Genders in Production: Making Workers in Mexico's Global Factories. Berkeley: University Press.
Scott, James
    1985 Weapons of the Weak: Everyday Forms of Peasant Resistance. New Haven, CT: Yale University Press.
Sharma, Nandita
    2003 Travel Agency: A Critique of Anti-trafficking Campaigns. *Refuge* 21(3):53–65.
    2005 Anti-trafficking Rhetoric and the Making of a Global Apartheid. *National Women's Studies Association Journal* 17(3):88–111.
Shirazi, Faegheh
    2003 The Veil Unveiled: The Hijab in Modern Culture. Gainesville: University Press of Florida.
Smilde, David
    2007 Reason to Believe: Cultural Agency in Latin American Evangelism. Berkeley: University of California Press.
Stack, Carol
    1974 All Our Kin: Strategies for Survival in a Black Community. New York: Harper and Row.
Tarlo, Emma
    2010 Visibly Muslim: Fashion, Politics, Faith. Oxford: Berg.
Tsing, Anna Lowenhaupt
    1993 In the Realm of the Diamond Queen. Princeton, NJ: Princeton University Press.
United Nations (UN)
    2000 Protocol to Prevent, Suppress and Punish Trafficking in Persons, Especially Women and Children, Supplemented by the United Nations Convention against Transnational Organized Crime. Available at: http://www.uncjin.org/Documents/Conventions/dcatoc/final_documents_2/convention_%20traff_eng.pdf. Accessed July 16, 2011.

United States Agency for International Development (USAID)
2007 USAID's Family Planning Guiding Principles and U.S. Legislative and Policy Requirements. Available at: http://pdf.usaid.gov/pdf_docs/PDACI438.pdf. Accessed July 16, 2011.

U.S. Congress
2000 Victims of Trafficking and Violence Prevention Act of 2000. Public Law 106-386. Available at: http://www.state.gov/documents/organization/10492.pdf. Accessed July 16, 2011.
2005 Acquisition & Assistance Policy Directive: Implementation of the United States Leadership against HIV/AIDS, Tuberculosis and Malaria Act of 2003—Eligibility Limitation on the Use of Funds and Opposition to Prostitution and Sex Trafficking. Available at: http://www.usaid.gov/business/business_opportunities/cib/pdf/aapd05_04.pdf. Accessed July 16, 2011.

U.S. Department of State
2004 Trafficking in Persons Report: The Tiers. Available at: http://www.state.gov/g/tip/rls/tiprpt2004/. Accessed July 16, 2011.

Vilaça, Aparecida
2010 Strange Enemies: Indigenous Agency and Scenes of Encounters in Amazonia. Durham: Duke University Press.

Wardlow, Holly
2006 Wayward Women: Sexuality and Agency in a New Guinea Society. Berkeley: University of California Press.

Weiner, Annette
1974 Women of Value, Men of Renown: New Perspectives on Trobriand Exchange. Austin: University of Texas Press.

Weitzer, Ronald
2005 Flawed Theory and Method in Studies of Prostitution. *Violence against Women* 11(7):934–49.

Winter, Bronwyn
2009 Hijab and the Republic: Uncovering the French Headscarf Debate. Syracuse: Syracuse University Press.

Zheng, Tiantian
2009 Red Lights: The Lives of Sex Workers in Postsocialist China. Minneapolis, MN: University of Minnesota Press.

5

Global Climate Change from the Bottom Up

Shirley J. Fiske

Introduction: Global Interconnections, Climate Change, and Local Peoples

The phenomenon of globalization provided an "afterburner" acceleration to the widespread sociocultural changes of the industrial revolution and explosive urbanization that followed. Globalization increased global trade and movement of capital through multilateral loans for major infrastructure projects for energy facilities, transportation arteries, and natural resource extraction. These in turn led to ever more energy-intensive development and manufacturing investments across the world, culminating in a steadily increasing release of carbon dioxide and other greenhouse gases and the popularly known phenomenon of global climate change.

The challenges for all of us presented by the phenomenon of global climate change are monumental, particularly for anthropologists. Anthropology is a field strongly influenced by social and environmental justice viewpoints. Climate change anthropologists consistently point out that people who are poor, have few resources for alternatives, are marginal to the economies of nation-states, and who depend on the local environment for their livelihood are the most vulnerable to impacts from climate change. Its impacts will be felt most intensely where people live in close relationship to the earth and oceans and depend on natural resources—people living in low-lying delta areas of major river systems such as the Ganges or Mississippi, pastoralists in the Sahel, people on island nations in the Pacific and Indian Oceans, and circumpolar Arctic peoples. These individuals, families, and communities will bear a disproportionate share of the brunt of changing climate.

Climate change is an international body of knowledge, belief, activities, and policies where anthropologists and other social scientists have been able to leverage their knowledge about culture, human interactions, and the environment. This chapter focuses on how anthropologists deal with the human issues and problems as a result of climate change, specifically carbon mitigation, carbon offset programs, and carbon trading.

Anthropologists use the theories and tools of ethnography, knowledge of social structure and kin networks, social capital, and peoples' traditional knowledge about the natural world to understand what is happening at the "bottom levels," to the world's vulnerable peoples where people live and work in close connection with nature and natural resources in a globalized world where climate change is a reality.

This is not to say that anthropologists do not also "study up", as in the classical challenge from Laura Nader (1974). Nader's point is that anthropologists need to look "upwards" to understand how power and responsibility are exercised, extending our research into institutions, corporations, and policy processes that affect us all. Anthropologists use this dual approach of studying up while focusing on "on the ground" impacts to connect the dots between what is happening at the "bottom" level and the decisions, economic agreements, and trade policies that are negotiated at national and international levels among state institutions, lending agencies, and multinational corporations. Anthropologists have been critical of carbon offsets as a way of reducing greenhouse gases from both perspectives. They have documented human rights abuses, in the worst cases, and unequal access to participation in programs in others. They also look upward to identify the implicit sources of power and influence, sometimes embedded in historically uneven political relationships between North and South, governance at multilateral lending institutions, and national/state politics and policies that shape the nature of programs that are available at the end of the pipeline.

How are seemingly remote peoples and livelihoods connected with climate change emissions and reductions programs that have been put in place through United Nations (UN) treaties such as the Kyoto Protocol?

The UN Framework Convention on Climate Change (UNFCCC) and the legally binding Kyoto Protocol have been more than a decade in the making and entered into force for most nations of the world in 2005.[1] Policies and programs developed in the last decade promote programs that reduce carbon emissions, such as the UN's Clean Development Mechanisms, through a global carbon-trading scheme to allow nations that produce *too much* carbon to acquire credits from countries that are *sequestering* (reducing) carbon. Carbon, or more correctly, the lack of it, thus becomes a commodity, which trades on international markets. Intermediaries such as the World Bank, U.S. Agency for International Development (USAID), and international and national nongovernmental organizations (NGOs) are institutional enablers that knit together carbon reduction programs through state-based (national) policies, agricultural communities, tribal and indigenous populations, and pastoralists into the world of global financial flows and ebbs and market trades of carbon credits. Carbon offset and "cap and trade" programs and policies interconnect the local and the international in a world where market transactions among financial institutions happen almost instantaneously. These interconnections have brought the carbon markets directly into contact with indigenous groups in the Amazon, forest dwellers in Vietnam, or herders in Siberia as examples (see Nash 2007). This chapter is the story of how anthropologists are involved and build their cases regarding global interconnections from the bottom up.

The next section situates this discussion in the context of environmental anthropology and anthropologists' work in climate. I highlight the conceptual contributions that have been made to core concepts like vulnerability, adaptation, and resilience, the approaches and roles taken by anthropologists, and concerns that have been raised.

In the case study on carbon policies and programs I will provide examples from anthropologists who are based in research institutes, academia, the government, NGOs, and international organizations—not solely practitioner examples. Climate change involves a broad swath of anthropologists in different roles, and to get the full picture of anthropological engagement, I want to show the dynamic relationship between knowledge produced in organizational settings outside of academia and the critical analyses and insights generated by scholars and researchers in academia.

I conclude the chapter with comments on the disciplinary cycle of theory-building and practice within the field of anthropology. I expand on the role of practicing anthropologists in building theory (see for example Hill and Baba 2006) by suggesting that professional anthropologists "leverage knowledge" at a variety of different program and policy levels. Copeland-Carson in this volume has excellent insights into the "blending of scholarship" from both sources into a field of knowledge and action she refers to as "anthropological praxis" (see also Wulff and Fiske [1987] on praxis). I agree with exhortations that more anthropologists should put "anthropology into use" and engage directly in political and policy decision making (as suggested in Rylko-Bauer et al. 2006), and am optimistic that in this manner we have a chance to promote anthropologically informed knowledge, social change, and policy reform that has the ability to improve lives of vulnerable and marginalized peoples globally.

An Anthropological Perspective on Environment, Climate, and Carbon

The field of environmental anthropology developed from several foundational bodies of work, indeed going back to the early twentieth century.

Cultural ecology is a primary theoretical underpinning. Cultural ecology understood human societies and culture as adaptations to their environments (including climate) that cultures worked out over time. Varying ecological niches the world over provided opportunities for different kinds of subsistence and social adaptations, whether it was hunting in tropical rainforests, shifting agriculture, wet rice farming, or living on coral atolls. Cultural ecologists described how people adapted to their immediate surroundings and their knowledge about it (ethnoecology), their decision making, and their adaptive strategies. Humans were seen as a biocultural element within larger ecosystems, an important part of the overall flow and use of energy in the ecosystem, and environmental anthropologists generally saw cultural practices as allowing optimal adaptation to their local environment in a fairly stable fashion (Netting 1986; Steward 1955).

Sometimes referred to as the new ecological anthropology (Kottak 1999), environmental anthropologists in the 1980s began to see human adaptation in its larger context—beyond adaptation to immediate physical surroundings—including adaptation to forces outside the community such as political and economic systems in which they were imbedded (Netting 1993). Political ecology gradually emerged as an insightful framework to understand cultural behavior and interactions with the environment at the local ecosystem level. Political ecology goes farther in clearly identifying the consequential role of supralocal factors on local cultures, and the importance of understanding them—including monetary and trade policies, development investments by international aid institutions, foreign investment by multinational corporations, structural adjustments required by lending institutions, and national policies (Greenberg and Park 1994; Stonich and DeWalt 1996).

This shift in understanding cultures and communities was dramatic and took environmental anthropology in new directions—to focus on power relationships, external policies, access to resources, and flows of technology, capital, and information to understand peoples' relationships with the environment. It is a critical step and component. This conceptual shift occurred simultaneously with the aftermath of World War II, the Green Revolution, the Washington Consensus for trade liberalization and market fundamentalism, and the unleashing of forces of globalization (Stiglitz 2003). Anthropologists have used the framework of political ecology to understand how policies established at international levels, within international financing institutions such as the International Monetary Fund and the World Bank have cascading effects on nations and rural communities, villages, and tribal peoples. Tribal groups in Amazonia, for example, are not isolated cultural groups no matter how distant they are from contact. Understanding their "world" means knowing how international development loans and national policies (international trade pacts, internal economic growth policies) have affected available hunting areas, paved roads, allowed settlements or ranching to encroach, caused migration to their areas, and so on. Agriculturalists, similarly, find themselves responding to extension agents, regional production incentives, or policies that promote export crops over crops for local markets.

Climate and Carbon

With respect to climate change and carbon offset programs, anthropologists share a common approach: they rely on deep ethnographic understanding of local peoples' way of life, their cultural and social systems that support it, and the nuanced number of ways that they perceive and deal with environmental change—and how it will affect their livelihoods and quality of life in the future. These are communities, families, and people who are often "under the radar" of national and international decision makers. Anthropologists document the depth and breadth of traditional ecological knowledge (TEK) inherent in peoples' long-standing understandings about and interactions with the natural world, and have advocated for its importance and relevance for culturally appropriate climate policies and programs (Crate and Nuttall 2009; Strauss and Orlove 2003). They work with traditional peoples but also use their insights with developed nations, such as helping decision makers understand how rural communities in the American southwest will react to perceptions of climate change (Finan et al. 2002; Nelson et al. 2009).

Anthropologists have broadened our understanding of the core concepts of climate change—*adaptation, resilience, vulnerability,* and *sustainability.* For environmental anthropologists, sustainability means *social* and *cultural* sustainability, not solely biological sustainability. The anthropological component of sustainability means that people are able to continue to maintain a livelihood from the land or sea, and maintain the integrity of social institutions that support their customary ways.

Likewise, adaptation does not refer to building homes on higher ground, or buying a motor to go out farther to fish for different species. To environmental anthropologists, adaptation is rooted in a social context where any adaptation means also changing ways of relating to people, or having access to family groups' resources, or access to external assistance. Adaptation is *a social process* that stems from a "web of social reciprocities and obligations" that informs peoples' decisions about what to do under uncertain circumstances (Roncoli et al. 2009:101). For anthropologists, adaptation does not refer to a technological or engineering fix, such as building dikes to keep the ocean out as sea levels rise. In addition, anthropologists have shown that "social capital" is a valuable cultural asset for adaptation and natural disasters, like having social insurance or a support network, leading to resilience and adaptability during the stress of climate change (Galvin et al. 2007; Vásquez-León 2009).

Anthropologists have helped put a historical face on the concepts of adaptation and vulnerability in the context of climate change. Archaeologists in particular have broadened the understanding of adaptation by interpreting the failures of civilizations and colonies during climate swings. As an example, the fate of the early Norse colonies in Greenland has pointed lessons about the key role of cultural adaptation. The inability to adapt and to adopt cultural components from their neighbors, the Inuit—such things as hunting tools and protective clothing, and to shift from agriculture and herding of ruminants to fishing and sealing like their neighbors—was the crucial factor in the colonies' demise (McGovern et al. 2007). Jared Diamond has popularized the sagas of how and why civilizations disappear in *Collapse,* and among the five points in his framework is the response of the society to its environmental problems (Diamond 2005).

In reviewing the ways that environmental anthropologists have approached climate change I argue that a predominant role is to parse the effects of policy and programs, asking, "who really benefits?" and "what are the distributional effects?" Because of this attention to how communities and families operate in the real word (compared with theoretical models), environmental anthropologists look for undetected or unanticipated economic or institutional barriers that may be embedded in program design and implementation. Will pastoralists, for example, be able to take advantage of carbon sink programs as designed? Among agricultural families in a community, will all families have equitable access to the programs? What are the social and cultural barriers, like gender, to participation? (Perez et al. 2007)

In addition, anthropologists have a long-standing concern with environmental justice, beginning with the research done on the enormous toll on communities such as Zambia's Gwembe Tonga, by large-scale, World Bank–financed hydropower dams in the 1960s and 1970s (Colson 2003; Scudder 1973). River basin development and involuntary resettlement created "development refugees" who were relocated to unfamiliar lands, where the next generation never saw the lands and villages their elders described (Scudder 1993). Today, environmental anthropologists continue to document forced migration to unsuitable sites, loss of property, and death from large-scale development projects, including road building. Anthropologists have provided critical analyses of climate impacts and carbon-related projects, including the effects on indigenous tribal Amazonians and the forced relocations of Arctic peoples from coastal villages (Marino 2009) and of villagers in Uganda whose human rights are ignored due to carbon plantations (Checker 2008).

In the following section, I include a focused discussion of anthropological work related to carbon sequestration and offset projects as examples of policy-relevant work that practicing and applied anthropologists are undertaking. Much of the work is done through funded research projects from an academically affiliated research base, although it is often funded by mission-oriented agencies like USAID.

At the same time, important work is going on in the U.S. federal government (including USAID), the World Bank, and NGOs where practitioners are working. As an example, in my career both at the National Oceanic and Atmospheric Administration (NOAA) and in Congress, I was closely involved in the development of and advocacy for the human dimensions of climate change from the early days of the U.S. Global Change Research Program in the 1990s. My association with climate change policy continued through my legislative work on cap and trade and carbon emissions legislation. The focus and direction I identified for my personal and professional actions in the climate change policy and research stream was (and still is) clearly influenced by my anthropological training (Fiske 2009a).

Global Forces and Climate from the Bottom Up

Anthropologists, who tend to see things from the bottom up (while also looking to the top), have been deeply critical of the processes of globalization because of the inequitable distribution of benefits and costs—including costs to the environment—across the ethnic and socio-economic sectors of nation-states. Arturo Escobar's searing critique anticipates many of the themes in current discourse—that globalization and development are versions of imperialism and a way of spreading Western influence to capture natural resources, wealth, and political power over nation-states (1995).

I also recommend a gripping indictment of the process of globalization in the best-selling autobiographical *Confessions of an Economic Hit Man* by John Perkins (2004). In his compelling book, he gives personal detail on how globalization led to opening up vast sectors of indigenous territory for oil exploration, the building of large dams (displacing thousands of people) and infrastructure to support the development of national electricity grids, and other carbon-intensive modernization efforts. While not new insights, I recommend his first-hand observations of U.S. influence and implications in regime changes at critical junctures in the early globalization process.

Global forces have economic, social, and ecological ramifications that cascade down the streambed to bury and cripple local communities. Neoliberal policies imposed by the International Monetary

Fund and the Bolivian government in 1985—such as privatization of government-owned tin mines—resulted in the development of grass-roots social resistance movements by tin miners and their families (Nash 2007:165–96). Jonathan Friedman and other anthropologists have called attention to the underbelly of globalization, not just the widening disparities between the rich and the poor, but a much darker side: global transformations of a much more fundamental and divisive nature, involving redistribution of capital, loss of hegemony among developed nation-states, and increasing violence—"both everyday domestic, local, and regional violence" (Friedman 2003a:xiv, 2003b). Friedman's argument is that globalization derives from the rise and fall of hegemonic states, and is but one phase as the world's civilizations expand and contract, as capital of the world moves from one region to another. Today's globalization is the phase in which capital is moving from the United States and Western Europe to Asia and other parts of the world (Friedman 2003a:1–34). This view is shared in part by June Nash's interpretation of globalization, in which she sees the creation of a Hobbesian world of terror and violence from the "disruption of subsistence economies and the fragmentation of the moral economy without construction of institutional controls on the emerging global economy" (2007:9).

Sustained environmental change means cultural loss in profound ways. It is almost common knowledge that many indigenous and traditional peoples in nonwestern cultures generally see themselves as an integral part of nature in which an individual's existential being is part of natural forces, not *separate* from them, as we tend to think of the cultural order in industrialized societies where nature is "out there," apart from humans.

The corollary to this among traditional peoples is that persistent environmental change erodes the prominent cultural icons and stories of long-established cosmologies, destroying the fundamental value base of their culture. Stories, memories, evocative symbols, or rituals become inconsistent, irrelevant, or lost. In her provocative articles, Susan Crate shows how the complex set of feelings, beliefs, and affinities for peoples' immediate environment is being challenged or lost as people can no longer count on the long, hard, cold winters of Northeastern Siberia—"Gone the Bull of Winter"—but must reorient their way of life and culture to a new reality undergirded by climate changes. These changes threaten thousands of years of knowledge, both symbolic and practical, that allows them and their reindeer herds to survive (Crate 2008; Crate and Nuttall 2009).

In the Pacific, the Marshallese experienced enormous cultural losses as they were forcibly removed from their islands after thermonuclear testing in the 1950s made their islands uninhabitable and their lives horrific. Their losses ranged from the harvesting of familiar fish, shellfish, and plants on which they depended to the disruption of social relationships and meanings connected with sharing those resources. These losses contributed to a sense of displacement, alienation, and bereavement (Johnston and Barker 2008).

Similarly, residents of the circumpolar North are experiencing a different world than their elders did, as revealed in the book *The Earth is Faster Now* (Krupnik and Jolly 2002). The retreat of sea ice, higher sea levels, different species availability, new weather cycles, and events more difficult to predict all combine to make life more susceptible to surprises. I suggest that cultural loss will be experienced among the growing number of peoples in all areas whose very cultures are threatened by the environmental change around them. Cultural loss of many magnitudes is related to the hypothesis that the "globalization package" of increased energy development and use (weaponry in the case of the Marshallese), and energy-intensive (high-carbon) manufacturing processes distributed across the globe are bringing us global changes in culture and climate.

How do societies adapt to change, particularly long-term climatic stresses such as changes in rainfall, prolonged drought, changes in growing season, or wetness and dryness of the growing season? (Roncoli 2006) Kathleen Galvin and her coauthors have called attention to the importance of *social capital* under conditions of land fragmentation (Galvin et al. 2007) and its importance in providing pastoralists with resilient adaptive strategies in the face of changing climate or changing access to pasturage. In addition, anthropologists have shown that "social capital" is a valuable cultural asset, like having social insurance and a support network, that leads to resilience and adaptability during the stress of climate change (Vásquez-León 2009).

As anthropologists become more active in international policy, and as they become advocates for indigenous and marginalized peoples, a number of important concerns surfaced with respect to climate change, globalization, and human rights. At the international level, Gutierrez (2007) argues that the very process of developing the governance of climate change through the UNFCCC was flawed from the beginning because it was heavily influenced by developed countries imposing Western science-based theories of global climate change over the perspectives of developing nations. Anthropologists are particularly suited to see embedded assumptions of equity and power framed in arguments surrounding scientific issues because anthropologists view Western science is a cultural construction—a way of knowing about the universe, which is one of many.

In addition, the Kyoto Protocol and U.S. dialogue on carbon regulation rely on "market-based" principles of cap and trade, in which countries and polluters (e.g., utilities, manufacturers, and others) can meet their emissions targets by buying or selling their credits—their rights to a certain amount of emissions (pollution by carbon dioxide or other green-house gases). Anthropologists raise the issues of whether this market-based principle is fundamentally flawed, leading to commodification of rights to pollute, and uses a colonial model to "farm out" carbon reductions to developing countries? Anthropologists are very good at raising critical analyses and questions: that's what we do. But we also have great challenges in providing responses in ways that enhance agency for people affected by climate change and in creating an actionable pathway for decision makers.

Case Example: Climate Change Policy from the Bottom Up

A number of changes in the last decade have laid the groundwork for greater anthropological participation in and critique of carbon reduction and carbon abatement. After a brief contextual history on the status of UNFCCC process, I will focus on anthropologists' work in this area.

The recent UNFCCC negotiations include policies to decrease carbon emissions. Earlier UN programs promoted Clean Development Mechanism projects, most of which can be described as highly capitalized renewable energy projects such as wind farms, hydroelectric dams, and monocrop plantations for carbon sequestration. The role of forests was limited to reforestation and afforestation projects.

Subsequent agreements (Bali Action Plan in 2007; Conference of Parties [COP] 15 in 2009; and COP16 in 2010) are aimed at reducing carbon emissions from *deforestation* and *degradation*, enlarging the scope of forests in reducing carbon and the types of groups that are involved in carbon mitigation projects. Reduced Emissions from Deforestation and Degradation (REDD) and REDD-plus are key components of the agreements; REDD-plus emerged from COP16 in Cancun in December 2010 and calls for activities directed toward local communities, indigenous people, and forests that reduce emissions from deforestation and forest degradation, such as increasing forest cover and enhancing existing forests. It includes some form of payments to decrease deforestation; President Obama pledged $1 billion U.S. dollars. In theory, these projects are amenable to the participation of and benefits to local communities; however, there is widespread concern that the rights of indigenous forest dwellers and forest communities be safeguarded and that the projects truly are "pro-poor."

Steve Schwartzman is an environmental anthropologist working for the Environmental Defense Fund (EDF). He described the EDF's policy approach, "Compensated Reduction," which was adopted to reduce emissions through deforestation—a policy to which he contributed his long experience in Amazonia and his anthropological knowledge and insights. He is concerned that the benefits of REDD reach local indigenous communities and that they are implemented in ways that safeguard their rights.

> The idea behind Compensated Reduction is to bring countries with large tracts of tropical rainforests to the table and to begin to reduce deforestation rates in the same way we hope to reduce industrial emissions in the U.S.
>
> It starts with establishing a historical baseline deforestation rate and then creating compensation programs in the form of global warming pollution credits that are earned every year that deforestation rates go down. It's a powerful tool for bringing down deforestation on a large scale.
>
> One real risk here and something we need to get right is to make sure the credits these countries earn for reducing deforestation don't just go down bureaucratic sinkholes. That wouldn't be efficient or sustainable.
>
> In the Amazon, you have a lot of indigenous and traditional peoples who live in the forest who have their own cultures and traditions. They understand the benefits of keeping forests standing, but they want access to markets and modern technology. They want to strike the right terms. They want their land rights recognized and they also want income. Therefore, they want to be entitled to earn credits and due compensation from the forest offsets.
>
> And, this involves governance on the frontiers. Government institutions need to be strengthened to better enforce the laws and protect the interests of forest populations.
>
> We need to support the economic alternatives that show promise, and to make sure the international agreements don't unintentionally harm vulnerable forest communities (EDF 2008).

In the same vein, Diane Russell works at USAID in natural resource management amid daunting political complexity and budgetary uncertainty. Her job includes managing a set of activities—hopefully a program of actions—that will help design and implement social and environmental safeguards for USAID's REDD investments. These efforts are critical because the World Bank and bilateral donors have yet to adopt a clear rights-based framework that provides for maximum transparency, accountability, and inclusive decision making across REDD programs (Russell, personal communication, 2011).

The Cancun principles for social safeguards are very general; more specific guidance and methodologies need to be developed. This time period is a historic opportunity to use anthropological approaches to understand and engage local communities in a way that safeguards their rights in the midst of global forces.

Somewhat predating REDD, my experience with carbon capture stems from my work as legislative aide and advisor from 1999 to 2007 for Senator Daniel K. Akaka (D-HI), who was deeply concerned about climate change and the vulnerabilities of Hawaii and Pacific island nations to the effects of global warming and sea level rise. Senator Akaka was a senior member of the Senate Committee on Energy and Natural Resources, which took a lead role in formulating groundbreaking cap and trade legislation, holding hearings, briefings, and crafting carbon emissions bills. My work included research, analysis, and recommendations on the regulatory options (e.g., auctions, offsets, allowances) and impact of climate change and climate emissions in hearings, statements, and on the Senate floor.

As part of my work on climate change legislation and policy options, I began to look at provisions for carbon sequestration and the *usefulness of markets* for carbon for conservation goals in the state of Hawaii. At the start of the new millennium on Capitol Hill, the U.S. Congress was beginning to consider ways to use market principles to reduce our carbon emissions domestically and participate in global carbon markets, even though carbon was not regulated domestically (the Administration did not support the Kyoto Protocol or regulation of carbon emissions).[2]

Multiple bills were introduced that would make it attractive for landowners to sequester carbon through reforesting their lands, for example. The carbon reductions would be offered as carbon credits in the global carbon market. This could be done by increasing acreage devoted to forests, as in Hawaii's tropical forests, where biological conversion is rapid compared with temperate forests; it could also be done by "fertilizing" the oceans with nutrients in an effort to grow algae, which would sequester carbon and "sink" it in the oceans.[3] There were a variety of options for sequestering carbon, and clearly it was an opportunity for entrepreneurs and forest owners to harness sequestration for commercial purposes.

With the entering into force of the Kyoto Protocol in 2005, carbon offsets and carbon markets, led by the establishment of the carbon exchange in the European Union (EU), emerged on the U.S. Congressional radar screen and a full plate of legislative options, including numerous cap and trade bills. Carbon markets are based on limits on the amount of carbon that can be released into the atmosphere (e.g., under the Kyoto Protocol or potential domestic legislation). The regulated entities can buy and sell emission credits to meet their ceiling/limit (metric tons of carbon);

hence, the market sets a price for carbon reductions that can be bought and sold on several exchanges.

Carbon reduction became a centerpiece of environmental conservation efforts worldwide. National and international NGOs such as the World Wildlife Fund, the International Union for the Conservation of Nature (IUCN), EDF, and Conservation International have launched ambitious programs for pro-poor carbon capture (EDF 2009). Today, the most extensive funding for sequestration projects come from the World Bank carbon funds. The World Bank has launched extensive programs that endorse carbon capture and has made increasingly sizeable investments in carbon programs and offsets.[4]

From my vantage point in Congress, I observed the generation of billions of dollars in revenue through the Chicago Carbon Exchange and the European Trading System carbon trading market. At the time, I questioned who should rightfully benefit from this revenue—beyond financiers and trading firms, brokers, industry CEOs, and countries that needed to meet their carbon ceilings, predominantly developed countries in Europe. The generation of this revenue seemed a windfall that should be shared equitably with those who bear the brunt of climate change—particularly those who live close to the land. I believed it could be a potential redistributive mechanism.

Perhaps idealistic, my quest became finding models that illuminated how carbon offset projects could usefully return carbon dollars to the producers of carbon at the ground level. Working in the U.S. Congress, I was particularly mindful of applications to domestic legislation that could benefit small farmers, tree farmers, and others in rural communities and neighborhoods across the nation and also serve conservation goals.

Regardless of whether the United States becomes a signatory of the Kyoto Protocol, or whether the nation enacts carbon cap and trade policies, federal agencies are already implementing a small number of carbon offset projects as a way to generate revenue for agency priorities, such as restoring and enhancing native forest and wildlife habitat on national wildlife refuges (U.S. Fish and Wildlife Service; see Fiske 2009b). As U.S. policy makers and agencies approach the question of carbon offsets and carbon reductions, anthropologists in domestic federal agencies (as well as USAID) are using their skills to engage local communities in carbon projects (see Charnley 2008 with respect to the U.S. Forest Service) and otherwise inserting the consciousness of human dimensions into official concepts like "vulnerability."

As environmental anthropologists, we have already benefited from the research of early leaders in this area and have learned from their work. In Africa, Carla Roncoli and colleagues reported critical reservations about potential carbon projects in the Sudan-Sahel region. Their analyses with small-scale dryland farmers living in semiarid lands of Senegal and Mali showed that participation in carbon projects was highly unequal, as were benefits (Tschakert 2007). Not surprisingly, families with greater resources were more able to take advantage of participation in land management experiments. Pastoralists in the same region, compared with dryland farmers, faced a number of barriers to participation, including increasing difficulties herding over other peoples' lands, and the lack of supralocal institutions to aggregate and negotiate carbon credits that would accrue from rotational grazing (Brown and Cobera 2003; Perez et al. 2007). Recommendations included "adequate and equitable funding...and... a careful rethinking of the institutional structures necessary to enhance rural livelihoods and natural resource management" in a variety of settings (Tschakert 2007:75).

In addition, carbon projects tend to make assumptions about land tenure (e.g., single use, clearly defined ownership, and distinct boundaries within one jurisdictional unit), most of which do not apply to pastoralists. Roncoli notes "The potential [for successful use] will likely be greater if the design and implementation of similar carbon sequestration projects involving pastoralists is informed by a good understanding of past and current land and livestock management practices, local ecology and social dynamics" (Roncoli et al. 2007:106). One of the lessons from this work is that projects will need to fit local circumstances and will have to deal with lack of legally recognized land tenure.

Roncoli and others emphasize the critical role of supralocal institutions, those that are external to local communities, including central governments, local administrative units, and growers' cooperatives, or the creation of mediating organizations that can organize and bundle carbon credits and access a carbon market. They also point out that conflict management and access to social capital are key elements of a carbon sequestration projects if they are expected to be sustainable and equitable in the Sahelian region (Roncoli 2006).

Anthropologist Stephanie Paladino completed a socioeconomic assessment of a grassroots-generated and NGO-assisted carbon offset effort in Chiapas, Mexico, called *Scolel Te'*. Her research, which looked at the social, economic, and any unanticipated socioenvironmental impacts (such as increased use of agrochemicals), was part of a larger project to further develop the technical aspects of monitoring and assessing the amount of carbon produced by participants in the project (Paladino 2008a).

Scolel Te' began as a collaborative project between a well-established *campesino* (rural farmer and producer) organization, *Pajal Yakactik,* which was later joined by research scientists from El Colegio de la Frontera Sur (ECOSUR) and the University of Edinburgh, Scotland.[5] In 1994 and 1995, the parties began a collaborative, participatory process that ultimately led to the creation of the *Scolel Te'* project. By 1997, the first eight communities began establishing agroforestry plots and receiving annual carbon payments, and became administered by Ambio, a local Chiapas NGO.

A key part of the success of this project is the "Plan Vivo" process, a planning process that allows farmers to propose agroforestry options that meet their own needs while including carbon production as part of their agricultural goals. The planning process is a dialogue between project technical staff and farmers, and ensures that they have enough land and resources to be successful. As of 2007, up to 677 agroforestry plots based on Plan Vivos were being undertaken in Chiapas and the neighboring state of Oaxaca (Paladino 2008a).

Although *Scolel Te'* has brought carbon revenue to campesinos on a consistent basis, in a relationship of trust and mutual respect, data show that as a percentage of family incomes, the range is from one-quarter to less than 1 percent of families' annual income. Most people see it as a supplement or "gratuity" to their yearly round of agricultural activities. Importantly, however, it is not a net drain on their income. Labor costs tend to be absorbed into ordinary operating costs, with most of the costs in the first-year establishment period; after that, the costs of maintenance become minimal (Paladino 2008b).

Paladino recognizes that there are important potential synergies for project participants beyond the small income from carbon; she recommends that Ambio (which provides technical assistance and services and mediates between carbon producers and brokers) become a more aggressive protagonist in addressing how the project can become transformational, including preparing campesinos for the long-term goals of timber harvesting on a sustainable basis through training and knowledge transfer (Paladino 2009).

Other researchers have also commented on the organizational evolution and effectiveness of *Scolel Te'*, observing that, among other things, the project continues to work after 10 years, in spite of the fact that decision-making power with respect to the market has shifted from "shared decision making incorporating farmer representatives" (Nelson and de Jong 2003:20) to more centralized decision making by the carbon broker and Ambio (mediated by two other organizations). They also note that *Scolel Te'* is strongly supported by its participants.[6]

For an alternative experience, Costa Rica's national approach provides an instructive lesson. Costa Rica is one of the few nations that initiated a state-run environmental services package early, in concert with opportunities after the Kyoto Protocol entered into force in 2005. Carbon payments were included as one type of environmental service that was compensated.

> In Costa Rica...the federal government serves as the broker for a complete package of environmental services including carbon mitigation, watershed protection, and biodiversity among others...the Costa Rican government pays for environmental services provided by government parks, large tracts of forested land in corporate ownership, as well as community forests (Nelson and de Jong 2003:27).

Maria Gutierrez documented the creation of carbon markets and evaluated the Costa Rican government's use of environmental services as an income transfer mechanism. She notes Costa Rica's early leadership on carbon offsets, and the creative and ambitious development of state projects that were intended to contribute to Costa Rica's environmental and economic goals simultaneously (Gutierrez 2007:285–310). However, she notes extensive problems in the way the program has worked on the ground with respect to small and medium landowners. The biggest problem is that access is inequitable. The data show that 72 percent of the areas financed represented projects greater than 100 hectares, whereas only 3.9 percent of those with less than 20 hectares were financed with payment for environmental services (PES) projects (Gutierrez 2007:303; see also Castro et al. 2000).

Participation is also problematic due to lack of clear title to the land, especially among small landowners. Banks in Costa Rica automatically put liens on property designated as PES (e.g., carbon offset projects), an enormous disincentive for small landowners to participate. The Costa Rican program is characterized by lack of participation in decision making and lack of accumulation of knowledge and training. Gutierrez concludes that "the production and trade of a new commodity resulted in reproduced inequality and the further marginalization of those people who, for social and ecological reasons, it made most sense to incorporate" (2007:316).

Anthropologists tend to see things from the viewpoint of people at the bottom of the production chain—the *producers* of carbon credits: indigenous people, small landholders, forest dwellers, and traditional rural communities. I have not found many anthropologists who endorse carbon offsets, at least for practical objectives of eradicating poverty in the short term or increasing social equity in the longer term—not to mention the environmental objective of decreasing the rate of greenhouse gas accumulation. When seen through lenses that are critical of neoliberal policy, carbon offsets are seen as one more step toward alienating natural resources from nature and from the people who depend on them.

Nonetheless, it is worthwhile to point out that there is diversity among types of community- or producer-based carbon projects, ranging from experimental or speculative projects, such as those in Africa, to well-established projects in Mexico and Costa Rica, and from agricultural communities and pastoralists to large monocrop plantations. Given this diversity in project scope and design, Stephanie Paladino and I organized a panel for the 2009 Society for Applied Anthropology Annual Meeting that would allow us to learn from collective experiences of a number of anthropologists engaged with carbon offsets.[7] Eight central points about community-based participation emerged from review and discussion of the panel:

(1) Transaction costs to participate in carbon offset process are usually too high for small producers and must to be kept to a minimum. Anthropologists have noted the negative effects of steep transaction costs on indigenous and smallholder participation.

(2) Carbon payments and PES will not alleviate poverty, and they must be realistically assessed and presented. The income stream to small producers and co-ops is likely to be very small, ranging from 25 percent to as low as 2 percent of annual income for families in Chiapas (Paladino 2008a). To benefit from an income stream, the price of carbon must be high, and to date it has hovered between $2 and $7 per metric ton in the U.S. voluntary market and $28 per tonne in Europe, prior to the 2008 global economic recession.

(3) Access to carbon projects tends to be inequitable, favoring well-off families and individuals, so the design of carbon projects must take into consideration how to encourage participation by low-income families, and both genders, and make it possible to do so.

(4) Secure land tenure is an assumption made in planning carbon projects, but the reality is that land tenure at the bottom level is in flux in most countries outside of the most developed core of nations. Land ownership in the newly opened areas of the Amazon, for example, is a highly negotiated status between migrant settlers and state officials, often "created" with landmarks, documents, and use of specific areas. There are social and institutional barriers to participation if land ownership is not clear, and unintended consequences for participants where land is not held in the traditional property ownership mold of Western Europe. In Mexico, much of the forested land is held communally (e.g., in *ejidos*), but carbon payments ended up going to families instead of the *ejido,* undercutting communal ownership (Shapiro 2009).

(5) Aggregative or supralocal institutional capacity is needed to package and broker carbon credits effectively (e.g., Asquith et al. 2002; Roncoli et al. 2007:98). Experience in Mexico shows that active engagement of NGOs as intermediaries at the community level is crucial (Paladino 2008a; Shapiro 2009).

(6) Each implementation of PES/carbon offset programs will be shaped by the role of the state (Mexico and Costa Rica have different experiences) and rural social movements. McAfee and Shapiro (2010) point out the strong role of social movements in changing the thrust of Mexico's PES programs, a phenomenon not apparent in Costa Rica's experience. Rural resource users and producers of environmental services eventually forced the PES program officials in Mexico to reconsider how they evaluated rural livelihoods, the role of agriculture, and rural life in Mexico's economic development (Shapiro 2009).

(7) Carbon projects need to provide capacity-building mechanisms for providers if they are to be transformative (Paladino 2009).

(8) Local participation in designing and implementing the cooperatives is critically important, and it cannot be top-down (see Asquith et al. 2002 for a case study of how *not* to do carbon projects in Bolivia).

Typically, carbon offsets are seen as the "bad boys" of climate policy. They are criticized by journalists and satirized by the media as a dubious way to reduce carbon emissions and a nonconstructive way to assuage the guilt of Western consumers who wish to reduce their carbon footprint (Fahrenthold 2008). They are accused of perpetuating the problems of colonialism, as European nations "contract" with developing nations to reduce their carbon emissions to meet their targets under the Kyoto Protocol (Bond 2007; Checker 2008). Anthropologists with experience in the field question whether carbon projects are transformative opportunities—that is, creating long-lasting changes in land use or its social and political ecology (Gutierrez 2007; Paladino 2009). Anthropologists also question the extent to which environmental services programs are a distraction from the root causes of environmental degradation, pollution, and poverty. Finally, anthropologists ask, are carbon projects or PES approaches ultimately another way of commodifying nature, of "selling nature to save it," with the potential for transforming indigenous and resource-dependent peoples' relationships and rights to nature and natural resources? (Igoe 2008)

U.S. legislators were concerned enough about carbon markets and carbon credits in 2007 to request a special analysis from the Government Accountability Office (GAO), which found the supply of offsets generated from projects based in the United States grew rapidly from about 6.2 million tons in 2004 to about 10.2 million tons in 2007. The report concluded that carbon markets can provide tracked, verifiable, and accountable carbon credits to investors and nation-states; however, they also concluded that in the United States, the market is not fully transparent, not regulated, and that caveat emptor reigns—but did not recommend further Congressional action (GAO 2008).

Anthropologists are well positioned to engage in the development of policy—especially as it may affect or engage small landowners (farmers, tree farmers, or grasslands), rural communities, and public and private rangelands and forest lands. For example, we know that a cookie-cutter, one-size-fits-all approach will not work, and that carbon capture programs will have to be created in regional or even more highly localized circumstances, contexts, and landscapes. "Producer-friendly" programs will have to vary by livelihood, whether it be subsistence trapping and gathering or small organic farmlands. Intermediary organizations, non-profits, aggregators, and brokers (e.g., NGOs) will need to reach out to communities to find families and small landowners that might not otherwise engage.

This contribution to this book has focused on the work of anthropologists producing insights from the bottom up, hopefully influencing the policy stream—making it more "human-responsive"—to make it more able to inform and direct activities that protect human rights rather than destroy them, and protect livelihoods and enhance living conditions rather than diminish them.

Has the work of anthropologists actually affected climate policy and carbon programs, either in the United States or in other countries? I believe it probably has and will, in a cumulative way: the work of anthropologists in NGOs, in the federal workforce, and in the World Bank, as examples, will have an iterative and cumulative effect on the development of guidelines, definitions of concepts, legislative priorities, funding priorities, and public thinking about human dimensions and social equity. These steps are iterative with the research findings coming from Collaborative Research Support Programs (USAID), Regional Integrated Sciences and Assessments units, and other university-affiliated and federally funded research institutes, and from numerous perspectives, critiques, and project assessments from academia and public anthropologists. At the domestic level, the U.S. Forest Service is engaging communities, family farmers, and owners of forest lands in carbon offset projects (Charnley and Diaz 2009), something that reflects anthropological values in conjunction with forest and carbon conservation. At the international level, a sign of growing anthropological involvement is the fact that there were more anthropologists participating in the UN COP15 meeting in Copenhagen in December of 2009, than have collectively participated in a UNFCCC event at any time in the past (see Chernela et al. 2010). Anthropologists are monitoring and advocating on behalf of indigenous and tribal peoples for the most part, and some anthropologists at least see incremental progress on involving indigenous peoples in the carbon emissions reductions regime of REDD. REDD was introduced at the COP meeting in Montreal in 2005; it was instituted in 2007 through the Bali Action Plan, and in Copenhagen (2009), $3.5 billion was pledged for REDD funds. Each of these are small steps, but forward ones, in bringing traditional peoples' interests more in line with climate and carbon policy.

Conclusions

It is perhaps a well-known story that anthropologists have made important contributions to the human dimensions of climate change, and one of those contributions is "institutionalizing" the human dimensions in the U.S. climate change research program. This is a significant accomplishment by social scientists, including numerous anthropologists, that often does not get recognized because of its incremental nature. Anthropologists have been involved at every step, from the formation of interagency committees in the 1990s, to membership on National Academy of Sciences studies, to contemporary efforts to insert the social and power dimensions into concepts like "vulnerability assessment" that are building blocks of the National Climate Assessments required by statute. It is not just one person, but the continuing insertion of the "bottom up" approach with awareness of "top level" factors and external constraints on a number of different levels and opportunities. It is a good example of how environmental anthropology has influenced research and policy directions for global climate change. This is a first step, which is "getting to the table" as a player.

The steps continue as the carbon policy stream continues to evolve politically and presents needed avenues for perspective and work of anthropologists, from the bottom up and looking upward as well. I argue that anthropology has deepened our understanding of how people will be affected by market-based climate policy options such as cap and trade systems and carbon offset projects—demonstrating the complexity of these systems as they are implemented in the real world under varying national, local, and livelihood contexts and conditions. I have included some of the important concepts and lessons learned from carbon projects and programs earlier in this chapter.

I believe that anthropologists collectively are having an effect through their critical analyses, evaluations of operational carbon projects, design and implementation of new approaches to projects, and growing activist participation in international meetings. In addition, a growing number of public anthropologists, commenting critically on carbon issues and natural disasters, are monitoring human rights, analyzing distributional effects, assessing access to programs, and adapting concepts so that the concerns noted above are dealt with in the design process for carbon projects. I am optimistic that as anthropologists continue to write, work in organizations, and speak up, their perspectives will begin to be integrated into policies and programs that will lead to more progressive effects across the globe (Fiske 2011).

How Anthropological Knowledge is Augmented and Leveraged

I have gone into some detail on my engagement with global climate change to provide greater transparency about what practicing anthropologists do. In many instances, we are hidden in the intestines of large organizations, whether it is a federal agency, the World Bank, a consulting firm, or a large NGO such as the EDF. My point is that practicing anthropologists' work on the "inside" is an important part of knowledge development, policy selection, and implementation. Work such as fostering human dimensions of global change as a part of climate modeling and articulating policy options inside Congress to inform national debate is perhaps not apparent on the surface; nor is changing the agenda inside conservation NGOs to be more pro-poor. However, the cumulative positioning of many anthropologists in the policy stream leads to an important "leveraging" effect when combined with the actions of colleagues "outside," in academia, research institutions, and other locales. The leveraging effect occurs not just in getting things done or funded, but also with the production of knowledge and development of theory.

Knowledge is leveraged when anthropologists add value by pushing a conceptual or theoretical envelope, whether on terms like "adaptation," "vulnerability," or "social capital." It is also leveraged when anthropologists knowledgeably push the policy envelope with political ecology analysis. Rylko-Bauer et al. speak of an "anthropology in use, united by the goal and practice of applying theories, concepts, and methods from anthropology to confront human problems" (2006:179). The "anthropology in use" concept, it seems to me, encompasses the work of program officers at the National Institutes of Health, the National Science Foundation, the Minerals Management Service, and the GAO, whose research projects refine theory and concepts. It includes anthropologists working in NGOs with World Bank funding to expand the social development programs and policies. It also includes academically based anthropologists as important links in publicizing and expanding knowledge and in investigating the nuances of concepts and theories. Examples of leveraged knowledge include the work of anthropologists in NOAA's National Marine Fisheries Service, who have led the effort to develop conceptual approaches for understanding community dependency and social impact assessment on fishing communities (Clay and Olson 2007; Ervin 2000:98–111; Pollnac et al. 2008).

Anthropologists in the U.S. Bureau of the Census, as another example, have worked together with academics and others to advance understanding of complex ethnic households and household diversity within the United States (Schwede et al. 2005), ideas that are important for accurate census efforts in the future. Practitioner anthropologists bring ethnographic approaches and critical perspectives to natural resource issues such as fisheries, traditional cultural properties in national parks, and forest management (Fiske 1990; see also The George Wright Forum [2009a, 2009b] for special issues on traditional cultural properties and ethnography).

Practitioner and applied anthropologists are closely attuned to questions of equity and sustainability in environmental management policies, for example highlighting the social and economic effects of privatization. The conceptual and theoretical insights mentioned earlier are examples of *leveraged knowledge* about concepts such as family and community structure, ethnicity, and the nature of common property and common pool resources.[8]

Climate change is an international body of knowledge, beliefs, and policies where anthropologists and other social scientists have been able to leverage their knowledge about human interactions with the environment. The human dimensions were noticeably absent in the early stages of global climate change, but with the persistent insertion of human dimensions into climate change dialogue and modeling, we now have a greater understanding of the complexities of human adaptation, resilience, risk, vulnerability, and land use change, and which policies and mechanisms work and which will not.

We have an opportunity currently to take advantage of the leveraging possibilities with anthropologists who are now well distributed inside federal agencies and NGOs and can make links with policy. The fact is that there are more anthropologists working in the federal (and state) government and possibly in NGOs than ever before (Fiske 2008). Good models of such leveraging include government partnerships with anthropologists in academic institutions such as Regional Integrated Sciences Assessments (NOAA) and collaborative research projects (funded in academia), the National Sea Grant College Program (a federal-academic partnership), Cooperative Studies Units funded by the U.S. Department of the Interior and Agriculture/U.S. Forest Service, and the U.S. Department of Agriculture's Cooperative Extension Service.

Practitioners have been criticized by other anthropologists as being, well, too practical. I will admit a bias toward research and policy that is useful, or relevant in concrete ways, and my views are informed by the desire to improve policy outcomes for people who do not have access to or voice in the policy process. My hopes are based on the belief that policies can be changed, that people can learn, and that social change and environmental justice are desirable goals. The former president of the American Anthropological Association, James Peacock, made the point that if anthropology is to maintain a valuable identity and gain recognition in the twenty-first century, it must do things beyond analyze and critique—it must accomplish things, which I understand to mean produce useful knowledge and results. He offers the hopeful salvo: "Pragmatism and searching critique need not be mutually exclusive" (1997:12).

Acknowledgments

I would be remiss not to acknowledge the helpful reviews of anonymous reviewers of this chapter, but particularly the insightful critique and suggestions of Jennifer Collier at Left Coast Press, which helped me enormously. I would like to mention the extremely valuable collaborative assistance of Stephanie Paladino in reviewing versions of this manuscript. Her experience, review, and suggestions added greatly to the substance and accuracy of this manuscript. I would also like to thank Carla Roncoli for her supportive help in networking and understanding carbon projects in the field. I am grateful for the thoughtful and thorough review of Roberto Escobar's classic work by Robert Packwood, which he undertook on behalf of the authors in this book. I greatly appreciate the comments and editorial insights of Mary O. Butler, Christina Wasson, and Jackie Copeland-Carson, my patient reviewers and editors in the production of this volume, who helped me see how to make my chapter much more readable and understandable.

Notes

1. The United States and China are two notable exceptions. Neither has ratified the Kyoto Protocol.
2. During the period 1997–2007, U.S. climate change policies provided *incentives*, but few if any *requirements*, to reduce greenhouse gas emissions. A variety of voluntary and reporting actions were in place, including monitoring of power plant carbon emissions, improved appliance efficiency, and incentives for renewable energy; however, carbon dioxide emissions continued to increase (Parker and Yacobucci 2007).
3. For ocean sequestration, there were too many environmental unknowns to be successful, although interested parties lobbied heavily.

4. In 2011, The World Bank Climate Investment Funds were $6.4 billion, operating through several subfunds that focus on technology (Clean Technology Fund, $4.5 billion) and the Strategic Climate Fund ($1.9 billion) for forest emissions reductions programs and renewable energy in low-income countries (http://www.climateinvestmentfunds.org/cif/, accessed May 11, 2011).

5. *Pajal Yakaktik* had coffee production as its main focus, but also provided services such as a credit union for members. ECOSUR had a scientist working on carbon capture in forest issues, and there was the desire to use the mechanism of carbon capture payments in such a way that it could contribute to campesino well-being, maintain or preserve the ecosystem services of the rural landscape, and provide carbon capture as well. The carbon capture element was to be added to *Pajal Yakaktik's* portfolio of things it did for its membership.

6. Other conclusions address the changes in the general objective of the projects from community well-being and economic development in the early years to a more narrow focus on the banking function of the projects, and from a weak administration of the trust fund and brokering organization—the *Fondo Bioclimatico*—to a strong administration in terms of monitoring and assessing the climate projects (Nelson and de Jong 2003).

7. Carbon Capture and Environmental Services Projects: Who and What Do They Serve? Panel I and II. Society for Applied Anthropology annual meetings, March 17–21, 2009, Santa Fe, New Mexico.

8. Although outside the scope of this chapter, a significant conceptual and theoretical contribution of anthropologists both inside and outside of academia has been the reframing of the debate over the genesis and meaning of the "tragedy of the commons." Led by insights and research from anthropology, with plenty of interdisciplinary dialogue, the original tragedy of the commons has been drastically redefined over a 20-year span, beginning with McCay and Acheson's 1987 classic, *The Question of the Commons.*

References

Asquith, N. M., M. T. Vargas Rios, and J. Smith
    2002 Can Forest-protection Carbon Projects Improve Rural Livelihoods? Analysis of the Noel Kempff Mercado Climate Action Project, Bolivia. *Mitigation and Adaptation Strategies for Global Climate Change* 7(4):323–37.
Bond, Patrick
    2007 Privatisation of the Air Turns Lethal: Carbon Trading as a Non-Solution to Climate Change. Presentation at Dartmouth College, New Hampshire, November 13–14. Available at: http://www.nu.ac.za/ccs/files/Bond%20climate%20change%20paper.pdf. Accessed November 8, 2007.

Brown, K., and E. Cobera
2003 Exploring Equity and Sustainable Development in the New Carbon Economy. *Climate Policy* 3(S1):41–56.

Castro, R., F. Tattenbach, L. Gamez, and N. Olson
2000 The Costa Rican Experience with Market Instruments to Mitigate Climate Change and Conserve Biodiversity. *Environmental Monitoring and Assessment* 61:75–92.

Charnley, Susan
2008 The Role of Rural Communities in Climate Change Mitigation in the U.S.: Policies and Practices. Paper presented at the annual meeting of the American Anthropological Association, San Francisco, California, November 19–23.

Charnley, Susan, and David Diaz
2009 Mitigating Climate Change through Small-scale Forestry in the U.S.: Forest Management Practices and Market Opportunities. *In* Seeing the Forest Beyond the Trees: New Possibilities and Expectations for Products and Services from Small-scale Forestry, K. B. Piatek, B. D. Spong, S. Harrison, and D. W. McGill, eds. Proceedings of the 2009 IUFRO 3.08 Small-scale Forestry Symposium. June 2009, Morgantown, WV: West Virginia University, Division of Forestry and Natural Resources.

Checker, Melissa
2008 Carbon Offsets: More Harm than Good? Pulse of the Planet. Counterpunch. Available at: http://www.counterpunch.org/checker 08272008.html. Accessed September 11, 2009.

Chernela, Janet, Susan Crate, Brandon Derman, et al.
2010 Documenting COP-15: Modes of Participation and Knowledge Flows. *Anthropology News* 51(4):21–22.

Clay, Patricia, and Julia Olson
2007 Defining Fishing Communities: Issues in Theory and Practice. *In* Anthropology and Fisheries Management in the United States: Methodology for Research. Pp. 27–41. NAPA Bulletin 28. Washington, D.C.: American Anthropological Association.

Colson, Elizabeth
2003 Forced Migration and the Anthropological Response. *Journal of Refugee Studies* 16(1):1–18.

Crate, Susan A.
2008 Gone the Bull of Winter? Grappling with the Cultural Implications of and Anthropology's Role(s) in Global Climate Change. *Current Anthropology* 49(4):569–95.

Crate, Susan A., and Mark Nuttall (eds.)
2009 Anthropology and Climate Change: From Encounters to Actions. Walnut Creek, CA: Left Coast Press.

Diamond, Jared
2005 Collapse: How Societies Choose to Fail or Succeed. New York: Viking.

Environmental Defense Fund (EDF)
2008 The Anthropologist: Steve Schwartzman. Fighting Global Warming by Slowing Tropical Deforestation. EDF Publications Archive. Available at: http://www.edf.org/article.cfm?contentID = 7652. Accessed February 15, 2010.

Ervin, Alexander M.
2000 Applied Anthropology: Tools and Perspectives for Contemporary Practice. Boston: Allyn & Bacon.

Escobar, Arturo
1995 Encountering Development: The Making and Unmaking of the Third World. Princeton, NJ: Princeton University Press.

Fahrenthold, David A.
2008 There's a Gold Mine in Environmental Guilt: Carbon-offset Sales Brisk Despite Financial Crisis. Washington Post, October 6, 2008, p. A01.

Finan, Timothy J., C. T. West, T. Maguire, and D. Austin
2002 Processes of Adaptation to Climate Variability: A Case Study from the U.S. Southwest. *Climate Research* 21:299–310.

Fiske, Shirley J.
1990 Resource Management as People Management: Anthropology and Renewable Resources. *Renewable Resources Journal* 8(4):16–20.
1999 The Value of Ground Truth. *In* Common Ground: Archaeology and Ethnography in the Public Interest. Washington, D.C.: National Park Service.
2008 Working for the Federal Government: Anthropology Careers. *In* Careers in Applied Anthropology: Advice from Practitioners and Academics, Carla Guerron Montero, ed. National Association for the Practice of Anthropology Bulletin 29:110–30. Washington, D.C.: American Anthropological Association.
2009a Global Change Policymaking from Inside the Beltway: Engaging Anthropology. *In* Anthropology and Climate Change: From Encounters to Actions, Susan A. Crate and Mark Nuttall, eds. Pp. 277–91. Walnut Creek, CA: Left Coast Press.
2009b Domesticating Carbon Offsets. Paper presented at the Annual Meeting of the Society for Applied Anthropology, Santa Fe, NM, March 17–21, 2009.
2011 Anthropology's Voice in the Public Policy Process. *Anthropology News* 54(4):17.

Friedman, Jonathan
2003a Globalization, Dis-integration, Re-organization: The Transformation of Violence. *In* Globalization, Violence, and the State, Jonathan Friedman, ed. Pp.1–34. Walnut Creek, CA: AltaMira Press.
2003b Globalizing Languages: Ideologies and Realities of the Contemporary Global System. *American Anthropologist* 105(4):744–52.

Galvin, Kathleen A., Jim Ellis, Robin S. Reid, et al.
2007 Fragmentation in Semi-Arid and Arid Landscapes: Consequences for Human and Natural Landscapes. NY: Springer Press.

Government Accountability Office (GAO)
2008 Carbon Offsets. The U.S. Voluntary Market is Growing, but Quality Assurance Poses Challenges for Market Participants. August. Washington, D.C.: GAO-08-1048.

Greenberg, James B., and Thomas K. Park
1994 Political Ecology. *Political Ecology* 1:1–12.

Gutierrez, Maria
2007 All That Is Air Turns Solid: The Creation of a Market for Sinks under the Kyoto Protocol on Climate Change. Ph.D. dissertation, City College of New York.

Hill, Carole E., and Marietta L. Baba
2006 What's in the Name "Applied Anthropology"? An Encounter with Global Practice. *In* The Globalization of Anthropology. National Association for the Practice of Anthropology Bulletin 25:178–207. Washington, D.C.: American Anthropological Association.

Igoe, James
2008 Environmental Anthropology and Neoliberal Conservation. *Anthropology News* January:49–50.

Johnston, Barbara Rose, and Holly M. Barker
2008 Consequential Damages of Nuclear War: The Rongelap Report. Walnut Creek, CA: Left Coast Press.

Kottak, Conrad
1999 The New Ecological Anthropology. *American Anthropologist* 101(1):23–55.

Krupnik, I., and D. Jolly
2002 The Earth is Faster Now: Indigenous Observation on Arctic Environmental Change. Fairbanks, Alaska: Arcus (Arctic Research Consortium of the U.S.).

Marino, Elizabeth
2009 Losing Ground: Understanding Environmental Relocations and the Struggle for Local Control. Paper presented at the 2009 Annual Meeting of the Society for Applied Anthropology, Santa Fe, New Mexico, March 17–21, 2009.

McAfee, K., and E. N. Shapiro
2010 Payments for Ecosystem Services in Mexico: Nature, Neoliberalism, Social Movements, and the State. *Annals of the Association of American Geographers* 100(3):579–99.

McGovern, Thomas H., Orri Vésteinsson, Adolf Fridriksson, et al.
2007 Landscapes of Settlement in Northern Iceland: Historical Ecology of Human Impact and Climate Fluctuation on the Millennial Scale. *American Anthropologist* 109(1):27–51.

Nader, Laura
    1974 Up the Anthropologist—Perspectives Gained from Studying
    Up. *In* Reinventing Anthropology, Dell Hymes, ed. Pp. 284–311.
    New York: Random House. Vintage Books Edition.
Nash, June C.
    2007 Practicing Anthropology in a Globalizing World: An Anthropological
    Odyssey. Lanham, MD: AltaMira Press.
Nelson, Donald R., Colin Thor West, and Timothy J. Finan
    2009 Introduction to "In Focus: Global Change and Adaptation in Local
    Places." *American Anthropologist* 111(3):271–74.
Nelson, Kristen C., and Ben H. J. de Jong
    2003 Making Global Initiatives Local Realities: Carbon Mitigation
    Projects in Chiapas, Mexico. *Global Environmental Change* 13:19–30.
Netting, Robert McC.
    1986 Cultural Ecology. Long Grove, IL: Waveland Press.
    1993 Smallholders, Householders: Farm Families and the Ecology of
    Intensive, Sustainable Agriculture. Palo Alto, CA: Stanford University
    Press.
Paladino, Stephanie
    2008a An On-the-Ground View of Carbon Capture for Smallholders:
    Transformation, Exploitation, Mitigation, or None of the Above? Paper
    presented at the Annual Meeting of the Society for Applied Anthropology,
    Santa Fe, New Mexico, March 17–21, 2009.
    2008b The Social and Economic Impacts of Campesino Adoption of
    Agroforestry Systems for Carbon Capture—Case Study of Participants in
    Scolel Te', Chiapas, Mexico. El Colegio de la Frontera Sur (ECOSUR),
    San Cristóbal de las Casas, Chiapas, Mexico and Consejo Nacional de
    Ciencia y Tecnología (CONACYT), Mexico City. Internal Report.
    2009 Farming Carbon in Mexico: Can Carbon Agroforestry Projects
    Support Rural Development? (unpublished manuscript in preparation)
Parker, Larry, and Brent D. Yacobucci
    2007 Greenhouse Gas Reduction: Cap-and-Trade Bills in the 110th
    Congress. RL 33846. Washington, D.C.: Congressional Research Service.
Peacock, James L.
    1997 The Future of Anthropology. *American Anthropologist* 99(1):9–17.
Perez, Carlos A., Carla Roncoli, Constance Neely, and Jean L. Steiner
    2007 Can Carbon Sequestration Markets Benefit Low-income Producers
    in Semi-arid Africa? Potentials and Challenges. *Agricultural Systems*
    94(1):2–12.
Perkins, John
    2004 Confessions of an Economic Hit Man. NY: Penguin Group. A
    Plume Book.
Pollnac, Richard B., Susan Abbott-Jamieson, Courtland Smith, et al.
    2008 Toward a Model for Fisheries Social Impact Assessment. *Marine
    Fisheries Review* 2006(68):1-4–1-18.

Roncoli, Carla
2006 Ethnographic and Participatory Approaches to Research on Farmers' Responses to Climate Predictions. *Climate Research* 33:81–99.
Roncoli, Carla, K. Ingram, P. Kirshen, and C. Jost
2003 Meteorological Meanings: Understandings of Seasonal Rainfall Forecasts by Farmers of Burkina Faso. *In* Weather, Climate and Culture, S. Strauss and B. Orlove, eds. Pp. 181–202. Oxford: Berg.
Roncoli, Carla, C. Jost, C. Perez, et al.
2007 Carbon Sequestration from Common Property Resources: Lessons from Community-based Sustainable Pasture Management in North-Central Mali. *Agricultural Systems* 94:97–109.
Roncoli, Carla, Todd Crane, and Ben Orlove
2009 Fielding Climate Change in Cultural Anthropology. *In* Anthropology and Climate Change, Susan A. Crate and Mark Nuttall, eds. Pp. 87–115. Walnut Creek, CA: Left Coast Press.
Rylko-Bauer, Barbara, Merrill Singer, and John van Willigen
2006 Reclaiming Applied Anthropology: Its Past, Present, and Future. *American Anthropologist* 108(1):178–90.
Schwede, Laurel, Rae Lesser Blumberg, and Anna Y. Chan (eds.)
2005 Complex Ethnic Households in America. Lanham, MD: Rowman and Littlefield Publishers, Inc.
Scudder, Thayer
1973 The Human Ecology of Big Projects: River Basin Development and Resettlement. *Annual Review of Anthropology* 2:45–55.
1993 Development Induced Relocation and Development Studies: 37 Years of Change and Continuity among Zambia's Gwembe Tonga. *Journal of Refugee Studies* 6(2):123–52.
Shapiro, Elizabeth
2009 But How Will They Harvest It? Barriers to Participation in the International Carbon Market by Rural Communities in Mexico. Paper presented at the Annual Meeting of the Society for Applied Anthropology, Santa Fe, NM, March 17–21, 2009.
Steward, Julian
1955 Theory of Culture Change: The Methodology of Multilinear Evolution. Urbana, IL: University of Illinois Press.
Stiglitz, Joseph E.
2003 Globalization and its Discontents. New York: W. W. Norton & Company.
Stonich, Susan C., and Billie R. DeWalt
1996 The Political Ecology of Deforestation in Honduras. *In* Tropical Deforestation: The Human Dimension, Leslie E. Sponsel, Thomas N. Headland, and Robert C. Bailey, eds. Pp. 187–215. New York: Columbia University Press.
Strauss, Sarah, and Benjamin S. Orlove (eds.)
2003 Weather, Climate Culture. Oxford: Berg.

The George Wright Forum

2009a Traditional Cultural Properties: Putting Concept into Practice. *GWS Journal of Parks, Protected Areas & Cultural Sites* 26(1).

2009b Ethnography in the National Park Service. *GWS Journal of Parks, Protected Areas & Cultural Sites* 26(3).

Tschakert, Petra

2004 The Costs of Soil Carbon Sequestration: An Economic Analysis for Small-scale Farming Systems in Senegal. *Agricultural Systems* 81:227–53.

2007 Environmental Services and Poverty Reduction: Options for Smallholders in the Sahel. *Agricultural Systems* 94:75–86.

Vásquez-León, Marcela

2009 Hispanic Farmers and Farmworkers: Social Networks, Institutional Exclusion, and Climate Vulnerability in Southeastern Arizona. *American Anthropologist* 111(3):289–301.

Wulff, Robert M., and Shirley J. Fiske (eds.)

1987 Anthropological Praxis: Translating Knowledge into Action. Boulder, CO: Westview Press.

6

Aging and Transnational Immigration

Madelyn Iris

Introduction

For more than a decade, globalization has been a hot topic in the popular press, focused mostly on the effects of internationalization of commercial markets and local economies (Stiglitz 2003), environmental challenges (Friedman 2008), and technology and communications (Friedman 2007). One important dimension of globalization concerns the consequences for immigration and the ways in which family life and social systems are altered in the aftermath of transnational relocation. Transnational immigration refers to relocation that crosses national boundaries, whether permanently or temporarily, as opposed to internal immigration, such as urbanization within one's native land. Transnational immigration has a new importance in understanding the effects of relocation on refugees and immigrants, as well as on those who remain behind, given the rapid expansion of technologies that break down historic obstacles to international communication. As we witnessed during the revolutionary uprisings of 2011 in Tunisia, Egypt, and Libya, communication platforms such as Twitter, Skype, and Facebook challenge us to find new ways of thinking about what it means to be a "citizen" and to live within a demarcated geographic space, or what Copeland-Carson, Butler, and Wasson (this volume) call a "global locality."

Appadurai (1996) coined the term "ethnoscapes" to talk about the shifting world in which people live, a world comprising an ever-changing set of actors and landscapes. Such changes have a particular effect on the lives of families, where, as Appadurai (1996) notes, children may move before older generations, traditional or usual patterns of economic exchange and reciprocation of both material and immaterial support are interrupted or totally abandoned, and cultural mores and practices related to marriage, habitation, and socialization may be profoundly altered. All these factors are active in the current circumstance of global integration of economic markets and especially in the concomitant movements of people and accompanying transformation of lifeways.

Gardner (1995) asserts that by the late twentieth century, migration had become a prominent characteristic of life, such that geographic mobility is now the norm rather than the exception. She discusses the transformative impact of migration, and the reinvention and redefinition of self that results from shifting personal and social boundaries (see Fry 2005; Phillipson 2007; Walker 2005). The impact of such transformation and accompanying reinvention and redefinition is potentially vast. According to Torres, "the emergence of transnational communities is likely to challenge the manner in which we think about culture" (Torres 2006:232). In particular, globalization has made irrelevant the notion of culture as embedded within the practices and lifeways of persons living within bounded, geographic settings or "fixed localities." This is due largely to the primacy of the Internet and other electronic mechanisms for instant, multisensory information sharing.

In addition to information or knowledge sharing, the last decades have seen an explosion in "people-sharing" as well because of unprecedented numbers of transnational immigrants and refugees (Martin and Taylor 2001). This phenomenon is worldwide, but has been especially marked in the United States. Aday (2001) documents a steady increase in documented immigrants and refugees, whereby between the 1960s and the 1990s, there was a more than 100 percent increase in numbers, from 3,321,700 to 7,605,077 (Aday 2001:52). The Pew Hispanic Center notes that more recent trends indicate a spike in immigration in the first years of the past decade (2000–2001) followed by a decline back to a level akin to that of the 1990s, with a small spike in 2004 (Passel and Suro 2005). Internationally, United Nations (UN) data indicate that the percentage of all international migrants increased from 150 million to 214 million between 2000 and 2008 (International Organization for Migration 2011).

The study of immigration constitutes its own field of inquiry, but one factor especially relevant for this chapter and its focus on aging is that immigration is a potentially disruptive event in the overall life course experience and can have great impact and grave consequences for how older adults live out their years in new or shifting environments (Gorospe 2006). Whereas relocation and the resulting disjunction of social space were once features that permanently altered the ways in which family members interacted across space and time, we increasingly see that immigrants are redefining the patterns and forms of social and family structures. Torres notes that this challenges us to rethink culture's impact on the experience of growing old, "because if the fixed locality of culture is no longer tangible, neither are, for example, assumptions regarding cultural differences about the way in which old age is conceived and experienced" (Torres 2006:232). According to Baars, "migrating workers or asylum seekers and their families will inevitably age and develop ambivalent patterns of integration and disintegration, both with the new country of residence and their origins. Multicultural aging is the complicated result of international migration" (Baars 2006:19). Crystal (2006) describes events that shape late-life outcomes include occupational and labor-force participation histories, health changes, marriage, divorce, widowhood, etc. Immigration, in a sense, "forces" individuals to experience these major life course events in an unfamiliar, sometimes misunderstood, and potentially even hostile context (see also Estes and Phillipson 2002).

Immigration also provokes a disruption or at least disjuncture in the anticipated life course that can be particularly stressful for older immigrants (Gelfand 1989). The ethnographic literature is replete with reports that illustrate this point: Yee (1997) recounts the experiences of Southeast Asian elders who fled Vietnam, Cambodia, and Laos in the months and years after the end of the Vietnam War and the rise of the Khmer Rouge in Cambodia; Hegland and Associates (2009) describe the sadness experienced by Muslim Iranians in California as they struggle with the emotional aftermath of relocation; and Martinez (2009) writes about Cuban elders who are "aging in exile."

In this chapter I explore issues related to relocation, immigration, and evolving family structures as they relate to older adults. I examine the ways in which globalization and immigration, along with greater opportunities for maintaining transnational identities, have influenced the position of older adults within their familial and larger social systems, and how these factors have created new perceptions of what aging means for these individuals within the context of their social support networks. I focus on older immigrants and refugees in the United States, using examples from my own ethnographic and applied work and older adults living in a highly diverse urban area.

As an applied anthropologist, my approach in both research and evaluation studies has been to examine the aging process and its effects by drawing upon the experiences of older adults in their own words, and to then provide a contextualizing framework for these experiences that accounts for multiple, interacting layers of influence, from the level of the individual to the family, neighborhood, community, and larger social and political-economic system. The intimacy of the ethnographic encounter allows for the development of trust between anthropologist and older adult, leading to the potential revelation of positive as well as negative experiences and relationships within and across these multiple levels. Because older adults, particularly those with some degree of physical and/or cognitive impairment, are more likely to withhold negative information, this trust is extremely important in elucidating all aspects of their lives; the good, the not-so-good, and the outright bad. In addition, open-ended interviewing allows participants to tell their stories according to their unique experiential frame. This "focused reminiscence-like" experience reinforces the value of their lives, and is often perceived as validating and confirmatory.

I started my career working on an ethnographic evaluation to learn about how a parent/child drop-in program in Chicago benefited parents of children from birth to age three, and in what ways. At the time, using qualitative methods in evaluation was a relatively new practice; as we explored this methodology, I was contacted by a multiagency project designed to provide guardianship services to low-income older adults through cross-agency collaborations. I was hired to conduct an "impact" evaluation that would supplement the more traditional, quantitative evaluation that monitored and tracked service costs. This was my first introduction to the field of gerontology, and it caught my interest.

At the conclusion of the guardianship project, I went on to work as a qualitative evaluation specialist on several other age-related studies, particularly within the subfields of guardianship and elder abuse. Eventually, I joined the faculty at the Buehler Center on Aging at the Feinberg School of Medicine at Northwestern University, where I worked for 16 years. However, my passion was always with applied research in collaboration with community-based organizations. In 2005 I joined CJE SeniorLife in Chicago, a large multiservice organization, as Director of the Leonard Schanfield Research Institute. My focus now is on program evaluation, the development and testing of new service models, and the generation of new knowledge about the aging experience that can help guide policy and practice. Through this work I have been privileged to work with older adults from many different cultural and ethnic backgrounds.

This chapter examines aging and globalization at the micro-level of local communities and individuals. The examples are drawn from ethnographic and other research with individuals from the former Soviet Union, Cuba, Korea, and other countries, and were chosen to highlight the changing nature of older adults' relationships with their families and communities as well as altered expectations of aging in their new social settings. A case study describes a mutual aid association located in a multiethnic community on the north side of Chicago that serves immigrants and refugees from numerous countries and thus represents the "global" neighborhood as a new demographic reality. In the conclusion, I discuss the potential effects of macro-level forces such as neoliberalism on the lives of older immigrants and refugees (for a detailed discussion of neoliberal ideology, see Passmore, this volume).

An Anthropological Perspective on Aging and Globalization

In his preface to the latest edition of *The Cultural Context of Aging*, Sokolovsky (2009) comments that aging as a focal area of study was long neglected in anthropology, despite the fact that many anthropologists conducting fieldwork worked with elders as primary cultural interpreters (see also Ikels and Beall 2001). Yet the experience of aging, as a topic in itself, was rarely of interest to these researchers (see Cohen [1994] for counter-arguments). In the last 30 years or more there has been significant growth in the numbers of anthropologists who study aging from a subdisciplinary perspective, supported by the establishment of the Association of Anthropology and Gerontology in 1978, and the *Journal of Cross-Cultural Gerontology* in 1986 (Ikels and Beall 2001). Sokolovsky's edited volume provides an impressive compilation of work at the intersection of anthropology and gerontology, from both academic as well as applied perspectives. Issues related to globalization are addressed, either through comparative cross-national studies or by including studies of elders in various communities and societies around the world.

The area of particular interest for this chapter is the aging experience for immigrants and refugees (Ikels and Beall 2001). Given the aging of the world's population overall and projections that by 2050 as many 20 to 25 percent of people will be 60 years of age or older (Weinberger 2007), attention to the issues of growing old, as a topic in itself and with regard to how such societal aging affects traditional as well as emergent customs, beliefs, and practices in local communities, will become imperative in any ethnographic setting.

The authors in Sokolovsky's edited volume (2009), as well as other publications in the anthropological literature (e.g., Becker and Beyene 1999; Wong et al. 2006) provide diverse examples of the ways in which anthropology and its focus on emic understandings of individuals' cognitive constructions of their social worlds can be used to explore how the aging experience is played out among those who, in a sense, live a bicultural existence, either explicitly or de facto. Some older adults are acutely aware of the push and pull of living with competing value systems, languages, cultural practices, and even the conduct of everyday personal and instrumental functions (i.e., bathing, cooking, cleaning, money management). Others may not be able to specifically point to or describe the underlying causes or sources of such tensions or conflicts, especially when physical disability or cognitive impairment limits personal agency, but the effects of such stresses are demonstrated in their medical, psychological, and emotional conditions.

Around the world, whether in developed or developing nations, expansion of the aging population (i.e., those 65 and older) is attracting more and more attention (Mukherjee 2008; Wegman 2006). In European nations, there has already been a marked growth in the percentage of elders, such that by 1995, 20 percent of the population was already 60 years of age or older (Hayward and Zhang 2001). By 2050, the world's population aged 60 and older will hit the 21 percent range; in Western and Southern Europe, the percentage is expected to rise to 31 percent, or about every one in three persons will be 60 or older.

In the United States, for the next 30 years or so, we expect to see a burgeoning older population, as the Baby Boomers turn 65. Hence, by 2050, demographers project that 27 percent of the population will be 60 or older (Hayward and Zhang 2001), and access to programmatic and financial entitlements are anticipated to produce significant challenges to those social institutions created to ensure the health and economic security of older adults, particularly Social Security and Medicare (Hayward and Zhang 2001).

Regardless of location, the expansion of the older segment of the population comes from three primary forces: first, more people are surviving to achieve older age; second, life expectancy is increasing, especially after age 70 (Serow 2001); third, low fertility results in fewer births to offset the expansion of the older population (Hayward and Zhang 2001; Weinberger 2007). In nonwestern nations in particular, outmigration of younger adults also contributes to local pockets of elder-dominated communities (Barker 1994), which are sometimes split between the older generation and the young children left in their care (Ice et al. 2008).

Migration and immigration of both younger and older adults lends an added dimension to the already complicated portrayal of an aging world population. In the past, it was most common for the oldest generation to remain in place while younger family members moved across continents, often without any expectation that they would be able to remain in contact or to return. My own paternal grandfather and his numerous siblings left Lithuania at the end of the nineteenth century to escape religious persecution and seek opportunities for economic success; they never returned and never saw their parents again. Today, however, using the United States as an example, older adults are becoming increasing global due to temporary relocation or permanent immigration. Leach (2008–2009) reports that the number of foreign-born people in the United States who are 65 years of age or older has grown in raw numbers from 2.7 million in 1990 to 4.3 million in 2006, although there has been no change as a percentage of the total foreign-born population, which remains at approximately 11 percent. This is equal to 8 percent of all older adults in the United States, which now constitutes approximately 13 to 14 percent of the total U.S. population. Furthermore, Leach notes that estimates project a quadrupling of the size of the older adult immigrant population by 2050.

This burgeoning population group has also become more diverse. The older immigrant population in the United States has been dominated by growing numbers of older Mexicans and Chinese immigrants (about 25 percent of the group overall). During the last half of the twentieth century, there has also been a substantial influx of refugee elders, including those from southeast Asia, the former Soviet Union, Cuba, El Salvador, Bosnia, and, more recently, Iraq and Burma. Although individually these groups are small, when combined, they contribute to the increasingly multicultural face of older America.

Older immigrants and refugees in particular are often at a serious economic and social disadvantage. In the United States, 21 percent of non-citizens who are 65 and older live at or below the federal poverty line, compared with 9.9 percent of native-born Americans and 11.9 percent of naturalized citizens. More specifically, Porter and Malkin (2005) report that there were an estimated 710,000 Mexicans 60 and older living in the United States, a figure 63 percent higher than 10 years earlier, and that about 25 percent of these immigrants lived below the poverty line compared with 10 percent of the overall U.S. population aged 65 and older. Wilson (2001) notes that older migrants are highly disadvantaged in most countries (see also Walker 2005).

Globalization and Aging

These facts open the door to a number of concerns about the effects of globalization on older individuals and their well-being. According to Mukherjee (2008), even as globalization has led to improvements in quality of life, such as better housing, increased income, and greater availability of basic health care in at least some developing nations, none of these factors has prepared these nations to meet the new challenges associated with population aging (see also Wegman 2006; Wilson 2001). Most countries in the developing world do not have the social and economic support systems necessary to serve elderly people (e.g., some form of social security or pension as well as auxiliary community support services programs), and hence both the economic status and social position of older persons are likely to grow more dire as young adults relocate to urban centers within their own countries, or to western European and American nations, in search of greater economic opportunities. Mukherjee describes the situation in India as illustrative of this point. He writes, "the incipient social impact of globalization has led to disintegration of social protections for the elderly, which had been traditionally provided by the family and kinship networks because of cultural norms, religious values, and economic expediencies" (Mukherjee 2008:21). Lamb (2009) provides resonant ethnographic vignettes of the impact of globalization on elders in India, either directly due to their own immigration experiences, or indirectly as a result of their children's movements. In fact, because the vast majority of elderly persons (70 percent overall, and 85 percent female) are economically dependent on their children and other relatives, the government enacted the Hindu Adoption and Maintenance Act in 1956 to ensure protections for elderly parents (and other disabled persons) in the absence of a state-managed program (Mukherjee 2008) and in 2006 passed a law called "The Senior Citizens (Maintenance, Protection and Welfare) Bill" (Lamb 2009).

On the broader international stage, the International Plan of Action on Ageing 2002 (United Nations Programme on Ageing) cites a number of factors that can marginalize older people from the mainstream of development, thereby diminishing their purposeful economic and social roles and weakening traditional forms of support. These factors include migration; urbanization; the shift from extended to smaller, mobile families; lack of access to technology that promotes independence; and other socioeconomic changes.

Discussions of globalization generally focus on economic systems, supply chains, electronic and other communications, and development policies promulgated by large multinational organizations such as the World Bank and the International Monetary Fund (Sidorenko 2007; Stiglitz 2003). Most examine globalization and its effects on nation-states at the macro-level of analysis. But understanding the effects of globalization on older adults in particular requires an exploration of the interactions between micro- and macro-level factors. Baars et al. write, "[An adequate understanding of human aging] requires a recognition of how social forces operate at the macrolevel to shape the microlevel of everyday experience" (Baars et al. 2006:5). Anthropology is a discipline particularly well-suited to studying the ways in which macro-level policies and programs affect individual lives because of its focus on the "voice" of the individual and its effort to provide a rich contextual framework for examining local, or micro-level, impact. The anthropological perspective combines analysis of variations with the search for shared patterns of human behavior, including the intersection of belief systems, material culture, and sociopolitical practices. From these analyses, anthropologists are able to derive holistic understandings of sociocultural systems.

For the study of aging, this perspective drives the examination and explication of the ways in which group members (defined by the purposes of the examination) produce and describe behaviors as normative models of practice. These models can be interpreted as physical or material representations of underlying beliefs about the meaning and expectations of old age. At the macro-levels of analysis, local and national sociopolitical systems that support the elderly may be evaluated within the same type of framework.

Twentieth-century health and social policies around the world have had a significant influence on the lives of older adults and have also, directly or indirectly, affected elders' relationships with family and community. Recent attitudinal shifts in expectations regarding normative behaviors and the social context of growing old have generated a new model of aging that, while emphasizing strengths, may serve to marginalize those older adults whose physical and mental health status prohibits them from achieving the new social norms. The unique perspective of anthropology brings to light the ways in which aging is experienced within such larger cultural frames, and analyses such as those presented here help explain how we define aging to begin with, as well as how globalization and neoliberalism have recently affected these ideas (and related institutions). Some brief examples of these processes are provided here, followed by more in-depth case studies.

The evolution of the welfare state, defined here as "free access to fundamental social benefits" (Hastrup 2007), is one of the earliest examples of how social policy addressed individual needs at the local or micro-level of experience throughout Europe and in the United States. Over time, this ideology led to significant changes in the ways that societies as well as individuals perceived of and defined their responsibilities for care of the aged and, concomitantly, generated new expectations about socioeconomic entitlements. Walker describes the welfare state in Europe as emerging out of a concern for the well-being of older adults, noting "old age was acknowledged collectively as a risk status from the early part of the last century" (Walker 2006:61). This concern led to the implementation of a comprehensive old-age pension system that came to define old age itself. The linking of old age and social policy began when Bismarck initiated a public pension system in Germany in 1889, setting the age of eligibility at 65. This was followed by the start of similar programs in Great Britain in 1908 and France in 1910 (Walker 2006). The age of 65 became so widely accepted as representing the onset of old age that it became institutionalized as the chronologic delimiter of old age.[1] In the United States, Social Security was not established until 1935 as part of Franklin D. Roosevelt's New Deal, and was intended to keep older adults out of dire poverty. Although Social Security includes a number of programs that benefit more than just older adults (e.g., survivor benefits for children), it is the retirement benefit that is best known. In 1965, the U.S. Congress enacted Medicare, an "old age" entitlement intended to improve the health conditions of the elderly.

While these entitlement programs have been highly effective in reducing poverty among older people and in opening up access to health care for acute conditions (as well as some preventive care), they also led to socially and politically constructed images of older adults as dependent, frail, passive, and disengaged from larger social contexts, particularly the labor market (see Walker 2006). In addition, such programs shifted responsibility for support of elders from the family to the state, fostering the further displacement of elders from their central roles in family life to more peripheral and marginalized positions on the edges of family and community networks, a movement that began during the industrial revolution and continued in response to urbanization.

There are numerous examples of the social and structural effects of these processes. For example, subsidized senior housing with on-site service coordinators enables older adults with low incomes to live independently of their children and to need less day-to-day support from them compared with what they might receive if they were living together. Hence, instead of sharing family meals, now many frail elders receive home-delivered meals that they consume alone. Medicaid, the health insurance program for the indigent, also covers the cost of nursing home care for elders who qualify, shifting responsibility from family and community to a state-regulated institutional setting. In addition, Medicaid waivers fund in-home services such as homemakers and personal care providers for elders who would otherwise have to move to a long-term care facility or share housing with family members or others. Access to these publically funded services further supplants the traditional roles historically fulfilled by family members by reducing the need for assistance with various daily activities of life such as transportation, shopping, and bathing.

Social Security, Medicare, and Medicaid, as products of a "welfare state" ideology, helped stabilize the economic, social, and health status of older adults; Older Americans Act programs (instituted in 1965) provided a national infrastructure for psychological and social supports for older adults. These programs continue to be the three-legged stool upon which the U.S. response to aging rests. But in the context of severe economic stress combined with a neoliberal ideology, these entitlements and programs have come under significant threat of cutbacks, limitations on eligibility, or even elimination. These threats are supported or given credence by a shift in the public image of what it means to be old. The perception of old age as a period of decline, increasing need, and disengagement has been challenged by the promulgation of a new normative model, supported by macro-level ideology. The paradigm of "successful aging" popularized in last decade of the twentieth century has direct implications for the micro-level experience. Broadly speaking, successful aging posits "the expectation that later life can be a time of sustained health and vitality" (Moody 2009:68). Rowe and Kahn (1997) define successful aging as multidimensional, encompassing the avoidance of disease and disability, the maintenance of high physical and cognitive function, and sustained engagement in social and productive activities.

Moody (2009) notes that Rowe and Kahn include within this the ability to cope with normal changes related to chronological aging, called "decrement with compensation," meaning that individuals who age successfully demonstrate the ability to adjust and adapt to expected age-related changes, including illness and decline.

The successful aging paradigm challenges the portrayal of the elderly as frail, dependent, and needy, and promotes an image of older adults as financially secure, vigorous, healthy (due to medical innovations), and even sexually active. This new normative image lends credibility to the neoliberal threat to sustained support for older adults via social welfare programs. Polivka and Longino (2006) quote Gilleard and Higgs (2000), who write, "individuals themselves should take responsibility for achieving and maintaining health, wealth and well-being throughout their adult life. This perspective views later life as the culmination, or final reckoning, of how well such responsibilities have been exercised" (Gilleard and Higgs 2000:63).

The successful aging paradigm is not without its critics, who see it as stigmatizing those who are most in need, the frail and/or poor elderly, while favoring those who are affluent, fit, and socially engaged (Holstein and Minkler 2003). At worst, the model focuses on physical and mental health outcomes and supports neoliberal positions that "blame the victim" without recognizing the impact of continuous disadvantage across the life course, including lifelong health disparities and their cumulative effects over the life course (see Polivka and Longino 2006). It also fails to account for biological, physical, and cognitive changes associated with "normal aging," such as metabolic alterations, loss of muscle mass, and slowing of memory retrieval.

Importantly, the successful aging paradigm is blind to ethnic and cultural differences in goals and values regarding aging. Older immigrants and refugees, who may have suffered trauma as well as years of deprivation with little to no access to preventative health care, are at particular risk when confronted with the dominance of the successful aging paradigm. Given their poor economic status, inability to fully integrate into the majority culture due to language barriers, and high levels of psychological distress, they often fail to adapt to the predominant American values of independence, individualism, and autonomy. As one example, these factors can have significant influence on how well older refugees from the former Yugoslavia have been able to meet the demands of the successful aging paradigm, as it is well documented that Bosnian refugees have a high level of post-traumatic stress disorder, exacerbated by lack of English language skills (Vojvoda et al. 2008). Similarly, older refugees from countries within the former Soviet Union suffer higher rates of depression compared to U.S. norms (Miller and Chandler 2002) as well as somatization and demoralization (Kohn et al. 1989). Older refugees from Vietnam may show long-term effects of prearrival traumatic experiences with a higher risk of depression, even up to 18 months after immigration (Hinton et al. 1997).

Globalization can affect one's potential to achieve a "good old age" by putting significant pressure on an individual's ability to adapt and adjust, and by endangering the collective social transfers essential to elders in later life (Wilson 2001:121). The movement toward global neoliberalism has altered attitudes toward old-age support programs throughout the developed nations, and has weakened the traditional "safety net" of social and economic support programs. Characterizing globalization as a "destabilizing force in the lives of older people," Phillipson writes, "globalization has also played an influential role in the production of new forms of risk associated with the privatization of social policy" (Phillipson 2006:47). Especially important as a theoretical justification for neoliberal policies is the redefinition of the goals of aging at the individual and societal level, as well as culturally proscribed beliefs about old-age expectations, including the marketing of "successful" aging in the United States and the promotion of independence as the highest moral value.

Since my focus is on elderly immigrants (and refugees), one important consequence of neoliberal policies is the collapse of public support for the safety net and the disparities that result, especially for those elders who were not able to establish a secure future on their own prior to relocation to the United States. Wilson (2001) describes the "three pillars" of support for the elderly: work, family, and formal collective institutions. Globalization affects all three of these pillars as it changes the nature of work, dislocates families, and poses threats to the formal collective institutions. Wilson states, "the discourse that sees older people as an enormous and potentially uncontrollable burden on health systems, combined with the global financial bias against public expenditure, is a long-term threat to services for elders even in developed countries. In the developing world the outlook is worse" (Wilson 2001:127).

Case Examples: Older Immigrants and Refugees in Transnational Contexts

Learning more about how older immigrants adapt and adjust to their changing circumstances and environments is a critical step in the policy and service planning process. Various aspects of globalization have made this more complicated. For example, as described earlier, requirements that frail elders be citizens to be eligible for health services or financial supports (such as Medicaid and Supplemental Security Income [SSI]) raises the risk of poor or even catastrophic health outcomes. Moves toward privatization in both the social and health sector and proposals to transform Social Security and Medicare into a private sector programs threaten all older adults with vulnerabilities, but may be especially challenging for older immigrants and refugees who lack knowledge of such systems as well as the skills required to master them (Estes and Phillipson 2002).

Torres (2006) points out that transnationalism raises challenges to policy-making directed at programs and services for older adults, particularly when such policies directly affect the well-being and status of older immigrants and refugees. Because elderly immigrants and refugees in particular may lack a secure foundation upon which to build for old age, attention must be given to the cultural, historical, and social factors that have a direct influence on the aging process.

For example, lack of a work history in the United States usually precludes noncitizen immigrants from receiving Social Security benefits. Noncitizens are also not eligible for Medicaid and SSI unless they enter the United States with refugee status; even then, there are time limits for eligibility. Very often, elderly immigrants and refugees have no pension programs in their native countries, so their economic dependency is severe. In addition, when they are eligible for social support programs, these elders may have difficulty obtaining benefits due to language barriers or lack of cultural sensitivity on the part of service providers.

Practices such as the requirement that applicants disclose personal information as part of an assessment process may keep some of these elders from obtaining help. For example, in Illinois, the Community Care Program provides in-home services to low-income older adults who are at risk of nursing home placement. The program requires a detailed financial disclosure, and the comprehensive assessment instrument that determines need and intensity of service delves deeply into psychosocial and emotional status as well as health history and family relationships to identify other potential sources of support. Not only are the questions intrusive, but for persons from different cultural backgrounds and with nonmainstream familial values, they may not even be interpretable or translatable, especially for those with limited English proficiency.

In addition, many elderly immigrants and refugees are also struck by the loss of traditional roles and models for what it means to be old. Although this is a more "existential" than material issue, it remains a major obstacle to adjustment and adaptation to new environments and practices, and the meaning of the aging experience itself is subject to reinterpretation and renegotiation. Torres notes "old age, therefore, concerns the way in which elderly transnational migrants 'negotiate' the meanings they attach to the experience of aging when growing into old age takes place while being both Here-and-There and when both Either-Or applies" (Torres 2006:240). The dual constructs of Here-and-There and Either-Or directly reflect the struggle to maintain continuity of self across the life course. This is not an "out of awareness" experience: older immigrants and refugees often have a great deal of insight into this struggle, and their solutions are evident in their words and in their behaviors. Although this struggle is not unique to today's older immigrants and refugees, what is different is that it occurs within the context of a globalized world with almost instant, ongoing communication with individuals who reside not only in the homeland, but around the globe.

In the following examples I draw upon my own ethnographic and applied research studies to illustrate how older immigrants and refugees themselves talk about the struggle to create a balance between Here-and-There and Either-Or, and highlight some of the ways in which they achieve success. The first two examples are taken from the final report of the Qualitative Study of Aging in Chicago (Iris and Berman 1992), a three-year ethnographic investigation of aging in an urban environment. The project was funded by the Chicago Community Trust, which was seeking information to guide rethinking of funding priorities, fostering a shift from a "deficit" model of aging in which older adults as a sector of the population defined by chronological age alone were portrayed as socially and financially vulnerable as well as at risk for negative health outcomes. The social norm was that elders were unable to serve as their own advocates, a view that led to a complex structure of federal and local policies and programs for supportive services, known as "the aging net-work." A new set of social norms viewed older adults as vital contributors to community life, somewhat in line with the emerging dominance of the successful aging paradigm. This shift prompted the Trust to undertake a large-scale project to investigate how this new paradigm played out in the reality of people's lives. The purpose of our study was to explore, via multiple in-depth interviews, what aging meant to a group of 50 adults, aged 55 and older, and how they saw themselves growing older within their local community contexts. Immigrants from Ukraine, Lithuania, and Korea, who came to the United States for economic and familial pur-poses in the second half of the twentieth century, constituted one subset of participants. During the interviews there were repeated references to the differences these immigrants encountered in their own aging experi-ences compared with what they had anticipated based on the aging of their older relatives prior to emigration. In addition, I include examples from subsequent studies that involved older adults from Mexico, China, India, and the former Soviet Union. Although none of these studies focused on aging and immigration specifically, the effects of immigra-tion on family and social support systems and on the well-being of the older participants are undeniable and permeated almost all conversations, regardless of topic. As noted earlier, the changeable nature of the fixed locality of culture (as experienced by older immigrants and refugees) challenges assumptions about cultural differences and the ways in which old age is conceptualized and experienced (Torres 2006).

Elena Barreras[2] was one of the participants in the Qualitative Study of Aging in Chicago project. She came to Chicago around the time of Fidel Castro's rise to power in Cuba. In Cuba, she and her mother owned a small "trinket" store, but after arriving in the United States she did not work again. She and her husband lived on the near west side of Chicago in a subsidized senior housing building. They were well looked after by their daughter and grandchildren, who would accompany them whenever they left their apartment. Because Mrs. Barreras did not speak English, she tended to socialize only with other residents in her neighborhood who were Latina/o, although not Cuban. Thus, her social life was quite circumscribed, and she was not able, nor did she wish, to engage with the larger community in which she lived.

Mrs. Barreras spoke of how growing old in the U.S. was different from what her life would have been like in Cuba, as in the United States, "old people are very alone." Her primary coping strategy was to seek to maintain continuity with her previous life by adhering to a lifestyle that replicated that of her mother and grandmother in Cuba. She told stories about how her own mother and grandmother had aged in Cuba, and how she wished to grow old as they did. To achieve this, she dressed in very conservative clothing, commenting that she would never think of wearing short sleeve or sleeveless dresses. She disparaged those older women in her building who she thought dressed in this risqué fashion. She resisted acculturation and was generally successful in creating a comfortable life for herself that was at least partially congruent with her life-long expectations for a good old age. Her efforts bound her to a cultural environment she had long left behind, but through her constancy she was able to transcend, at least cognitively, both geographic and temporal distances. In this way she produced and maintained a consistent although limited "ethnoscape" of her own.

Two Korean women also interviewed during the Aging in Chicago project told a somewhat different story. At the time they were interviewed, they were both living in subsidized senior housing buildings on the north side of Chicago, in or near an area often referred to as Little Korea. Now in their mid-70s, both had come to the United States to provide care for grandchildren. However, once the grandchildren were older, these women moved out of their children's suburban homes and into their own apartments in Chicago. Their familial relationships became more tenuous and less supportive, especially in comparison with Mrs. Barreras'. One woman,

Sun Dong Jung, commented on the ways in which Americanization was affecting the next generation of Korean-Americans. She said, "when I first came here, that's when there weren't that many Korean people around. They were being really nice to old people.... But this second generation, who are completely Americanized, cannot understand the Korean way to treat senior citizens" (Iris and Berman 1995:188). This is a telling example of the dislocation experienced by these older Korean women, who had expected to spend their days living with their sons and daughters-in-law. These women came to the United States to provide support, but they lost that vital role as well as consistent familial connections when the grandchildren grew up. Hence, they became doubly displaced.

The circumstances of these two Korean women provide ethnographic evidence of theoretical constructs such as role loss and dislocation, and the reconfiguring of cultural values. In addition, their dependency on governmental programs, such as subsidized housing and senior centers, gives life to the earlier discussion of the importance of the welfare state in providing material and social support previously viewed as family responsibilities.

More positively, in the community where they now lived there were many Korean-owned businesses, including restaurants and grocery stores. There was also a Korean senior center nearby that Mrs. Jung attended almost every day. As Mrs. Jung Rahn Kim said, "English is not necessary to live around here. You don't need it that much" (Iris and Berman 1995:121). This is akin to Mrs. Barreras' experience in her neighborhood, with its wide variety of Latino-owned businesses and large population of Spanish-speaking residents. These two "global-local" enclaves exemplify how connections to cultural practices, language, and tradition are sustained and provide cognitive continuity despite geographic distance.

Although these two examples do not seem overtly related to issues of globalization, they in fact illustrate how social policies and practices (such as the provision of subsidized housing for low-income older adults) offer supports that enable immigrant elders to maintain themselves and even thrive, despite the disruption of the immigration experience. However, the emergence and rapid growth of a new "transnational reality" has threatened this social safety net by dismantling the security offered via the "global-local" enclave. For example, Chicago's "Little Korea" community underwent significant demographic shifts between 1990 and 2000, resulting in greater ethnic as well as racial diversity. During this decade, the Asian population dropped from 23.2 percent to 17.7 percent, and the enclave model was challenged by an influx of multiple immigrant and refugee groups in this formerly heavily Korean neighborhood such that by 2000, almost half the population was Hispanic, compared with only 31.8 percent in 1990 (the time of our study). There was also substantial growth in the Arab-American population, which is not captured in census statistics. Demographic changes were also seen on the near west side of Chicago, where Mrs. Barerras lived. In 1990, 62 percent of the population was Hispanic/Latino; however, by 2000, this percentage had dropped to just 46.9 percent, while the white, non-Hispanic population rose from 27.5 percent to 39.4 percent (Chicago Fact Finder 2009).

Refugees from the former Soviet Union present a different and somewhat unique example of older immigrants and their expectations. These highly educated immigrants came to the United States within a relatively limited span of years (late 1970s through the 1990s) via an international effort to "free" them from Soviet religious oppression and discrimination. As refugees, they qualified for government supports like Medicaid and SSI. Approximately 400,000 refugees from this region came to the United States over a period of about 25 years (United Jewish Communities 2009). Jewish communal organizations in major cities throughout the United States geared up to absorb them, and provided numerous types of aid both publically and privately funded, including housing, education, and social networking.

I had the opportunity work with a group of these refugees on a study I was conducting called "Beliefs About Alzheimer's Disease: Cultural and Social Factors" (Schrauf and Iris 2011). The project investigated conceptualizations of Alzheimer's disease, aging, and memory loss in three population groups: Mexican-Americans, African-Americans, and refugees from the former Soviet Union. During their interviews, the Russian-speaking refugees compared their lives in the United States with what they might have experienced had they remained in their homelands, such as the Ukraine and Russia. One participant, Eugene Egorov, made some very astute comments. He said, "they (the refugees) are getting older in different circumstances and the approaches of these people to ideas of getting old are different,"[3] and later added, "in the Russian-speaking community, people are becoming old early and much quicker because many of the immigrants experience stresses and depression… and easily accumulate a negative attitude…they are isolated, depressed, unsatisfied."

The theme of isolation was also seen in comments about relationships with family members. Mr. Egorov noted, "after immigration, the distance between the old and young generation becomes much greater…and finally the (older) person starts to recognize that he/she is abandoned and feels unneeded." Katrina Litovsky elaborated on this theme: "it's not very comfortable for the (Russian) elderly here, because they are taken out of their native environments… Language, new laws, broken connections with people." These statements speak to a life course experience that virtually precludes successful aging. They provide ethnographic support for arguments that advocate for the maintenance of public programs that foster socialization and mental health interventions.

As a counterpoint, some participants felt that the United States offered benefits they would not have experienced in the former Soviet Union, including a longer and more secure life. Arthur Andropov elaborated, "You know, in our homeland, the age 70 is extreme old age.... In our homeland the image of old people, at age 70, is the image of feeble people, people...in poverty, in need." One woman, Marta Alexandropov, said, "I remember our lives in Russia...living in one big family was just horrible for elder members." Mr. Andropov commented that in the United States there is more support for elders, more respect, and overall they enjoy a better life. He said, "...many have the great support of their children and friends and I think that the elderly here are healthier emotionally and physically.... They live longer and better."

One particular area where life has changed for these older refugees is interdependency. Several participants noted that while refugees from the former Soviet Union still maintained tightly knit families, "Russian immigrants are used to a much more interdependent family and expect much more in-depth interaction." But in the United States, although families remain close-knit, much of the interdependence is lost because elders live in their own apartments, often in the city, while their children live in the far suburbs. Like the participants from previous studies, instead of daily assistance from family members, these elders now rely on social service agencies for help with housekeeping, transportation, translation, and for socialization opportunities. Similarly, despite significant linguistic and cultural barriers vis-a-vis the larger community, refugees from the former Soviet Union appear able to maintain somewhat strong social networks comprising other older Russian refugees due to public policies and local contextual factors. For example, as refugees, they were given priority status for placement in subsidized senior housing, which resulted in small, highly local enclaves of Russian-speaking seniors and allowed for the maintenance of Russian-speaking social networks. Because many of these buildings are concentrated in contiguous neighborhoods, a critical mass of refugees from the former Soviet Union evolved that supported local Russian-speaking businesses and other institutions such as social centers and a synagogue. In addition, a variety of services and language-specific resources were developed by the Jewish community to provide health care, supportive services, and socialization opportunities.

These examples illustrate the ways in which the larger social and political context interacts with characteristics of the immigration experience itself to affect outcomes for individual refugees and immigrants. Those who emigrate alone, or with their nuclear family members, may lose the advantages of a preexisting cultural and social context into which they can be absorbed. Those who come as part of a large-scale migration may at least have the advantage of a solid social support system to stand upon. While the mass emigration of Jewish refugees from the former Soviet Union was somewhat unique in that it was accompanied by a massive mobilization of the Jewish communities in the United States, other groups, such as Cambodians, Vietnamese, and now Iraqis and Somalis, do have refugee resettlement agencies to which they can turn for assistance. One example from my work in community-based participatory research illustrates this point.

In this last example, I move from micro-level perspectives to a more macro-level effect, and describe a mediating institution that eases the tension between the individual experience of the immigrant/refugee and the larger societal institutions that shape such experiences. In the fall of 2008, I began working with the Chinese Mutual Aid Association (CMAA), a multiservice nonprofit organization operating out of a double storefront in what is commonly called the New Chinatown area of Chicago. This area is a neighborhood within the larger community of Uptown. Uptown covers approximately 3.5 square miles and has a total population of close to 64,000 people, of whom about half are non-Hispanic white. The remainder is composed primarily of African Americans, Asians, and Latinos (Encyclopedia of Chicago 2009). According to the 2000 U.S. Census, 33 percent of residents were foreign-born; 56 percent of these residents arrived in the 1990s (Encyclopedia of Chicago 2009), making Uptown one of the most culturally diverse communities in Chicago. Just over 11 percent of Uptown residents were 65 years of age or older, just slightly higher than the overall percentage of older adults in Chicago. Furthermore, more than 15 percent of persons 65 and older were living below the federal poverty level in 2000 (Chicago Fact Finder 2009), whereas 25 percent of all residents were at this level or below.

Beginning in the 1960s, Uptown became a "port of entry" for migrants from Appalachia as well as significant numbers of Native Americans. It also became a preferred area for the placement of hundreds of persons with mental illness, who were relocated from large residential mental health facilities under a policy of "deinstitutionalization" that emphasized a return to the community and residence in the least restricted environment. Large homes were subdivided into apartments, and numerous single-room occupancy hotels emerged in the area. Combined with the presence of a number of public housing buildings for both families and seniors, Uptown became an ideal location for resettlement of older refugees and immigrants who needed access to subsidized and below-market rate housing. Federal resettlement policies and the practices of local resettlement agencies led to higher proportions of newer refugees in the Uptown area compared with other communities in the city of

Chicago because of lower rental rates and the advantages of colocating refugees. This created a cycle of resettlement in which more immigrants and refugees sought out residence in this general area, driving an increase in the presence of food stores that carry specific products for particular populations as well as multilingual health clinics and ethnic-specific social service organizations, thereby making the community even more attractive for newly arrived immigrants and refugees.

My project, funded by the Community-Engaged Research Center at Northwestern University, was designed to assist the CMAA in moving forward on the creation of a standalone multicultural senior center, combined with a health survey to determine the baseline status of older clients at the agency. CMAA was established in 1981 by a group of ethnic Chinese refugees from Vietnam. Its mission is to "serve the needs, promote the interests, and enhance the well-being of Chinese and other immigrations and refugees in the Chicago area, and to foster their participation in and assimilation into American society" (CMAA 2009). CMAA now serves more than 13,000 children and adults each year through a wide variety of services, including after-school programming, benefits and legal aid assistance, and English language and citizenship classes. Senior services include a "golden age" club that has approximately 300 members, mostly Chinese, as well as state-funded homemaker services with Mandarin- or Cantonese-speaking aides, benefits assistance, health screenings, companion services, and counseling for older victims of domestic violence and other crimes. Besides ethnic Chinese, CMAA senior programs also assist Korean elders, and there are English as a Second Language classes specifically for Russians. In addition, CMAA houses the Bosnian-Herzogovenian American Community Center, which offers similar services to its target population, although there was only one staff member at the time of our collaboration. One of the important services she provides is support groups for older refugees, most of whom suffer from post-traumatic stress disorder. In all, there are more than 28 different languages and dialects spoken at CMAA, and the Executive Director reported that he is expecting to adapt their services to accommodate new refugees from Somalia, Burma, and Iraq. Hence, CMAA is an excellent example of the global character of the community it serves, as its constituency moves toward greater multiculturalism.

CMAA's older adult population is also transnational. In contrast to previous immigrant experiences, where it was assumed that once one had emigrated they were highly unlikely to return to their homeland (due to political or religious persecution), many of the seniors who come to CMAA now make annual trips back to their homeland, often staying for several months at a time. For example, we were advised to postpone our focus groups with older Bosnian women because so many had returned to Bosnia for the summer. Similarly, it is not uncommon for refugees from the former Soviet Union to now make visits back to their homelands, something that was unexpected prior to the collapse of the Soviet Union in 1990–1991. The seniors who attend CMAA programs are almost all immigrants and refugees who come together for socialization, information, and support in a nonthreatening environment that feels like "home" to them. In a survey completed by 124 participants at the center, we found that 63.4 percent lived alone or with a spouse, whereas only 30 percent lived with their children. In addition, 26.3 percent lived in subsidized housing. Their dependence on the organization is evidenced by the finding that when asked who or where they would go first if they needed help, 66 percent of the 124 respondents to the survey indicated they would go to the agency, despite the fact that 95 percent of the respondents had one or more children (Iris 2010). Within its walls they can speak their own language, practice their own cultural traditions, and share experiences with people who are living through the same situations. In addition, they also have the opportunity to learn about the lives and cultures of other older adults who have had the same experience of living in a second culture. In talking with these seniors about their vision of a multicultural senior center, they spoke of the desire to learn more about each other, including sharing food and celebrating cultural or religious holidays together (e.g., the Chinese August Moon and New Year's celebrations, songs, and dances). In the globalized setting proposed by CMAA, they found there was much to be gained.

To understand the larger programmatic and policy context affecting CMAA's effort to create a multicultural senior center, I drew upon anthropological theories regarding social networks and reciprocity, and helped the organization convene a meeting of representatives from other local organizations that served the ethnic elderly, as well as community leaders who could influence local policy and planning activities. The meeting was positioned as a first step in the process of building support for the new center and ensuring buy-in from community stakeholders through engagement and a sense of shared ownership, at least conceptually. Unfortunately, the economic downturn prohibited CMAA from moving forward with plans to acquire a property appropriate for the center; at the time of this writing, alternatives sources of funding were being explored.

Conclusions

The examples and case study described here were selected to illustrate the various ways in which older immigrants and refugees wrestle with the need to adapt to new geographic as well as cultural contexts, in particular via accommodation to increasing diversity and potential options for a cognitive as well as physical multilocality. Because it is increasingly easier to take advantage of opportunities to remain connected to social networks and cultural settings around the world, it has become possible for older people to "straddle" the real as well as imagined geographic divide that in the past would have been experienced as an impermeable barrier. Acceptance of technological innovations such as e-mail, Facebook, Skype, Twitter, etc., and the global proliferation of cellular phone service has made communication with family and friends still in their countries of origin, or dispersed throughout the world, quicker, cheaper, and easier to maintain, thereby fostering and sustaining linkages between the "here and there" of older immigrants' lives.

For example, several years ago I interviewed a Chinese woman who lived in a subsidized senior housing building in Philadelphia. She had come to the United States approximately 16 years earlier to be near her sister and brother; one son and his family followed soon after and settled in Alabama. Another son and several grandchildren remained in China. She "spoke" with both her sons and their children via e-mail and instant messaging, and anticipated "seeing" them once her sons arranged for webcams to be installed. She also followed news about China by reading online newspapers in Chinese. Another interviewee, an older gentleman from Russia, wrote regular emails to his friends in St. Petersburg as well as those who had migrated to Israel, and followed sports and politics by downloading a daily newspaper in Russian. He was as familiar with what was happening in these geographically disparate settings as he was with what was going on in the community in which he now lived.

Stories such as these illustrate how immigration is no longer a one-way street. Immigrants have the ability to establish lifestyles that are both "here-and-there" as well as "both," rather than "either-or." This includes personal contacts as well as connections with larger social functions and institutions such as politics and sports. They have become truly global in their outlook and in their practice. This is particularly so for the vast numbers of those who immigrate to the United States at an older age, at a time when they are unlikely to become self-sufficient or fully independent in their new geographic and social settings (Leach 2008–2009).

As demonstrated by the ethnographic examples presented here, globalization has a potentially disproportionate effect on the elderly, not only because of economic impacts, but also due to disruption in the anticipated norms of the life course model and associated challenges to the traditional roles, values, and expectations of aging. At the same time, globalization, as experienced via new communications systems in particular, can help to lessen the negative impacts of such disruption. The processes of adaptation, adjustment, and integration are complex, and often appear somewhat contradictory. For example, as the stories presented here illustrate, many immigrant and refugee elders feel disengaged from their families and disconnected from familiar cultural models of aging and old age; yet, at the same time, they feel they have a better life in their new setting. Globalization can help to ease their transitions.

However, neoliberalism, so closely associated with economic globalization, may have a hugely negative effect on the elderly overall, but especially on immigrant elders, if movements toward privatization succeed, particularly with regards to Medicare and Social Security. Elders have few options for economic growth or recovery, particularly when limited by chronic health problems and lack of English language skills. Dismantling the economic safety net, whether this means direct benefits or programmatic supports, could leave these elders in dire need.

As an applied anthropologist, I have drawn upon the methodological tools of the discipline (structured and unstructured interviewing, participant observation, surveys, network analysis, cognitive modeling and consensus analysis, and rapid assessment strategies) to help inform program planners and policy makers as they sought to address the needs of immigrant elders. For example, at CMAA, my work responded to the question, "How do we create a multicultural senior center that honors and respects the diverse cultures of the participants all within one setting?" To answer this question, I conducted focus groups with seniors who were active in the Golden Age Club and elicited their thoughts about what such a center should look like and what it should do. Similar discussions were conducted by staff members with Russian speakers and Bosnians. My analysis of the data provided CMAA leadership with a synthesis of opinions as well as information about how the physical space could be designed.

Work of this type contributes to the development of a new paradigm for examining what it means to grow old as an elderly immigrant or refugee. Rather than focusing on characteristics that differentiate such elders, such as ethnicity and/or language, it is now more meaningful to think about the ways in which such individuals coexist in common spaces that allow them to transcend difference and focus on what is shared. As Copeland-Carson, Butler, and Wasson note in the introduction to this volume, "People living in a locality move in a wide array of differing realms that overlap in multiple ways, are often dependent on one another, and are not cognitively recognized as distinct either by those who live in them or those who observe them." This argues against a reductionist model of culture and aging that looks at factors such as ethnicity and language as determinant characteristics.

The examples and case study presented in this chapter lend empirical evidence to support the familiar (though often unheeded) assertion that older immigrants constitute a heterogeneous population, whose experiences related to relocation are affected by a variety of factors, including the circumstances of immigration (e.g., whether they migrate as refugees or immigrants); the cultural mores they carry over from their countries of origin relating to family integration and support; the adjustments they are expected to make in their new homes (acculturation or enclave-building); and the resources available to help them in this adjustment. Anthropological theories and methods as they relate to both the explication of values and shared belief systems, as well as the interpretation of these in real-life settings, contribute to our understanding of the differing ways in which older immigrants and refugees manage relocation and how they maintain and validate their conceptualizations of what it means to grow older in a global, multicultural world.

The work of applied anthropology as manifested in real-life settings and contexts has helped program planners, policy makers, and direct service providers better understand the role and place of older adults in their adopted communities, and has elucidated the challenges these elders face as they adapt and adjust to the new social settings, social mores, and evolving, altered relationships within their families, neighborhoods, and the larger community described here. In particular, information about adjustment capacity and culturally appropriate older adult services and service delivery models can be invaluable in creating supportive environments that are flexible enough to incorporate the heterogeneity of cultural practices and lifeways that characterize older immigrants and refugees. The anthropological perspective helps elucidate the deeper-level contingencies and connections that draw people together to create and define social interactions within a specific context or situational framework, such as an encounter between an older immigrant from China and an older refugee from Moscow. In addition, the use of ethnographic methods in applied research studies contributes to a more sophisticated, nuanced, and multidimensional approach to aging that can inform and influence both policy and practice.

Notes

1. Given that the age of eligibility for full Social Security benefits is rising, depending on year of birth, it will be interesting to see if this alters perceptions of the onset of old age, particularly among younger persons. Even now, many older adults believe that old age is not chronologic, but rather is integrally tied to overall health status and outlook.

2. All the personal names used in the examples are pseudonyms. All of the studies from which these examples are drawn were approved by the Northwestern University Institutional Review Board (IRB) or the

CJE SeniorLife IRB. Funding for the various projects was provided by the Chicago Community Trust, the Alzheimer's Association, and the Northwestern University Community Engaged Research Center. My thanks to Rebecca Berman, Ph.D., my long-time partner in research, and to the numerous research assistants who helped conduct the interviews. I also thank the many, many older adults who volunteered to participate in these studies, and were so willing to share their stories.

3. Quotations from this study come from transcripts and have not been published elsewhere. Therefore, no citations on source are provided.

References

Aday, Lu Ann
    2001 At Risk in America: The Health and Health Care Needs of Vulnerable Populations in the United States. Second edition. San Francisco: Jossey-Bass.
Appadurai, Arjun
    1996 Disjuncture and Difference in the Global Cultural Economy. *In* Modernity at Large: Cultural Dimensions of Globalization. Pp. 27–47. Minneapolis: University of Minnesota Press.
Baars, Jan
    2006 Beyond Neomodernism, Antimodernism, and Postmodernism: Basic Categories for Contemporary Critical Gerontology. *In* Aging, Globalization and Inequality: The New Critical Gerontology, Jan Baars, Dale Dannefer, Chris Phillipso, and Alan Walker, eds. Pp. 17–42. Amityville, NY: Baywood Publishing Co.
Baars, Jan, Dale Dannefer, Chris Phillipson, and Alan Walker
    2006 Introduction: Critical Perspectives in Social Gerontology. *In* Aging, Globalization and Inequality: The New Critical Gerontology, Jan Baars, Dale Dannefer, Chris Phillipson, and Alan Walker, eds. Pp. 1–14. Amityville, NY: Baywood Publishing Co.
Barker, Judith
    1994 Home Alone: The Effects of Out-Migration on Niuean Elders' Living Arrangements and Social Support. *Pacific Studies* 17(3):41–81.
Becker, Gay, and Yewoubdar Beyene
    1999 Narratives of Age and Uprootedness among Older Cambodian Refugees. *Journal of Aging Studies* 13(3):295–314.
Chicago Fact Finder
    2009 Chicago Facts. Available at: www3.nd.exu/~chifacts. Accessed June 21, 2009, and June 26, 2011.
Chinese Mutual Aid Association (CMAA)
    2009 Mission. Available at: www.chinesemutulaid.org/mission. Accessed June 21, 2009.

Cohen, Lawrence
 1994 Old Age: Cultural and Critical Perspectives. *Annual Review of Anthropology* 23:137–58.

Crystal, Stephen
 2006 Dynamics of Late-Life Inequality: Modeling the Interplay of Health Disparities, Economic Resources, and Public Policies. *In* Aging, Globalization and Inequality: The New Critical Gerontology, Jan Baars, Dale Dannefer, Chris Phillipson, and Alan Walker, eds. Pp. 205–13. Amityville, NY: Baywood Publishing Co.

Encyclopedia of Chicago
 2009 Uptown. Available at http://www.encyclopedia.chicagohistory. org./pages/1293.html. Accessed June 21, 2009.

Estes, Carroll L., and Chris Phillipson
 2002 The Globalization of Capital, the Welfare State, and Old Age Policy. *International Journal of Health Services* 32(2):279–97.

Friedman, Thomas
 2007 The World is Flat: A Brief History of the Twenty-First Century. New York: Farrar, Strauss, and Giroux.
 2008 Hot, Flat and Crowded: Why We Need a Green Revolution—And How It Can Renew America. New York: Farrar, Straus and Giroux.

Fry, Christine
 2005 Globalization and the Experiences of Aging. *In* Aging Education in a Global Context, Dena Shenk and Lisa Groger, eds. Pp. 9–22. New York: Haworth Press.

Gardner, Katy
 1995 Global Migrants, Local Lives: Travel and Transformation in Rural Bangladesh. Oxford: Clarendon Press.

Gelfand, Donald
 1989 Immigration, Aging, and Intergenerational Relationships. *The Gerontologist* 29(3):366–72.

Gilleard, Chris, and Paul Higgs
 2000 Cultures of Aging: Self, Citizen and the Body. New York: Prentice Hall.

Gorospe, Emmanuel
 2006 Elderly Immigrants: Emerging Challenge for the U.S. Healthcare System. *The Internet Journal of Healthcare Administration* 4(1). Available at: http://www.ispub.com/ostia/index.php?xmlFilePath=journals/ijhca/vol4n1/elderly.xml. Accessed February 18, 2011.

Hastrup, Bjarne
 2007 Healthy Aging in Denmark? *In* Global Health and Global Aging, Mary Robinson, William Novelli, Clarence Pearson, and Laurie Norris, eds. Pp. 71–84. San Francisco: Jossey-Bass.

Hayward, Mark, and Zhenmei Zhang
 2001 Demography and Aging: A Century of Global Change, 1950–2050. *In* Handbook of Aging and the Social Sciences, fifth

edition, R. H. Binstock and L. K. George, eds. Pp. 70–85. San Diego: Academic Press.

Hegland, Mary Elaine, and Associates
2009 Losing, Using and Crafting Spaces for Aging: Muslim Iranian American Seniors in California's Santa Clara Valley. *In* The Cultural Context of Aging: Worldwide Perspectives, third edition, J. Sokolovsky, ed. Pp. 302–24. Westport, CT: Praeger.

Hinton, W. Ladson, Quyen Tiet, Carolee GiaouyenTran, and Margaret Chesney
1997 Predictors of Depression among Refugees from Vietnam: A Longitudinal Study of New Arrivals. *Journal of Nervous and Mental Disorders* 185(1):39–45.

Holstein, Martha, and Meredith Minkler
2003 Self, Society and the New Gerontology. *The Gerontologist* 42(6):787–96.

Ice, Gillian, Amy Zidron, and Elizabeth Juma
2008 Health and Health Perceptions among Kenyan Grandparents. *Journal of Cross-Cultural Gerontology* 23(7):111–29.

Ikels, Charlotte, and Cynthia Beall
2001 Age, Aging and Anthropology. *In* Handbook of Aging and the Social Sciences, Robert Binstock and Linda George, eds. Pp. 125–40. New York: Academic Press.

International Organization for Migration (IOM)
2011 About Migration. Available at: http://www.iom.int/jahia/Jahia/about-migration/lang/en. Accessed June 23, 2011.

Iris, Madelyn
2010 Status Report 2010: Health and Social Support of Seniors at Chinese Mutual Aid Association. November 2010. Unpublished manuscript.

Iris, Madelyn, and Rebecca Berman
1992 The Aging in Chicago Project. Paper presented at the Annual Meeting of the American Society on Aging, San Diego, California, March 1992.
1995 Qualitative Study of Aging in Chicago. Final Report. Chicago Community Trust, Chicago, IL.

Kohn, Robert, Joseph Flaherty, and Itzhak Levav
1989 Somatic Symptoms among Old Soviet Immigrants: An Exploratory Study. *International Journal of Social Psychiatry* 35(4):350–60.

Lamb, Sarah
2009 Elder Residences and Outsourced Sons: Remaking Aging in Cosmopolitan India. *In* The Cultural Context of Aging: Worldwide Perspectives, 3rd edition, J. Sokolovsky, ed. Pp. 418–40.Westport, CT: Praeger.

Leach, Mark
2008–2009 America's Older Immigrants: A Profile. *Generations* XXXII(4):34–39.

Martin, Philip, and J. Edward Taylor
2001 Managing Migration: The Role of Economic Policies. *In* Global Migration, Global Refugees: Problems and Solutions, Aristide Zolberg and Peter Benda, eds. Pp. 95–120. New York: Berghahn Books.

Martinez, Iveris
2009 Aging in Exile: Family Support and Emotional Well-Being among Older Cuban Immigrants in the United States. *In* The Cultural Context of Aging: Worldwide Perspectives, 3rd edition, J. Sokolovsky, ed. Pp. 325–45. Westport, CT: Praeger.

Miller, Arlene, and Peggy Chandler
2002 Acculturation, Resilience, and Depression in Midlife Women from the Former Soviet Union. *Nursing Research* 51(1):26–32.

Moody, Harry R.
2009 From Successful Aging to Conscious Aging. *In* The Cultural Context of Aging: Worldwide Perspectives, 3rd edition, J. Sokolovsky, ed. Pp. 67–76. Westport, CT: Praeger.

Mukherjee, Dhrubodhi
2008 Globalization without Social Protection: Challenges for Aging Societies Across Developing Nations. *The Global Studies Journal* 1(3):21–27.

Passel, Jeffrey, and Roberto Suro
2005 Rise, Peak, and Decline: Trends in U.S. Immigration 1992–2004. Washington, D.C.: Pew Hispanic Center.

Phillipson, Chris
2006 Aging and Globalization: Issues for Critical Gerontology and Political Economy. *In* Aging, Globalization and Inequality: The New Critical Gerontology, J. Baars, D. Dannefer, C. Phillipson, and A. Walker, eds. Pp. 43–58. Amityville, NY: Baywood Publishing Co.
2007 The "Elected" and the "Excluded": Sociological Perspectives on the Experience of Place and Community in Old Age. *Aging and Society* 27:321–42.

Polivka, Larry, and Charles Longino, Jr.
2006 The Emerging Postmodern Culture of Aging and Retirement Security. *In* Aging, Globalization and Inequality: The New Critical Gerontology, Jan Baars, Dale Dannefer, Chris Phillipson, and Alan Walker, eds. Pp. 183–204. Amityville, NY: Baywood Publishing Co.

Porter, Eduardo, and Elisa Malkin
2005 Aging Immigrants Could Strain 2 Countries. *International Herald Tribune*, August 14, 2005. Available at: http://www.iht.com/articles/2005/08/03/business/retire.php?page = 2. Accessed July 17, 2011.

Rowe, John, and Robert Kahn
1997 Successful Aging. *The Gerontologist* 37(4):433–40.

Schrauf, Robert, and Madelyn Iris
2011 A Direct Comparison of Popular Models of Normal Memory Loss and Alzheimer's Disease in Samples of African Americans, Mexican

Americans, and Refugees and Immigrants from the Former Soviet Union. *Journal of the American Geriatrics Society* 59(4):628–36.

Serow, William
2001 Economic and Social Implications of Demographic Patterns. *In* Handbook of Aging and the Social Sciences, 5th edition, R. H. Binstock and L. K. George, eds. Pp. 86–102. San Diego: Academic Press.

Sidorenko, Alexandre
2007 World Policies on Aging and the United Nations. *In* Global Health and Global Aging, Mary Robinson, William Novelli, Clarence Pearson, and Norris Laurie, eds. Pp. 3–14. San Francisco: Jossey-Bass.

Sokolovsky, Jay
2009 Preface. *In* The Cultural Context of Aging: Worldwide Perspectives, 3rd edition, J. Sokolovsky, ed. Pp. xiii–xiv. Westport, CT: Praeger.

Stiglitz, Joseph
2003 Globalization and its Discontents. New York: W. W. Norton and Co.

Torres, Sandra
2006 Culture, Migration, Inequality, and "Periphery" in a Globalized World: Challenges for Ethno- and Anthropogerontology [sic]. *In* Aging, Globalization and Inequality: The New Critical Gerontology, J. Baars, D. Dannefer, C. Phillipson, and A. Walker, eds. Pp. 231–44. Amityville, NY: Baywood Publishing Co.

United Jewish Communities
2009 Integrating Jews from the Former Soviet Union into American Jewish Life. Available at: http://www.jfns.org/page.aspx?id = 16773. Accessed June 28, 2009.

United Nations Programme on Ageing
2002 International Plan of Action on Ageing 2002. Global Action on Aging. Available at: www.globalaging.org/waa2/documents/international_plan2002.doc. Accessed July 16, 2011.

Vojvoda, Dolores, Stevan Weine, Thomas McGashan, et al.
2008 Posttraumatic Stress Disorder Symptoms in Bosnian Refugees 3½ Years after Resettlement. *Journal of Rehabilitation Research and Development* 45(3):421–26.

Walker, Alan
2005 Towards an International Political Economy of Ageing. *Aging and Society* 25:815–39.
2006 Reexamining the Political Economy of Aging: Understanding the Structure/Agency Tension. *In* Aging, Globalization and Inequality: The New Critical Gerontology, Jan Baars, Dale Dannefer, Chris Phillipson, and Alan Walker, eds. Pp. 59–80. Amityville, NY: Baywood Publishing Co.

Wegman, David Howe
2006 Aging and Globalization. *Medicina del Lavoro* 97(2):137–42.

Weinberger, Mary Beth
    2007 Population Aging: A Global Overview. *In* Global Health and Global Aging, Mary Robinson, William Novelli, Clarence Pearson, and Laurie Norris, eds. Pp. 15–30. San Francisco, CA: Jossey-Bass.
Wilson, Gail
    2001 Globalisation and Support in Old Age. *Education and Ageing* 16(2):121–34.
Wong, Sabrina, Grace Yoo, and Anita Stewart
    2006 The Changing Meaning of Family Support among Older Chinese and Korean Immigrants. *Journals of Gerontology Series* B 61(1):S4–S9.
Yee, Barbara W. K.
    1997 The Social and Cultural Context of Adaptive Aging by Southeast Asian Elders. *In* The Cultural Context of Aging, 2nd edition, J. Sokolovsky, ed. Pp. 293–303. Westport, CT: Bergin and Garvey.

7

Defining Family: Anthropological Contributions to Practice and Policy in Child Welfare

Susan Racine Passmore

Introduction

Since the economic "meltdown" that began in 2007, there has been a sharp rise in the level of public doubt about the neoliberal policies of deregulation. However, whether other neoliberal values such as the belief in privatization and the general principles of the "ownership society" have seen a similar decline in their popularity is still an open question. Ironically, these values may have even broader implications for defining the relationships between nation and citizen, community and individual. This chapter explores the application of neoliberal principles to an arena of society and policy that has always had an awkward relationship to these ideas: human services in general and child welfare services (CWS) in particular.

I will illustrate, with observations gained through many years of work as a professional consultant in the field and the work of other social scientists, that global neoliberalist ideology has introduced both dramatic and subtle shifts in the seemingly very local concerns of CWS. I will also show that anthropology, applied anthropology, and the scholar-practitioner perspective have distinct contributions to make to the body of knowledge about the impacts of neoliberal ideology in human services. One key contribution has been to show how such ideologies become "standard operating procedure" and how they are spread through an organizational culture. By extension, these same means are potential avenues for contributing to the well-being of children and families from within the system.

Neoliberal Principles from Global to Local

David Harvey (2005) defines neoliberalism as the economic "configuration" of globalization. It is "a theory of political economic practices that proposes that human well-being can best be advanced by liberating individual entrepreneurial freedoms and skills within an institutional framework characterized by strong private property rights, free markets and free trade" (Harvey 2005:2). Many scholars trace the birth of neoliberalism—portrayed as a "rebirth" of the beliefs of Adam Smith and other economists in the liberal tradition—to the policies of Ronald Reagan in the United States and Margaret Thatcher in the United Kingdom. In the United States, neoliberal policies were pursued by the Reagan administration as an expression of a general critique of the "welfare state," and others were extended by the Clinton administration, including the 1996 Welfare Reform Act. The George W. Bush administration is responsible for some unique twists on the theme, and the Obama administration's policies on education and economic stimulus have also been labeled as neoliberal (Platkin 2009). It is important to realize that neoliberalism and the concomitant ideologies are not strictly associated with any particular political party (Harvey 2005).

Some basic principles of neoliberalism include:

1. The rules of the market (competition) will lead to ideal conditions that will result in higher quality and efficiency in all circumstances and situations; the market can create better public services, schools, prisons, retirement savings plans, and military forces.
2. Everyone will benefit in a neoliberal system, as quality, service, and everything positive will increase due to increased efficiency. In addition, everyone will benefit because profits will trickle, theoretically, down to all.
3. Government should have a limited role. For the free market to work, it needs to be truly free. In an ideally neoliberal system, the role of government is to step out of the way of the "natural" flow of capitalism. This is accomplished through divestment or "load shedding," deregulation, and privatization. In particular, governments must stay out of the way of global trade. (Ironically, as Harvey [2005] points out, government actually has an increased role in neoliberal systems, since they support the market in the form of subsidies and, of course, bailouts.)

Any discussion of such an incredibly pervasive system can attend only to small piece of the overarching, and decidedly global, pie. Neoliberalism has become a powerful and global economic and ideological framework that touches many parts of our lives. Just as we can't talk about trade—or information, or popular culture, or climate change—without reference to global forces, we cannot speak of anything but *global* neoliberalism. Indeed, the system depends on trade unrestricted by national boundaries, which in turn creates the need for global acceptance (if not devotion) to neoliberal ideology.

What began in the 1980s with Thatcher and Reagan spread to continental Europe and created widespread reform of the social democratic/welfare state (Bortolotti and Milella 2008). In Eastern Europe, global neoliberalism became the driving ideology behind the transition of the former Soviet bloc (Roland 2008). Neoliberal ideology also drove International Monetary Fund (IMF) and World Bank policies, tied to massive international lending and development programs, and therefore spread throughout the "global south."[1] Nations in Asia, Africa, and Latin America and the Caribbean have responded to IMF pressure to denationalize industries, open markets to international trade, and cut back on social programs (Di Leonardo 2008; Ferguson 2006; Ong 2006; Roland 2008). We see expressions of global neoliberalism everywhere in the form of shrunken state-run utilities and services, withdrawn support of unions (as barriers to the free reign of the market), and the turning back of "welfare state" regulations (Di Leonardo 2008:6).

Neoliberalism in Family Services: The Ownership Society and Privatization

> An ownership society values responsibility, liberty, and property. Individuals are empowered by freeing them from dependence on government handouts and making them owners instead, in control of their own lives and destinies. In the ownership society, patients control their own health care, parents control their own children's education, and workers control their retirement savings (David Boaz, Cato Institute, n.d.).

The "ownership society" is a phrase tied to the administration of George W. Bush, but it has roots that extend back to back to Thatcher (Boaz n.d.) and Reagan (Freundlich and Gerstenzang 2003) and is, in some ways, the foundation of neoliberal perspectives in human services. The concept of the ownership society is one of the ideological pillars that "makes sense" of neoliberalism (Fraser 1993). Key to the ownership society is the importance of civic engagement that encourages communities to organize and solve problems without federal assistance (Hyatt 2001). For example, under the first Bush administration, home ownership for all was a specific goal intended to tie citizens to their communities and, thereby, increase volunteerism and civic responsibility (Office of the Press Secretary 2004).

In practice, however, many analysts believe it contributed substantially to the foreclosure crisis, with the result of heightening alienation.

Ownership also implies that the poor and in-need "own" their problems. Hyatt argues that "in this age of neoliberalism, government is increasingly becoming operationalized through the creation of new kinds of subjects, whose own goals as 'free' individuals become aligned with the state" (Hyatt 2001:212). The neoliberal argument that government is a threat to its own citizens (Kahn and Minnich 2005) supported the dismantling of welfare with the Personal Responsibility and Work Opportunity Reconciliation Act (PRWORA) in 1996 (Piven 1998). Proponents of this reform argued that "big" government in general, and the Aid for Families with Dependent Children (AFDC) program in particular, created dependence and lowered self-efficacy and self-esteem among the poor (Collins 2008; Goldstein 2001; Piven 1998). Once government's role was more limited, the poor and in-need would have the "power" and "freedom" to help themselves. They argued that government should not provide direct services but rather "empower" community organizations, churches, volunteers, and the poor to help themselves (Berger and Neuhaus 1977:7; Hyatt 2001).

The complex privatization of CWS is a natural extension of neoliberal thinking and is the focus of much discussion and reform in the field. CWS include four types of services designed to protect and serve children at risk for abuse and neglect: child protective services (CPS), adoption, foster care, and family preservation services. Each local agency[2] providing CWS provides CPS. CPS receives reports of abuse or neglect and is responsible for investigations and assessments of future risk. If reports are substantiated, a child or children may be removed from the home and be placed in foster care temporarily. Family preservation services help families improve their situations through parenting education, drug treatment, and other types of support so that reunification may be achieved. If abuse, neglect, or the assessed risk of abuse or neglect persists, a termination of parental rights (TPR) may be sought. At that point, the child welfare system is responsible for seeking adoption while supporting the child in foster care. These services are complicated by their interrelated nature as well as by the unique problems and needs of individual families. Another unique and complicating characteristic of CWS is that, although they are designed to serve and support families, they are also potentially punitive.

Privatization in CWS, as in all human services, has had its critics, although no one would argue that the involvement of private organizations in CWS is new. In fact, CWS were originally provided solely by private philanthropic organizations such as the New York Aid Society and the New York Society for the Prevention for Cruelty to Children (Myers 2006). Even after CWS became a public responsibility, discrete services such an adoption placement or foster care homes have been provided by private, nonprofit agencies. The current move to privatization, however, involves two significant shifts: the ideas that all services would be better provided by private agencies, and that private agencies could take over decision making and responsibility for caring for children.

Proponents of privatization in CWS argue that private agencies can move children through faster and reduce workloads (Freundlich and Gerstenzang 2003). Mountjoy (1999:1) suggests that under privatization children will no longer be "lost in the cogs." Others argue that privatization will result in better quality and lower cost of services, reduced government monopoly, increased flexibility and responsiveness, and a reduction in the number of government employees (Freundlich and Gerstenzang 2003). Opponents argue that privatization is potentially corrupting and that contractors can default or go bankrupt, leaving children and families with no access to services. In fact, there has been no clear evidence to support either increased quality or cost efficiency in privatization (Freundlich and Gerstenzang 2003).

Critics also worry about the implications for families. Some worry that corruption is more common in the private sector and might contribute to the victimization of vulnerable populations. There are questions about the professional judgment needed in human services, especially regarding high-risk cases that a private system would inappropriately streamline because of its attention to cost (Freundlich and Gerstenzang 2003). Sullivan (1987) points out that because private agencies, unlike their public counterparts, are not bound to protect citizen's rights, privatization and protection of civil liberties may prove to be mutually exclusive goals. Finally, many critics ask whether cost efficiency is an appropriate goal in social services at all. For example, Blank (2000) suggests that family and other social relationships are inherently "inefficient" and that social workers who take time to form relationships and make informed decisions are equally inefficient but effective.

Despite substantial criticism, privatization is widespread in the field of CWS. A few states, such as Kansas and Florida, have made dramatic reforms; many more have implemented more limited projects. By 2000 McCullough and Schmitt (2000) had found that at least 50 percent of states were planning or had already implemented managed care reforms. By 2010, the Reason Foundation reported that:

> Rather than simply contracting for a subset of specific child welfare services, the trend has also favored transferring case management to the private providers, thus giving them primary decision-making authority over day-to-day case decisions. Child welfare privatization is increasingly defined as the degree to which these essential functions are managed by the private provider versus the public agency (Gilroy et al. 2011:41).

There is also support for neoliberal shifts at the federal level. For example, federal support for privatization is implicit in funded projects such as the National Quality Improvement Center for the Privatization of Child Welfare Services. In addition, Roberts (2008:155) points out that the emphasis on the timely "freeing" of children for adoption rather than on family preservation services under the Adoption and Safe Families Act of 1997 is itself a reflection of neoliberal principles. This policy, she argues, encouraged shortening stays in foster care through concurrent planning[3] and earlier petitions for the termination of parental rights, all of which weakens state responsibility and encourages private families to take on the responsibility of caring for abused and neglected children. Roberts (2008:156) argues that "like welfare policy's promotion of marriage, the reliance on adoption furthers the neoliberal agenda to replace state support for families with private remedies for social and economic inequality."

Although CWS privatization may still be debated, neoliberalist perspectives are now part of "doing business" in CWS both locally and nationally. Given this circumstance, whole-cloth objections to neoliberal thinking in CWS are neither heard nor effective. More helpful approaches are (1) to gain a deeper understanding of why neoliberal ideologies are so accepted even in areas in which they seem to be a "bad fit" and (2) to explore what avenues are available to ameliorate the negative effects of such policies and to strengthen positive outcomes for children and families.

An Anthropological Perspective on Neoliberalism in Human Services

> One of the reasons for the drive for privatization is simple-minded ideology… ungrounded in theory or empirical evidence. But another of the motivations for the drive for privatization is special interests (greed) (Stiglitz 2008:xi).

In the lines quoted above, Stiglitz offers an answer to a particularly difficult question in understanding neoliberalism. Why does the ideology endure? There exists little evidence that neoliberal policies work in many circumstances and contexts—and certainly no evidence that they work in all. Abuses and difficulties attributed to neoliberal shifts are numerous (Harvey 2005; Ong 2006; Stiglitz 2008). Authors such as Harvey (2005) and Ong (2006) have argued convincingly that neoliberalism is inherently contradictory and difficult to coherently support. It is clear that despite the advertised "cost-saving" benefits of privatization, actual transformations of publicly administered services are difficult and expensive to implement and manage (Stiglitz 2008). There are also intrinsic problems associated with managing contracted services of all types, and contracts focus on the achievement of simple outcomes that tend toward the simply measurable rather than the logical. For example, as Stiglitz (2008:xii) points out, success achieved by military contractors in Iraq is not measured by the "winning of hearts and minds" of Iraqis or even military achievements but by minimizing costs. Even more broadly, while privatization has created revenue for some western European governments, neoliberal policies have also led uniformly to increased inequality in family incomes (illustrated by worldwide Gini indices; Stiglitz 2008).

Why, then, does global neoliberalism endure? One could make an argument, as Stiglitz does, that greed plays some role but it has certainly been effectively argued that ideology is a powerful factor as well (Kahn and Minnich 2005; Roland 2008). However, neoliberalist ideology is more than a set of "simple-minded" wrong-headed beliefs held by the powerful. In reality, neoliberal ideology is complex and fluid and embedded in the perspectives of many throughout the world, including the poor and powerless, and relates to many more subjects than economics or politics.

It is in this question of understanding the ideological underpinning of neoliberalism that the field of anthropology offers its most valuable contribution related to the anthropological focus on the local. Ong (2006) made this observation as well, and credited the anthropological connection to ethnography:

> As anthropologists, we are skeptical of grand theories. We pose big questions through the prism of situated ethnographic research on disparate situations of contemporary living...our approach may still be characterized as low-flying, an analytical angle that stays close to discursive and non discursive practices (Ong 2006:13).

Although cognizant of neoliberalism as a global artifact, this "low-flying" perspective of anthropologists provides a unique insight to the understanding of local meanings of global processes including the complexities of neoliberal belief.

Anthropological contributions to the privatization debate have focused on neoliberal reforms in healthcare (Boehm 2005; Lamphere 2005; Rylko-Bauer and Farmer 2002) and welfare (Collins 2008; Fraser 1993; Morgen 2001; Morgen and Wiegt 2001). Like other critics, anthropologists have challenged the assumed cost benefit of privatization (Boehm 2005) and deeply question claims of improved quality of services (Collins 2008; Fraser 1993; Lamphere 2005; Morgen 2001; Morgen and Wiegt 2001; Rylko-Bauer and Farmer 2002), but they have also established that neoliberalism is not reducible to privatization or even a preference for market analogies in policy. Rather, anthropologists have demonstrated neoliberal shifts in meaning in many more arenas of social life.

In the discussion of neoliberalism in the United States, Judith Goode and Jeff Maskovsky's edited volume, *The New Poverty Studies: The*

Ethnography of Power, Politics and Impoverished People in the United States (2001) highlighted research on the impacts of neoliberal policies on American families and the growing gap between the lived experience of the poor and wealthy. Authors such as Williams (2008), Stack (2001), and Hyatt (2001) explored shifts in the economic structure of the financial life of American families caused by increasing consumer debt and the increasing difficulty of "getting ahead." These authors also reported the necessary reshaping of informal and social support networks in response.

Similarly, Micaela Di Leonardo's *New Landscapes of Inequality: Neoliberalism and the Erosion of Democracy in America* (2008) introduced ethnographic evidence of the changing economic context of life in the United States and its impact on sociocultural contexts. In particular, Di Leonardo demonstrated how recent years have brought substantial changes in the "responsibilities" of employers to care for their employees (2008:12). Following the work of Hyatt (2001) and others in the earlier Goode and Maskovsky volume, authors presented new ethnographic evidence of shifting systems of support and related definitions of family and, interestingly, "social services." For example, Roberts (2008) reported a growing dependence of the poor on "punitive" services such as prison and CWS. Similarly, Collins (2008:141–42) reported the necessary manipulation of social services by the working poor to survive in conditions of low pay and shrinking benefits. Another line of observations has followed the transformation of growing economic insecurity into fear and even "suburban panic" in American middle-class communities (Hyatt 2001; Lancaster 2008; Zavella 2001). Overall, contributors to each of these volumes revealed the "on the ground" realities of neoliberalist policies and ideologies.

The anthropological focus on the local provides an insight into how meaning is manipulated and reshaped in response to new realities. For example, Ong (2006:2) connects global shifts in the concepts of citizen, sovereignty, and personhood to the spread of "American neoliberalism." Ong describes how the "ownership society" of the Bush administration reshaped the concept of a "responsible" citizen as individualistic, competitive, and entrepreneurial but still subject to manipulations at the local level. Ong is not alone in this observation. Hyatt (2001) also noted that neoliberal ideology has "produced a series of new technologies designed to reconfigure the relationship between citizen and the state" (Hyatt 2001:205). Similarly, Collins (2008) observed the emergence of a definition of citizenship contingent on involvement in paid work as a byproduct of welfare reform. Others have documented the growing saliency of values such as "self-sufficiency" (Morgen 2001) and "responsibility" (Willging 2005).

The discussion of these shifts has provided valuable insight into neoliberalist ideology "in practice." As Ong (2006) suggested, the anthropological emphasis on the discursive aspects of neoliberal ideology—such as those involving concepts like "self-sufficiency" and "responsibility"—have posed a solution to the question of the creation and reification of neoliberal values. While it may be tempting to see ideas related to the "ownership society" as "top-down" beliefs forced into the collective conscious by politicians, ethnography instead trains the perspective on how people at all levels of the "system" participate in the ongoing process of "making sense" of neoliberalism.

For example, Morgen's (2001), Morgen and Weigt's (2001), and Morgen et al.'s (2010) research on welfare reform provides a unique "grounded" example of neoliberal discourse in practice. Like other researchers, these authors reported the rise of such concepts as "freedom," "power," "self-sufficiency," and "choice" as important concepts in the rhetoric of neoliberalism but also charted the saliency of these concepts for actual social workers dealing with welfare reform in Oregon over the course of more than a decade. In this way, they demonstrated both the process through which these concepts became "part of doing business" in social work, as well as the role individual social workers and supervisors played in the reification of these ideas. Morgen et al. (2010) demonstrated how transformative policies that emphasized neoliberal ideals came to seem good and positive to individual social workers. As the authors suggest, this research relates directly to Lipsky's (1980) assertion that "street-level" bureaucrats are a moving force in the implementation, and therefore, reality, of policy.

For example, Morgen (2001) traced the importance of the concept of "choice" that emerged with welfare reform. It is adopted because the concept "makes sense" and "works" with both ideology and practice.

> The emphasis on choice works in two ways: it portrays the agency as fostering highly cherished values associated with freedom and citizenship, and it absolves the agency of responsibility for what happens to clients who "choose" not to cooperate. This language of choice pervades agency documents and discussions. Administrators, managers, and workers return frequently to the theme of client choice to justify decisions ranging from a client's "choice" not to be in the assessment program (and therefore not to be eligible to collect cash assistance) to the "choice" to go through the disqualification process by not cooperating with agency policies (Morgen 2001:574).

Morgen's ethnographic exploration found that over time social workers grew to accept and in turn use more "ownership society–like" perspectives such as "choice." One caseworker she interviewed, for example, felt that:

> Everybody should be free to choose. There are always consequences for our choices. And the fact that the agency can't support a choice that refuses to move ahead is still respectful to the person.... It's based more on mutual respect and less on the agency being a parent. And the client has more self-respect, more self-esteem and we are not enablers anymore (Morgen 2001:571).

In this case, the concept of choice in social services is connected to the more pervasive value of choice in American society. It "makes sense" on many levels and, in turn, became a nearly unavoidable concept in social services. In the same way, other concepts came to be embedded in practice building a complex discursive system of support for neoliberal perspectives. Morgen et al.'s (2010) research with social workers a decade later revealed the development of a similar, nearly irrefutable value placed on "self-sufficiency" as a social services outcome. For social workers, "self-sufficiency" came to be defined as an invaluable aspect of a "better life," "responsible adulthood," and centrally important to "positive modeling for children" (Morgen et al. 2010:87). Over time, "self-sufficiency" became positioned as the opposite of (clearly detrimental) "dependency," whereas "choice" and "helping" were similarly juxtaposed with "coercion" and "enabling" (equated with pre-reform practices).

Overall, anthropological work on neoliberalism has been an exploration of individuals and social life that adds a grounding perspective for other views that tend to stress policy, politics, and economics in the abstract. Through ethnography, the multifaceted impacts of neoliberal policies, which also may be highly variable and localized in a global system, become apparent. Critically, anthropologists understand neoliberalism as policies and ideologies that are not just enforced from the "top-down" but also reproduced at the level of individuals and communities. Beyond developing critical social theory, this anthropological understanding can improve the well-being of children and families even when there may be no way to turn back completely from neoliberal policies.

The case examples that follow both illustrate the complexity of the problems that neoliberal policies pose and demonstrate how an anthropological perspective can serve in the objective of ameliorating some of the complex impacts from within the field of CWS. An anthropological perspective can clarify local conditions and needs that are especially important to understand in the application of broad political ideologies and ideas such as those associated with neoliberalism. More important, such insights may be employed in the service of the goals of all CWS agencies—improving outcomes for vulnerable children. Key to this discussion is the idea that change is possible from a position of "pragmatic engagement" from within—even from within a flawed system (Rylko-Bauer et al. 2006:186).

Case Examples: Privatization and Ownership Principles in Action

As a research and evaluation consultant, my work in child welfare has largely consisted of providing technical assistance to local demonstration projects funded by the Administration of Children and Families (ACF).

Demonstration grants are designed to give agencies and organizations serving families the opportunity to try out new and innovative ideas such as providing specialized services to children and families in the child welfare system, trying out new ways to encourage families to adopt older children, or, in the case of the Healthy Marriage and Responsible Fatherhood initiatives, exploring whether the actions of private individuals can alleviate big problems on a national scale, such as poverty. All of these programs are about the local application of big ideas—like neoliberalism. Some of the grantees I have worked with have been funded by ACF through the Children's Bureau Adoption Opportunities, Child Abuse and Neglect, and Promoting Safe and Stable Families (PSSF) programs, the Early Head Start and Child Welfare Services Program, and the ACF Healthy Marriage and Promoting Responsible Fatherhood Initiative. I have also participated in research directly exploring the local realities of privatization in CWS. I have provided guidance in evaluation research design for local service providers as well as participated in broader initiative evaluations and needs assessments.

As a research consultant in child welfare, I am in an interesting position for several reasons. Initially, my work is about demonstration grants and about research exploring applied directions, and therefore important to the creation of future directions in the field. In addition, when I work on federal initiatives, I am brought into contact with child welfare professionals working in the field in communities all over the country, so I am knowledgeable about service goals and barriers as well as common experiences across space and with varied target populations. However, I am neither a federal officer nor a local service provider, so I am not central to the organization of the funding initiatives themselves. As a consultant, I am positioned as both insider and outsider—very much like a traditional anthropologist.

Like any other anthropologist entering the field, when I begin work with a local project my first objective is to establish rapport with local staff, who nearly always are fearful and suspicious. Although I am not a direct representative of the granting agency, I am often seen as such. At the very least, I am (correctly) identified as someone who will report back to the federal agency controlling their funding. It is my anthropological training that is directly responsible for the connections I am able to make in the "field," and these, in turn, create circumstances in which local voices may be accurately heard and needs met. The examples that follow illustrate other benefits of a perspective focused on the complexities of the local.

Perspectives on Privatization

That neoliberalism is woven through the cultural fabric at the federal level is not to say that those people working and thinking at the national level are simple dupes of a false consciousness. Nor should local initiatives for CWS privatization be seen as the forced imposition of macro-level theories. On the contrary, policy makers generally value the voice of the local. In fact, I was introduced to the topic of CWS privatization when I was asked to conduct informal interviews with local administrators of CWS to assess their "needs" regarding privatization. I took this initiative to be a sincere effort to move away from more top-down approaches, although, as a local administrator pointed out, using terms like "needs" and "barriers" did imply a certain position on the part of those at the federal level that wielded power to those that the local level.

The view of privatization at the local level is as complicated as is the field of CWS generally. Each local administration of CWS has a unique circumstance and history that confounds the implementation of any blanket fix, neoliberal or otherwise. In the first place, not all local public CWS agencies are structured in the same way. Some agencies are administered at the state level, whereas others are county-run, which makes comparisons or broad recommendations impractical if not impossible. Whereas CWS agencies in regions such as the northeast might have a range of private CWS agencies with which to partner, in more rural regions there may be no private agencies available, making the whole discussion quite pointless. In some parts of the county, strong local unions make privatization a publically debated issue, whereas in others, there is little public awareness. In still others, a strong belief in the "shrinking" power of government may influence local policy in favor of privatization. The uniqueness of each local CWS service region negates the ability to create the "hard evidence"—either positive or negative—that everyone would like to see regarding the implementation of privatization and that would provide the field with clearer direction.

For example, the idea that privatization will lead to lower costs is largely theoretical and often difficult to quantify. In fact, we find significant increases in costs at least initially. Depending on the type of privatization, there may be a significant restructuring of services. Often there is the cost of capacity building, including staff training, staff hiring, and the expansion services in private agencies. Communities have varying levels of existing private capacity to take over public CWS, which negates the possibility of free market competition—one of the important theoretical conditions of neoliberal theories.

Each local situation and experience is unique, making charting a "course" for privatization across the county an arduous task. For example, Kansas—the first state to pursue CWS privatization—initially contracted out its adoption services in 1996 to Lutheran Social Services, the single bidder for the contract. The stress of the transition, bulk of services to be provided, and restraints of the contract brought Lutheran Social Services close to bankruptcy. Rather than lose the services provided by Lutheran Social Services, Kansas supported the private agency through state funds. The agency continued to experience difficulty, and the contract was eventually awarded to another agency (Freundlich and Gerstenzang 2003). In other privatization efforts in other regions, local public agencies have had to step back in to provide funds or services when private agencies performed inadequately. The constant possibility that this might happen means that monitoring and quality control are a continual public responsibility and a costly duplication of tasks.

The very concept of public responsibility is another vital part of the context of privatization discussions at the local level. CWS organizations everywhere exist in a difficult relationship with the public that they serve. There has been much criticism of past and present mistakes in CWS, including the mass removal of Native American children from their homes until the Indian Child Welfare Act of 1978 (Myers 2006:99), a long history of bias against the African-American community (Myers 2006:184; Roberts 2008), and the 2008 removal of 400 children from a polygamist sect in San Angelo, Texas (MSNBC 2008). The foundation of such mistakes is the hegemonic standard of childrearing and definition of family based on a dominant social perspective that is embedded in CWS decisions. The hard reality is that decisions must be made on some criteria—and they are not always the right ones. They are endlessly debatable, and these debates are frequently louder in local communities than on the national stage.

Local CWS administration is fraught with public scrutiny, a fact that is always on the minds of staff in local agencies, who seem constantly to be dealing with public outcry surrounding a child welfare tragedy. For example, in 2008, there were two cases in the Washington, D.C. area in which caregivers killed more than one child. One was a mother who had been previously reported to the local CWS agency; the other was an approved foster care parent who had killed children in her care while continuing to collect subsidy funds. These incidents resulted in rounds of firings and increased scrutiny (Dvorak 2008). Because the risk of catastrophic consequences from CWS failures is ever-present, the duplication of monitoring and supervision tasks may not be avoidable in most local contexts. It is a constraint on local agencies that frequently is not clear to observers at the national level.

Harvey (2005) and Ong (2006) point out that there are many contradictions inherent in neoliberal globalization. One of these is that although neoliberalism seeks to create stronger communities through civic engagement and sustainability through community-based collaboratives, there are aspects of privatization that actually undermine community innovation. Overall the problem is that in a privatized system, the focus is on individual tasks and simple outcomes rather than on the well-being of children or families or the community as a whole. Under privatization, individual CWS become in some ways "closed shops." There may be limited ability for parts of the same system—adoptions and foster care handled by different private agencies, for example—to communicate. Moreover, if families move across county lines they may move into the service area of yet another private agency—or multiple agencies.

CWS operates at multiple levels, including the personal, national, and community levels. At the community level, the complication of providing the complete range of CWS is significantly compounded by the fact that these services actually exist within a larger local system, and that many CWS families have multiple and complex needs. Under privatized systems, other service providers serving the same families may be limited in their ability to communicate and collaborate with a private agency or agencies. Thus, privatization can be a substantial barrier to community-based innovation and collaboration. For example, in an initiative to provide specialized services to families involved in the child welfare system, one local project failed to establish a formal relationship with their local CWS provider because that provider was a private agency. By contrast, similar projects in other communities did work with their local public CWS agencies to identify and refer families to their services. Those without CWS "buy-in" could not gain appropriate access to the families they were hoping to serve.

By highlighting the local conditions and circumstances of neoliberal impacts at the local level, challenges are made possible. Evidence of this complexity can help guide policy makers and funders to reasonable decision-making at the national level. Thus, I have seen my role as one of critical translator and cultural broker. Without entering into a debate about the relative appropriateness of private or public CWS—a dead-end approach certain to end in stalemate—I use on-the-ground experiences and examples to demonstrate how the inflexible, blanket approach with which neoliberal policies are often pursued is simply impractical. The examples discussed here, such as the importance of public opinion in the local context and the threat to the local provider community posed by neoliberal shifts, are not apparent to those at the federal level, but may still be considered valuable to them and play a role in policy decisions.

Mine is not the only opinion, of course, and other researchers doing similar work and who are privy to similar observations do not make a critical leap away from the cultural perspectives of their (federal or private) clients. Some may consciously present a more positive view of privatization or other shifts. Others, probably the majority, may not recognize neoliberal ideological shifts at all. For example, some collaborators on one project exploring the perspectives of local administrators advocated for a more narrow focus on the "nuts and bolts" of privatization, such as the intricacies of payment structures, because they felt that all larger problems lie outside the definition of "data." After all, hired guns charged with undertaking a "needs assessment" might not be in the position to question the nature of the "need" itself. Nonetheless, an anthropologist, or anyone, in such a position, has a unique ability to present data that encourages evidence-based rather than ideologically based decision-making. This must be done from a critical but engaged vantage point. Equally impractical and unproductive would be a perspective so critical of the framework so as to preclude the possibility of solution.

The Ownership Society in CWS

One of the most interesting and common ways that the ownership society has seeped into child welfare and family-based services is through shifts— sometimes subtle, sometimes dramatic—in project outcomes or theories of change that reflect neoliberal thinking that influences professionals working in the field. For example, "self-sufficiency" may be considered an appropriate goal for a project providing parenting support and education to families that have been investigated by their local CPS agency. Such goals may be assessed by standardized instruments developed by local responses to the Results-Oriented Management and Accountability (ROMA) initiative, which promotes outcome-based management strategies for community, state, and federal programs participating in the Community Service Block Grant programs. In this way, the saliency of "self-sufficiency" as a goal of social service projects grows across the service community.

The goal of self-sufficiency makes sense because of the embedded ideological power of neoliberalism, as well as the knowledge that joblessness, low education, poverty, and drug use are all risk factors for child abuse. Behind the pursuit of this goal is the well-meaning belief that "self-sufficiency" will decrease stress and result in end of child maltreatment. As Morgen et al. (2010) among others have noted, neoliberal ideology is culturally embedded and pervasive. Self-sufficiency seems to "make sense" intuitively. This cultural value is reified and made stronger when institutionalized as an outcome goal. In essence, we become what we measure. In this small way, significant shifts are advanced.

The goal of self-sufficiency is also found in higher-level policy discussions and has been used to alleviate government responsibility for difficult social problems like poverty. An illustrative example of this is the Healthy Marriage and Responsible Fatherhood Initiatives sponsored by the ACF.

> To encourage marriage and promote the well-being of children, I have proposed a healthy marriage initiative to help couples develop the skills and knowledge to form and sustain healthy marriages. Research has shown that, on average, children raised in households headed by married parents fare better than children who grow up in other family structures. Through education and counseling programs, faith-based, community, and government organizations promote healthy marriages and a better quality of life

for children. By supporting responsible child-rearing and strong families, my Administration is seeking to ensure that every child can grow up in a safe and loving home (President George W. Bush, A Proclamation on Marriage Protection Week, 2003).

Under the Bush administration, there were several such programs within the ACF since 2002. One of these was managed by the Office of Family Assistance (OFA), which is also responsible for the management of the Temporary Assistance for Needy Families (TANF) program (the current U.S. "welfare" program). With the reauthorization of TANF in 2006, 150 million dollars were designated to support programs to "help couples form and sustain healthy marriages," principally through relationship education (OFA n.d). Fifty million dollars of this amount was designated for programs to "encourage responsible fatherhood," and 226 organizations received federal grants to provide Healthy Marriage and Responsible Fatherhood projects in communities across the country.

McClain explains, "the social movement known as the 'marriage movement' argues that shoring up the institution of marriage is vital to the nation's social health and urges a return to a 'marriage culture' to stem the tide of divorce, cohabitation and nonmarital childbearing" (2006:1). In other words, the Healthy Marriage and Strong Families movement seeks to avoid a host of social ills that might otherwise fall on the backs of American taxpayers. Some of these social ills are included in the Institute for American Values' "Twenty-Six Conclusions from the Social Sciences" (n.d.), which is quoted on the OFA website in support of the Healthy Marriage Initiative. Without citations, the list argues that marriage solves problems of the family ("marriage increases the likelihood that fathers and mothers have good relationships with their children" and "marriage is a virtually universal human institution"), economics ("divorce and unmarried childbearing increase poverty for both children and mothers" and "parental divorce reduces the likelihood that children will graduate from college and achieve high-status jobs"), physical health and longevity ("parental marriage is associated with a sharply lower risk of infant mortality" and "marriage is associated with reduced rates of alcohol and substance abuse for both adults and teens"), and mental health and emotional well-being ("boys raised in single-parent families are more likely to engage in delinquent and criminal behavior" and "a child who is not living with his or her own two married parents is at greater risk for child abuse") (Institute for American Values n.d.). Perhaps not surprisingly, most of the 26 "conclusions" reached by the Institute of American Values are factors that correlate with poverty (as does marriage).

I have provided technical assistance to both Healthy Marriage and Responsible Fatherhood projects. These experiences offer another example of the importance of local circumstances in the implementation of wide-reaching policies and, interestingly, the potential of varying levels of "success" among projects rooted in the same ideological foundation. Both Responsible Fatherhood and Healthy Marriage projects were designed to serve low-income communities and to affect the same ultimate outcome—reduce dependence on public support for poor families. Yet, the meaning and impact of these projects are quite different on the ground.

At the local level, Healthy Marriage programs provided marriage education in an attempt to strengthen the relationships between romantic partners in lower-income families. They offered classes in conflict resolution and communication skills in more or less traditional educational settings. Many funded programs provided the same services before their involvement with the Initiative but switched their focus to lower-income communities. In fact, some projects struggled with curricula designed for middle-class white families that had been roughly adapted to the new target population.

One of the struggles experienced by some Healthy Marriage projects was in the recruitment of participants. Solutions included offering transportation, meals, and babysitting. Also suggested was providing financial incentives to participants to be staggered along the curriculum so that couples had to participate at each stage to get "paid." On the face of it, these projects seem to have struggled because they did not gain enough acceptance in the community to be able to recruit participants. But the problem was more than a lack of rapport between project staff and the communities that they hoped to serve; the projects also suffered because they attempted to provide a service that was not valued in the target population using culturally inappropriate models—of both marriage and classroom instruction—that were developed with very limited definitions of "healthy" family relationships.

An interesting contrast is the Responsible Fatherhood approach. Although they are perceived by some as born of the same ideology as Healthy Marriage, they were immediately more "owned" by their target communities. Initially and, perhaps, more important, the goals of Responsible Fatherhood projects reflected already existing values in the community. In fact, the value of increased father involvement and the associated difficulties of single motherhood have long been an important issue in the African-American community—a principal target population of Responsible Fatherhood projects. Not surprisingly, many Responsible Fatherhood programs were established by organizations already serving the community. Another success of the Responsible Fatherhood approach—although one more challenging to measure in evaluations—is that services provided were often tailored not only to the community but also to the needs of the individual father. Fathers received services they needed such as mentoring, help navigating the child support system, or some limited job training. There was no one "set" of services that everyone received. More important, perhaps, the projects paid attention to the structural barriers to parental involvement, such as limitations based on visitation and child support agreements, and offered fathers avenues to alter them to allow for greater father-child interaction. Whereas Healthy Marriage projects were tightly focused on communicating a certain cultural family style, Responsible Fatherhood worked on less culturally bound project outcomes such as improving contact and removing structural barriers (such as child support noncompliance). Not only were Responsible Fatherhood projects more "culturally appropriate," but their success was tied to the existence of community acceptance of project goals along with a reasonable understanding of the structural barriers of poverty.

An interesting and important point about these differences between Healthy Marriage and Responsible Fatherhood is that they are not easily evident to those making policy-level decisions. Data provided by local evaluations and even initiative-wide evaluations are only as good as their research design. For example, in a local evaluation, Healthy Marriage projects can focus on "mid-range" outcomes such as improving knowledge of conflict resolution skills even if they cannot show a connection between their services and broader goals. In fact, many projects are evaluated in this way and assess knowledge outcomes through curriculum-supplied "tests." Although many Responsible Fatherhood projects, I believe, provided needed services and more closely achieved initiative goals, they are extremely difficult to evaluate. This is partly because they tailored services to individual needs, but also because qualitative outcomes such as "improved father involvement" are very hard to demonstrate. If such an outcome is operationalized as economic support (which might be attractive to those at the federal level), structural limitations such as poverty obscure the impact of the project, and the outcome (although measurable) substantially misrepresents the actual focus of the efforts. Similarly, there are also serious structural limitations if an outcome is defined as "increased father-child interaction" because the fathers served may or may not be removed from their children. In fact, some projects targeted incarcerated fathers, whose face-to-face interaction with their children is, of course, strictly controlled. Nearly all outcomes in Responsible Fatherhood projects (parental involvement, nonfinancial contribution to household) are complex and difficult to define. The ability to demonstrate the considerable value of the Responsible Fatherhood approach is dependent on the availability of sophisticated evaluation design. Because many evaluations are limited to the resources of individual service providers, some projects that actually produce positive outcome may, ironically, appear "unsuccessful." Such projects need evaluation support and advocacy from those recognized as knowledgeable such as experienced evaluators and researchers.

In this case, the potential for error is considerable. At the level of ideology, one could easily conclude that "ownership society" projects are uniformly bad for families, missing that Responsible Fatherhood projects have a potential to truly help at a time when other services are being cut. It is specifically from a "low-flying" vantage point that the relative "fit" of projects with the community in need become visible. As Ong (2006) and others have demonstrated, an understanding of neoliberalism is simply not available without knowledge of local manipulations. Similarly, a purely "evidence-based" approach may be equally misguided by convincing data produced through inappropriate evaluation designs or its reverse. Both a complex view of the local and an ability to communicate evidence to decision-makers are necessary to produce positive outcomes for families.

Conclusions

Making Sense and Change: Scholar-Practitioner Contributions

Privatization and other neoliberal trends in human services are an important opportunity for practicing anthropologists. These changes, like those associated with welfare reform, are not only about the distribution of services. They also shape who we are as communities, as families, and as individuals. In human services, to an even larger extent than elsewhere, the role of ideology might be greater precisely due to the ill fit of free-market analogies to the care of those in need—and in the case of CWS, of children. An anthropologist can carefully parse the local impacts of macro-level decisions and sees cultural construction where others might see "common sense." Each is important to critical assessment and discussion. Moreover, the anthropological concept of holism—that is, seeing the interconnectedness of the levels of individual, community, and nation—is a valuable asset to the evaluation of developments in the field, as is solid evidence to those in policy-making positions.

One of the missing pieces in our understanding of neoliberal policies is insight into how and why neoliberal trends are pursued in the first place. Even analysts who see privatization and similar trends as threatening see them as driven by relatively simple mechanisms—greed and bad ideas. Anthropologists have pointed out how cultural construction and discourse give power to the ideas of neoliberalism in practice (Morgen 2001; Morgen et al. 2010; Willging 2005). Through this work, we see that many actors may play a role in determining the reality of policy, and that ideology is continuously shaped and reshaped. Indeed, as Mary Douglas has argued, "To acquire legitimacy, every kind of institution needs a formula that founds its rightness in reason and nature" (1986:45). Scholar-practitioners working from an anthropological perspective help us understand how the neoliberal "formula" has become integrated into practice of CWS. Certainly, the use of ethnography and qualitative methodologies can capture what surveys cannot about the "on the ground" realities of policy and practice (Rylko-Bauer and Farmer 2002). Finally, through the study of neoliberal policies in application, change may be encouraged in small ways as well as large ones. As Rylko-Bauer et al. (2006) suggest,

> practitioners [may] find spaces within structures that are open to beneficial input. If carried out with a critical eye rather than accepting structures of inequality as a given, this provides an opportunity for meeting Laura Nader's (1972) challenge to "study up." In the process, practitioners can gain insights into policies and programs often only accessible to those willing to go "inside" (Rylko-Bauer et al. 2006).

Although there are restrictions, the potential for change is, perhaps, the most important strength of the scholar-practitioner perspective in that offering knowledge in the form of both data and experience is considerably more effective in creating change than abstract criticism. As Rylko-Bauer et al. go on to suggest, "pragmatic engagement requires a willingness to not only shape public discourse but also offer evidence-based solutions to social problems" (2006:186). Turning back to the welfare state is not a pragmatic solution for the problems of today social services. If change is to be achieved, alternatives must be advanced. Such alternatives may be developed by truly collaborative research that builds on the knowledge and experience of those in the social service field with reference to complex local realities.

Notes

1. This is not to say that there is not substantial global resistance to the principles of neoliberalism. In fact, there has been a turn back from privatization policies in Latin America and significant resistance in many parts of the world (Stiglitz 2008).
2. Local public CWS offices may be run by states, by counties, or regionally. It depends on the historical development of local government and CWS.
3. In concurrent planning, plans for adoption and reunification are developed and pursued at the same time. If one plan falls through, no time will be lost in the resolution of the child's case.

References

Berger, P., and R. Neuhaus
1977 To Empower People: The Role of Mediating Structures in Public Policy. Boston: University Press of America.

Blank, R. M.
2000 When Can Public Policy Makers Rely on Private Markets? The Effective Provision of Social Services. *Economic Journal* 110:34–49.

Boaz, David
n.d. Ownership Society: Responsibility, Liberty, and Prosperity. Available at: http://www.cato.org/special/ownership_society/boaz.html. Accessed October 14, 2008.

Boehm, Frédéric
2005 Privatization and Corruption. *In* Limits to Privatization: How to Avoid Too Much of a Good Thing, E.U. von Weizsäcker, O. Young, and M. Finger, eds. Pp. 263–65. London: Earthscan.

Bortolotti, Bernardo, and Valentina Milella
2008 Privatization in Western Europe: Stylized Facts, Outcomes and Open Issues. *In* Privatization: Successes and Failures, Gerard Roland, ed. Pp. 32–75. New York: Columbia University Press.

Bush, George W.
2003 A Proclamation by the President of the United States of America. Marriage Protection Week, 2003. Available at: http://www.acf.hhs.gov/programs/cse/pubs/2003/csr/csr0310.html#e. Accessed June 2, 2009.

Collins, Jane
2008 The Specter of Slavery: Workfare and Economic Citizenship of Poor Women. *In* New Landscapes of Inequality: Neoliberalism and the Erosion of Democracy in America, Micaela Di Leonardo, ed. Pp.131–52. Santa Fe: School for Advanced Research Press.

Di Leonardo, Micaela
2008 Introduction: New Global and American Landscapes on Inequality. *In* New Landscapes of Inequality: Neoliberalism and the Erosion of Democracy in America, Micaela Di Leonardo, ed. Pp. 3–20. Santa Fe: School for Advanced Research Press.

Douglas, Mary
1986 How Institutions Think. New York: Syracuse University Press.

Dvorak, Petula
2008 New Cases Strain Child Welfare Agency After Deaths of Four D.C. Girls, Firings. Washington Post, February 2.

Ferguson, James
2006 Global Shadows: Africa in the Neoliberal World Order. Durham: Duke University Press.

Fraser, Nancy
1993 Clintonism, Welfare and the Antisocial Wage: The Emergence of a Neoliberal Political Imagery. *Rethinking Marxism* 6(1):9–23.

Freundlich, Madelyn, and Sarah Gerstenzang
  2003 An Assessment of the Privatization of Child Welfare Services: Challenges and Success. Washington, D.C.: CWLA Press.
Gilroy, Leonard, Harris Kenny, Lisa Snell, et al.
  2011 Annual Privatization Report 2010: State Government Privatization. Reason Foundation. Available at: http://reason.org/files/state_annual_privatization_report_2010.pdf. Accessed May 24, 2011.
Goldstein, Donna
  2001 Microenterprise Training Programs, Neoliberal Common Sense, and the Discourses of Self-Esteem. *In* New Poverty Studies: The Ethnography of Power, Politics and Impoverished People in the United States, Judith Goode and Jeff Maskovsky, eds. Pp. 236–72. New York: New York University Press.
Goode, Judith, and Jeff Maskovsky (eds.)
  2001 The New Poverty Studies: The Ethnography of Power, Politics and Impoverished People in the United States. New York: New York University Press.
Harvey, David
  2005 Brief History of Neoliberalism. Oxford: Oxford University Press.
Hyatt, Susan Brin
  2001 From Citizen to Volunteer: Neoliberal Governance and the Erasure of Poverty. *In* New Poverty Studies: The Ethnography of Power, Politics and Impoverished People in the United States, Judith Goode and Jeff Maskovsky, eds. Pp. 210–35. New York: New York University Press.
Institute for American Values
  n.d. Why Marriage Matters: Twenty-Six Conclusions from the Social Sciences. Available at: http://www.americanvalues.org/pdfs/wmmsnapshot.pdf. Accessed May 24, 2011.
Kahn, Si, and Elizabeth Minnich
  2005 The Fox in the Henhouse: How Privatization Threatens Democracy. San Francisco: Berrett-Koehler Publishers, Inc.
Lamphere, Louise
  2005 Providers and Staff Respond to Medicaid Managed Care: The Unintended Consequences of Reform in New Mexico. *Medical Anthropology Quarterly* 19(1):3–25.
Lancaster, Roger
  2008 State of Panic. *In* New Landscapes of Inequality: Neoliberalism and the Erosion of Democracy in America, Micaela Di Leonardo, ed. Pp. 39–64. Santa Fe: School for Advanced Research Press.
Lipsky, Michael
  1980 Street Level Bureaucracy: Dilemmas of the Individual in Public Services. New York: Russell Sage Foundation.
McClain, Linda
  2006 The Place of Families: Fostering Capacity, Equality, and Responsibility. Cambridge, MA: Harvard University Press.

McCullough, C., and B. Schmitt
2000 Managed Care and Privatization: Results of a National Survey. *Children and Youth Services Review* 22(2):117–30.

Morgen, Sandra
2001 The Agency of Welfare Workers: Negotiating Devolution, Privatization, and the Meaning of Self-Sufficiency. *American Anthropologist* 103(3):747–61.

Morgen, Sandra, and Jill Wiegt
2001 Poor Women, Fair Work, and Welfare to Work that Works. *In* New Poverty Studies: The Ethnography of Power, Politics and Impoverished People in the United States, Judith Goode and Jeff Maskovsky, eds. Pp. 152–78. New York: New York University Press.

Morgen, Sandra, Joan Acker, and Jill Weigt
2010 Stretched Thin: Poor Families, Welfare Work and Welfare Reform. Ithaca: Cornell University Press.

Mountjoy, J. J.
1999 The Privatization of Child Welfare: Saving Children, Saving Money. *Spectrum* 72(2):1–4.

MSNBC
2008 534 Women, Kids Leave Polygamist Ranch. April 8. Available at: http://www.msnbc.msn.com/id/23993440/ns/us_news-crime_and_courts/. Accessed May 24, 2011.

Myers, John
2006 Child Protection in America: Past, Present and Future. Oxford: Oxford University Press.

Nader, Laura
1972 Up the Anthropologist—Perspectives Gained from Studying Up. *In* Reinventing Anthropology, Dell H. Hymes, ed. Pp. 284–311. New York: Pantheon Books.

Office of Family Assistance (OFA)
n.d. Healthy Marriage Initiative (HMI): Background. Available at: http://www.acf.hhs.gov/healthymarriage/about/mission.html#background. Accessed October 14, 2008.

Office of the Press Secretary
2004 Fact Sheet: America's Ownership Society: Expanding Opportunities. Available at: http://www.whitehouse.gov/news/releases/2004/08/20040809-9.html. Accessed October 14, 2008.

Ong, Aihwa
2006 Neoliberalism as Exception: Mutations in Citizenship and Sovereignty. Durham: Duke University Press.

Piven, Francis
1998 Welfare Reform and Low Wage Labor Markets. *City and Society Annual Review* 10(1):21–36.

Platkin, Richard
2009 The Urban Policy of the Obama Administration: Cash-infused Neo-Liberalism or Another New Deal? Paper presented at the Annual Meeting

of the Sociological Association, Hilton San Francisco, San Francisco, CA, August 8.

Roberts, Dorothy
2008 The Racial Geography of State Child Protection. *In* New Landscapes of Inequality: Neoliberalism and the Erosion of Democracy in America, Micaela Di Leonardo, ed. Pp.153–68. Santa Fe: School for Advanced Research Press.

Roland, Gerard
2008 Introduction. *In* Privatization: Successes and Failures, Gerard Roland, ed. Pp. 9–31. New York: Columbia University Press.

Rylko-Bauer, Barbara, and Paul Farmer
2002 Managed Care or Managed Inequality? A Call for Critiques of Market-based Medicine. *Medical Anthropology Quarterly* 16(4):476–502.

Rylko-Bauer, Barbara, Merrill Singer, and John Van Willigen
2006 Reclaiming Applied Anthropology: Its Past, Present, and Future. *American Anthropologist* 108(1):178–90.

Stack, Carol
2001 Coming of Age in Oakland. *In* New Poverty Studies: The Ethnography of Power, Politics and Impoverished People in the United States, Judith Goode and Jeff Maskovsky, eds. Pp. 179–200. New York: New York University Press.

Stiglitz, Joseph
2008 Foreword. *In* Privatization: Successes and Failures, Gerard Roland, ed. Pp. i–x. New York: Columbia University Press.

Sullivan, H. J.
1987 Privatization of Public Services: A Growing Threat to Constitutional Rights. *Public Administration Review* 47:461–67.

Willging, Cathleen
2005 Power, Blame, and Accountability: Medicaid Managed Care for Mental Health Services in New Mexico. *Medical Anthropology Quarterly* 19(1):84–102.

Williams, Brett
2008 The Precipice of Debt. *In* New Landscapes of Inequality: Neoliberalism and the Erosion of Democracy in America, Micaela Di Leonardo, ed. Pp. 65–90. Santa Fe: School for Advanced Research Press.

Zavella, Patricia
2001 The Tables are Turned: Immigration, Poverty and Social Conflict in California Communities. *In* New Poverty Studies: The Ethnography of Power, Politics and Impoverished People in the United States, Judith Goode and Jeff Maskovsky, eds. Pp. 103–34. New York: New York University Press.

8

From Internationalism to Systemic Globalism in Health Leadership Training

Eve C. Pinsker

Introduction: Health Leadership Training

"Health," like the anthropological concept of culture, is one of those concepts that relates to almost any area of human life at both individual and collective levels. The administration of health services delivery; assuring the health of the community via monitoring crucial public resources such as safe water, a nontoxic environment, and safe food systems; or setting goals for health policy require skills in interacting with multiple players and a range and depth of knowledge and insight not always given in the formal degree programs that provide high-level entry to such positions, which often only provide narrow clinical training. Furthermore, in the United States and elsewhere, given the breadth of activities subsumed under health, including grassroots-level community health promotion or outreach, although many people (such as myself) have found their ways to health-related positions with little formal training in specifically health-related disciplines, they may still find themselves in leadership positions. Thus, there has been a need for health leadership training programs geared toward working professionals that support those who have assumed the tasks of directing public and community health–related activities. Health leadership training offers an instructive viewpoint for reflection on how changes in international and global perspectives affect the concerns of those whose goal is to improve health and reduce health inequities as well as those who teach and mentor them.

Health leadership training specifically for working professionals stands at the intersection of a number of disciplines and sources of curricula, among them academic-based health professions education, including medical, nursing, and public health education; adult learning; public health workforce development; and organizational development and the practices of leadership training that have emerged in corporate as well as nonprofit and government contexts. In more than a decade of involvement with this field, I have seen, in my corner of it at least, a movement toward a greater articulation of the importance of a systemic and global perspective on health for emergent health leaders. The attention garnered by physician anthropologist Paul Farmer's work is only one small example (Farmer 2003; Kidder 2003).

Within the discipline of public health, the transition to curricula for the training of practitioners based on a broad, multidisciplinary view of health leadership was facilitated by the fact that by the mid-2000s, a "networked" vision of the public health workforce and its development via leadership training had been implemented. This perspective was articulated in the 1998 and 2003 Institute of Medicine (IOM) reports (1988, 2003a) on the practice and teaching of public health (referenced elsewhere in this volume by Odell Butler). This vision asserted that the public health workforce consists not only of employees of state or local departments of public health, but also of workers in other agencies and nonprofit, community, and educational organizations, which collaborate with public health departments to fulfill the public health core functions and essential services. As part of the development of training for the public health workforce called for by these IOM reports, the U.S. Centers for Disease Control (CDC) began sponsoring regional Public Health Leadership Institutes in 1991.

In the past decade, health leadership training curricula have also been shaped via private foundation involvement. Beginning in 1999, the Robert Wood Johnson (RWJ) and Kellogg Foundations worked with public health partners to develop collaborative leadership training materials relevant to a broad spectrum of people working or volunteering in the health arena, such as clinical health professionals, grassroots peer educators and activists, public health department employees, mental health and social services personnel, and those working in other nonprofits, community-based organizations, and agencies relevant to health (The Turning Point Leadership Development National Excellence Collaborative n.d.). The collaborative leadership model developed through Turning Point recognized the importance of local knowledge and community-based expertise as well as academic-based health expertise, and the need for working together in an participatory, egalitarian, and inclusive process across organizations and community groups, rather than a top-down command-driven fashion, to improve community health and empower those to whom health services and education are targeted.

On the global scene, an international group of 10 academic institutions for health professions education had come together in 1979 as The Network of Community-oriented Education Institutions for the Health Sciences, with the support of the World Health Organization (WHO) and the Pan American Health Organization, to foster more effective partnerships between centers of academic health professions education and the communities they were meant to serve. In 1999, to reflect the increasing role of their community partners and the expansion of the original group, they were renamed The Network: Community Partnerships for Health through Innovative Education, Service, and Research. In 2001, this network merged with an existing European-based network, and in 2002 it merged with another existing WHO initiative and became The Network: Towards Unity for Health (The Network: TUFH; http://www.the-networktufh.org).

In 1997, Ronald Richards, a medical educator active in both the Kellogg Foundation's early effort to develop community-university partnerships in health leadership training and the early development of the precursors of The Network: TUFH, received a grant to develop an International Center for Health Leadership Development (ICHLD), and an associated fellowship program for working professionals, including non–U.S.-based fellows, housed at the University of Illinois at Chicago (UIC), and promoting a "bridge-building" partnership approach to health leadership. The ICHLD programs are described in the case study portion of this chapter.

The implications of the "bridge-building" approach to leadership that was taken by ICHLD and affirmed by its fellows is that leaders (as opposed to "managers") do more than shore up existing organizational structures and practices for allocating services and distributing resources: they aim to support systems change, or change in the underlying relationships generating those structures and practices, such as those that prevent a more equitable and just distribution of resources. Taking systems change seriously means challenging the dominant modes of thinking about leaders as essential, atomic, heroically individual agents (the CEO model), and emphasizing the team, organizational, and cross-organizational levels of leadership as well as the competencies of the individual leader (Rowitz 2006). The ICHLD model emphasized the relationships leaders have with those under their supervision and mentorship as well as with other leaders in other organizations, and in grassroots community-based as well as institutional contexts: it was a collaborative leadership model, developed in parallel with the collaborative leadership training concurrently developed under the sponsorship of the RWJ and Kellogg Foundations. The RWJ and Kellogg collaborative leadership materials were used in later incarnations of the ICHLD program and, following the end of the

ICHLD- and Kellogg-sponsored fellowship program, became part of the resources drawn on by the UIC School of Public Health (SPH)–based health leadership programs for practitioners (under its current MidAmerica Center for Public Health Practice) as well as other public health leadership institutes across the United States.

In the remainder of this chapter, I will first briefly describe some conceptual frameworks from systems theory and systems thinking useful for creating an understanding of what is necessary to foster collaborative leadership that will support systemic change and a more equitable distribution of health, not merely the reproduction of an (unsatisfactory) status quo. In a world in which the global and the local interact in ways that more frequently or markedly affect everyday lives, the core ideas of systems thinking—including, for instance, the concept that the proximity or distance of a cause in time or space does not necessarily predict the magnitude of the effect it engenders—are needed, not only for inclusion in the contents of a leader's "toolkit," but to understand how to go about developing more effective contexts as well as content for leadership training programs. Then, after some comments on the previous and prospective contributions of anthropological perspectives to both systems theoretical frameworks and to approaching health leadership development, I will continue by describing my own role (as an evaluator and contributor to curriculum development) in the 1998–2004 ICHLD International Health Partners Fellowship program and what I learned from that experience. In the conclusions, I will come back to the need to develop both theory and practice to support health leadership development in an increasingly interconnected world.

Systems Thinking Frameworks for Approaching Health Leadership and Intentional Systems Change

Within the last decade, public health researchers and activists have come to appreciate the importance of understanding and analyzing the multiple socioecological as well as biological levels that affect public health issues, from the cellular and tissue level affected by chronic disease, viruses, and bacteria; to the individual human level as both organism and person; to the levels of family and local community; to the broader political and economic community, which controls access to resources and social as well as geographic mobility, including across national borders (Krieger 2001). This inclusion of the political as well as the social and biological in public health thinking is parallel to the movement that Fiske describes elsewhere in this volume from ecology to cultural ecology and finally to political ecology. The need to analytically separate these levels is a necessary preliminary to a deeper understanding of the relationships between and among them, which is perhaps the more challenging task, and one which the multiple schools of systems theory[1] (which I subsume here under the rather vague title "systems thinking," as used in both academic and popular contexts, in health leadership training, and in organizational leadership training in general) are only now beginning to have useful ways of approaching.

Louis Rowitz, a sociologist by training who has significantly contributed to the field of public health leadership both through the Midwest regional public health leadership programs he has directed and his books (Rowitz 2006, 2009), has brought Peter Senge's version of systems thinking, widely applied in the corporate world, into public health leadership training (Senge 1990). Senge was a student of Jay Forrester, the founder of system dynamics, but departed from Forrester in deemphasizing computational simulation models and in translating the terms "positive feedback" and "negative feedback," making these foundational concepts clearer for the general public by calling them "reinforcing feedback" and "balancing feedback." Senge has also been influential in supporting the idea of fostering "learning organizations" and bringing into organizational development an emphasis on the usefulness of identifying and analyzing "mental models" that influence intra- and interorganizational interactions and outcomes.

Since Senge changed the field of organizational development by introducing system dynamics concepts, other organizational development practitioners have drawn on complexity theory as a newer variant of systems theory (although sometimes more metaphorically than rigorously), emphasizing multiple ecological levels, emergence, and the importance of attending to communication and human relationships (Wheatley 2006; Wheatley and Kellner-Rogers 1996). In the public health leadership programs hosted by Rowitz in the past several years, this literature and its developers have been a growing part of the curriculum: for example, both Margaret Wheatley and Myron Rogers have been presenters.

The new appreciation in public health for systems thinking, for trying to understand and model the nonlinear relationships between multiple hierarchical levels—biology, social organization (as in social network analysis), and the differential access to resources imposed by political and economic systems—became more visible in academic public health in the 2006 special issue of the *American Journal of Public Health* devoted to systems thinking (Leroy et al. 2006). This current work goes far beyond earlier attempts to apply variants of systems theory, such as "world systems" theory, which discounts the importance of local conditions. Milstein has worked with system dynamics modelers to create computer simulation models of diabetes and obesity as well as options in health reform policy that enable the projection of the effects of alternate choices in allocations of resources (more "upstream" or preventive versus "downstream" or reactive interventions, for example) given the multiple feedback loops which describe the interactions between the multiple factors (environmental as well as social and biological) affecting these chronic conditions. Milstein has explicitly recognized the connections among systems perspectives, systems modeling, and social/political as well as biological perspectives, explicitly articulated values, and more effective and proactive health leadership in his book *Hygeia's Constellation* (Milstein 2008). Milstein introduces the term "social navigation" and "public strength" and "public work" as variables involved in the relationships in his models. (The work of the modeling itself, however, because it is outside the frame of the model, does not affect the increase or decrease of public strength or public work.)

Other public health professionals have also recognized the implications of systems thinking perspectives for leadership training: the core competencies for public health identified by the Council on Linkages in 2001 already titled Domain No. 8 as "Leadership and Systems Thinking Skills" (Council on Linkages 2001). The connections between more sophisticated conceptions of agency and leadership implied by a complex systems perspective that includes the spectrum of socioecological levels from the individual, to the team, to the organizational, to the societal, to the global, have not gone unnoticed, although the implications for developing more effective health leadership training have yet to be fully explored.

For instance, at a conference on Population Health and Complex Systems held in Ann Arbor, Michigan, in 2007 (Center for Social Epidemiology and Population Health, in collaboration with the Center for the Study of Complex Systems, University of Michigan 2007) the visualization of computer-based simulation models showing the connection between the season of the year in which a contagious disease epidemic (such as SARS or avian flu) initializes, seasonal patterns in airplane travel, and changes in the rate and geographic spread of an epidemic, viscerally demonstrated the importance of networks connecting the global to the local, and the complex systems principle of sensitivity to initial conditions (Koopman 2007). Public health topics gaining importance today include how global warming is affecting disease-causing insects, as well as other changes portending new kinds of health crises. In today's world, international interchange in public and community health is no longer only for the sake of insight, but is about all of us having to join together to face threats that are not going to stay in one place or stay far away. This has become a predominant theme in leadership training for disaster preparedness.

In summary, the importation of various traditions of systems thinking into health leadership training has begun to change ideas about what a public or community health intervention is or needs to be. It is not simply identifying deficits and giving people needed information, needed care, or needed resources. There is a recognition that multiple inter-secting interrelationships need to be at least partially understood for an intervention to have a chance of having the desired effect; that those relationships run the gamut from the biological, to the social, to the political, and include connections between the local and the global; and that no one does it alone, or even with a small team of homogenous professionals.

An Anthropological Perspective on Health Leadership and Systems Thinking

To understand how things work at the local level, and the effect that changes instituted from above have on that level as well as what emerges from it, it is still important to understand culture in the anthropologi-cal sense, and how it operates at global, national, and state as well as local levels. So far, that has largely been left out of contemporary systems thinking–based models (both computer simulation models and concep-tual, qualitative models). This is partly because anthropology as a disci-pline in the past 20 years has largely abrogated its job of formulating a concept of culture that the general public sees as useful (except for those of us practicing anthropologists who are still trying to figure out how to explain it to the people with whom we work). At the 2007 conference on Population Health and Complex Systems, sociologist Michael Macy spoke about his "meme" theory: his version of modeling culture is that monad-like ideas—memes—spread throughout social networks. This dis-counts, however, that the memes themselves have any internal structure that matters. It implies, for instance, that practices like female circumci-sion, or stopping it, are propagated throughout a population the same as bacteria would: via networked contacts that privilege contact as a variable, without an understanding of the differing kinds of filters or thresholds that might pertain to culturally versus biologically mediated processes. This ignores the ethnographic evidence, such as that given by anthro-pologist Janice Boddy, that there are other factors than social contact and organization involved in stopping or starting the practice, beyond just someone in a social position contiguous or even superior to you telling you that you can or cannot. An understanding of indigenous cultural models connecting circumcision to valued conceptions and meanings, for instance, the link between "smoothness" and fertility (as in eggs), is key to understanding the success or failure of attempts to alter the practice (Boddy 1989).

What is now known as complexity theory is one contemporary variant (or several linked variants) of "systems thinking" resulting from multiple strands of development that go back at least to the early twentieth century (Capra 1996; Mitchell 2009; Richardson 1991). Within complexity theory, complex adaptive systems theory constructs models of systems that adapt, learn, and evolve. Complex adaptive systems theory is perhaps the most potentially useful development within complexity theory for more deeply understanding social systems and how they change over time, although it can certainly be applied to biological systems and of course machine intelligence and machine-based models of cognition and perception (because its methodology is computer-simulation based) as well as to the interactions between biological and human systems, as the anthropologist Stephen Lansing (2007) has.

Complex adaptive systems learn, and moreover "complex adaptive systems form and use internal models to *anticipate* the future, basing current actions on expected outcomes" (Holland 1992:24; emphasis in original). The use of internal models here is not reserved for conscious models in the way we understand them in ourselves, or even sense in other mammals: Holland also includes such phenomena as bacteria moving along a gradient, or a butterfly whose form mimics that of another species that predators avoid. Complex adaptive systems can be modeled through describing distributed, interacting parts governed by multiple rules (as opposed to a single, overarching rule). Those multiple rules, through recombination and competition, allow the system as a whole to produce novelty, and to adapt and evolve in response to a changing environment (Holland 1992). The aggregate behavior emerging from the interactions of the parts of a complex system is not easily predictable by more linear types of models or thinking: hence emergence—what seems like discontinuous change on the level of the whole made up of the parts—is seen as a fundamental characteristic of complex adaptive systems (Holland 1998). When the individual parts are seen as agents, computer simulation modeling of complex adaptive systems becomes agent-based modeling in contrast to other types of computer simulation–based systems modeling, which take a more aggregate level as the basic unit, such as system dynamics models (see Richardson 1991).[2]

George Peter Richardson (1991) has identified a key bifurcation in variants of systems theory that occurred in the post–World War II period, which relates to anthropology's (and culture's) place in the development of contemporary systems theory: the split between the "servomechanisms"-based thread of systems theory and the cybernetics thread. The servomechanisms thread includes Jay Forrester's systems dynamics (originating in engineering approaches to systems analysis, transferred to business management) and its popularization by Senge. The cybernetics thread includes the work of Norbert Wiener and the group that coalesced around him at the Macy conferences held from 1946 to 1953 (Conway and Siegelman 2005).

Unlike the current developments in complexity theory centered around the Santa Fe Institute, which have centered around an initial exchange between physicists and economists, with input from computer science and other disciplines (Mitchell 2009; Waldrop 1992) and much lesser representation from anthropologists via cultural anthropologist Stephen Lansing and some archaeologists, the cybernetics group included major representation from the social and behavioral sciences as well as biology. This included psychologists, educators, and the anthropologists Margaret Mead and Gregory Bateson. (Among contemporary historians and disseminators of systems theory, Capra [1996] and Richardson [1991] both recognize the significance of Mead's and Bateson's contributions.) Unfortunately, the incorporation of cultural perspectives into visible activity within systems theory initiated within the cybernetics thread largely dead-ended by the 1980s for multiple reasons, including the (mistaken) Cold War association of cybernetics with the Soviet bloc by potential U.S. government sponsors (Conway and Siegelman 2005) and the (also mistaken) association of cybernetics with out-of-fashion "structural functionalism" by leading American anthropologists (D. Schneider, personal communication, 1981).[3]

However, complex adaptive systems theory takes up some of the same issues raised by Bateson and Mead in the 1940s and 1950s, and in Bateson's subsequent work: learning as something that extends beyond the individual and which is potentially reflexive and hierarchical (learning how to learn, etc.), evolution as learning, mind and mental processes as not confined to the brain, and the importance of internal models in understanding the constraints on what kinds of behavior will emerge from a system (Bateson 1972). Nevertheless, what has largely been missing, on both the anthropology and the systems theory sides, is building an understanding of culture as an emergent property of a group of communicating humans, with the provision that a culture is not a set of individual organisms: a person can participate in multiple cultures. If cultures are seen rather as sets of interrelated cultural models, then the recombination of models and parts of models across boundaries in response to coevolving contexts can produce novel and radical change: the analog of new species. However, for preserving diversity (and the resources to respond to novel change), the maintenance of and respect for cultural boundaries can be important, and there is justification for bemoaning the McDonaldization of the world. This leads to a new perspective on cultural diversity training for health leaders than what is commonly given in existing cultural competency training for health professionals.

Social and political boundaries that contribute to inequity (and increase it, with positive feedback loops making the situation worse over time), however, can and should be challenged. Bobby Milstein, who has led efforts to incorporate systems modeling into the CDC's work, has credited and disseminated medical anthropologist Merrill Singer's conception of "syndemics" (Singer 2009): the confluence and interrelationship among multiple infectious and chronic disease vectors that cannot be understood apart from the social, cultural, economic, and political conditions which contextualize and exacerbate them. This has had an important impact on discussions of the relationships between what is biologically "under the skin" and what is at the organizational and societal levels beyond the individual. (Milstein 2008; see also the Syndemics Prevention Network website at http://www.cdc.gov/syndemics/). (Examples of "syndemics" include HIV/AIDS, drug abuse, sex work and the economic, cultural, and political contexts that foster it and the vulnerability of its practitioners; or diabetes, heart disease, and differential access to sources of healthy food.)

From an initial focus on bridging boundaries in community-university partnerships, and an insistence on recruiting diverse, multiethnic classes of fellows, the ICHLD curriculum developed to allow fellows to support each other in bridging resource gaps while respecting different kinds of expertise. Nonetheless, I sometimes found the focus on "leadership" itself to be somewhat antithetical to my own training as a political anthropologist. I came to realize that dominant modes of leadership training (before the importation of systems thinking perspectives) implied a focus on individual agency. As an anthropologist, I was used to thinking more in terms of how leaders are shaped by their cultural and social context, or rather how both leaders' and followers' conceptions and practices of leadership are shaped by cultural models and by social organization (that is, by cultural differences in leadership as an anthropologist would understand them).

Case Example: The ICHLD's Health Partners Fellowship Program

In 1997, an anthropological colleague and I were recruited to become evaluators for the ICHLD, housed at UIC. This was my introduction to the field of health leadership training.

The initial director of ICHLD was a medical educator, with experience as a Foundation officer as well as a medical school faculty member, who developed ICHLD's programs with a cadre of community- as well as university-based professionals from other fields. The ICHLD was subsequently directed (beginning in 2000) by a lawyer with a background in community development work and advocacy, particularly in Latina/o and women's issues. Also in 2000, the Center was moved from the Vice-Chancellor's office to UIC's SPH. The move to the SPH made that discipline's perspective on leadership training central to the development of ICHLD's programs, with the help of a key SPH and ICHLD faculty member (Louis Rowitz, cited in the previous section) who concurrently was directing several state and regional public health leadership fellowship programs and institutes of his own.[4]

ICHLD's signature program was the Health Partners Fellowship (HPF) program, a two-year leadership development program focused on developing skills in collaboration for the purpose of improving the health of communities. Participants in the program were professionals from a variety of disciplines and backgrounds, including those based in university as well as community settings. They met periodically for approximately five weeks each year, taking knowledge and skills learned through the fellowship sessions back to their ongoing work. These sessions used a variety of strategies, including site visits, learning contracts, didactic presentations, exercises, group discussion, and group projects.

This was an intensive small-group program for working professionals, with 12 fellows in each two-year class. From 1998 to 2004, there were three classes of fellows (1998–2000, 2000–2002, and 2002–2004). Each of these classes had two fellows recruited from outside the United States. Their airfares and expenses were paid for, as were the other fellows'. They were recruited through the director's ties with the international group of health professions educators and their community partners now called The Network: TUFH. Of the three classes of fellows that followed this model, the international fellows came from South Africa, Malaysia, the Philippines, Lebanon, Chile (via Australia), and Colombia. (The Chilean fellow had been a political exile, was practicing as a physician and faculty member in Australia at the beginning of his fellowship tenure, and later was able to return to Chile.)

My anthropologist colleague and I were recruited as evaluators for ICHLD because we had previously been involved in the evaluation of community-university partnership programs (Pinsker and Lieber 2005), and the founder of the fellowship program, Ronald Richards, had been involved in initiatives from a major foundation (Kellogg) to foster community-university partnership programs focusing on improving relationships between health professions schools and community organizations (Richards 1996). The "international" aspect of the program came from his involvement with parallel community–health professions education partnership initiatives in countries across the world, with members of the aforementioned The Network: TUFH (Richards and Sayad 2001). The Kellogg Foundation had supported initiatives in South Africa and South America.

Through his work with both organizations, Richards had become convinced that a key aspect in the successful formation, development, and sustainability of such partnerships was leadership. Therefore, he determined to start a fellowship program for working professionals, both university- and community-based, who shared an interest in health and a commitment to building bridges between local communities and the resources embodied in academic health centers or other resource-rich health institutions. His thesis was that a particular sort of leadership, collaborative leadership, was needed and that training could help with this—such leaders could indeed be made and not just born. Although the people drawn to such a program would already have values commensurate with this, presumably there were skills, information, and experiences that it would benefit them to have. Part of what he thought would benefit them was exposure to similarly inclined health professionals in other parts of the world.

The ICHLD HPF program had evaluation built into it from the outset. From October 1997 (when the fellowship was being developed) to October 2001, fellow cultural anthropologist Michael D. Lieber and I conducted the evaluation through a contract under UIC's Office of Social Science Research. From October 2001 to the end of the international version of the fellowship program in 2004, I alone conducted the evaluation as internal evaluator and ICHLD staff member. The evaluator(s) observed most of the fellowship sessions and initially observed the fellowship staff meetings as well. Later, when the evaluator became an internal position, I as evaluator assumed an active role in the staff meetings, reporting evaluation results and participating in the discussions about the ongoing curriculum. HPF faculty and the ICHLD director participated in the evaluation process as well, conducting pluses-and-wishes discussions with the fellows during fellowship weeks. Thus, the input of both fellows (directly and via oral and written comments collected by the evaluator) and faculty shaped the continuing development of the HPF curriculum and program.

Evaluation data included: fellows' session questionnaires, with Likert scale (1–5) ratings plus open-ended questions; observation of sessions by evaluator and faculty; learning contracts and other fellows' products; interim, final, and alumni questionnaires; interviews with HPF Class 1 and 2 fellows; site visits with a sample of fellows (two HPF Class 1 and two HPF Class 2 plus Chicago fellows and, in the year following submission of the 2004 report, one HPF Class 3 international fellow); and focus groups with HPF Class 3. Following standard practice among evaluation anthropologists (Copeland-Carson and Butler 2005), conclusions in the submitted evaluation report (Pinsker 2004) were based primarily on the interviews and site visits with HPF 1 and 2 alumni, focusing particularly on the evaluation questions relating to outcomes and determining what aspects of the fellowship were particularly successful in leading to changes in the fellows, their programs, and their communities (linking process to outcomes). The written interim, final, and alumni questionnaires provided corroborating evidence. As in all qualitative evaluation where one has the opportunity to collect data through multiple methods, the triangulation achieved through comparing comments gained through interviews with observations and with comments made on questionnaires and during HPF sessions was important in supporting the validity and reliability of the conclusions and recommendations.

Culture, Difference, Discrimination, and Leadership

Part of the challenge of this program was that the curriculum was not set at the beginning, and part of the interest in being an evaluator was being a participant-observer of how the curriculum developed. However, cultural differences in leadership, although one might think they would be a standard item in such a curriculum, were rarely directly addressed, at least as I understood them. Differences in privilege, racism, and ethnocentrism—the topics that have become conventionally addressed under "cultural competency" or "cultural diversity" training—did emerge as important topics in the curriculum.

Initial attempts to directly address this arena, however, resulted in some challenges to group process. In recruiting of all the classes of the HPF fellows, a conscious effort was made to diversify the group, not only among organizational bases (university, government agency, and community organizations), gender and gender orientation, and through the inclusion of the international fellows, but also in terms of race and ethnicity (as defined in U.S. contexts), with all classes including Latino/a, African-American, and in some cases Native American representatives as well as whites. Faculty was also recruited with an eye to diversity.

However, there were challenges: (1) A movie shown about racism toward the end of the series of meetings of the first HPF class resulted in a discussion fraught with tensions between nonwhite and white fellows that were never resolved. (2) Due to observation and feedback on this issue from the experience in the first class, an attempt was made in the second class to include a presentation (made by an African-American faculty member) explicitly addressing racism and ethnocentrism earlier in the sequence of sessions; but again, some of the white fellows resented the defensive posture in which they felt themselves placed. On the other hand, the connection among diversity, ethnic/race relations, community health, and social justice was an area in which there was demonstrable change within some fellows and changes at their home sites that they have helped to foster (Pinsker 2004). Some of the tension may be necessary—as one of the fellows said, being "comfortable" is not the goal—but one HPF 2 fellow said (and his supervisor corroborated this statement) that after the presentation on racism, he was seriously considering dropping out of the fellowship.

The leadership of the program did become better at dealing with this over time, helped, I hope, by the feedback given by the evaluators. Because at that point in the program we were evaluators and not faculty (subsequent to the HPF international program I presented as faculty in some ICHLD sessions as well as serving as evaluator), our attempts to introduce an anthropological concept of culture were sometimes made out-of-turn—although I can remember one occasion when one of the participants in the first HPF class, who self-identified as Native American and had a career in U.S. urban Indian health, turned around during a discussion in which we were observers sitting in the back and said something like, "well, you are anthropologists, you tell us what culture is...."

Looking back on the tensions involved in earlier discussions of racism and effects on the tasks and necessary competencies of health leaders, it is important to remember that the discussion of health disparities/inequities in the United States was then in its infancy—it was not nearly as mainstream a topic as it has since become among health professionals, subsequent to the IOM report *Unequal Treatment* (IOM 2003b), and attention in the media such as the PBS television series Unnatural Causes, broadcast in 2009 (http://www.pbs.org/unnaturalcauses/explore_learn.htm). The presence of the international fellows helped to provide an important comparative perspective on discussions of internal U.S. connections between race and ethnicity on the one hand and class and access to resources on the other. However, the potential for using this comparative perspective to reduce the tensions in U.S.-centric discussions of race and discrimination via a greater awareness that definitions of race and ethnicity are culturally and socially constructed, as are their connections to inequity in access to resources (and hence, hopefully subject to change by leaders who can envisage a different way of looking at this distinctions and implement actions based on a new perspective) was more fully realized with the third HPF class.

The first HPF class did go on an international trip, to South Africa; the evaluators did not accompany them. We had reservations about the trip as a learning experience because we felt the fellows had not been well prepared for a cross-cultural experience, and because the trip had been framed in terms of the fellows teaching the people in South Africa, who had been engaged in community-university partnerships in some cases longer than they had. In fact, when people came back, we heard stories of travel disasters and what we recognized as culture shock (but were usually attributed by participants to something else, such as not being taken care of by the organizers or, in one case, to sexual orientation differences rather than cultural ones). Although the director had hoped that international experiences and participants would help participants get new insights into intranational differences and experiences of inequality (e.g., among racial or ethnic groups in their home society), as discussed earlier in relation to the dissension following the movie on racism (shown in a session well after the international trip), such was not often the case with that first group.

It became easier for the fellows over the three classes of the HPF program to discuss racism and health in the United States—partly due to improvements in the way the faculty framed discussions, partly due to the emergence of "health disparities" as a recognized topic in the health professions, and partly due to increased awareness over time of the social and cultural construction of racial and ethnic categories among the recruited fellows (particularly the two international fellows in the third class). One way the consciousness of the socially constructed nature of these categories emerged was in the awareness by fellows that racial discrimination in the United States was not necessarily something that the non–U.S.-based fellows would want to spend a lot of time discussing.

The advantage of this double layer of cross-cultural comparison—between the experiences of people with different backgrounds in the United States talking about their experiences with social difference and inequality, with the international participants as witness and commentator, contributing their own experiences of inequality was increasingly realized over time, although it rarely reached the level of being able to talk about the "taken for granted" assumptions that I as an anthropologist think of as cultural. One memorable point in the discussion was when the Chilean family practice physician in the third HPF class told the group of his initial repudiation of his own family's indigenous roots (manifesting as "internalized colonialism," the devaluing of these roots), and subsequent embracing of them as part of his own personal as well as professional identity. He began a project to develop a medical school that would use anthropological approaches to combining indigenous and western approaches to medicine, including shamans as well as Western-trained doctors as respected professionals.

Part of what made this increased awareness in the third class possible was the development through collaborative discussion of a systemic framework for considering the genesis of inequalities and allowing their comparison across societies, including "capitalism" and how it plays out in different national contexts. This includes the contrast of the United States to other countries in the extreme extension of capitalist logic to health (parallel to discussions of the assumptions of neoliberalism elsewhere in this volume): considering health as a privilege to be bought rather than a basic right of all people within a society. In a focus group (facilitated by the evaluator) on collaborative leadership learning at the end of the first year of the third HPF class, the fellows identified "turf issues" and "the unwillingness to share resources due to capitalism" as key barriers to the success of collaborative leadership. Although the identification of "capitalism" brought us up against a seemingly invincible systemic barrier, the fellows did see avenues to systemic change through leadership. They identified the following as key in the role of the leader:

- Vision—seeing opportunities (where others see problems);
- Matching resources—people, not just money, with needs;
- Bringing people together in group discussion; and
- Knowing when to use perceived power.

Furthermore, they identified the following additional leadership lessons learned: networks extend resources; openness to "morphing" (program activities, goals, and participants evolving over time); and support for long-term and systemic view of problems. The fellows thus identified, out of their own experience, key facilitating factors in systems change identified by current reflective organizational development consultants and practitioners applying complex systems perspectives to leadership development, although this literature was not a part of the curriculum of their fellowship (Westley et al. 2007; Wheatley 2006; Wheatley and Kellner-Rogers 1996).

In my 2004 evaluation of ICHLD's HPF program, I addressed the question of how many of the fellows were able to accomplish some measure of "systems change" through applying skills and knowledge gained in the fellowship. More than 90 percent of the 23 fellows who completed the program (from Classes 1 and 2, 1998–2002) reported in the fall of 2003 that their participation in the fellowship resulted in not only changes in their own perceived abilities, but improved process and/or outcomes in their collaborations or the ways their home organizations participated in collaborations; these changes were linked to participation in the HPF through concrete examples of how learning was applied. These changes were coded as "enabling outcomes." Furthermore, for 30 percent of the fellows completing the program, there was strong evidence of significant contributions to farther-reaching improvements in their collaborations or home organizations, coded as "systems change." Systems change was defined as new collaborative programs or initiatives formed (not just modifications to existing programs) with tangible outcomes (participation from new populations, success in acquiring funding). Furthermore, the learning from the HPF, as seen by fellows with evidence corroborated by outside observer(s), was key in the creation of these new programs (Pinsker 2004). The definitions used in coding for these outcomes depended both on the reported strength of the outcome and the strength of the evidence linking that outcome to the HPF.

Not surprisingly, the success of "systems change" catalyzed by the fellow depended not only on the increase of their individual competencies as leaders via their participation in the program, but on their initial structural position in their home organizations: those fellows who were able to mobilize support from superiors and colleagues as well as those they supervised were more successful in implementing systems change than those who were not. In addition to initial organizational position (see the earlier comments from the focus group on "perceived power"), shared underlying conceptual models, or the ability to develop them through reframing, were part of the factors facilitating success for these fellows. For enabling deeper systems change, the fellows' ability to capitalize on relationships with other fellows (parallel to some definitions or models for increasing social capital) was also a facilitating factor.

Examples of systems change outcomes cited included the following (Pinsker 2004:8):

- HPF 1 Fellow, university based: fellow's increased ability to work with community agencies allowed three of those partnered with fellow to get an additional $500,000.
- HPF 2 Fellow, health system based: percentage of Hispanic pediatric clients served increased from near 0 percent to 30 percent, through hiring an outreach coordinator (new position) and the creation of a coalition.
- HPF 3 Fellow, minority-serving and staffed community organization based: 783 percent increase in the organization's budget (from $230,000 to $1.8 million), increasing clinic hours, clients served, and range of services offered, including new roles for the organization in partnerships (e.g., contracting as consultant).

From Comparative Internationalism to Systemic Globalism in Health Leadership Training

At the beginnings of the ICHLD health leadership program, the emphasis was on the possibilities for international exchange: the faculty probably considered themselves enlightened for realizing that the exchange does not go in just one direction, that the First World has things to learn from the Third World. The Alma Ata declaration and "health for all" were seen as precursors to the movement toward health equity in the United States. Given U.S. morbidity and mortality statistics versus how much the

United States spends on health care, it is of course difficult for U.S. health professionals, at least for those working in chronically underserved primary care and public health settings, to aver that the U.S. health system is the one that should be spread to the rest of the world. The faculty and fellows saw the Third World's experience with community health workers as a viable model that could work with underserved groups in the United States. Furthermore, the program had been started in the first place by the realization on the part of the original director that the United States did not have a premium on expertise in the community-university health professions schools partnership arena. But at the beginning, we were not yet talking about "global" health, although it emerged as a topic during the final years of the international program.

For me personally, the high point of being able to compare my own society with another, in the context of health leadership discussions about the provision of health care, was my interaction with the family practice doctor from Colombia, a member of ICHLD's third class of fellows, whom I later got a chance to visit (in 2005). I observed his work placing medical students in elementary schools in small towns in the *sabana*, the rural area outside of Bogota, where many people have come as refugees from the violence in other parts of Columbia. I went with the medical students to a meeting in the local social welfare office (run by a Ph.D. sociologist who was very supportive of the medical students and their work), which was coordinating the students' work with the community development work directed by the town municipal offices. The Colombian fellow had also had a chance to meet, in Chicago, the family practice residency faculty of the county public hospital and clinic system in which I was also working (at the same time I was still an evaluator for the health fellowship program based at the university). Hearing about our travails in working at the local level in Chicago—not having coordinated resources, having to separately deal with the local community-based organizations, the alderman's office, and the schools to try to do anything—he commented that in his country, although they had the equivalent of civil war at the national level, at the local level things were more organized and more responsive to community needs than they were in Chicago. In 2006 and 2007, I came to increasingly agree with him, as severe cuts in personnel and services in the public hospital and associated clinics in which I was working (administering the family practice physician faculty development program) decimated our local clinical public health system. The differences between the First and the Third World increasingly seem overrated. (That part of the "flat world" argument I agree with, although I agree with those who say that Thomas Friedman overemphasized the positive part of that message.)

One of the things that I learned in Bogota was that despite the under-nourishment and stunted growth displayed by some of the school children my colleague and his students were treating in the *sabana*, elsewhere in the metropolitan region obesity and diabetes were also surfacing as prob-lems in the low-income underclass. In the past several years, in working with projects aimed at reducing obesity and diabetes in underserved pop-ulations in the Midwest, I have learned that this is part of a global—not just domestic—pattern (Popkin 2009). Systemic relationships between modes of food production and consumption of nutrient-poor, calorie-dense food and beverages, and attitudes as well as practices underlying both consumption and production, extend beyond the United States as a "fast food nation" to the rest of the world. This is another example of how the growing development and application of systems theory–based analyses have benefited public health and thus need to be part of the train-ing of health leaders.

In the ICHLD program, back in 2004, earlier discussions about social categories and differential privilege and a differential access to health care were carried through to our developing understandings of what "global" health might mean. For instance (see Butler's comments on border health in this volume), when we had a reunion including all three classes of fel-lows from the international program, the theme was border health, and we held the meeting on the U.S.-Mexico border. We had site visits on both sides of the border, in El Paso, Texas, and Ciudad Juarez, Mexico. But what participants came to realize was that the "border" didn't just exist at the southern boundary of the United States. With seasonal migration patterns for many urban as well as rural U.S.-based Mexican-American families traveling between the United States and Mexico, the "border" was also in Chicago, and Oregon, and anywhere else where the health care system was dealing with people who go back and forth (with the challenges Butler describes). Furthermore, differential access to care has been compounded by demands for documentation, while drug-resistant tuberculosis and other bacteria infect people regardless of their legal status.

This degeographization of the "border" is what I think a lot of writers mean when they talk about a qualitative difference between "globalization" or "globalism" in the contemporary world and the kinds of cross-national traffic that happened before. When I first heard talk of "globalization" in public intellectual discourse I was skeptical—as anthropologists, don't we know that people have always managed to travel great distances, even if not by plane? And that food, ideas, music, religion, and medical practices have always traveled from one group of people to another? And that not all the immigrants to the United States, for instance, went one way—some people came to the United States and then went back to Poland or

Italy, even if others could not return, for political or economic reasons, to where they came from, although they may have preferred that? (See Thomas and Znaniecki 1920.) The idea that our world was the only one in which people and ideas have gone back and forth seemed ludicrous.

However, some people have argued that the pace of the exchange has increased, and that it is a "tipping point" kind of phenomenon—what the complexity theorists call "emergence"—where a quantitative increase gets to the point of a qualitative difference, a quantum leap. I am beginning to think there is something to that, that when distance is replaced by instant and cheap communication, such as Skype, and airline travel can make the path of a pandemic spread much more rapidly than our public health systems, with their multiple jurisdictions, can currently handle—something has indeed dramatically changed. The connection between geography and difference has changed—unlike the way Friedman (2005) portrays travel as a succession of McDonald's restaurants in cities around the world, difference is still there—cultural, social, and economic—but the difference between the south side of Chicago and the north side might be greater than the difference between someone on Chicago's wealthy Gold Coast and the new skyscrapers in Shanghai, or someone living in the skyscraper apartments in Zone 6 of Bogata (Bogata has zones that determine both tax rates and services available to residents, with Zone 6 being the highest income, highest tax, and highest service zone). Despite this, the bottom in the First World is still not as far down, on average, as the bottom in the Third (although the First World is not homogenous; Europeans have more of a safety net than Americans do).

As implied by the previous discussion of complex systems and the spread of epidemics, the public health professionals I work with are increasingly concerned about "disaster preparedness" and the potential of systems modeling and network analysis for increasing our ability to anticipate and respond to crises. However, national boundaries are still important, for political reasons more than strictly geographical ones. Decisions about who can go where and policies about who is quarantined, or not, and who gets care, or not, are still mediated by national governments. But, in a seeming paradox, the local becomes even more important, for how local authorities handle a burgeoning epidemic or other disaster has consequences that can reverberate outward very quickly (bringing us back to sensitivity to initial conditions). So, there are more reasons for local leaders from faraway jurisdictions to get together: it is not just for trading "best practices" anymore, it is because what local leaders do can actually influence what happens to people in a different country.

In the MARPHLI (MidAmerican Regional Public Health Leadership Institute) fellowship program based in UIC's SPH, the 2007–2008 program, for the first time, included an international fellow, based in

Prague, Czech Republic (International Collaborative for Public Health Emergency Preparedness n.d.). Participation of this fellow, as well as several exchanges (both virtual and face-to-face) between public health leaders and leadership trainers based in Prague and in Chicago, was based on the recognition that the theme of the institute ("Meta-Leadership and Collaboration in a Global Health Environment") spoke to the recognition that public health professionals in both cities and their regions are linked via existing biological and commercial exchanges, rendering them vulnerable to global epidemics and other potential disasters in similar and interconnected ways. ("Meta-leadership" is a term for leadership crossing multiple organizations and sectors.) Although at first glance it might not seem to make sense why a Prague-based fellow would come to Chicago rather than New York or Washington, D.C., with any international airport being a port of entry, it was useful for him to understand how things work here in the "heartland" of the U.S. Midwest, which has some parallels to the region surrounding Prague.

Conclusions: Anthropological Perspectives, Systems Thinking, and Leading Systems Change in an Intricately Connected World

The interrelationships among the systemic processes that we label as "social organization" and "culture" are not simple, but any effort to increase the effectiveness of attempts to lead social change, or to train others to do so, will have to address them. One of the doctors I have worked with went to Texas after Hurricane Rita. After sitting idle for some time, he was finally sent to a small Texas town. There was a local doctor there, sitting with a cash box, demanding $75 up front from anyone who sought his services. It is not mere greed that is going on here, or unmediated social networks—it is local assumptions about privilege, and what people are or are not entitled to. As cognitive linguist George Lakoff has recognized, "framing"—linking policy issues to the underlying cultural models that shape how they are viewed—is a strategy that must be mastered by anyone who would link with others to become a successful agent of social change (Lakoff 1996). Senge, the organizational development leadership guru whose books have popularized Forrester's systems dynamics, emphasizes the importance of understanding "mental models" for effective organizational leaders (Senge 1990), as noted earlier. Formal complex adaptive systems models include "internal models," as also noted in this chapter.

Margaret Mead's often-cited quotation "Never doubt that a small group of thoughtful, committed citizens can change the world. Indeed, it is the only thing that ever has," contains more systemic wisdom than is usually realized. The quote brings into question the cultural assumptions behind the predominant (in our society), heroic individual as agent model of social change, privileging instead the relationships among a small group and what can emerge from them. Efforts in public health to look at what makes for successful change in smoking cessation or obesity reduction, for example, have pointed to the influence of close interpersonal networks. However, small groups, such as the family, are also a prime locus for learning cultural models, as Mead and Bateson both realized.

What is learned can be modified, particularly if embodied via interpersonal practice as well as explicitly discussed. In the ICHLD leadership development program, in modifying attitudes as well as behavior involved in cross-ethnic/cross-racial collaborations, it was the informal relationships outside of the formal session that developed among fellows that mattered, in some cases supplanting or overcoming tensions resulting from explicit classroom presentation. The fellow who nearly dropped out due to dissatisfaction with the classroom presentation on racism told me that what made a difference in his own practice, and helped him successfully link some of the African-American churches in his community, was informal interaction with one of his African-American colleagues in the HPF, which provided the basis for a useful consulting relationship.

In the global context, too, regime change can come from the top down, but truly revolutionary systems change rarely does (although apparently, it can be stifled from the top). In this increasingly interconnected world, where every city becomes a port-of-entry for ideas as well as disease vectors, if we learn to couple the creation of local-to-global networks with the reframing of the meanings that result in changed models for what is possible, we may yet become more effective in fostering the development of small groups of committed leaders who can indeed transform the multiple challenges facing us toward greater health and well-being for all.

Notes

1. It does take at least a book to describe the variants and history of different schools of systems theory. I allude to only a few in this chapter. For readers interested in more detail, I recommend G. P. Richardson's book, *Feedback Thought in Social Science and Systems Theory* (Richardson 1991) as well as Fritjoff Capra's *The Web of Life* (Capra 1996). For applied systems theory approaches taken mainly from organizational and community development contexts and transferred to evaluation practice, see the collection edited by Bob Williams and Iraj Imam (Williams and Imam 2007).

2. Although computational modeling of complex adaptive systems can become very, well, complex, relatively simple agent-based computer models can be developed that display surprising emergent adaptive behavior: see Uri Wilensky's work in using Net Logo/Star Logo to develop models that high-school students and even middle-school students can use to learn about how to think about multileveled systems and understand such phenomena as why traffic jams can travel backwards when the cars are only going forwards (Wilensky and Resnick 1999; also see the current website for Uri Wilensky's center at Northwestern University, the Center for Connected Learning and Computer-based Modeling, at http://ccl. northwestern.edu/uri/).

3. Aside from Lansing, there have been some other cultural anthropologists who have built on some of the cybernetic concepts used by Bateson and Mead, or others from within the Macy circle; but this work has not found a place within the discussions of the Santa Fe group or other highly visible system theorists. See, for instance, Michael D. Lieber (*More than a Living: Fishing and the Social Order on a Polynesian Atoll,* 1994), which deals with many of the same themes that Lansing's work does, though the analysis is based on conceptual models rather than computer simulation modeling: the feedback loops among biological, social, and cultural/ritual factors which can sustain a healthy ecological balance in the absence of top-down human coordination consciously directed at maintaining that balance.

4. I have subsequently participated in these public health institutes as a presenter and mentor, which has given me a window onto the development of leadership training as interpreted through the evolving discipline of public health. From 2000 to 2007, I also was the program director for a family practice physician faculty development program (funded by the U.S. Health Resources and Services Administration [HRSA]) based in a public hospital and oriented to primary care physicians working in underserved contexts. We included leadership as a topic within this program, and I used my other contacts in health leadership training for presenters and resources. The dedicated physicians I met through this work, both as fellows and colleagues, have also informed my understanding of what health leadership can be.

References

Bateson, Gregory
    1972 Steps to an Ecology of Mind. San Francisco: Chandler Books.
Boddy, Janice
    1989 Wombs and Alien Spirits: Women, Men, and the Zār Cult in Northern Sudan. Madison, WI: University of Wisconsin Press.

Capra, Fritjof
    1996 The Web of Life: A New Scientific Understanding of Living Systems. New York: Anchor Books.
Center for Social Epidemiology and Population Health, in collaboration with the Center for the Study of Complex Systems, University of Michigan
    2007 Complex Systems Approaches to Population Health. Available at: http://sitemaker.umich.edu/complexsystemspopulationhealth/home. Accessed May 1, 2011.
Conway, Flo, and Jim Siegelman
    2005 Dark Hero of the Information Age: In Search of Norbert Wiener, the Father of Cybernetics. New York: Basic Books.
Copeland-Carson, Jacqueline, and Mary Odell Butler
    2005 Creating Evaluation Anthropology: Introducing an Emerging Subfield. NAPA Bulletin No. 24.
Council on Linkages
    2001 TRAIN National, 2001 Core Competencies. Available at: https://www.train.org/Competencies/compWOskill.aspx?tabID = 94. Accessed May 1, 2011.
Farmer, Paul
    2003 Pathologies of Power: Health, Human Rights, and the New War on the Poor. Volume 4. California Series in Public Anthropology. Berkeley, CA: University of California Press.
Friedman, Thomas L.
    2005 The World is Flat: A Brief History of the Globalized World in the Twenty-first Century. New York: Picador/Farrar, Straus and Giroux.
Holland, John H.
    1992 Complex Adaptive Systems. *Daedalus* 121(1):17–30.
    1998 Emergence: From Chaos to Order. Jackson, TN: Perseus Books.
Institute of Medicine (IOM)
    1988 The Future of Public Health. Washington, D.C.: The National Academy Press.
    2003a The Future of the Public's Health in the 21st Century. Washington, D.C.: The National Academy Press.
    2003b Unequal Treatment: Confronting Racial and Ethnic Disparities in Health Care. Washington, D.C.: The National Academy Press.
International Collaborative for Public Health Emergency Preparedness
    n.d. Announcing the First International Fellow at the 2007–2008 MARPHLI 16th Annual Leadership Institute, "Meta Leadership and Collaboration in a Global Health Environment." Available at: http://www.icphep.org/pdf/Anncemt_1st_Intl_Fellow_R_Olejnik.pdf. Accessed May 1, 2011.
Kidder, Tracy
    2003 Mountains Beyond Mountains. New York: Random House.

Koopman, J.
  2007 Applications in Epidemiology. Paper presented at Complex Systems Approaches to Public Health, Center for Social Epidemiology and Population Health, in collaboration with the Center for the Study of Complex Systems, University of Michigan, Ann Arbor.
Krieger, Nancy
  2001 Theories of Social Epidemiology in the 21st Century: An Ecosocial Perspective. *International Journal of Epidemiology* 30:668–77.
Lakoff, George
  1996 Moral Politics: What Conservatives Know but Liberals Don't. Chicago: University of Chicago Press.
Lansing, J. Stephen
  2007 Priests and Programmers: Technologies of Power in the Engineering Landscape of Bali, 2nd edition. Princeton, NJ: Princeton University Press.
Leroy, Kenneth, Scott Leischow, and Bobby Milstein
  2006 Special Issue on Systems Thinking in Public Health. *American Journal of Public Health* 96(3).
Lieber, Michael D.
  1994 More than a Living: Fishing and the Social Order on a Polynesian Atoll. Boulder, CO: Westview. Available at: www.questia.com.
Milstein, Bobby
  2008 Hygeia's Constellation: Navigating Health Futures in a Dynamic and Democratic World [electronic book]. Atlanta: U.S. Dept of Health and Human Services, Centers for Disease Control Syndemics Prevention Network.
Mitchell, Melanie 2009
  Complexity: A Guided Tour. Oxford, New York: Oxford University Press.
Pinsker, Eve C.
  2004 Evaluation of ICHLD Health Partners Fellowship Program, 1998–2004. April 2004. Evaluation report forwarded to WK Kellogg Foundation, Chicago: International Center for Health Leadership Development, University of Illinois at Chicago.
Pinsker, Eve C., and Michael D. Lieber
  2005 Anthropological Approaches to the Evaluation of Community-University Partnerships, Jacqueline Copeland-Carson and Mary Odell Butler, eds. NAPA Bulletin 24:107–24.
Popkin, Barry
  2009 The World is Fat: The Fads, Trends, Policies, and Products that are Fattening the Human Race. New York: Penguin.
Richards, Ronald
  1996 Building Partnerships: Educating Health Professionals for the Communities They Serve. San Francisco: Jossey-Bass Publishers.
Richards, Ronald, and Judith V. Sayad
  2001 Addressing the Needs of People: Best Practices in Community-oriented Health Professions Education. Maastricht, Netherlands: Network Publications.

Richardson, George P.
 1991 Feedback Thought in Social Science and Systems Theory. Philadelphia: University of Pennsylvania Press.
Rowitz, Louis
 2006 Public Health for the 21st Century: The Prepared Leader. Sudbury, MA: Jones and Bartlett.
 2009 Public Health Leadership: Putting Principles into Practice, 2nd edition. Sudbury, MA: Jones and Bartlett.
Senge, Peter
 1990 The Fifth Discipline: The Art and Practice of the Learning Organization. New York: Doubleday.
Singer, Merrill
 2009 Introduction to Syndemics: A Critical Systems Approach to Public and Community Health. San Francisco: Jossey-Bass.
The Turning Point Leadership Development National Excellence Collaborative
 n.d. Turning Point: Collaborating for a New Century in Public Health. Leadership Development. Available at: http://www.turningpointprogram.org/Pages/leaddev.html. Accessed May 1, 2011.
Thomas, W. I., and Florian Znaniecki
 1920 The Polish Peasant in America: Model of an Immigrant Group. Volume V: Organization and Disorganization in America. Boston: Richard G. Badger: The Gorham Press.
Waldrop, M. Mitchell
 1992 Complexity: The Emerging Science at the Edge of Order and Chaos. New York: Simon and Schuster.
Westley, Frances, Brenda Zimmerman, and Michael Quinn Patton
 2007 Getting to Maybe: How the World is Changed. Toronto: Vintage Canada, a division of Random House Canada.
Wheatley, Margaret J.
 2006 Leadership and the New Science: Discovering Order in a Chaotic World. San Francisco: Berrett-Koehler.
Wheatley, Margaret J., and Myron Kellner-Rogers
 1996 A Simpler Way. San Francisco: Berret-Koehler.
Wilensky, Uri, and Mitchell Resnick
 1999 Thinking in Levels: A Dynamics Systems Approach to Making Sense of the World. *Journal of Science Education and Technology* 8(1):1–24.
Williams, Bob, and Iraj Imam
 2007 Systems Concepts in Evaluation: An Expert Anthology. Port Reyes, CA: Edge Press/American Evaluation Association.

9

Localizing the Global in Technology Design

Christina Wasson and Susan Squires

Introduction

The spread of information and communication technologies (ICTs) constitutes a fundamental dimension of globalization. The proliferation of these technologies has been encouraged by the private sector, resulting in the increasing penetration of markets around the globe. Despite the profit orientation of corporations promoting ICT use, ICTs can also empower local populations, mitigate some of the problems created by inequalities within the marketplace, and improve communication access at the local level.

Based on many years of combined experience in the field as well as interviews with 15 design anthropologists, we identified two interrelated contributions that practicing anthropologists have made in the field of technology and globalization. Most fundamentally, anthropological perspectives counter what we term the "universalist globalization logic," widespread in corporations, that it would be a good business strategy to sell the same product all over the world. Anthropology practitioners argue for the need to consider differences between cultures with regard to the daily routines in which a product is used, as well as the symbolic structures and political economy in which its use is embedded. Simply put, while technologies are often viewed as being independent from culture, anthropologists show that the two are intimately intertwined. As one of our interviewees put it,

> You can build a widget that looks the same in Alaska, and send it to Patagonia and Chile, and it looks like the same widget but it ain't the same widget, because Nancy Munn was right and there's a thing called a value

transform and every time an object in a system of exchange moves in an exchange, it changes its meaning and its value. It becomes empirically a different object that's used differently.

Second, and more specifically, anthropologists provide technology organizations with understandings about how users in a *particular* culture engage with technologies, and recommendations for how to design products targeted to the lifeways and cultural meanings of that group (Cliver et al. 2010; Kimura 2010; Rangaswamy 2007; Salvador et al. 2007; Thomas and Lang 2007).

Anthropologists have increasingly been involved in the research and design process for ICTs because of the unique research perspective they offer. They collaborate with local populations to identify the impact of globalizing processes as well as the ways in which local groups innovate new ways of using ICTs to accomplish culturally constituted goals. They balance an examination of culture change with a consideration of cultural continuities. The impetus for change may come from a globalizing political economic system as well as from the availability of new technological tools that are able to support political, economic, religious, or family activities in novel ways. The result is often the development of translocal practices and social structures that integrate traditional and modern dynamics in sometimes unexpected ways. Rather than seeking to impose western capitalist norms of consumerism on nonwestern populations, anthropologists strive to respect local values. Working together with local research participants, they try to identify significant problems that new, culturally appropriate technologies might alleviate. Such problems could range from health care to bank access.

In this chapter, we examine the contributions of anthropologists who have worked with populations around the world to design technologies that improve the quality of life for these groups. We describe how they integrate theory and practice, the constraints that shape their work, and how they extend their insights through collaboration on interdisciplinary teams. We offer three case examples of projects to illustrate these themes, and conclude by arguing that while the field is still young, it shows great promise for the future.

In the summer of 2008, we interviewed 15 anthropologist practitioners who work at the intersection of technology and globalization. All were selected for an interview because they had international research experience working in the field of information and communication technologies. Six of the interviewees were external consultants or contractors, and nine worked for large corporations as "in-house anthropologists." One interviewee worked for a nonprofit organization, one held a research position within an academic institution contracted to conduct research with a private corporation, and the rest worked in the private sector under diverse titles. Ten of the interviewees were based in the United States, two in Ireland, and one each in the United Kingdom, Norway, and India. The companies most often represented were Intel, with four interviewees; Microsoft, with two, and IDEO (a large design firm) with two. Other large corporations represented included Motorola, Pitney Bowes, and Telenor, a Norway-based international telecommunications firm. There were seven women and eight men in the group interviewed. Although the group provided a representative range of experience, it was by no means an exhaustive list of practitioners in this field.

In the interviews, we explored these anthropologists' experiences with projects that addressed new technologies in the context of globalization, including their work process, theories used, and whether the projects led to new theory development. Each interview lasted about 45 minutes on average. They were audio recorded, transcribed, and coded using the qualitative analysis software Atlas.ti. We also collected publications, websites, videos, and other available materials from the interviewees. Although we discovered quite a range of work experiences, we were able to identify key patterns in those experiences that make the contributions of anthropology to ICT design so valuable.

An Anthropological Perspective on Technology and Globalization

The development and broad distribution of ICTs is widely recognized as one of the central elements of globalization. For example, anthropologists often draw on Arjun Appadurai's framework of globalization, which consists of five types of cultural flows: movements of peoples, media, technologies, finance, and ideologies (1996:33). As Appadurai notes, "technology, both high and low, both mechanical and informational, now moves at high speeds across various kinds of previously impervious boundaries" (1996:34).

Recent years have seen a burgeoning use of technologies to address various problems associated with globalization processes in developing countries. Often these technologies work through mobile phones, since those are the most widespread ICT products in many parts of the world. The challenges addressed by these technologies vary widely; examples include:

- The use of mobile phones to transfer money. In these cases, mobile phones can be of great help for families living in rural areas with no banking services who may have a relative working hundreds of miles away to earn money to support the others. This practice is most widespread in Africa, and is spreading in South Asia.

- The use of mobile phones to provide health services. For instance, one program in South Africa "uses a sensor-equipped pill bottle with a SIM card to advise healthcare workers if their patients aren't taking their tuberculosis medicine. The percentage of people keeping up with their medicine rose from 22 percent to 90 percent" (Bhatia 2009).
- The use of mobile phones to find the best market for one's products. For example, "The Kenya Agricultural Commodity Exchange… provides crop growers with up-to-date commodity information via text message (SMS). This allows farmers to access daily fruit and vegetable prices from a dozen markets, and many have quadrupled their earnings because they have access to information about potential buyers and prices before making the often arduous journey into urban centers to sell their produce" (Massachusetts Institute of Technology 2009).

In each of these three examples, the problems being addressed may be traced back to processes associated with globalization and the spread of capitalism in developing countries: the worker's need to migrate several hundred miles to find paying work that can support his/her family; the spread of modern diseases and the inadequate numbers of medical personnel; and the increasing degree to which local farmers deal directly with larger markets.

Often, the technologies that mitigate such problems are developed without any involvement from anthropologists. However, an understanding of the cultural context in which the technologies will be used is a prerequisite for their success. Many new technologies fail because their developers lacked such cultural insights. For instance, in an article, one of our interviewees cites a "mobile-based project in southern Africa aiming to provide SMS alerts to villagers [that] has so far failed…mainly due to suspicion, lack of trust and lack of understanding of the project" among its intended users (Banks 2007:4).

When anthropologists participate in the development of such products, they are able to ensure that technologies will be designed in a way that fits local cultural beliefs and practices, and that they are introduced into local communities in a culturally and politically appropriate manner. Anthropologists also work with technology developers to ensure that their products or services fit comfortably with ongoing changes in cultural norms, work practices, family relationships, and so forth.

The anthropologist practitioners who work in this area generally belong to the emerging applied field of "design anthropology" or "ethnographic praxis in industry" (anderson and Lovejoy 2005; Salvador et al. 1999;

Squires and Byrne 2002; Wasson 2000). Whereas some design anthropologists work in academia, most are employed by corporations or consulting firms. Design anthropologists most often work together with designers and technology developers, conducting ethnographic research with potential users of new technologies to ensure a good fit between the cultural beliefs and practices of the users and the products being developed for them. In addition, there are people who conduct ethnographic research in the area of technology and globalization who are not trained in anthropology, but who are clearly influenced by it.

The vast majority of design anthropologists are employed in the private sector. We are not sure why so few technology-focused anthropologists are employed by nonprofit organizations; there are many anthropologists who work with developing countries in other capacities (such as those represented in other chapters of this volume). Therefore, this area appears to represent an opportunity for future employment of anthropologists.

With regard to the private sector, companies have become interested in developing countries for several interrelated reasons. One is that they are looking for new markets, since Western markets have become fairly saturated by products such as mobile phones. Another is that countries like India, China, and Brazil are doing well economically and are therefore regarded as growth opportunities in the near future that are worth cultivating today. A third reason is that the private sector is discovering innovations in developing countries that have potential applications in the west. "Innovation now trickles up from emerging to advanced economies. And it may be the way of the future" (Fitzgerald 2009:33).

Anthropologists tend to be concerned about ethical issues, and there is certainly a potential for anthropologists working in business to participate in unethical practices, in the sense that their work might be part of a larger organizational effort to promote forms of consumption that could harm rather than benefit consumers. It is our experience that the vast majority of design anthropologists thinks carefully about ethical considerations, and do their best to ensure that the projects they work on do not lead to harm. This was certainly the case for our 15 interviewees. The flip side is that their work often has the potential to improve users' lives, and they are enthusiastic about such opportunities to contribute to society (Baba 2009).

The Field of Design Anthropology

Design anthropology emerged in the United States in the 1990s (Wasson 2000). It built on earlier anthropological studies of consumption, which can be traced back to Mauss's distinction between gifts and economic exchanges (1990 [1925]), and which experienced a resurgence in the 1980s and 1990s (Carrier 1994, 1997; de Certeau 1984; Miller 1994, 1997, 1998). Mauss first articulated the close symbolic linkages that exist between artifacts and individuals, and the ways that objects are centrally embedded in the enactment of social relationships. Ever since, when anthropologists have studied consumption, they have focused on the symbolic meanings of objects and on the roles that these objects play in social relationships. In the same vein, the anthropologists who contribute to technology development help the designers and engineers on their teams understand how a particular technology could be designed to fit with the existing practices, social interactions, and cultural frameworks of the intended users.

The first significant engagement between anthropologists and designers occurred through research on computer-supported cooperative work (CSCW) in the 1980s. The Xerox Palo Alto Research Center (PARC) was a major locus of such work. A group of eight or so anthropologists at PARC pioneered the use of ethnographic methods to understand how users interact with computers and related technologies (Blomberg et al. 1993, 1997; Suchman 1987). These anthropologists collaborated with engineers and designers to improve the design of various products. With regard to their theoretical approach, the anthropologists who worked in the CSCW field were particularly influenced by ethnomethodology, conversation analysis, and activity theory (Garfinkel 1967; Goodwin and Heritage 1990; Nardi 1996; Sacks et al. 1974). They emphasized the close examination of interactions between people and machines as well as the role that sociality plays in shaping tool use. At the same time, they contextualized such microlevel investigations in a critical consideration of corporate work processes and late capitalism (Blomberg et al. 1996, 1997; Suchman and Trigg 1991; Suchman et al. 1999).

The initial link between PARC and industrial design was forged in 1991 when PARC collaborated with a design firm called the Doblin Group on a project for Steelcase (Goodwin 1996; Goodwin and Goodwin 1996; Suchman 1992, 1996). Subsequently, Doblin's head of research left to create a new firm called E-Lab, based on the novel vision of using ethnographic research as a basis for all design recommendations. This approach was extensively publicized in the business and design press (Coleman 1996; Hafner 1999; Heath 1997; Nussbaum 1997; Robinson 1993, 1994a, 1994b; Robinson and Nims 1996; Smith 1997; Weise 1999; Wells 1999). Designers at other firms recognized the value of learning about consumers' everyday interactions with their products, and by the late 1990s, every major design firm in the United States claimed to include ethnography as one of its approaches (Wasson 2000). At the same time, several large high-technology corporations such as Intel and Microsoft also began to hire anthropologists to contribute to innovation and product development processes.

It is worth noting that anthropologists working in the public sector—nongovernmental organizations (NGOs) and government-sponsored research—have also used ethnography to understand technology in different cultural settings. Since at least the mid-1970s, anthropologists working in rural development projects requiring quick results have developed approaches referred to as rapid appraisal, rapid assessment, or rapid rural appraisal (Beebe 1995; Chambers 1983; Hildebrand 1982; Honadle 1979; Rhoades 1982; Shaner et al. 1982). Three important characteristics are shared by design and development anthropologists: "(1) a system perspective, (2) triangulated data collection, and (3) iterative data collection and analysis" (Beebe 1995:42). However, design anthropology also differs from development approaches in three important ways. First, design teams are usually small, whereas rapid rural appraisal requires the participation of more sizable teams. Second, the outcomes of a design team's work are most likely products rather than complex state-subsidized programs and public policies. Third, design teams use video whenever possible to document interviews and activities, so that team members and clients who could not participate in the fieldwork might review and exchange information (Squires 1999).

By 2005, the interdisciplinary community of researchers, designers, and others concerned with ethnographic studies of consumers had coalesced sufficiently to produce its own conference, the Ethnographic Praxis in Industry Conference (EPIC). An examination of conference proceedings reveals five widespread themes pertaining to the theory and practice of design anthropology.

First of all, design anthropologists have frequently identified one of their most fundamental contributions as the ability to bring local practices and the cultural contexts of product use to life through rich ethnographic narratives. Suchman initially articulated the need for such a contribution in 1995, when she noted that "how people work is one of the best kept secrets in America" (1995:56). She argued that such information was vital for workplace products (such as copiers and printers) to be designed in accordance with actual usage patterns. Anthropologists such as Suchman showed that they were able to uncover work practices and reveal how they were embedded in cultural norms and organizational politics.

In subsequent years, many anthropological studies for corporations described the ways in which various products and technologies were embedded in the lives of consumers around the world, from mobile phone use in China to computer use in Brazilian schools. Anthropologists became known for the ability to bring their portraits to life through the use of photographs, video clips, and other narrative tools. At the same time, design anthropologists did not want to be perceived as *only* contributing culturally situated stories of product use; they emphasized the importance of their analytical and theoretical work as well.

Second, the value placed on the integration of theory and practice was visible from the start, as the very first EPIC opened with a session on this topic. In the introduction, Robinson argued:

> [A]rticulating and developing theory is action. This is especially true of the representations of theory we develop and deploy. Because we are in this conversation with the people and organizations who will populate the future with artifacts, affordances, tools, and ways of thinking, we are actively engaged in shaping the future. We are not simply observers, describers, or contemplators of it.
>
> Where there is active engagement, there is both power and responsibility.... [W]e act in a way that inflects the directions of the companies and institutions who make the everyday world, who shape power and politics, whose values are literally "materialized" in a thousand ways each day. We cannot ignore the fact that we have both considerable influence on the future nor the consequent responsibility for using it (Robinson 2005:7).

Robinson positioned design anthropologists as developers of theoretical frameworks that can have a direct impact on the design of future products and technologies. This interest has continued in subsequent conference; for instance, in 2010 Cefkin considered the value of the concept of "practice" for comparing theoretical concerns with practical business agendas (Cefkin 2010).

A third theme commonly found in design anthropology discourse is the topic of methodological innovation (anderson and de Paula 2006; Faulkner and Zafiroglu 2010; Flynn et al. 2009; Metcalf and Harboe 2006). Influenced by conversation analysis, design anthropologists were early in adopting video recording as a data collection tool (Wasson 2000). The field also pioneered the development of photo diaries, video diaries, logbooks, and other data collection techniques (Faulkner and Zafiroglu 2010; Graham and Rouncefield 2010; Wasson 2000). Various practitioners have also developed software to analyze video and other forms of data (Di Leone and Edwards 2010; Ducheneaut et al. 2010; Mack and Mehta 2005).

A fourth topic of widespread interest is the question of how design anthropologists should strategize their work process and deliverables to maximize their influence on employers and clients. A valuable innovation has been the development of "experience models," "visual representations depicting key analytic relationships of the underlying behavioral structure of the organization or of an experience for the people involved. Their purpose is to distill the important aspects of behavior in a form that aids the development of concepts, prioritizes and evaluates design directions, and acts as a shared reference tool" for researchers, designers, and clients (Jones 2006:88; Robinson 1994a). More generally, the question of representation—how findings can be framed and communicated effectively among researchers, study participants, designers, and clients—has drawn a great deal of attention. In 2008, a session at EPIC was dedicated to this topic. In the introduction, Sunderland noted the importance of providing

> a space for mutual shared experience—spanning not just ourselves and those with whom we conduct our research, or between ourselves and our contracting clients, but among all parties. The papers in this section… implicitly and explicitly address the dynamics of power that are implicated in our methodological and representational choices, choices which simultaneously always implicate both theoretical and political considerations (2008:101).

Further consideration of how design anthropologists can work effectively in corporate contexts is presented below.

A final theme in the design anthropology literature is a debate about the relationship between ethnography, anthropology, and other disciplines. In the field of design, ethnography is practiced not only by anthropologists, but also by a wide range of other social scientists and designers. Anthropologists have been caught between a desire to gain recognition for their unique training and expertise, and a wish to be open to interdisciplinary collaboration. Many have expressed concern that ethnography may not deliver on its promise when practiced by those with limited training in theory, method, and cultural analysis. Yet in 2006, Tim Malefyt (an anthropologist) caused a stir at EPIC when he made critical comments about "pseudo-ethnography"; many non-anthropologists in the audience felt disparaged and alienated. Over time, this tension has diminished, and the sophistication of the interdisciplinary community engaged with ethnographic praxis in industry has significantly increased. Recently, Tunstall compared ethnographic practice across the fields of anthropology, marketing, and design by examining the questions, assumptions, methods, and evidence characteristic of each field. She concluded that "we cannot clearly articulate our value as a community of ethnographic practitioners until those distinctions are made visible and then subsumed within a transdisciplinary desire to create a unity of knowledge" (Tunstall 2008:230). It should be noted that the term "design anthropology" is not used by all anthropologists working in this field; some prefer to refer to themselves as "ethnographers" to downplay disciplinary distinctions.

Integrating Theory and Practice

In our 15 interviews with anthropologists working on globalization and technology issues, one of the striking patterns we found was how articulate the interviewees were about the relationship between theory and practice in their work. As in academia, theory provides the bedrock for the work of these anthropologists. Furthermore, they also contributed to new theory development with practical applications. For example, Nimmi Rangaswamy at Microsoft India was in the process developing new understandings of the "gray markets" through which technology products are often purchased in emerging economies. She argued that these markets should not be framed as piracy, but rather should be recognized as a form of entrepreneurship that operates through informal networks. "It's too expensive for the middle class and lower middle class. They just cannot buy it…companies have to engage with this."

Second, ken anderson at Intel developed the notions of "plastic time" and "distracted computing" to explain that "the kind of time that we live in now is really not that kind of scheduled, I mean it looks like it on your Outlook calendar but it's really not…. It sort of molds to activities and melts into cracks and things creep into it." Through ethnographic research, he found that most people were using their computers for short bursts of time in between other activities. This framework had implications for how Intel should plan power management in chip designs; instead of planning for hours of continuous use, he recommended a "turbo model of chip design, so…when you start up you have a burst of acceleration."

Almost all of the interviewees published their research findings. By doing so, they demonstrated the scholarly side of their professional identities, and contributed to a variety of disciplines. Their publications appeared in a mix of anthropology, human-computer interaction, design, and engineering venues. Only two had not published in traditional scholarly venues such as journals or conference proceedings. We present their stories to illuminate potential publishing issues for practitioners. We do not consider their situations as exceptions, but two ends of the curve. It is not that they do not or will not publish, but that they simply have not yet found where to publish.

Tatyana Mamut is a recent Ph.D. working for IDEO, a large design consulting firm. She has several articles in progress, and plans to publish them. However, she is in the process of thinking about her long-term career direction: whether she wishes to seek a traditional academic job, or remain in the world of practice. She is keenly aware of the different expectations for publications in these two worlds. Her decision about where to publish will depend on how she resolves this larger question; her publishing activities are on hold until she makes this decision.

I definitely do want to publish, and that was actually the whole reason why I went to grad school…. My problem is that I'm not really sure who I want to speak to at this point…. [I]f I want to get back into…academia, you know, it could be a liability, right, to position oneself as a practitioner…. I can't figure out who my audience is or who I want my audience to be in the future, because I want it to be all of that. The fissures between those different aspects of scholarship…seem to be much more fractured and fragmented and judged than they need to be.

Tatyana's experience with anthropology at elite institutions, such as her Ph.D. program, was that applied work was poorly understood and accorded low status. Although there are quite a few anthropology departments that focus on applied anthropology, they are located within second-tier universities.

At the other end of the continuum, Jared Braiterman actively publishes his research findings; however, his strong commitment to engaging with the general public has led him to turn away from publishing in anthropology journals. He makes his work accessible via websites, videos, design and computer conferences, newspapers, magazines, and participation in art exhibits. Publishing venues that cater to an anthropology audience are too narrowly targeted for his purposes.

I'm not really interested in contributing to the discipline of anthropology. Although I identify myself as a trained anthropologist, I don't see myself as part of academic anthropology. And because of that outlook, I really embrace self-publishing and adjacent communities including business, public policy, experience design, new technology, and the art world. With self-publishing I have had more freedom to experiment with new ways of telling stories, of communicating new ideas, and of reaching people who aren't necessarily interested in anthropology, per se. They might be interested in China, they might be interested in technology, they might be interested in urban green spaces. So those are the audiences I focus on. And I think when you talk about contributing to theory…it returns to the question of whom you want to engage in your research and with your ideas. I prefer to go beyond a narrow audience of anthropologists, who are often rewarded for limiting their conversations to each other, and instead to reach out to multi-disciplinary academics, practitioners, businesses, and a wider public audience concerned about technology, culture and global ecology.

Jared's preference is to make his findings widely accessible. That decision has influenced *where* and *how* he publishes, and shapes *what* he publishes as well. This does not mean he has abandoned theory. The theory is present in the questions he explores, the international approaches he takes, and the way he engages with a wide public audience. However, his insights are framed around the topics he is interested in, such as green spaces, rather than being framed as contributions to the discipline of anthropology.

The key factor that shaped Jared's applied orientation was his experience with homophobia in graduate school at Stanford University. His department made it clear that:

> my academic career was limited, basically because of homophobia.... I was told in my second year of graduate school that I could have an academic career if I were closeted. This contradicted the so-called reflexivity in anthropology movement and was voiced not by social conservatives but by self-described liberals, feminists, Marxists and post-colonialists.... I decided to choose an applied field because of that experience of exclusion, and have found the business world far more open to diversity than academic anthropology.

This interest in reaching a wider audience was not unique to Jared, although he was the only one of our interviewees who chose to make it his exclusive focus. Others we interviewed engaged in both academic publications and communication with the general public. Quite a number of our interviewees had a strong web presence, including websites, videos, and blogs. It was also common for the interviewees to frame their contributions in terms of practice-oriented topics, although many did participate in anthropology-focused activities as well, such as attending anthropology conferences.

Interdisciplinary Collaboration

Although each anthropologist we interviewed participated in a somewhat different work process, we also identified shared patterns across the interviewees. All of them collaborated with a variety of partners. Typically, they worked on interdisciplinary teams that included social scientists, designers, technologists, and perhaps other specialists. Team membership was generally described as highly fluid and varying over time, based on shifting needs of the project. Those who worked in consulting firms also collaborated closely with their clients; those who worked in corporations might or might not work closely with internal clients, depending on the company and the project. The work process for the interdisciplinary teams typically involved ethnographic fieldwork followed by analysis and the development of findings that were meaningful to internal or external clients (Squires and Byrne 2002; Wasson 2002). The findings ranged from general recommendations about the cultural practices that a new product should articulate with, to actual prototypes of new products.

One of our interviewees pointed out that the collaborative process of developing insights in this field of practice was markedly different from her experience in the university setting:

> the primary mode of theory development is kind of an adversarial one in academia.... [C]ritique is the primary method through which theory gets developed...there isn't a whole lot of room for critique in this particular job. It's more...collaboration and building upon.

Developing theories and models that integrate the perspectives of multiple disciplines, the client, and the cultures of the intended users is a challenge that our interviewees regularly faced and negotiated. As another interviewee commented,

> I think there is a challenge in worldviews, in different worldviews. Like it's often quite hard to communicate across the disciplines. And so that's really a challenge, especially with the engineers and the business people...for them to grasp...that we have different kinds of rationalities and [they]... come from a more positivist background where you see things as set and the world as like, one.

This interviewee noted that worldviews included not only different disciplinary perspectives within her organization, but also the perspectives of research participants from diverse cultural contexts, which had been revealed through fieldwork. The organization's social scientists tried to represent these voices within the organization.

Another interviewee illustrated the contrast between an engineering approach and an ethnographic approach by noting that engineers might respond to ethnographic findings by saying, "Just tell me what to do." In such a situation, the ethnographers would respond, "We're not really here to say...you should...move this from here to there. But we're here to provide strategic guidance." Whereas engineers wanted solutions that could easily be operationalized, the ethnographers sought to challenge taken-for-granted cultural assumptions.

Crysta Metcalf, an anthropologist at Motorola Labs who was one of our interviewees, portrayed the challenges of developing an interdisciplinary analysis in her presentation at the 2008 Society for Applied Anthropology conference. Figure 9.1 shows four consecutive slides from this presentation. As you can see, she portrayed the challenges of integrating the perspectives of the three disciplines represented on her research team: engineers, human computer interaction (HCI) specialists, and the anthropologist (herself). Members of each of these disciplines had different theoretical orientations and asked different research questions. Engineers drew on American folk theories to explain study participants' behaviors. They focused on logical coherence in sequences

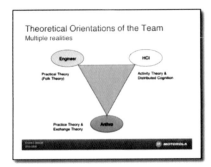
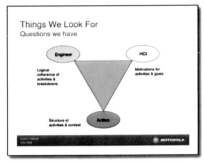
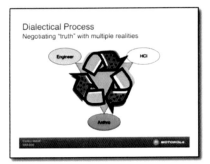

Figure 9.1. Slides from Crysta Metcalf's Presentation, "Interdisciplinary Research, Anthropological Theory and Software Innovation: Bringing it all Together"(Metcalf 2008). Illustration by Crysta Metcalf, Motorola Mobility, Inc.

of actions, and noted breakdowns as indicators of usage problems. HCI specialists approached research from the perspective of activity theory and distributed cognition (Hutchins 1995; Nardi 1996). They focused on users' motivations for engaging in particular activities. Crysta, the anthropologist on this team, drew on practice theory and exchange theory in her approach to analysis (Blau 1964; Bourdieu 1990). This allowed her to examine the social practices of users and the objective structures within which such practices took shape. Since the technologies being investigated by Crysta's team were highly social in their use, an anthropological perspective added an important dimension to the team's analytic capabilities.

Constraints That Shape Their Work

Most of the practitioners we interviewed identified two major kinds of constraints in their work process. One was based on their place in the product development cycle. The other resulted from the priorities of their employers and clients. Each of these constraints is described in turn, and then we present a counterexample to the overall patterns.

First Constraint: Working at the "Fuzzy Front End" of Innovation

Originally, we hoped to find the perfect case study for this chapter. In this ideal situation, we would interview someone who had participated in an interdisciplinary team that had conducted ethnographic research, discovered novel insights regarding local culture and technology use, and then used the insights to design a technology, which would now be making a significant difference in the lives of users.

We never found this story. Why not? Because most of our interviewees—most anthropologists working in this field—work at the "fuzzy front end" of a complex and lengthy product development cycle. The "front end" is where exploratory research takes place that may lead to the conceptualization of new products; it precedes the actual product development process (see Figure 9.2). Those of our interviewees who worked for design consulting firms were, by definition, providing such preliminary, advisory "front-end" information that would subsequently be used by their clients' internal product development organizations. Those of our interviewees who worked in corporations were usually located in labs or other "front-end" units of the business. Thus, whether in corporations or consulting, most of our interviewees had little control over how a product might evolve later in the development process. All they could do was try to influence key decision makers by evangelizing their insights and ideas. As one in-house practitioner explained, "You come up with some inspiration and some direction, and then you try to direct it in places where you think it will have influence. But at some point, you set it free."

As a result of where anthropologists were located in the product development cycle, it is often hard to trace their direct influence on the ultimate product. Products might also get sidelined or canceled later in the development process for reasons that have nothing to do with research. For example, new managers, changing corporate priorities, budget constraints, and technical issues could all have an impact on the continued development of a product concept.

In recognition of the challenges that employees located at the front end of innovation face in influencing product development, Donna Flynn and Tracey Lovejoy, two anthropologists at Microsoft, started to strategize ways of inserting their contributions all the way through the development process. They presented their approach at the 2008 Ethnographic Praxis in Industry Conference (Flynn and Lovejoy 2008), and we interviewed Donna for this chapter. She explained:

> What we've tried to do is identify ways in which having a robust understanding of who you're building something for is inserted in the product cycle all the way through. And so that also means we have to

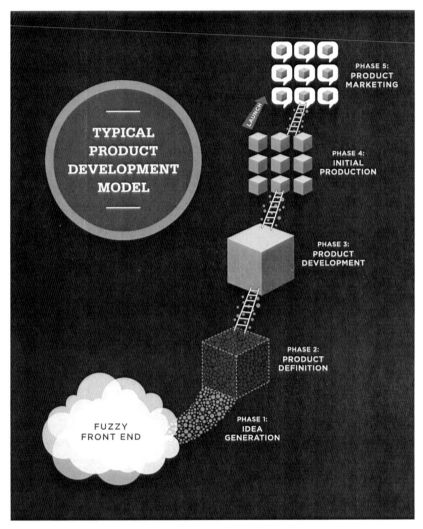

Figure 9.2. The Fuzzy Front End of Innovation. Illustration by Jeff Joiner/ Rocketlab Creative, based on Squires and Wall (2002).

map our research plans and our work plans very much to the product cycle. And so part of that...I mean that's sort of a long-winded way of saying we kind of find ourselves doing both the big strategic work and the very focused iterative—improving a little bit here, improving a little bit there—type of work at the same time. Because we have to stay with the product team as well as kind of a step ahead of the product team.

Second Constraint: Priorities of Employers and Clients

Interviewees were also constrained by the priorities of the corporations that employed them, or, if they worked for a consulting firm, by the priorities of their clients. The work these practitioners undertook was always framed by global markets and by their employer's or client's needs, goals, strategies, and understandings of where the best opportunities for profit and market share might be. As one in-house anthropologist put it,

> We don't always get to revel in the complexity of that global landscape as much as we would like to. Because as a business we also have to stay focused on top business priorities and business strategy. And that tends to be, kind of our top money-making markets: U.S., Europe, China. And so we, as anthropologists, sometimes feel a struggle between wanting to really embrace and understand the larger patterns of globalization within our business, and yet our business priorities and fiscal constraints often prevent us from going as broad as we would like to.

Constraints—A Counterexample

Not all of our interviewees were constrained by working at the front end of innovation or by the priorities of an employer. One of them, Ken Banks, the only interviewee who did not work for the private sector, provided an interesting counterexample. Ken has formed his own business working on issues of technology, conservation, and development in the nonprofit field (www.kiwanja.net). He had a strong background in technology design before he received his training in anthropology, so he combined the ability to conduct ethnographic research and develop technology solutions to a particular problem within a single person. As a consequence, he is not limited to working only at the front end of the product development cycle and can oversee the whole development process; and, being self-employed, he does not need to limit himself to the priorities of an employer. Of course, he still needs to work closely with clients, other nonprofit organizations he collaborates with, and the local people he seeks to assist. This produces constraints in terms of his need to maintain good relationships with clients and stakeholders, ensure that a range of voices are heard, and work within with funding limitations.

An example of his work is FrontlineSMS, an innovative technology for conducting surveys using the text-messaging feature on mobile phones. He is responsible for both the idea and the development of this technology, in which a computer sends questions to large numbers of mobile phones and receives responses in a format that can be analyzed using Excel or a variety of other software programs. FrontlineSMS has been adopted for many purposes, including for health organizations to communicate with nurses in remote areas, and for monitoring the vote process in several African countries.

Case Examples

In this section, we provide three examples of projects where our interviewees led ethnographic research to develop new product ideas that responded to the specific circumstances of particular cultural groups. These are all partial examples; none is a "perfect" case study. The stories are often incomplete, both because our interviewees tended to work at the "fuzzy front end" of innovation, and because most of the product ideas they described have not reached the point of commercialization yet. The contributions of these anthropologists weave together applied and theoretical strands. Their insights have emerged from their work as practitioners, and have helped to solve real-world problems. At the same time, we found that their relationship to theory was not, in fact, fundamentally different from that of academics. Like any anthropologist, they engage in an inductive, holistic research process that encompasses field research, analysis that draws on existing theory, and the development of interpretive frameworks and new theories.

Case Example 1: Communication Needs of Rural Low-income People in India

Crysta Metcalf, an anthropologist at Motorola Labs, worked on a project designed by a team at the Motorola Labs facility in Bangalore, India. Since this project emerged from a research lab, it was exploratory in nature, located at the "fuzzy front end" of innovation. The broader context of this project was Motorola's concern to become successful in the large Indian market. Since poor rural villagers were the largest part of the market, Motorola decided to focus on the needs of this group of potential users. Furthermore, Motorola wanted to take advantage of the expertise of employees at its Indian labs to do India-specific research.

> The topic was the communication needs of extremely rural, extremely low-income people in India. So, what we were really trying to figure out is not "How can we sell them something?" but instead, "What do they need?" And so we started off with this idea—well, let's go and, you know, spend some time with people in rural villages and figure out their communication patterns and their communication needs and see what we can design that will actually help them in their lives.

The team included three members from the Indian facility, a Ph.D. in political science and two interface designers, plus Crysta, who was there to mentor the team on how to conduct fieldwork. The team spent about five days intensively interviewing inhabitants of a rural village, and then returned to Bangalore to develop their analyses and identify new product ideas. Their findings encompassed four main topics.

First, they discovered that agriculture was organized into a three-level hierarchy, with day laborers at the bottom, tenant farmers in the middle, and (largely absentee) landowners at the top. The day laborers had a significant unmet need: "to know which plots of land are going to need the weeding, the sowing, the harvesting, at what time, on what day, and who's ready to pay them." Their current system was simply to walk around looking for work, often over long distances, and try to learn from each other which tenant farmers were hiring laborers that day. The Motorola team envisioned a communication tool that would allow day laborers to locate where the jobs were on a given day.

Second, the research team found that there was a shortage of doctors. Almost all of the villagers with whom they spoke identified this as a problem. One of their key research participants had lost a husband when he had a heart attack and died because there was no means to get him to a hospital. "From our perspective, we can't really help with getting them doctors, but we can help with some sort of communication, either for transportation to the doctors or communication with the necessary medical personnel, for...triage in the meantime."

Third, the research team identified an opportunity to make life a bit easier for villagers planning weddings or other large celebrations. They found that invitations to such events needed to be more personal than a phone call or a letter.

> They actually go to this other person's village and invite them in person. This can take two days out of their wage earning.... So we were trying to toy with the idea of...making...a more formal, acceptable invitation system...where the display on the phone allows the invitation to maybe open, and be more of a formal kind of [visual display].

Fourth, the researchers discovered a need for travelers to let their families back home know that they were okay. At present, communicating even simple messages was cumbersome. "They'd find somebody who had a phone, to call somebody in their village who had a phone, to give the message 'I arrived safely.'" The Motorola team envisioned a kiosk that could provide communication services for a whole village.

The theoretical frameworks that Crysta brought to this project were primarily economic theory and practice theory developed by both anthropologists and sociologists. She has been particularly influenced by Peter Blau's insight that "you can look at other things besides economic systems in an economic way." This resonated with Pierre Bourdieu's practice theory, in which he analyzed society using a marketplace metaphor. The project team integrated Crysta's theoretical frameworks with the perspectives of the other team members, who represented the disciplines of political science and interface design.

In addition to such theoretical framings, Crysta believes that her anthropology background contributed to the project in several other ways. She added a rigorous approach to ethnographic data collection and analysis, and a holistic emphasis on exploring relationships between themes. Furthermore, she believes that her training in cultural relativism helped her recognize the value of the different disciplinary perspectives offered by team members, and contributed to her ability to effectively manage interdisciplinary collaborations. Crysta's ability to share the outcomes of these projects with us was limited, partly by the need to protect Motorola's interests, and partly by the fact that products were still being envisioned and prototypes were still being developed.

Reflecting on ethical issues, Crysta mentioned a large multinational firm that is famous for having sold products that were harmful to consumers in Third World countries, and characterized the business strategy of such companies as: "We've got this product...what's our globalization plan? Oh, it's to sell it in all of these places." She continued:

> And what I really like about Motorola is that they don't seem to have that philosophy. It's, "What is needed in this area?" And then, it will sell itself, because it's needed. And sure you have to market it, and you have to do all of these things, but let's figure out what's needed. And actually they put together a phone specifically for India, and they thought it was, you know, what was needed, and it wasn't and it didn't sell. And instead of ramping up and trying, "Oh well then let's take it to the rural areas."... It was just like, "OK. Fine, take it off the market and do something else."

Case Example 2: Water Technologies for Low-income Farmers

Tatyana Mamut is an anthropologist at IDEO, a leading design firm. She described a four-month project, the Human-Centered Design Toolkit, when it was about halfway completed. It was a partnership with the Gates Foundation and an NGO called IDE, which designs, markets, and distributes water technologies to farmers who earn less than a dollar a day, primarily in Africa and Southeast Asia. The Gates Foundation had asked IDEO to help IDE develop a process for engaging with particular farming communities and learning about their needs and constraints. Such a process will enable IDE to develop water technologies that are targeted to local needs, and will also help IDE distribute the technologies effectively. Tatyana noted that this project will help IDE and similar NGOs address questions such as:

> How do they better engage...dollar a day farmers, and understand what their needs and their...constraints are, what their lifeworlds are like.... Also to take...previously existing designs from around the world and apply

them to contexts where it's appropriate, and understand in which contexts it's not appropriate, right, to do that kind of technology diffusion from other regions.

The IDEO team consisted of Tatyana, a mechanical engineer, and a curriculum specialist. They worked closely with their colleagues at IDE and the Gates Foundation. Members of all three organizations participated in fieldwork trips, including visits to Ethiopia, Kenya, and Cambodia. "We share all the tools with them. We do a workshop with them, out there [in the field].... [I]t's really all about collaboration through every step of the way."

The intended outcome of this project is a toolkit that NGOs can use to "walk through the process of need-finding on the ground.... [T]here will be findings about what processes or what methods are most salient and most useful in different contexts and in engaging...dollar-a-day farmers in really honest conversations about their lives and what they need." The methods being developed were quite ethnographic; they included community meetings, family home stays, semi-structured interviews, and participant observation. Furthermore, Tatyana also wanted to help NGO employees develop an anthropologist's ability to notice and question what is taken for granted: "how do you come into a new area with the anthropologist's eye of...making the strange familiar and the familiar strange."

The theoretical frameworks that Tatyana brought to this project were primarily practice theory and development anthropology. She said, "I really see practice theory...coming in over and over and over again in my work...habitus and fields, the individual and the system and how they interact, is...a constant theme in our work, understanding the relationships between system constraints and individual actions." Tatyana's training in the theories of Michel Foucault was also useful for this project. Like practice theory, Foucault's notion of governmentality provided a way to articulate the relationship between individuals and the political and economic contexts that shaped their perspectives and through which they navigated. She joked that "the actual phrase 'Foucauldian analysis' came up in the field in Ethiopia."

In addition to such theoretical framings, Tatyana believes that her anthropology background contributed to the project in three ways: she provided expertise in ethnographic data collection, skill in analysis, and familiarity with the ethnographic literature on development issues across a variety of cultures. With regard to data collection, she pointed out that it has become popular in design firms to "do quote-unquote ethnographic research, but the nuances of when to use what, for what purpose, and... what do you yield from different methodologies...is more nuanced with an anthropological background." With regard to analysis, she said that her training in anthropology contributed to her skill in "translating the information that we gain into...theoretical structures—what we call 'frameworks' at IDEO." Finally, her familiarity with ethnographic literature helped her direct other team members to useful background readings. For instance, to prepare American designers who had never experienced the practical logics of developing countries for fieldwork in such settings, Tatyana had her whole team read the work of development anthropologist James Ferguson, as well as Tania Li's *The Will to Improve* (2008), an ethnography of development in Indonesia.

Since the time of the interview, this project has been completed and has started to receive considerable public notice, including an article in *Fast Company* (Walker 2009) and a 2009 International Design Excellence Award.

Case Example 3: Missed Calls in Bangladesh

Hanne Cecilie Geirbo is an anthropologist at Telenor, a Norway-based international telecommunications firm. Hanne Cecilie works at Telenor Research and Innovation, "an innovation hub...with a long-term perspective. The purpose is to strengthen Telenor's global competitive strength" (Telenor 2008). In other words, Hanne Cecilie's position is similar to Crysta Metcalf's at Motorola, in the sense that she also works in a lab environment conducting exploratory research at the "fuzzy front end" of innovation.

Furthermore, Hanne Cecilie told us that because Telenor is an international company, with interests around the world, most of her research is conducted in countries other than Norway. Indeed, Telenor Research and Innovation opened a facility in Malaysia in 2006 (Telenor 2008). Hanne Cecilie described most of her research as a translation activity.

> Lots of technologies [were] actually developed in the West and for a certain purpose. You develop [a technology] with a certain purpose in mind and then it goes out to people who practice or use it totally differently...in different ways that were not intended and there was no past business case built on that kind of use.

So, the task of Hanne Cecilie and her colleagues was to understand cultural communication practices that affected the use of Telenor services, and to recommend new technologies and services that would support such practices while creating a profit opportunity for Telenor.

As an example, Hanne Cecilie described a "missed calls project" that she conducted in Bangladesh in April 2007. She explained that missed calls are a major concern for phone companies in Asia and Africa, where the practice of sending missed calls is widespread. Essentially, people call and hang up before the phone is answered, in order to send a signal to the person being called without incurring any charges. For phone companies, this is a challenge because it causes network congestion. Operators are compelled to scale their networks to accommodate not only revenue-generating traffic, but also missed calls. A contributing factor was that people were able to send several hundred missed calls at a time. Jonathan Donner at Microsoft research first wrote about missed calls as a social practice (2007). Elaborating on Donner's observations, the Telenor team thought it would be interesting to look more closely at the various motivations behind the practice, combining qualitative research with quantitative analysis of call data records.

Hanne Cecilie's research team went to Bangladesh "to explore why people [send missed calls], and how they do it, and who does it," with the goal of developing win-win solutions that would support the cultural communication practices of users as well as saving Telenor money and reducing traffic on the network. In addition to Hanne Cecilie, the project team included a psychologist with whom she conducted the fieldwork, which consisted of focus group discussions as well as semi-structured interviews with random people in public space, as well as a mathematician who conducted quantitative analysis of call data drawn from Grameen Phone's records. Back home, the analysis process consisted of iterations between the quantitative analysis that revealed large-scale patterns of missed calling, and the qualitative analysis that illuminated the social practices behind the numbers and graphs. During this process, the team was in regular communication with a business unit that contributed an economic and regulatory framework and pointed out issues to explore further. Since Hanne Cecilie had previously lived and worked in Bangladesh, she also contributed expertise on Bangladeshi culture.

Through their ethnographic research, the research team made a series of discoveries. First of all, they found that sending missed calls was a common practice among members of all classes of Bangladeshi society, from richest to poorest. This finding was contrary to what Hanne Cecilie called the "myth" that the team had encountered when they set out for fieldwork, namely "that this is something poor people do, only poor people, and they do it only to save money." The implication of the research team's discovery was that sending missed calls was not simply motivated by economic necessity; more complex cultural logics were at play.

Second, they identified four major reasons for sending missed calls: economic, practical, entertainment, and social/relational, which included flirting and expressive communication. With regard to entertainment, Hanne Cecilie said that people would "send each other like a hundred missed calls just to tease and have these missed call competitions to see who can send the most amount of missed calls and that kind of thing." For flirting purposes, she explained that "as a way to pick up people you send missed calls to random numbers so someone will call you back.... Even girls do that.... And then people develop phone affairs.... There's all these stories about people ending up getting married."

Perhaps most important, the research team found that sending missed calls was a way for friends to maintain the high level of sociality that was traditional in Bangladeshi society in the face of a modern lifestyle that no longer permitted such time-taking face-to-face practices. For instance, friends traditionally would drink tea together in informal gatherings that could continue for many hours. During such events, the conversation would to a large extent consist of what Hanne Cecilie called "expressive communication" rather than "instrumental communication." What she meant was that participants were making conversation merely to be social, rather than because they needed to communicate particular facts to each other. "The words will just flow between the people and the group, and it will go from more serious issues to more just nonsense and back.... It's just this thing about being together...the flow of communication, that's the point." When friends could not be together in person, sending each other missed calls was a way for them to engage in "expressive communication"; the caller was simply letting the recipient know that the caller was thinking of the recipient. It was a way for two people to feel connected without the need to communicate anything more than each other's presence. "That explains a lot of this missed call behavior and it also points probably to a solution.... [W]e need to give people...some kind of service where they can express this...kind of communication."

These research findings generated a great deal of attention within Telenor. The project "gained a lot of interest from different people—business people, and technologists, and other people on these issues, there's been a lot of attention." The solutions for avoiding financial losses were still under development at the time of the interview; technologists had taken the lead on this part of the project, but the research team remained in communication with them to ensure the cultural appropriateness of solutions as they emerged.

Hanne Cecilie's theoretical background reflects her training in anthropology at the University of Oslo. She is interested in topics that have long been a focus at this university—where Fredrick Barth worked for many years—such as identity, ethnicity, nation-building, and related ideologies. However, she feels that these topics were not as central to the missed calls project as they have been for some of her other Telenor projects, for instance in the Balkans. Publications about the missed calls project have been framed in the theoretical perspective of digital literacy (Fjuk 2008; Fjuk et al. 2008). In addition, Hanne Cecilie believes that a key contribution of her anthropological training is the ability to take advantage of "serendipity" during fieldwork, a lovely term that eloquently evokes the inductive and exploratory nature of ethnographic research (Wolcott 2010).

> We're perhaps more open than other social scientists to explore what we find when we're there. I mean, that we have this idea of what we're going to look at, we go to the field, and we might end up finding something completely different…. And then to be open to explore it and take the time to actually check it out and perhaps find something that we had no idea was there. And then so I think that's an advantage…being a little laid-back in the field in that way, that you open up for whatever is out there and have set aside time for hanging out, and just informal chatting, and, yeah, exploring whatever might come out of that.

Conclusions: The Potential of Anthropology for Translocal Technology Design

Localizing the Global

In many technology companies, there are some decision makers who assume that the same product can be sold around the world unproblematically. We refer to this as a "universalist globalization logic." Such logic rests on assumptions of cultural homogeneity with respect to technology use. Anthropologists have made significant contributions to technology companies by arguing that instead, technologies should be customized to the cultures of the regions in which they will be used. They have demonstrated that local understandings and uses of products can differ widely from group to group (Cliver et al. 2010; Kimura 2010; Rangaswamy 2007; Salvador et al. 2007; Thomas and Lang 2007). Such differences may range from users' goals, to a product's symbolic meanings, to the ways that a product supports or hinders local forms of sociality. Furthermore, these differences are embedded in the local social structures and political economies that people need to navigate on a daily basis.

Technology companies are increasingly recognizing the value of understanding local consumer cultures and the importance of using this understanding as a basis for product development. They are turning to anthropologists as experts in the analysis of cultural practices and beliefs. The companies that have gone farthest along this path are using ethnographic insights not only to adapt existing products, but also to develop entirely new products. This approach is described in the three case studies presented here.

Applied anthropologists' contributions to global-local technology design include both theoretical and practical elements. With regard to theory, design anthropologists fill a gap in the literature on the value of customizing technologies to their cultural context. This literature spans the fields of business strategy, design, marketing, and HCI (Aykin 2005; Chavan et al. 2009; Del Galdo and Nielsen 1996; Diehl and Christiaans 2006; Jansson 2007; Marcus 2006). Work in these fields is typically sophisticated with regard to business strategy, design, and so forth. However, this literature tends to undertheorize concepts of culture. The writings of design anthropologists fill this gap by contributing a more nuanced portrait of how cultural practices, meanings, and social structures shape product use.

Design anthropologists also contribute to science and technology studies (STS). STS scholars have conducted extensive research on how the development and use of existing technologies is embedded in a complex web of cultural and social phenomena. Design anthropologists build on this scholarship and extend it by showing how such insights can be used to actively shape the design of new technologies. In other words, they illustrate the integration of theory and practice and thereby contribute to a theory of practice (Baba 2000).

Design anthropologists' applied contributions to global-local technology design include both humanitarian and profit-related aspects. On the one hand, design anthropologists strive to ensure that the voice of local consumers is heard in the design of particular technologies. In doing so, they may contribute to the empowerment of local groups by providing them with tools to improve their economic, political, medical, or social situations. More generally, design anthropologists work to shift corporate business strategies away from the "universalist globalization logic" and toward greater recognition of cultural diversity in product use. They may seek to have an impact on their organizations not only at the "fuzzy front end of innovation," but also at other points along the product development process (Flynn and Lovejoy 2008). At the same time, design anthropologists contribute to the profitability of their employers by helping ensure that products are developed in a way that maximizes the likelihood that they will be widely purchased.

The Popularity of Ethnography

In the field of technology and globalization, the research approach known as "ethnography"—historically developed within anthropology—has become highly popular among corporations and design firms. In the process, however, it has become oddly disassociated from the field of anthropology. Many people now claim to conduct ethnography without any formal training; they may have been educated in the disciplines of design or psychology, or simply have a business background. Such people engage in a practice that we humorously refer to as "ethnography lite," an approach that tends to overemphasize data collection, especially video ethnography, while lacking an understanding of data analysis, anthropological theory and literature, and how to integrate research findings with theory to produce powerful, paradigm-changing insights. "Ethnography lite" leads to more superficial and less accurate conclusions than an approach grounded in cultural theory and analysis.

This disassociation between ethnography and anthropology represents a clear failure on the part of our discipline to communicate to the general public what anthropology is and does. It has resulted in a certain degree of competition between anthropologists and others who conduct ethnography. When we asked our interviewees what their anthropology training contributed to projects, they often answered by differentiating their work from that of non-anthropologist ethnographers. For example, one said, "What I rail against is…people with absolutely no background in the social sciences whatsoever claiming to be ethnographers…. There are people out there who…claim that ethnography can be done without theory, which I think is…bankrupt as a concept…you can't just have the methods and then execute on them. You have to have a framework, a theoretical framework in which those methods are applied." Another stated, "I think there's going to be probably a sorting out within the next five to ten years of [design] companies that can't provide more than just going into people's houses and videotaping them, and companies that can really demonstrate that they hold something that's resonant from that." As these quotes show, the anthropologists we interviewed regarded their knowledge of theory and analytical skills as central characteristics distinguishing their work from "ethnography lite." Theory plays a key role in their practice, their ability to develop far-reaching recommendations for their clients and employers (Sunderland and Denny 2007).

Furthermore, the business sector is at the vanguard of a broader phenomenon. Ethnography is increasingly becoming popular in other domains as well, such as public health. Anthropologists in these settings will most likely start to face the same kinds of competition from untrained "ethnographers" and will need to differentiate their skills. We would suggest to anthropologists in such contexts that what sets them apart is not so much their data collection abilities as their skill in cultural analysis, grounded in an extensive knowledge of cultural theory.

The Challenges of Participatory Action Research

A trend in applied anthropology is the effort to involve research participants in the design and execution of ethnographic research, a practice often known as "participatory action research." We asked our interviewees whether any of them were engaging in this practice. None were, and several provided insightful comments about their wish to do so, their hopes for doing so in the future, and the challenges that had prevented them from doing so until that point. The challenges emerged from the complexities of examining globalization as well as the constraints of working in the private sector. As one pointed out, "you need to set apart quite a bit of time to do it and you need to be…a lot in the field. You need to have close cooperation with the local people…. It's an ideal, we'd like to do that." In other words, participatory action research in the space of technology and globalization would require long visits to parts of the world that were far from corporate headquarters, and this was difficult to arrange. In addition, as discussed earlier, our interviewees were constrained by the priorities of the corporations that employed them, or, if they worked for a consulting firm, by the priorities of their clients; their work was never driven solely by the priorities of their research participants.

A New Field

The applied anthropology of globalization and technology is a young and growing field. The youth of the field, as well as the constraints placed on practitioners by corporate sponsors, mean that details of anthropology's contributions may not be immediately available. But practitioners are well positioned to keep pushing the envelope due to their thoughtful understandings of the feedback relationship between theory and practice.

Furthermore, we are confident that more and more case studies will emerge in coming years showing how anthropologists are working to ensure that new technologies are designed to support diverse cultural practices around the world. Such practitioners are already sharing information about completed projects through venues such as the Ethnographic Praxis in Industry Conference (EPIC), a venue designed for stories just such as these.

Acknowledgments

We extend our deep appreciation to the 15 anthropologists who were kind enough to allow us to interview them. We were impressed by the depth of their insights, and thank them for being willing to share their perspectives with a wider audience. All of them gave permission for us to use their real names. Everyone whom we quoted reviewed this chapter to ensure that we represented their views accurately and did not reveal any confidential information. We also wish to express our gratitude to our research assistant, Robert Packwood, for his excellent transcriptions of the interviews. His timeliness and good communication made him a pleasure to work with.

References

anderson, ken, and Rogerio de Paula
2006 We We We All the Way Home: The "We" Effect in Transitional Spaces. Ethnographic Praxis in Industry Conference Proceedings. Pp. 60–75.

anderson, ken, and Tracey Lovejoy (eds.)
2005 Ethnographic Praxis in Industry Conference Proceedings. Arlington, VA: American Anthropological Association.

Appadurai, Arjun
1996 Disjuncture and Difference in the Global Cultural Economy. *In* Modernity at Large: Cultural Dimensions of Globalization. Pp. 27–47. Minneapolis: University of Minnesota Press.

Aykin, Nuray (ed.)
2005 Usability and Internationalization of Information Technology. Hillsdale, NJ: Lawrence Erlbaum.

Baba, Marietta L.
2000 Theories of Practice in Anthropology: A Critical Appraisal. NAPA Bulletin 18:17–44.
2009 Disciplinary-professional in an Era of Anthropological Engagement. *Human Organization* 68(4):380–91.

Banks, Ken
2007 Mobile Web in the Developing World Vol. Available at: http://www.kiwanja.net. Accessed June 7, 2009.

Beebe, James
1995 Basic Concepts and Techniques of Rapid Appraisal. *Human Organization* 54(1):42–51.

Bhatia, Juhie
2009 Global Health: Mobile Phones to Boost Healthcare. Available at: http://globalvoicesonline.org/2009/02/23/global-health-mobile-phones-to-boost-healthcare/. Accessed July 6, 2009.

Blau, Peter
1964 Exchange and Power in Social Life. New York: Wiley.

Blomberg, Jeanette, Jean Giacomi, Andrea Mosher, and Pat Swenton-Wall
1993 Ethnographic Field Methods and Their Relation to Design. *In* Participatory Design: Principles and Practices, D. Schuler and A. Namioka, eds. Pp. 123–55. Hillsdale: Lawrence Erlbaum Associates.

Blomberg, Jeanette, Lucy Suchman, and Randall Trigg
1996 Reflections on a Work-oriented Design Project. *Human-Computer Interaction* 11:237–65.
1997 Back to Work: Renewing Old Agendas for Cooperative Design. *In* Computers and Design in Context, M. Kyng and L. Mathiassen, eds. Pp. 267–87. Cambridge: MIT Press.

Bourdieu, Pierre
1990 The Logic of Practice. R. Nice, translator. Stanford: Stanford University Press.

Carrier, James G. (ed.)
    1994 Gifts and Commodities: Exchange and Western Capitalism since 1700. London: Routledge.
    1997 Meanings of the Market: The Free Market in Western Culture. Oxford: Berg.
Cefkin, Melissa
    2010 Practice at the Crossroads: When Practice Meets Theory, a Rumination. Ethnographic Praxis in Industry Conference Proceedings. Pp. 46–58.
Chambers, Robert
    1983 Rapid Appraisal for Improving Existing Canal Irrigation Systems. Discussion Paper Series No. 8. New Delhi, India: Ford Foundation.
Chavan, Apala, Douglas Gorney, Beena Prabhu, and Sarit Arora
    2009 The Washing Machine that Ate My Sari: Mistakes in Cross-cultural Design. *Interactions* 16(1):26–31.
Cliver, Melissa, Catherine Howard, and Rudy Yuly
    2010 Navigating Value and Vulnerability with Multiple Stakeholders: Systems Thinking, Design Action and the Ways of Ethnography. Ethnographic Praxis in Industry Conference Proceedings. Pp. 227–36.
Coleman, Cindy
    1996 Perverse Fascination. *Perspective* 3(Fall):37–39.
de Certeau, Michel
    1984 The Practice of Everyday Life. S. Rendall, translator. Berkeley: University of California Press.
Del Galdo, Elisa, and Jakob Nielsen (eds.)
    1996 International User Interfaces. New York: John Wiley & Sons.
Di Leone, Beth, and Elizabeth Edwards
    2010 Innovation in Collaboration: Using an Internet-based Research Tool as a New Way to Share Ethnographic Knowledge. Ethnographic Praxis in Industry Conference Proceedings. Pp. 122–35.
Diehl, Jan Carel, and Henri Christiaans
    2006 Globalization and Cross-cultural Product Design. Proceedings of the International Design Conference "Design 2006." Dubrovnik. Pp. 503–10.
Donner, Jonathan
    2007 The Rules of Beeping: Exchanging Messages via Intentional "Missed Calls" on Mobile Phones. *Journal of Computer-Mediated Communication* 13(1):Article 1.
Ducheneaut, Nicolas, Nicholas Yee, and Victoria Bellotti
    2010 The Best of Both (Virtual) Worlds: Using Ethnography and Computational Tools to Study Online Behavior. Ethnographic Praxis in Industry Conference Proceedings. Pp. 136–48.
Faulkner, Susan A., and Alexandra C. Zafiroglu
    2010 The Power of Participant-made Videos: Intimacy and Engagement with Corporate Ethnographic Video. Ethnographic Praxis in Industry Conference Proceedings. Pp. 113–21.

Fitzgerald, Michael
    2009 As the World Turns. Fast Company, March. Pp. 33–34.
Fjuk, Annita
    2008 New Artifacts—New Practices: Putting Mobile Literacies into Focus. *Nordic Journal of Digital Literacy* 01. Available at: http://www.idunn.no.
Fjuk, Annita, Anniken Furberg, Hanne Cecilie Geirbo, and Per Helmersen
    2008 New Artifacts—New Practices: Putting Mobile Literacies into Focus. *Digital Kompetanse* 1(3):21–38.
Flynn, Donna, and Tracey Lovejoy
    2008 Tracing the Arc of Ethnographic Impact: Success and (In)visibility of Our Work and Identities. Ethnographic Praxis in Industry Conference Proceedings. Pp. 238–50.
Flynn, Donna K., Tracey Lovejoy, David Siegel, and Susan Dray
    2009 "Name that Segment!": Questioning the Unquestioned Authority. Ethnographic Praxis in Industry Conference Proceedings. Pp. 81–91.
Garfinkel, Harold
    1967 Studies in Ethnomethodology. Englewood Cliffs: Prentice-Hall.
Goodwin, Charles
    1996 Transparent Vision. *In* Interaction and Grammar, E. Ochs, E. A. Schegloff, and S. A. Thompson, eds. Pp. 370–404. Cambridge: Cambridge University Press.
Goodwin, Charles, and Marjorie Harness Goodwin
    1996 Formulating Planes: Seeing as a Situated Activity. *In* Cognition and Communication at Work, Y. Engeström and D. Middleton, eds. Pp. 61–95. Cambridge: Cambridge University Press.
Goodwin, Charles, and John Heritage
    1990 Conversation Analysis. *Annual Review of Anthropology* 19:283–307.
Graham, Connor, and Mark Rouncefield
    2010 Acknowledging Differences for Design: Tracing Values and Beliefs in Photo Use. Ethnographic Praxis in Industry Conference Proceedings. Pp. 79–99.
Hafner, Katie
    1999 Coming of Age in Palo Alto: Anthropologists Find a Niche Studying Consumers for Companies in Silicon Valley. New York Times, June 10. Pp. D1, D8.
Heath, Rebecca Piirto
    1997 Seeing is Believing: Ethnography Gets Consumers Where They Live—And Work, and Play, and Shop. *In* Marketing Tools March:4–9.
Hildebrand, Peter
    1982 Summary of the Sondeo Methodology Used by ICTA. *In* Farming Systems Research and Development: Guidelines for Developing Countries, W. W. Shaner, P. F. Philipp, and W. R. Schmehl, eds. Pp. 89–291. Boulder, CO: Westview.
Honadle, George
    1979 Rapid Reconnaissance Approaches to Organizational Analysis for Development Administration. Paper presented at the Conference on

Rapid Rural Appraisal at the Institute of Development Studies, University of Sussex, Brighton, United Kingdom, December 4–7.

Hutchins, Edwin
1995 Cognition in the Wild. Cambridge: MIT Press.

Jansson, Hans
2007 International Business Marketing in Emerging Country Markets: The Third Wave of Internationalization of Firms. Cheltenham: Edward Elgar.

Jones, Rachel
2006 Experience Models: Where Ethnography and Design Meet. Ethnographic Praxis in Industry Conference Proceedings. Pp. 82–93.

Kimura, Tadamasa
2010 Keitai, Blog, and Kuuki-wo-yomu (Read the Atmosphere): Communicative Ecology in Japanese Society. Ethnographic Praxis in Industry Conference Proceedings. Pp. 199–215.

Li, Tania
2008 The Will to Improve: Governmentality, Development, and the Practice of Politics. Durham: Duke University Press.

Mack, Alexandra, and Dina Mehta
2005 Accelerating Collaboration with Social Tools. Ethnographic Praxis in Industry Conference Proceedings. Pp. 146–52.

Marcus, Aaron
2006 Cross-cultural User-experience Design. In Proceedings of the 4th International Conference, Diagrams 2006: Diagrammatic Representation and Inference. Pp. 16–24. Berlin: Springer.

Massachusetts Institute of Technology
2009 Why Africa? In Entrepreneurial Programming and Research on Mobiles. Available at: http://eprom.mit.edu/whyafrica.html. Accessed May 14, 2009.

Mauss, Marcel
1990 [1925] The Gift: The Form and Reason for Exchange in Archaic Societies. W. D. Halls, translator. New York: W.W. Norton.

Metcalf, Crysta
2008 "Interdisciplinary Research, Anthropological Theory and Software Application: Bringing it All Together." Paper presented at the Society for Applied Anthropology Annual Meeting, Memphis, TN, March 28.

Metcalf, Crysta J., and Gunnar Harboe
2006 Sunday is Family Day. Ethnographic Praxis in Industry Conference Proceedings. Pp. 49–59.

Miller, Daniel
1994 Modernity, an Ethnographic Approach: Dualism and Mass Consumption in Trinidad. Oxford: Berg.
1997 Capitalism: An Ethnographic Approach. Daniel Miller, ed. Oxford: Berg.
1998 Material Cultures: Why Some Things Matter. Chicago: University of Chicago Press.

Nardi, Bonnie A. (ed.)
  1996 Context and Consciousness: Activity Theory and Human-Computer Interaction. Cambridge, MA: MIT Press.
Nussbaum, Bruce
  1997 Annual Design Awards: Winners—The Best Product Designs of the Year. *Business Week*, June 2. Pp. 92–95.
Rangaswamy, Nimmi
  2007 Representing the Non-formal: The Business of Internet Cafés in India. Ethnographic Praxis in Industry Conference Proceedings. Pp. 115–27.
Rhoades, Robert E.
  1982 The Art of the Informal Agricultural Survey (Training Document 1982-2). Lima, Peru: Social Sciences Department, International Potato Center.
Robinson, Rick E.
  1993 What to Do with a Human Factor: A Manifesto of Sorts. Special Issue: New Human Factors. *American Center for Design Journal* 7(1):63–73.
  1994a Making Sense of Making Sense: Frameworks and Organizational Perception. *Design Management Journal* 5(1):8–15.
  1994b The Origin of Cool Things. *In* Design that Packs a Wallop: Understanding the Power of Strategic Design. American Center for Design Conference Proceedings. Pp. 5–10. New York: American Center for Design.
  2005 Let's Have a Conversation: Theory Session Introductory Remarks. Ethnographic Praxis in Industry Conference Proceedings. Pp. 1–8.
Robinson, Rick E., and Jason Nims
  1996 Insight into What Really Matters. *Innovation* (Summer):18–21.
Sacks, Harvey, Emanuel A. Schegloff, and Gail Jefferson
  1974 A Simplest Systematics for the Organization of Turn-taking for Conversation. *Language* 50:696–735.
Salvador, Tony, Genevieve Bell, and ken anderson
  1999 Design Ethnography. *Design Management Journal* 10(4):35–41.
Salvador, Tony, John W. Sherry, L. Wilton Agatstein, and Hsain Ilahiane
  2007 ICT4D [rArr] ICT4X: Mitigating the Impact of Cognitive Heuristics and Biases in Ethnographic Business Practice. Ethnographic Praxis in Industry Conference Proceedings. Pp. 128–37.
Shaner, W. W., P. F. Philipp, and W. R. Schmehl
  1982 Farming Systems Research and Development: Guidelines for Developing Countries. Boulder, CO: Westview.
Smith, Alison
  1997 Shoppers under the Microscope: Watching How Different Types of People Use Goods and Services Can Supply Useful Information. *Financial Times*, December 5. P. A1.
Squires, Susan
  1999 Rapid Ethnographic Assessment, American Breakfast and the Mother-in-law. Paper presented at the Annual Meeting of the American Anthropology Association, Chicago, November 17–21.

Squires, Susan, and Bryan Byrne (eds.)
2002 Creating Breakthrough Ideas: The Collaboration of Anthropologists and Designers in the Product Development Industry. Westport: Bergin & Garvey.

Squires, Susan, and George Wall
2002 From Discovery to Launch: Unpacking the Fuzzy Front End. *In* Presentation at the Annual International Conference of the Product Development Management Association, Orlando, FL, October.

Suchman, Lucy
1987 Plans and Situated Actions: The Problem of Human-Machine Communication. Cambridge: Cambridge University Press.
1992 Technologies of Accountability: Of Lizards and Aeroplanes. *In* Technology in Working Order: Studies of Work, Interaction, and Technology, G. Button, ed. Pp. 113–26. London: Routledge.
1995 Making Work Visible. *Communications of the ACM* 38(9):56–65.
1996 Constituting Shared Workspaces. *In* Cognition and Communication at Work, Y. Engeström and D. Middleton, eds. Cambridge: Cambridge University Press.

Suchman, Lucy, Jeanette Blomberg, Julian E. Orr, and Randall Trigg
1999 Reconstructing Technologies as Social Practice. *American Behavioral Scientist* 43(3):392–408.

Suchman, Lucy A., and Randall H. Trigg
1991 Understanding Practice: Video as a Medium for Reflection and Design. *In* Design at Work: Cooperative Design of Computer Systems, J. Greenbaum and M. Kyng, eds. Pp. 65–89. Hillsdale: Lawrence Erlbaum Associates.

Sunderland, Patricia
2008 Session 2—Representation in Practice: Utilizing the Paradoxes of Video, Prose, and Performance. Ethnographic Praxis in Industry Conference Proceedings. Pp. 101–03.

Sunderland, Patricia L., and Rita M. Denny
2007 Doing Anthropology in Consumer Research. Walnut Creek: Left Coast Press.

Telenor
2008 Telenor Research and Innovation. Available at: http://www.telenor.com/rd/. Accessed July 6, 2009.

Thomas, Suzanne L., and Xueming Lang
2007 From Field to Office: The Politics of Corporate Ethnography. Ethnographic Praxis in Industry Conference Proceedings. Pp. 78–90.

Tunstall, Elizabeth (Dori)
2008 The QAME of Trans-disciplinary Ethnography: Making Visible Disciplinary Theories of Ethnographic Praxis as Boundary Object. Ethnographic Praxis in Industry Conference Proceedings. Pp. 218–33.

Walker, Alissa
2009 Open-source Innovation: IDEO's Human-centered Design Toolkit. Available at: http://www.fastcompany.com/blog/alissa-walker/designe-rati/human-centered-design-toolkit-shares-information. Accessed July 7, 2011.

Wasson, Christina
2000 Ethnography in the Field of Design. *Human Organization* 59(4):377–88.
2002 Collaborative Work: Integrating the Roles of Ethnographers and Designers. *In* Creating Breakthrough Ideas: The Collaboration of Anthropologists and Designers in the Product Development Industry, S. Squires and B. Byrne, eds. Pp. 71–90. Westport: Bergin & Garvey.

Weise, Elizabeth
1999 Companies Learn Value of Grass Roots: Anthropologists Help Adapt Products to World's Cultures. *USA Today*, May 26. P. 4D.

Wells, Melanie
1999 New Ways to Get into Our Heads: Marketers Ditch Old Focus Groups for Video Cameras, Chats over Coffee. *USA Today*, March 2. Pp. 1B–2B.

Wolcott, Harry
2010 Ethnography Lessons: A Primer. Walnut Creek: Left Coast Press.

Conclusion

Toward a Practice-based Ethnography in the Global Village

Jean J. Schensul and Mary Odell Butler

These remarks conclude a collection of chapters based on the integration of anthropological practice and the lived experience of global change, in which anthropologists as actors and observers describe the theoretical and practical implications of their work and illustrate with case examples. A close reading of the case studies suggests common questions and themes and raises salient issues in confronting the challenge of building an applied anthropology that can write analyses and interpretations of global/local changes through an ethnographic and experiential lens in a way that is both insightful and useful.

Key questions focus on the relationship between global phenomena and local communities, anthropological identities, and the integration of theory and intervention or practice. For example, how can we define, create, and apply models of globalization that link broad national and international phenomena with more localized situations? How has our understanding of "community" changed with the increased interlinking of local, national, and international networks of people? How do we determine where to situate ourselves and locate our personal and professional energies to maximize our effectiveness? How do we frame our work to capture the human experience of the global as it intersects with the local, and how do we link recorded human experience to policy? What methods are appropriate for our work and to what extent do they involve research, interventions, and/or other types of activities? What is the meaning of the concept of scholar-practitioner and how does it relate to other ways of conceptualizing the association between research and practice in a global-local applied anthropology? In what ways can we integrate theory and method with our practice to contribute to knowledge related to the forces of globalization that are affecting the present and future of societies, communities, and people and their environments? In the face of neoliberalism and international capitalism, can we really make a difference for the most economically marginalized and ecologically vulnerable populations, and what does it take to do so? Each of the chapters in this book attempts to address some or all of these questions.

Interconnectivity: The Global Village

The idea of the village brings up images of closely interconnected local communities in which people provide mutual support to one another on the basis of kinship or personal knowledge of their neighbors. As a number of the chapters illustrate, for many of the world's people, the experience of globalization has been quite different. At the same time, the term "globalization" also denotes constant and intense interconnection based on daily communication and exchange in a territorial space (Burawoy et al. 2000). It is in this sense in that we use the term "global village" in this volume, although now the territorial space, once local, has expanded to cover the globe.

The chapters in this book reinforce the idea that communities are no longer local. In a world where geosocial localities intersect with other broader sociopolitical entities, communities, individuals, and groups are networked across nations and around the world (Iriye 2002). This new global framing of the meaning of community is a challenge to anthropologists, who have been trained to think about conducting their work in geosocially bounded locations within which they can conduct ethnography, build relationships, and join forces to move toward improved quality of life for the people with whom they work. For decades, most anthropologists have clearly understood that the local communities in which they do their research are linked to broader national sociopolitical and economic dynamics (Kearney 1995). Now, however, the processes of migration, immigration, cross-cultural exchanges, and media and electronic communication suggest that most people live their lives in interaction with an ever-changing mosaic of local, regional, national, and global influences, which are experienced as part of ongoing life in local communities. Regardless of whether or not people not consider themselves to be global citizens, they are affected by global dynamics. If they wish, they can find ways to engage with and have an effect upon these dynamics (Castells 2005). Recent national independence/prodemocracy movements, influenced by multiple external as well as internal factors, are examples of the ways in which media interact with local populations and nongovernmental organizations (NGOs) to promote local changes on a global stage. The new perspective that we are endorsing thus requires that we look at local communities from the "outside in" as well as the "inside out"; that we use a systems model that reminds us to link sectors of our local community settings to wider national and global events, policies, and environmental issues and conditions; and that we go beyond the national to the global.

To differentiate the influences coming from different levels of socio-political organization requires that we navigate these levels, sectors, networks, and settings. Navigation, as we note later, is a boundary-spanning function. It refers to the capacity to understand cultural, social, and structural dynamics across levels and to bringing people together across the boundaries that demarcate differences. As Jacqueline Copeland-Carson points out in her chapter, anthropologists bring a local perspective that is sensitive to cultural and other innovations that arise in the globalized city. She describes how she, as an anthropologist working at the interface of multiple interests and a specific religious group, brings representatives from key sectors together to solve an important community problem—lending without interest—using skills and knowledge derived from her own navigation of a variety of governmental, private sector, international, and local community encounters. Mary Odell Butler, a program evaluator, points out that programs as implemented on the ground are always molded by local needs, whatever the state, national, or international concepts of a policy or intervention approach might be, and conversely, that the alternatives available to localities are critically shaped by national and international policies. Understanding, translating, and building on these differences is part of the anthropological navigational or "boundary-spanning" role.

The Human Experience of the Globalized Locality

Much of anthropology is concerned with understanding and theorizing the processes that affect people living in communities. A full consideration of globalization processes requires that we consider many global dynamics that are translocal and can have a significant effect on people's lives: the arms trade, local, regional, and cross-national wars, and the quest for control over land; the ever-increasing demand for natural resources to feed the desires of developed countries in the west and the growth and development of newly industrialized countries and economically advancing countries including Brazil, Russia, India, and China; migration and immigration stemming from the intersection of war, free trade, and the quest for work; the expanding production and marketing and use of legal (tobacco and alcohol) and illegal drugs; the interface between the holistic practices of traditional medicine and the segmented, technologically driven approaches to western medicine; and the flow of diseases, pollution, global warming agents, and radiation across national boundaries.

In the face of these macro-level challenges, the chapters in this volume are concerned with the well-being of human communities, however they are defined. As applied anthropologists, we often try to improve the lives of individuals or to contribute to activities that improve the contexts in which people negotiate change. The strategies described in these chapters that address both of these endeavors are broad and diverse. They include processes such as forging local partnerships with community-based organizations to accomplish specific objectives and outcomes, conducting evaluations and using the results, forming change-oriented vertical or intersectoral alliances, transferring and translating cultural knowledge and technology from one part of the world to another, and synthesizing knowledge to influence national policy makers and legislators to make changes beneficial to community welfare. All strategies take into consideration local organizational structures, priorities and needs, links with national and international agencies, and the dynamic global contexts that influence local settings. This process of negotiating local and global is facilitated by ethnographic research methods that make a point of soliciting the views of local people experiencing the effects of globalization as well as the institutions that affect, improve, or reduce the quality of their lives. Soliciting and recording the direct and immediate experiences of people who live the process of globalized dislocation and relocation, adaptation, and accommodation is central to efforts to mediate changes that improve their quality of life (LeCompte and Schensul 2010).

Neoliberalism's Global/Local Face

David Harvey defines neoliberalism as the economic "configuration" of globalization (Harvey 2005). It is a theory of political economic practices that proposes that human well-being can best be advanced by liberating individual entrepreneurial freedoms and skills within an institutional framework characterized by strong private property rights, free markets, and free trade (Harvey 2005:2).

The tenets of neoliberalism have been formulated and enacted in the past four decades. Neoliberal ideology was first implemented through the gradual disempowering of the labor movement as companies began to expand into nonunionized areas of the U.S., Latin America, and southeast Asia in search of markets and cheap labor. In the 1970s and 1980s, U.S. and European companies were building industrial complexes in Latin American and southeast Asian countries. Following similar principles, businesses were shifting headquarters from smaller cities of the United States to larger urban areas where tax breaks were better. Industries were moving from the unionized north to the nonunionized south, taking workers and capital with them. By the mid-1990s, as the full effects of the neoliberal agenda were emerging and public services were being outsourced and privatized, it became clear that labor unions were losing ground, and that greater efforts were required to support a strong international movement to protect the interests of workers in newly industrializing countries. Several of the chapters in this volume discuss the negative effects of neoliberal agendas on the lives of the poor and disempowered.

Most large businesses today are globalized. Their success is influenced by local political conditions, tax breaks, the cost of labor, and other factors over which local workers have little influence. A supportive international business climate has resulted in the emergence of a large wealthy global elite (Freeland 2011) that now has a major impact on urban development and global financial markets. At the same time, there are currently an unprecedented number of educated young adults who cannot be supported by work opportunities in their own countries and who are increasingly unable to be absorbed in the countries to which they have traditionally migrated. These young people, whose expectations and hopes are shaped by their education and the media and constrained by the restrictions inherent in their local situations, constitute a major force for change in countries where neoliberal policies have produced an increasing gap between the wealthy elites (government, international business, and the military) and an emergent middle class. This process applies to western countries as well as to others. These global phenomena should be of great interest to applied anthropologists as well as to policy makers in and outside of government.

The ethic of "self-sufficiency" and the supremacy of free-market forces, embodied in neoliberal thought, are costly to the poor who lack the resources to access the global economy and who are constrained by a variety of structural causes. Clarke discusses transportation policies that limit the participation of women in markets, educational opportunities, and new kinds of trade. Passmore carefully outlines the role of privatization—a neoliberal policy—in hampering the coordination of child welfare services when the multiple services needed by families and individuals are distributed among disconnected private organizations. She also notes the many ways in which neoliberal philosophy has come to be embedded in the viewpoints and lived experience of child welfare workers undergoing privatization. Pinsker describes the reactions of leadership trainees from other countries to the prospect of extending capitalist logic to the provision of health care to the poor in the United States and elsewhere in the world. These experiences suggest a need for a reconsideration of the neoliberal perspective and its potentially negative impacts on local low-income or disenfranchised communities in the West and beyond (Stiglitz 2007).

Geographically marginalized and indigenous peoples and the long-term urban poor constitute increasingly vulnerable populations under economic globalization. The chapters in this volume also reveal the many costs of global change to these populations. Clarke, for example, notes that inequities in access to transport in developing nations build on long histories of discrimination and devaluing of women so that women become invisible to transportation planners. Dewey highlights the powerlessness of trafficked women to violence and abuse by both clients and police because of their roles as sex workers. Iris's compelling chapter describes the plight of those immigrant older adults who have lost traditional supports as they age, and are forced to come to terms with the reality of life in the United States. In particular, the essentially middle-class American paradigm of "successful aging" creates a standard for independence that many immigrants cannot meet because of language barriers, limited economic resources, broken connections with kindred, and the difficulty of navigating new and unfamiliar laws.

As anthropologists, our primary ethical responsibility is to the welfare and safety of our work for the people involved (American Anthropological Association [AAA] 2009). Under the structural constraints of neoliberal capitalism, both dedicated scholars and practitioners make ongoing choices about their positionality with respect to endorsing, critiquing, neutralizing, adapting to, or countering neoliberal forces through multiple forms of resistance. Our choice of research and intervention/practice partner(s) requires a deep ethnographic analysis of any situation, using political ecology or other personal and/or critical frameworks. It also requires an assessment of whether and how agencies, informal groups, and individual activists accommodate to, endorse, or directly or indirectly critique the translation of neoliberal policies into local settings. Positioning ourselves relative to those who fund our research and the population we work with and study calls for an ongoing assessment of the structures of power and control that shape, influence, and often determine who speaks and whose voice is heard. Establishing positionality and engaging in practice calls for an evaluation of our own values with respect to science and social change. The authors of the chapters in this publication describe for us the ways in which they have made their own decisions with respect to their positions, vantage points, and ability to observe, learn, and act. Although they do not provide guidelines for others, their shared experiences suggest criteria for decision making that others can use when deciding where to work and how to apply their expertise in relation to their personal values and what they hope to accomplish professionally.

Western cultural and scientific notions related to the promotion of neoliberal agendas have made their way around the world. There is considerable literature that shows how these ideas have been adapted and co-opted, changing into cultural resistance movements, indigenous control over the production and use of local knowledge, and new ways of defining science and research agendas to meet indigenous and local needs rather than the requirements of international capital (Crane and Dusenberry 2004; Drainville 2008; Mato 2000). Rhoads and Alberto-Torres, for example, refer to "globalization from below" or antiglobalization, by which they mean movements that are opposed to neoliberal approaches to corporate globalism but not to increased international integration (Rhoads and Alberto-Torres 2006). Globalization "from below" can also refer to social movements that counter hegemonic institutions, including the media, political structures, oppressive governments, and limitations on freedom of expression. Castells, in a review of the history of social movements throughout the colonial and postcolonial period, reminds us that just as neoliberalism—a set of economic institutions, beliefs, and practices—influences cultural practices and the way people imagine and define themselves, so the enactment of social movements can transform culture through engagement in the transformation and enactment of new ideologies, and in the process (Castells 2005) transform identities.

Social media are a powerful mediating force organizing communities for connection and for change. Cell phones, email, the Internet, Facebook, Twitter, and other social media have been crucial to the rapid transmission of information, the catalyzing of action, and the organization of activities resulting in dramatic emergent transformations of government and society. The recent events that mark "the Arab Spring" illustrate the critical importance of social media in the generation of antihegemonic social movements around the globe. The ways in which indigenous peoples mobilize locally and at the same time link to national and international movements provide insights into ways that applied work can enhance such efforts at multiple levels (Durr 2005; Jackson and Warren 2005; Rubin 2004). At the same time, social media can influence individual and community identities in a variety of different ways. For example, as Iris points out in her chapter, immigrant populations can use Facebook, Twitter, the Internet, and cell phone technology to resist assimilation by providing them with daily connectivity to their communities of origin. At the same time, the same immigrant populations use social media to mobilize resources to confront political issues and institutions with which they disagree. Dialogues, differences, disagreements, and conflicts across generations and families are the result of these processes, all forming part of an ongoing process of dramatic and rapid cultural change.

Leveraging Knowledge to Influence Global/Local Policy

Much of the work of applied and practicing anthropologists is related in one way or another to policies that increase the access of people to resources, or production processes that have negative effects on local populations, sometimes in favor of globalized needs. The case examples in this volume offer insight into the complex dynamics and multiple levels of bureaucracy that result in policy decisions and policy changes with both beneficial and negative effects on communities, networks of communities, countries, and regions of the world. They demonstrate how external national, international, and transnational/global factors intersect to promote alternative directions, and how local dynamics and links across local and regional settings and issues can be used to bring about specific changes in favor of local populations.

In her insightful chapter on global climate change, Fiske models globalization processes and their effects on local infrastructure and the psychological well-being of vulnerable groups and the use of leveraged knowledge to influence policy development that reduces the negative effects of global climate change on environmentally marginal indigenous populations. Her multilevel theory begins with global trade and the availability of capital through multiple sources, including private investment, leading to increasingly energy-dependent and -intensive manufacturing. This in turn affects local environmental systems of production in vulnerable communities. Breakdowns in systems of production disrupt social relationships and produce alienation and cultural loss, which are partially resolved through drawing upon social capital. This theoretical framework provides an excellent example of an approach to systematic tracking of the macro components of a multilevel (international/national/regional/local) dynamic system that emerges through leveraged knowledge—in this case interdisciplinary, but with significant ethnographic material at the local level. Leveraged knowledge—the knowledge brought to bear on a problem by social scientists within and outside of the policy-making arena—provides the basis for conceptual models that can then be refined mathematically and tested against changes at every level. Testing models mathematically produces alternative results that cannot be assumed to be correct. Fiske argues that they must be reviewed by anthropologists, and others should be those affected directly by the problem, among others.

Today, there are many anthropologists working to formulate policy in health, education, environmental protection, and design, and these numbers have grown rapidly in the past two decades. The chapters in this volume demonstrate clearly that policies, often developed with the best intentions to improve, change, or increase the quality of life of local populations, may have the opposite effect. Further, as Dewey, Iris, Passmore, and others note, policies around trafficking, the rights of children, indigenous peoples, youth, women, and older adults always will be translated through local bureaucracies and negotiated and adapted at the local level. Anthropologists whose unique experience at the local level positions them to critique the negative or misplaced effects of national and international policies or to promote the development of new and more responsive policies can have a considerable effect on the process of policy formulation. To do this, though, they must be engaged with the policy-making arena. Fiske and Copeland-Carson's chapters, for example, show that the interplay of "insider" and "outsider" anthropology can mobilize knowledge to mediate the negative effects of well-intentioned policy and to support the development of new policies that promote the welfare of human populations.

Other examples in these chapters shows us how visionary anthropologists can serve to act as brokers or boundary spanners between policy makers, administrators, and local researchers and research partnerships to bring local knowledge to bear on global problems. A globalized policy-oriented applied anthropology should pay attention to forging stronger connections among these networks of anthropologists and their allies based in different types of organizations to strengthen the production and use of "leveraged knowledge." Coupled with advocacy efforts at the local and international levels, social scientists *can* make a difference in the quality of local community life.

Global changes are putting pressure on public policies. However, many public policies work in the best interests of people and should not be changed. Butler points out that protection of global health—that is, appropriate responses to infectious diseases—requires that public health remain a government function. Privatization of these functions would leave large populations vulnerable to epidemics if governments fail to sustain their vigilance. Passmore's critique of the child welfare system arrives at a similar conclusion.

Policy serves people if it is grounded in a consideration of multiple interacting elements: a system of forces interacting and constantly adjusting to changed circumstances. The fairly simple systems models that sufficed in the past are not adequate to accommodate the multiple and changing forces that impinge on communities today. Increasingly, anthropologists are turning toward new systems models adapted from other disciplines to model sociocultural change.

Butler, for example, speculates on the potential application of complex adaptive system (CAS) models, derived from physics and mathematics, in the context of global health planning. In anthropology, they have been applied to simulate the formation of settlements among the thirteenth-century Anasazi (Dean et al. 2000) and to understand Balinese farmers' management of very large irrigation systems (Lansing 2003). In a similar vein, Eve Pinsker described a conference on systems that included a workshop on computer-based simulation models showing the connection between the season of the year, a contagious disease epidemic (such as SARS or avian flu), seasonal patterns in airplane travel, and changes in the rate and geographic spread of an epidemic (Ness et al. 2007). This presentation compellingly demonstrated the importance of networks connecting the global to the local, and the complex systems principle of sensitivity to initial conditions (Lansing 1998, 2003; Schensul 2009).

There is an emergent anthropological literature on intervention science (Hahn and Inhorn 2009; Schensul and Trickett 2009). Intervention science introduces theoretically driven strategies for social change into specific local settings. Anthropologists working in this arena build theory both inductively and deductively, drawing from local settings and from the literature. The dynamic models that Pinsker and Butler describe are increasingly being used in community intervention research because social scientists recognize that communities are complex and dynamic and affected by multiple forces simultaneously over and above planned change efforts. All of the chapters in this book use ethnography to capture the dynamic character of the globalized local. Ethnography has much to offer in documenting the complexity of the system in which planned projects are being introduced. It also can monitor to assess the interaction of multiple factors on an ongoing basis, the reasons for progress or lack of progress toward a desired goal, and the emergence of new goals.

The Glass Half Full

The discussions here may imply that globalization has resulted in a downward spiral toward inevitable catastrophic outcomes for human populations, but the picture is not entirely grim. To quote Stiglitz in his most recent publication: "For most of the world, globalization as it has been managed seems like a pact with the devil...., that is not how it has to be. We can make globalization work not just for the rich and powerful but for all people, including those in the poorest countries" (Stiglitz 2007:8).

Stiglitz is hopeful. And the stories told in this volume give us some reason to join him. For example, Wasson and Squires as well as Clarke recognize some of the disadvantages of globalized transportation and technology industries, but they also see new opportunities to reach formerly isolated or marginalized people with appropriate transportation innovations and low-cost communication technologies that have direct bearing on their economic and general well-being, social integration, and empowerment. Copeland-Carson demonstrates how the process of negotiating changes in economic practices to resolve problems of immigrant groups—in this case development of interest-free loans for Muslims—can help to address the challenges and needs of specific populations with economic values and practices that differ from U.S. mainstream business practice, even in such seemingly "culture-proof" arenas as housing finance and economic development.

One way anthropologists who work with vulnerable populations can contribute to transformative change is by bringing affected community members to the table to participate as active partners in critiquing ineffective policies, defining health and other problems, and specifying alternative solutions. As William Partridge noted in 1985, and again in 2008: "it is in the interplay of theory and practice—to advocate, advance, or empower political effectiveness, economic power, and social influence in concert with the participants in our research—that more robust theories of individual and collective human development are to be generated (Dokecki 1996). Our understanding of praxis asserts that community researchers are participants in the action, joining other participants in designing and executing interventions, the unfolding choreography of which informs and enriches both scientific understanding and our lives and those of our collaborators" (Partridge 2008:162).

Often, anthropologists can build or work with communities to build interventions that will serve people better. Iris's article theorizes her setting by predicting the emergence of new issues likely to confront older adults in a globalized urban environment. At the same time, much of her "daily life" is dedicated to the development of social and other types of "interventions" that have meaning for and can improve the quality of life of older adults living in diverse community settings. Many of the authors in this volume, such as Copeland, Fiske, and Wasson and Squires, describe similar experiences.

Where Do We Go From Here?

Most of the chapters in this volume reflect the concept of the scholar-practitioner, a concept first articulated by Jacqueline Copeland-Carson (2005). It has been a central concern of this volume to build on this idea that practice must be driven by scholarship and that it should contribute to the anthropological understanding of how things work. As applied and practicing anthropology goes forward into this century, it is our hope that this grounding of practice in anthropological theories and methods will continue to grow (Hahn and Inhorn 2009).

Anthropologists in recent years have been taught that to be true scholars, they must produce theory. It is extraordinarily difficult to convince anthropologists wedded to the notion of scholarship resulting from individual theorizing and publication that there are other forms of knowledge production and representation that "count." We prefer to argue that scholarship should involve the production of knowledge through action and the conduct of theoretically driven and evaluated approaches to change, in addition to the conduct of research to produce a more abstract knowledge. As we attempt to shift the lens to more "engaged" anthropology, we must be careful to conceptualize practice as the constant and ongoing development of socially constructed theory, produced through the interaction of the anthropologist(s) with collaborators including partners from those communities with which the anthropologist is working most closely. This vision enables anthropologists to move to shared ownership of both practice and "theory" and "theory making" with the participants in our research (Schensul 2010).

Moreover, the results of the work must find public visibility beyond the realm of policy and the immediate benefits of local community collaborators. Ways of making researched practice results accessible and available include public journals, foundation publications, handouts and booklets, and presentations in community settings, or knowledge-based campaigns. Such dissemination activities can assist communities with a strong vested interest in planned and managed change to become more effective actors shaping their own future. One responsibility we can take on, as advocates for globalized applied anthropology, is to redefine the notion of scholarship by promoting it as an understanding of all of these forms of dissemination and use of knowledge.

Copeland-Carson's chapter reminds us that it is the responsibility of applied and practicing anthropologists to support but not to speak for underrepresented or marginalized peoples. The civil rights movements of the past 50 years and the ongoing postmodern concern with positionality and representational rights require that we reflect continuously on our identities and our roles in relation to the people with whom we are working and that we avoid "speaking for" while we are "speaking with." As anthropologists, we facilitate the production of new cultural forms by bringing together vertical or horizontal alliances of people representing different sectors that have the capacity to apply resources to the solution of a problem that requires innovation. We try to draw upon training, knowledge, lived experience, exposure to the cultures of local institutions, familiarity with the cultural needs of a local constituency, ethnographic methodology, and good social skills to implement a complex role. This role can include selecting partners in an alliance; facilitating of dialogue that clearly identifies the problem to be addressed (interest-free loans for example); forging research strategies or leveraged knowledge to enhance the information base for planned interventions; a discussion of the pros, cons, and challenges of various approaches; and forward movement through action/practice. A good facilitator, navigator, or boundary spanner will begin with the desire to find a joint solution that improves the life of a specific group of people, using ethnography as a tool to understand the concerns and needs of the broader community and to facilitate a discussion that searches for a "win-win" solution. This role, highlighted by a number of the chapters in this volume, is understudied and underdefined in applied anthropology, and few if any students are trained in the navigational skills that would enable them to function well in these increasingly complex situations.

It is abundantly clear from the chapters in this volume that the anthropological practice in the global locality will be interdisciplinary as well as intersectoral. Anthropology *is* an interdisciplinary discipline, connecting the physical/biological, the cultural/political, the linguistic, and the historical/archaeological dimension of the human experience. Continued training in the four fields approach, with specialized learning and certification in subfields, gives anthropologists an advantage when tackling interdisciplinary problems. Methodologically, ethnography calls for careful listening and the ability to analyze inductively as well as deductively: to synthesize the "pieces of the puzzle" over and over again, with others, to find the so-called best fit, the interpretation that works to explain and to solve a problem.

Finally, the face of anthropological practice can be expected to change as the century progresses. Wasson and Squires describe for us a new subfield of anthropology known as "design anthropology," which came into existence to meet the burgeoning needs of Information and Communication Technology (ICT) companies to understand better how people around the globe, including those representing new markets, articulate with ICT. Other anthropologists are noting the importance of research on social movements linking social network media to community organizing (Edelman 2001; Escobar 2000). Escobar's concept of "meshwork" is a strategy used by political campaign strategists, health reform policy makers, and global-social and protest movement organizers as ways of countering neoliberal and other restrictive ideologies and national structures (Escobar 2000). Still others, like Iris, are interested in ways in which electronic forms of communication can ensure and enhance global communication from local settings. Advancing these fields should be part of our mission.

Applied anthropologists working in the context of global change are well positioned to link with others at multiple levels to forge new relationships, new knowledge, and to work with existing and new global agencies that have the power to regulate. An applied anthropology of the global can foster new and alternative means of communication and new forms of resistance that address and attenuate the most negative consequences of globalization and reinforce the most positive.

Finally, we must strive to remain receptive to emergent forms of our discipline, to be open to change even if we cannot anticipate the outcomes. Since social and environmental problems are multifaceted, we must be able to judge the potential of innovations in our own and other fields for the welfare of those with whom we work. We must learn to be comfortable at the global frontier where disciplines, fields, practices, and problems intersect in new and complex ways. We must learn to do better and more collaborative research using methods and tools drawn from anthropology and other fields. We must create roadmaps that guide us and those who follow to explore and influence the process of engagement with globalized/local social and ecological situations that emerge in the global village. To accomplish these goals, we must listen carefully to our many research partners around the globe, to our students, and to the new members of our profession, for they know things that we do not and may lead all of us in new directions that are not yet envisioned.

References

American Anthropological Association (AAA)
  2009 Code of Ethics of the American Anthropological Association, February 2009. Available at: http://www.aaanet.org/csupload/issues/policy-advocacy/27668_1.pdf. Accessed June 1, 2011.
Burawoy, Michael, Joseph A. Blum, Sheba George, et al.
  2000 Global Ethnography: Forces, Connections and Imaginations in a Postmodern World. Berkeley: University of California Press.
Castells, Manuel
  2005 Global Governance and Global Politics. *In* 2004 Ithiel de Sola Pool Lecture. Berkeley, CA: Available at http://arkkitehtuuri.tkk.fi/YKS/fin/opetus/kurssit/yks_teoria/luennot/Castells/2005Global-Castellas.pdf. Accessed January 10, 2010.
Copeland-Carson, Jacqueline
  2005 Theory-building Evaluation Anthropology. NAPA Bulletin 24:7–16.
Crane, Barbara B., and Jennifer Dusenberry
  2004 Power and Politics in International Funding for Reproductive Health: The US Global Gag Rule. *Reproductive Health Matters* 12(24):128–37.
Dean, Jeffrey S., George J. Gumerman, Joshua M. Epstein, et al.
  2000 Understanding Anazazi Culture through Agent-based Modeling. *In* Dynamic in Human and Primate Populations, T. Kohler and G. Gumerman, eds. Pp. 179–205. Oxford: Oxford University Press.
Dokecki, Paul R.
  1996 The Tragicomic Professional: Basic Considerations for Ethical Reflective-Generative Practice. Pittsburgh: Duquesne University Press.

Drainville, André C.
  2008 Resistance to Globalisation: The View from the Periphery of the World Economy. *International Social Science Journal* 59(192):235–46.
Durr, Eveline
  2005 Translating Democracy: Customary Law and Constitutional Rights in Mexico. *Sites: New Series* 2(2):91–118.
Edelman, Mark
  2001 Social Movements: Changing Paradigms and Forms of Politics. *Annual Review of Anthropology* 30:285–317.
Escobar, Arturo
  2000 Notes on Networks and Anti-Globalization Social Movements. *In* Prepared for Session on Actors, Networks, Meanings: Environmental Social Movements and the Anthropology of Activism. San Francisco. November 15–19. http://www.unc.edu/oldanthro/faculty/fac_pages/escobarpapers/notesnetwork.pdf
Freeland, Chrystia
  2011 The Rise of the New Global Elite. The Atlantic Monthly, January–February issue. Available at: http://www.theatlantic.com/magazine/print/2011/01/the-rise-of-the-new-global-elite. Accessed May 12, 2011.
Hahn, Robert A., and Marcia C. Inhorn
  2009 Anthropology and Public Health Bridging Differences in Culture and Society. New York: Oxford University Press.
Harvey, David
  2005 A Brief History of Neoliberalism. Oxford: Oxford University Press.
Iriye, Akira
  2002 Global Community: The Role of International Organizations in the Making of the Contemporary World. Berkeley, CA: University of California Press.
Jackson, J. E., and K. B. Warren
  2005 Indigenous Movements in Latin America, 1992–2004: Controversies, Ironies, New Directions. *Annual Review of Anthropology* 34:549–73.
Kearney, Michael
  1995 The Local and the Global: The Anthropology of Globalization and Transnationalism. *Annual Review of Anthropology* 24(Annual Reviews):547–65.
Lansing, J. Stephen
  1998 System-dependent Selection, Ecological Feedback and the Emergence of Functional Structure in Ecosystems. *Journal of Theoretical Biology* 192:377–91.
  2003 Complex Adaptive Systems. *Annual Review of Anthropology* 32:183–204.
LeCompte, Margaret D., and Jean J. Schensul
  2010 Designing and Conducting Ethnographic Research, 2nd edition. Lanham, NJ: AltaMira Press.

Mato, Daniel
2000 Transnational Networking and the Social Production of Representations of Identities by Indigenous Peoples' Organizations of Latin America. *International Sociology* 15(2):343.

Ness, Roberta B., James S. Koopman, and Mark S. Roberts
2007 Causal System Modeling in Chronic Disease Epidemiology: A Proposal. *Annals of Epidemiology* 17(7):564–68.

Partridge, William L.
2008 Praxis and Power. *American Journal of Community Psychology* 36(2):161–72.

Rhoads, R. A., and C. Alberto-Torres
2006 The University, State and Market: The Political Economy of Globalization in the Americas. Stanford: Stanford University Press.

Rubin, Jeffrey W.
2004 Meanings and Mobilizations: A Cultural Politics Approach to Social Movements and States. *Latin American Research Review* 39(3):106–42.

Schensul, Jean J.
2009 Community, Culture and Sustainability in Multilevel Dynamic Systems Intervention Science. *American Journal of Community Psychology* 43:241–56.
2010 Engaged Universities, Community Based Research Organizations and Third Sector Science in a Global System. *Human Organization* 69(4):307–20.

Schensul, Jean, and Ed Trickett
2009 Multi-level Community Based Culturally Situated Interventions. *American Journal of Community Psychology* 43:232–40.

Stiglitz, Joseph E.
2007 Making Globalization Work. New York: W. W. Norton and Co.

Index

About the Authors

Mary Odell Butler is an anthropologist with 35 years of experience in research design, management, and supervision of public health evaluation projects. She is currently employed as a Senior Study Director with Westat and serves as an adjunct Professor of Anthropology at the University of Maryland. She is retired from the Battelle Centers for Public Health Research and Evaluation (CPHRE), where she served as Office Director of Battelle CPHRE's Arlington Office and as a Research Leader. As Principal Investigator, she provided technical leadership to multiple projects. She was project Principal Investigator for a Centers of Disease Control (CDC) evaluation project to assess the adherence to CDC guidelines for preventing sexually transmitted diseases in HIV-infected men who have sex with men (MSM) in 12 clinical settings in 6 cities. She directed a project to conduct a participatory evaluation of the U.S.-Mexico Binational Tuberculosis Referral and Case Management Project, which seeks to ensure continuity of tuberculosis (TB) treatment along the length of the U.S.-Mexico Border by collaboration in case tracking and case management. She was Principal Investigator on a project to document the readiness of state health departments for comprehensive state-level cancer planning and a project to provide guidance to state TB program coordinators in the management, implementation, and use of program evaluations of their programs and supported CDC in preparing an evaluation manual for use by TB program staff at the federal, state, and local levels. She has led several projects to assess the role of professional training programs in building programmatic capacity in local, state, national, and international contexts, including an evaluation of CDC's Field Epidemiology Training Program conducted in four countries. She has completed evaluations of the public health usefulness of infectious disease surveillance activities at CDC and in the United States, the process of computerizing national public health surveillance, and the accuracy and completeness of the CDC Mortality Reporting System. She has also completed studies of the effects of technological and economic change on reproductive health and human fertility in Latin America.

Mari H. Clarke has more than 25 years of international development experience with a focus on gender in a range of sectors, including infrastructure, environment, agriculture, education, health, and microenterprise. She is currently a senior gender consultant for the World Bank, working on gender and infrastructure as well as gender and climate change. She worked with the U.S. Agency for International Development (USAID), Office of Women in Development, for eight years on monitoring and evaluation and donor coordination, and participated in two delegations to the United Nations Commission on the Status of Women and the Vienna regional preparatory conference for the Beijing World Conference on Women. She also served as Senior Advisor for Development, Centre for Development and Population Activities; Director of the technical support contract for the USAID Office of Private and Voluntary Cooperation; Executive Director of the USAID U.S.-Egyptian Education Secretariat; Director for Development of the Peace Corps Child Survival Manual for health volunteers (prepared in collaboration with the World Health Organization [WHO] and CDC); and worked as an instructional designer, developing training materials development for the Program for International Training in Health. In addition to the World Bank, her consulting experience includes the Asian Development Bank, German Technological Corporation (GTZ), USAID, Catholic Relief Services, and Winrock International. She has authored numerous articles and book chapters as well as technical reports for development agencies. She has been active in the Washington Association of Professional Anthropologists as a former president, secretary, treasurer, and Praxis Award Chair. She also served as secretary of the National Association for the Practice of Anthropology. She holds a Ph.D. in Economic Anthropology from the University of North Carolina at Chapel Hill (UNC); M.Ed. in Instructional Design, UNC Chapel Hill; M.A. in Anthropology, University of Pennsylvania; and B.A. in Anthropology, Michigan State University.

Jacqueline Copeland-Carson is the USA executive director of the African Women's Development Fund USA. An anthropologist and urban planner, she has worked as a philanthropy scholar and practitioner for almost 30 years in Africa, Brazil, India, the Caribbean, Europe, and the United States. She has been an executive, evaluator, or researcher with numerous foundations, including the Philadelphia Foundation, Noyes, Women's Funding Network, Grantmakers Concerned with Immigrants and Refugees, Institute for the Future, Bertelsmann, and U.S. Bank Private Client Group. Dr. Copeland-Carson's influential writings examine issues in transnationalism, social theory, evaluation, diaspora studies, women's leadership, and development. Also a philanthropy blogger for The Huffington Post, her publications include *Pan-Africanizing Philanthropy* (coedited by Mojúbàolú Olufunke Okome and Olufemi Vaughan; Palgrave 2011), *Kenyan Diaspora Philanthropy* (TPI/Harvard University 2007), *Promoting Diversity in Contemporary Black Philanthropy* (Indiana University 2004), *Creating Evaluation Anthropology* (with Mary O. Butler; Wiley & Sons/NAPA 2005), and *Creating Africa in America* (University of Pennsylvania 2004). In 1998, she was a recipient of the Bush Foundation's prestigious Leadership Fellowship for her contributions as an activist scholar. As a volunteer, she has been on the boards of more than 20 nonprofit organizations, and in 2003 founded the Pan-African Women's Philanthropy Network (PAWPNet), a growing 400-member diaspora philanthropy community. Dr. Copeland-Carson holds two master's degrees, one in urban planning and the other in cultural anthropology, with a Ph.D. in anthropology (African/African diaspora and South Asian concentrations), all from the University of Pennsylvania. Her undergraduate degrees are from Georgetown University in literature, with a certificate in African studies from its School for Foreign Service.

Susan Dewey is an Assistant Professor in Gender and Women's Studies at the University of Wyoming. She is the author of three books that address the complex intersections between feminized labor and public policy: *Neon Wasteland: On Love, Motherhood, and Sex Work in a Rust Belt Town* (University of California Press 2011); *Hollow Bodies: Institutional Responses to Sex Trafficking in Armenia, Bosnia and India* (Kumarian Press 2008); and *Making Miss India Miss World: Constructing Gender, Power, and the Nation in Postliberalization India* (Syracuse University Press 2008). Dr. Dewey has co-edited two volumes, the first with anthropologist Patty Kelly, of *Policing Pleasure: Global Reflections on Sex Work and Public Policy* (New York University Press 2011) and the second with anthropologist Karen Brison, *Super Girls, Gangstas, Freeters and Xenomaniacs: Gender and Modernity in Global Youth Cultures* (Syracuse University Press 2012). She has published articles in the journals *American Ethnologist, Journal of South Asian Popular Culture, Labor: Journal of Working Class History in the Americas,* and *Ethnography and Education,* and was guest editor of a 2011 special issue of the feminist journal *Wagadu: Journal of Transnational Women's and Gender Studies* titled "Demystifying Sex Work and Sex Workers." Her research, in book chapter form, has also appeared in nearly a dozen edited volumes, many of which have been published with university presses. Dr. Dewey's research has been supported by grants from Fulbright-Hays and the National Science Foundation, and she has endeavored to put this research to practical use through professional consulting work for the U.S. Census Bureau, the African Population Health Research Center (Nairobi, Kenya, and Johannesburg, South Africa), the International Organization for Migration (Yerevan, Armenia, and Sarajevo, Bosnia-Herzegovina), and U.N. Women (Suva, Fiji).

Shirley J. Fiske is an environmental and policy anthropologist with 21 years of experience working in executive and legislative branches of the federal government. She is currently a Research Professor with the Department of Anthropology, University of Maryland at College Park. Dr. Fiske worked for the National Oceanic and Atmospheric Administration (NOAA) in the NOAA Office of Policy and Planning, and subsequently in the research arm of NOAA, the Office of Oceanic and Atmospheric Research. She directed a number of program and research areas in the National Sea Grant College Program, including social sciences, marine policy, education, and marine extension. She was director of the Sea Grant's Outreach program (including marine extension, communications, and education) and the Sea Grant Fellows Program (Dean John A. Knauss Fellows Program). As an anthropologist, she championed the value of social sciences and anthropology for global climate change, ocean governance, marine fisheries, common pool resources, and coastal communities. Her legislative work in the U.S. Senate included energy, natural resources, public lands, climate change, and ocean and fisheries policy. Current research includes a National Science Foundation (NSF)–funded project on cultural models of climate change in the Chesapeake Bay region, on which she is co-principal investigator. Dr. Fiske's recent publications include "Global Change Policymaking from Inside the Beltway: Engaging Anthropology," in *Anthropology and Climate Change: From Encounters to Actions* (2009) and *The Changing Face of Anthropology*, a survey report on anthropology MA graduates' careers and education for the American Anthropological Association (2011). Dr. Fiske is co-editor of a casebook in applied anthropology, *Anthropological Praxis: Translating Knowledge into Action* (Westview Press 1987) among other publications.

Madelyn Iris is Director of the Leonard Schanfield Research Institute at CJE SeniorLife in Chicago, a social service organization serving more than 18,000 clients each year through a wide variety of programs. She is also an adjunct Associate Professor in the Departments of Psychiatry and Preventive Medicine at the Feinberg School of Medicine, Northwestern University, where she teaches qualitative research methods. Dr. Iris received her Ph.D. in Anthropology from Northwestern University. From 1989 until 2005 she was an Associate Professor in the Department of Medicine and at the Buehler Center on Aging, Feinberg School of Medicine, Northwestern University. Her research focuses on older adult protective services, including elder self-neglect, elder abuse, and guardianship. She has also directed various intervention studies targeted to caregivers of older adults, older persons with chronic pain, and those with memory loss. Her most current research includes investigations of cultural beliefs and values related to Alzheimer's disease, and decision-making pathways for diagnosis seeking for memory loss in older adults. Prior to joining the faculty at Northwestern University, Dr. Iris was a research associate at the Erikson Institute for Advanced Studies in Child Development, Chicago, Illinois. She also is the principal of Iris Associates, a private consulting and research company specializing in the non-profit sector and older adult services, with a focus on evaluation capacity building. Dr. Iris's research has been funded by the National Institute on Aging, the Alzheimer's Association, the Retirement Research Foundation, and the Chicago Community Trust, among others. She is a Past President of the National Association for the Practice of Anthropology and The Association for Anthropology and Gerontology.

Susan Racine Passmore is Project Director at the Maryland Center for Health Equity at the University of Maryland, College Park, and Adjunct Lecturer with the Department of Epidemiology and Public Health at the University of Maryland, Baltimore, School of Medicine. Previously, she held positions as Senior Research Associate and Evaluation Consultant with James Bell Associates in Arlington, VA. Her work has been in two fields—child welfare evaluation and health disparities research—reflecting a long-standing engagement with vulnerable populations in the United States. Her knowledge of child welfare comes from eight years of evaluation research in support of U.S. Administration of Children and Families (ACF) programs. These include the Adoption Opportunities, Child Abuse and Neglect, and PSSF (Promoting Safe and Stable Families) Demonstration Grant Programs and the Early Head Start/Child Welfare Services Grants funded by the Children's Bureau, and the ACF Healthy Marriage and Promoting Responsible Fatherhood Initiative administered by the Office of Family Assistance (OFA). She has provided evaluation technical assistance to hundreds of nationally funded but locally administered projects, providing a range of services to American families in need. In minority health, she has provided consultation for projects funded by American Cancer Society, the U.S. Agency for Healthcare Research and Quality (AHRQ), and the National Institutes for Health (NIH), among other organizations.

Eve C. Pinsker received her Ph.D. in cultural anthropology from the University of Chicago in 1997. Her work focuses on systems-based ethnographic and process approaches to the planning and evaluation of collaborative (multisectoral) initiatives, particularly those involving multiple levels of intervention (individual, organizational, community) and diverse organizational and community cultures. From 1991 to 1994, she applied the approach to conceptualizing community linkages developed in her previous overseas research on political development in Micronesia to the evaluation of Kellogg-funded collaborative programs building healthy communities. Subsequent projects included the evaluation of community-university partnership programs, evaluation of a homeless shelter partnership and U.S. Environmental Protection Agency (EPA) community outreach in Chicago, and community ethnographic assessment for the Department of Labor's Youth Opportunity Areas program. Her work in multicultural education and professional development programs includes serving as evaluator and faculty for the International Center for Health Leadership Development (University of Illinois at Chicago [UIC]) from 1997 to 2006, and evaluation of educational sessions on community and cross-cultural competence for physicians as part of her work as Program Director of Faculty Development for the Department of Family Medicine at the Cook County Bureau of Health Services from 2000 to 2007. She served as lead evaluator for the Cultural Connections program run by the Field Museum of Chicago's Center for Cultural Understanding and Change (now part of Environment, Culture and Conservation [ECCo]) from 2000 to 2009. Currently, she is Director of Evaluation and Research at the Mid-America Center for Public Health Practice, UIC School of Public Health. She has published on community-university partnerships evaluation and presented at the American Evaluation Association, the American Anthropological Association, and other professional meetings.

Jean J. Schensul, an anthropologist, is Founding Director (1987–2004) and currently full-time Senior Scientist (2005–present) at the Institute for Community Research (ICR), an independent community-based research organization of 50 to 80 employees based in Hartford, CT, where she has guided the development and implementation of its collaborative domestic and international health, education research, training, and public arts and gallery program. As principal investigator, Dr. Schensul has been awarded many NIH, Substance Abuse and Mental Health Services Administration (SAMHSA), and other federal and foundation community research and intervention grants that have helped to support the work of the Hispanic Health Council in Hartford (1978–1987), and the ICR, and has ongoing collaborations with the National Institute for Population Sciences, Mumbai; International Institute for Research on Women, Asia Office, Delhi; and the National Institute for Reproductive Health, Mumbai. Her personal research and intervention interests have focused on Latino and disparities health issues, adolescents and youth, older adults, and methodologies for collaborative and partnership research, including the training of youth and adults to conduct participatory action research as a means of social advocacy. A recipient of the Solon T. Kimball Award (with Stephen Schensul) and the 2010 Malinowski award, she has served as president of the Council on Anthropology and Education and the Society for Applied Anthropology, and is currently a member of the Executive Board of the American Anthropological Association. She regularly reviews for NIH and other funders. Among her publications are the seven-volume *Ethnographer's Toolkit* (AltaMira Press 1999; 2nd edition, 2011–12), and peer-reviewed articles and special issues on substance use, HIV, and mental health–related issues across the lifespan, participatory action research, community-based research, and interventions and democratization of social science research. In addition to her full-time appointment at ICR, Dr. Schensul holds affiliate appointments at Yale University and the University of Connecticut.

Susan Squires consistently demonstrates leadership in the technology sector, creating innovative product solutions, and is a recognized expert on customer insights research. Most recently, she joined the Department of Anthropology at the University of North Texas, where she is teaching applied business and design anthropology courses. She earned her Ph.D. from Boston University in 1990 and began her career teaching at the University of New Hampshire. Soon after she was drawn into practice, conducting evaluative research for the U.S. government's Initiative in Science, Math and Technology. From 1993 to 1997, she was at Andersen Worldwide Center for Professional Development and has written about Andersen's culture in her book *Inside Arthur Andersen* (2003), co-authored with C. Joseph Smith, Lorna McDougall, and William Yeack. Leaving Andersen in 1997, she led ethnographic research for a range of technology companies, including GVO, Yahoo, Sprint, and Ericsson. Her edited book *Creating Breakthrough Ideas* (2002), co-edited with Bryan Byrne, chronicles the application of anthropological theory and method in business and design. From 2004 to 2007 she worked at Sun Microsystems, where she was part of a unique research project studying end-user productivity for Sun's next-generation supercomputer. Following Sun Microsystems, she worked as a Senior Researcher/Team Lead at the Technology Research of Independent Living Centre (TRIL), a project within the Institute of Neuropsychiatry, Trinity College Dublin, in Ireland. This was an Intel-funded research initiative where she led a multidisciplinary team investigating new communication technologies as a potential intervention to prevent social isolation of older adults. Throughout her career, Dr. Squires has supported the work of practicing anthropologists within the American Anthropological Association (AAA), first as secretary and president of the National Association for the Practice of Anthropology, and then as a founding member of AAA Practicing Anthropology Working Group as well as the AAA Committee on Practicing, Applied and Public Interest Anthropology.

Christina Wasson is a professor in the Department of Anthropology, University of North Texas. Her work is motivated by a passion for three "C"s: communication, collaboration, and community building. She investigates how technology can bring together people who are geographically separated, applying her findings to the design of technologies and organizational change processes. She also actively participates in virtual collaborations and community building herself. Wasson's current research areas include virtual communities of environmental scientists, virtual communication and collaboration in business settings, and a comparison of online and on-campus student experiences. Wasson was trained as a linguistic anthropologist. After finishing her Ph.D., she worked for E-Lab, a design firm that used anthropological research to develop new product ideas. Here, she developed an interest in the emerging field of design anthropology. Her consulting work in this field continues, and she teaches the only course in design anthropology offered through an anthropology department. Clients have included Motorola, Microsoft, and the Dallas/Fort Worth International Airport. Wasson was also a founding member of the Ethnographic Praxis in Industry Conference (EPIC) Steering Committee, 2004 to 2010. For more information, see http://courses.unt.edu/cwasson.